FREE Study Skills DVD Offer

Dear Customer,

Thank you for your purchase from Mometrix! We consider it an honor and a privilege that you have purchased our product and we want to ensure your satisfaction.

As a way of showing our appreciation and to help us better serve you, we have developed a Study Skills DVD that we would like to give you for FREE. This DVD covers our *best practices* for getting ready for your exam, from how to use our study materials to how to best prepare for the day of the test.

All that we ask is that you email us with feedback that would describe your experience so far with our product. Good, bad, or indifferent, we want to know what you think!

To get your FREE Study Skills DVD, email freedvd@mometrix.com with *FREE STUDY SKILLS DVD* in the subject line and the following information in the body of the email:

- The name of the product you purchased.
- Your product rating on a scale of 1-5, with 5 being the highest rating.
- Your feedback. It can be long, short, or anything in between. We just want to know your impressions and experience so far with our product. (Good feedback might include how our study material met your needs and ways we might be able to make it even better. You could highlight features that you found helpful or features that you think we should add.)
- Your full name and shipping address where you would like us to send your free DVD.

If you have any questions or concerns, please don't hesitate to contact me directly.

Thanks again!

Sincerely,

Jay Willis
Vice President
jay.willis@mometrix.com
1-800-673-8175

PSAT

Prep Book 2020 and 2021

PSAT Test Study Guide Secrets with

Full-Length Practice Test

Step-by-Step Review Video Tutorials

3rd Edition

Written and edited by the Mometrix College Admissions Test Team

Printed in the United States of America

This paper meets the requirements of ANSI/NISO Z39.48-1992 (Permanence of Paper).

Paperback
ISBN 13: 978-1-5167-1329-5
ISBN 10: 1-5167-1329-X

Dear Future Exam Success Story

First of all, **THANK YOU** for purchasing Mometrix study materials!

Second, congratulations! You are one of the few determined test-takers who are committed to doing whatever it takes to excel on your exam. **You have come to the right place.** We developed these study materials with one goal in mind: to deliver you the information you need in a format that's concise and easy to use.

In addition to optimizing your guide for the content of the test, we've outlined our recommended steps for breaking down the preparation process into small, attainable goals so you can make sure you stay on track.

We've also analyzed the entire test-taking process, identifying the most common pitfalls and showing how you can overcome them and be ready for any curveball the test throws you.

Standardized testing is one of the biggest obstacles on your road to success, which only increases the importance of doing well in the high-pressure, high-stakes environment of test day. Your results on this test could have a significant impact on your future, and this guide provides the information and practical advice to help you achieve your full potential on test day.

Your success is our success

We would love to hear from you! If you would like to share the story of your exam success or if you have any questions or comments in regard to our products, please contact us at **800-673-8175** or **support@mometrix.com**.

Thanks again for your business and we wish you continued success!

Sincerely,
The Mometrix Test Preparation Team

TABLE OF CONTENTS

Introduction

Thank you for purchasing this resource! You have made the choice to prepare yourself for a test that could have a huge impact on your future, and this guide is designed to help you be fully ready for test day. Obviously, it's important to have a solid understanding of the test material, but you also need to be prepared for the unique environment and stressors of the test, so that you can perform to the best of your abilities.

For this purpose, the first section that appears in this guide is the **Secret Keys**. We've devoted countless hours to meticulously researching what works and what doesn't, and we've boiled down our findings to the five most impactful steps you can take to improve your performance on the test. We start at the beginning with study planning and move through the preparation process, all the way to the testing strategies that will help you get the most out of what you know when you're finally sitting in front of the test.

We recommend that you start preparing for your test as far in advance as possible. However, if you've bought this guide as a last-minute study resource and only have a few days before your test, we recommend that you skip over the first two Secret Keys since they address a long-term study plan.

If you struggle with **test anxiety**, we strongly encourage you to check out our recommendations for how you can overcome it. Test anxiety is a formidable foe, but it can be beaten, and we want to make sure you have the tools you need to defeat it.

Secret Key #1 – Plan Big, Study Small

There's a lot riding on your performance. If you want to ace this test, you're going to need to keep your skills sharp and the material fresh in your mind. You need a plan that lets you review everything you need to know while still fitting in your schedule. We'll break this strategy down into three categories.

Information Organization

Start with the information you already have: the official test outline. From this, you can make a complete list of all the concepts you need to cover before the test. Organize these concepts into groups that can be studied together, and create a list of any related vocabulary you need to learn so you can brush up on any difficult terms. You'll want to keep this vocabulary list handy once you actually start studying since you may need to add to it along the way.

Time Management

Once you have your set of study concepts, decide how to spread them out over the time you have left before the test. Break your study plan into small, clear goals so you have a manageable task for each day and know exactly what you're doing. Then just focus on one small step at a time. When you manage your time this way, you don't need to spend hours at a time studying. Studying a small block of content for a short period each day helps you retain information better and avoid stressing over how much you have left to do. You can relax knowing that you have a plan to cover everything in time. In order for this strategy to be effective though, you have to start studying early and stick to your schedule. Avoid the exhaustion and futility that comes from last-minute cramming!

Study Environment

The environment you study in has a big impact on your learning. Studying in a coffee shop, while probably more enjoyable, is not likely to be as fruitful as studying in a quiet room. It's important to keep distractions to a minimum. You're only planning to study for a short block of time, so make the most of it. Don't pause to check your phone or get up to find a snack. It's also important to **avoid multitasking**. Research has consistently shown that multitasking will make your studying dramatically less effective. Your study area should also be comfortable and well-lit so you don't have the distraction of straining your eyes or sitting on an uncomfortable chair.

The time of day you study is also important. You want to be rested and alert. Don't wait until just before bedtime. Study when you'll be most likely to comprehend and remember. Even better, if you know what time of day your test will be, set that time aside for study. That way your brain will be used to working on that subject at that specific time and you'll have a better chance of recalling information.

Finally, it can be helpful to team up with others who are studying for the same test. Your actual studying should be done in as isolated an environment as possible, but the work of organizing the information and setting up the study plan can be divided up. In between study sessions, you can discuss with your teammates the concepts that you're all studying and quiz each other on the details. Just be sure that your teammates are as serious about the test as you are. If you find that your study time is being replaced with social time, you might need to find a new team.

Secret Key #2 – Make Your Studying Count

You're devoting a lot of time and effort to preparing for this test, so you want to be absolutely certain it will pay off. This means doing more than just reading the content and hoping you can remember it on test day. It's important to make every minute of study count. There are two main areas you can focus on to make your studying count:

Retention

It doesn't matter how much time you study if you can't remember the material. You need to make sure you are retaining the concepts. To check your retention of the information you're learning, try recalling it at later times with minimal prompting. Try carrying around flashcards and glance at one or two from time to time or ask a friend who's also studying for the test to quiz you.

To enhance your retention, look for ways to put the information into practice so that you can apply it rather than simply recalling it. If you're using the information in practical ways, it will be much easier to remember. Similarly, it helps to solidify a concept in your mind if you're not only reading it to yourself but also explaining it to someone else. Ask a friend to let you teach them about a concept you're a little shaky on (or speak aloud to an imaginary audience if necessary). As you try to summarize, define, give examples, and answer your friend's questions, you'll understand the concepts better and they will stay with you longer. Finally, step back for a big picture view and ask yourself how each piece of information fits with the whole subject. When you link the different concepts together and see them working together as a whole, it's easier to remember the individual components.

Finally, practice showing your work on any multi-step problems, even if you're just studying. Writing out each step you take to solve a problem will help solidify the process in your mind, and you'll be more likely to remember it during the test.

Modality

Modality simply refers to the means or method by which you study. Choosing a study modality that fits your own individual learning style is crucial. No two people learn best in exactly the same way, so it's important to know your strengths and use them to your advantage.

For example, if you learn best by visualization, focus on visualizing a concept in your mind and draw an image or a diagram. Try color-coding your notes, illustrating them, or creating symbols that will trigger your mind to recall a learned concept. If you learn best by hearing or discussing information, find a study partner who learns the same way or read aloud to yourself. Think about how to put the information in your own words. Imagine that you are giving a lecture on the topic and record yourself so you can listen to it later.

For any learning style, flashcards can be helpful. Organize the information so you can take advantage of spare moments to review. Underline key words or phrases. Use different colors for different categories. Mnemonic devices (such as creating a short list in which every item starts with the same letter) can also help with retention. Find what works best for you and use it to store the information in your mind most effectively and easily.

Secret Key #3 – Practice the Right Way

Your success on test day depends not only on how many hours you put into preparing, but also on whether you prepared the right way. It's good to check along the way to see if your studying is paying off. One of the most effective ways to do this is by taking practice tests to evaluate your progress. Practice tests are useful because they show exactly where you need to improve. Every time you take a practice test, pay special attention to these three groups of questions:

- The questions you got wrong
- The questions you had to guess on, even if you guessed right
- The questions you found difficult or slow to work through

This will show you exactly what your weak areas are, and where you need to devote more study time. Ask yourself why each of these questions gave you trouble. Was it because you didn't understand the material? Was it because you didn't remember the vocabulary? Do you need more repetitions on this type of question to build speed and confidence? Dig into those questions and figure out how you can strengthen your weak areas as you go back to review the material.

Additionally, many practice tests have a section explaining the answer choices. It can be tempting to read the explanation and think that you now have a good understanding of the concept. However, an explanation likely only covers part of the question's broader context. Even if the explanation makes sense, **go back and investigate** every concept related to the question until you're positive you have a thorough understanding.

As you go along, keep in mind that the practice test is just that: practice. Memorizing these questions and answers will not be very helpful on the actual test because it is unlikely to have any of the same exact questions. If you only know the right answers to the sample questions, you won't be prepared for the real thing. **Study the concepts** until you understand them fully, and then you'll be able to answer any question that shows up on the test.

It's important to wait on the practice tests until you're ready. If you take a test on your first day of study, you may be overwhelmed by the amount of material covered and how much you need to learn. Work up to it gradually.

On test day, you'll need to be prepared for answering questions, managing your time, and using the test-taking strategies you've learned. It's a lot to balance, like a mental marathon that will have a big impact on your future. Like training for a marathon, you'll need to start slowly and work your way up. When test day arrives, you'll be ready.

Start with the strategies you've read in the first two Secret Keys—plan your course and study in the way that works best for you. If you have time, consider using multiple study resources to get different approaches to the same concepts. It can be helpful to see difficult concepts from more than one angle. Then find a good source for practice tests. Many times, the test website will suggest potential study resources or provide sample tests.

Practice Test Strategy

If you're able to find at least three practice tests, we recommend this strategy:

Untimed and Open-Book Practice

Take the first test with no time constraints and with your notes and study guide handy. Take your time and focus on applying the strategies you've learned.

Timed and Open-Book Practice

Take the second practice test open-book as well, but set a timer and practice pacing yourself to finish in time.

Timed and Closed-Book Practice

Take any other practice tests as if it were test day. Set a timer and put away your study materials. Sit at a table or desk in a quiet room, imagine yourself at the testing center, and answer questions as quickly and accurately as possible.

Keep repeating timed and closed-book tests on a regular basis until you run out of practice tests or it's time for the actual test. Your mind will be ready for the schedule and stress of test day, and you'll be able to focus on recalling the material you've learned.

Secret Key #4 – Pace Yourself

Once you're fully prepared for the material on the test, your biggest challenge on test day will be managing your time. Just knowing that the clock is ticking can make you panic even if you have plenty of time left. Work on pacing yourself so you can build confidence against the time constraints of the exam. Pacing is a difficult skill to master, especially in a high-pressure environment, so **practice is vital**.

Set time expectations for your pace based on how much time is available. For example, if a section has 60 questions and the time limit is 30 minutes, you know you have to average 30 seconds or less per question in order to answer them all. Although 30 seconds is the hard limit, set 25 seconds per question as your goal, so you reserve extra time to spend on harder questions. When you budget extra time for the harder questions, you no longer have any reason to stress when those questions take longer to answer.

Don't let this time expectation distract you from working through the test at a calm, steady pace, but keep it in mind so you don't spend too much time on any one question. Recognize that taking extra time on one question you don't understand may keep you from answering two that you do understand later in the test. If your time limit for a question is up and you're still not sure of the answer, mark it and move on, and come back to it later if the time and the test format allow. If the testing format doesn't allow you to return to earlier questions, just make an educated guess; then put it out of your mind and move on.

On the easier questions, be careful not to rush. It may seem wise to hurry through them so you have more time for the challenging ones, but it's not worth missing one if you know the concept and just didn't take the time to read the question fully. Work efficiently but make sure you understand the question and have looked at all of the answer choices, since more than one may seem right at first.

Even if you're paying attention to the time, you may find yourself a little behind at some point. You should speed up to get back on track, but do so wisely. Don't panic; just take a few seconds less on each question until you're caught up. Don't guess without thinking, but do look through the answer choices and eliminate any you know are wrong. If you can get down to two choices, it is often worthwhile to guess from those. Once you've chosen an answer, move on and don't dwell on any that you skipped or had to hurry through. If a question was taking too long, chances are it was one of the harder ones, so you weren't as likely to get it right anyway.

On the other hand, if you find yourself getting ahead of schedule, it may be beneficial to slow down a little. The more quickly you work, the more likely you are to make a careless mistake that will affect your score. You've budgeted time for each question, so don't be afraid to spend that time. Practice an efficient but careful pace to get the most out of the time you have.

Secret Key #5 – Have a Plan for Guessing

When you're taking the test, you may find yourself stuck on a question. Some of the answer choices seem better than others, but you don't see the one answer choice that is obviously correct. What do you do?

The scenario described above is very common, yet most test takers have not effectively prepared for it. Developing and practicing a plan for guessing may be one of the single most effective uses of your time as you get ready for the exam.

In developing your plan for guessing, there are three questions to address:

- When should you start the guessing process?
- How should you narrow down the choices?
- Which answer should you choose?

When to Start the Guessing Process

Unless your plan for guessing is to select C every time (which, despite its merits, is not what we recommend), you need to leave yourself enough time to apply your answer elimination strategies. Since you have a limited amount of time for each question, that means that if you're going to give yourself the best shot at guessing correctly, you have to decide quickly whether or not you will guess.

Of course, the best-case scenario is that you don't have to guess at all, so first, see if you can answer the question based on your knowledge of the subject and basic reasoning skills. Focus on the key words in the question and try to jog your memory of related topics. Give yourself a chance to bring the knowledge to mind, but once you realize that you don't have (or you can't access) the knowledge you need to answer the question, it's time to start the guessing process.

It's almost always better to start the guessing process too early than too late. It only takes a few seconds to remember something and answer the question from knowledge. Carefully eliminating wrong answer choices takes longer. Plus, going through the process of eliminating answer choices can actually help jog your memory.

Summary: Start the guessing process as soon as you decide that you can't answer the question based on your knowledge.

How to Narrow Down the Choices

The next chapter in this book (**Test-Taking Strategies**) includes a wide range of strategies for how to approach questions and how to look for answer choices to eliminate. You will definitely want to read those carefully, practice them, and figure out which ones work best for you. Here though, we're going to address a mindset rather than a particular strategy.

Your chances of guessing an answer correctly depend on how many options you are choosing from.

How many choices you have	How likely you are to guess correctly
5	20%
4	25%
3	33%
2	50%
1	100%

You can see from this chart just how valuable it is to be able to eliminate incorrect answers and make an educated guess, but there are two things that many test takers do that cause them to miss out on the benefits of guessing:

- Accidentally eliminating the correct answer
- Selecting an answer based on an impression

We'll look at the first one here, and the second one in the next section.

To avoid accidentally eliminating the correct answer, we recommend a thought exercise called **the $5 challenge**. In this challenge, you only eliminate an answer choice from contention if you are willing to bet $5 on it being wrong. Why $5? Five dollars is a small but not insignificant amount of money. It's an amount you could afford to lose but wouldn't want to throw away. And while losing $5 once might not hurt too much, doing it twenty times will set you back $100. In the same way, each small decision you make—eliminating a choice here, guessing on a question there—won't by itself impact your score very much, but when you put them all together, they can make a big difference. By holding each answer choice elimination decision to a higher standard, you can reduce the risk of accidentally eliminating the correct answer.

The $5 challenge can also be applied in a positive sense: If you are willing to bet $5 that an answer choice *is* correct, go ahead and mark it as correct.

Summary: Only eliminate an answer choice if you are willing to bet $5 that it is wrong.

Which Answer to Choose

You're taking the test. You've run into a hard question and decided you'll have to guess. You've eliminated all the answer choices you're willing to bet $5 on. Now you have to pick an answer. Why do we even need to talk about this? Why can't you just pick whichever one you feel like when the time comes?

The answer to these questions is that if you don't come into the test with a plan, you'll rely on your impression to select an answer choice, and if you do that, you risk falling into a trap. The test writers know that everyone who takes their test will be guessing on some of the questions, so they intentionally write wrong answer choices to seem plausible. You still have to pick an answer though, and if the wrong answer choices are designed to look right, how can you ever be sure that you're not falling for their trap? The best solution we've found to this dilemma is to take the decision out of your hands entirely. Here is the process we recommend:

Once you've eliminated any choices that you are confident (willing to bet $5) are wrong, select the first remaining choice as your answer.

Whether you choose to select the first remaining choice, the second, or the last, the important thing is that you use some preselected standard. Using this approach guarantees that you will not be enticed into selecting an answer choice that looks right, because you are not basing your decision on how the answer choices look.

This is not meant to make you question your knowledge. Instead, it is to help you recognize the difference between your knowledge and your impressions. There's a huge difference between thinking an answer is right because of what you know, and thinking an answer is right because it looks or sounds like it should be right.

Summary: To ensure that your selection is appropriately random, make a predetermined selection from among all answer choices you have not eliminated.

Test-Taking Strategies

This section contains a list of test-taking strategies that you may find helpful as you work through the test. By taking what you know and applying logical thought, you can maximize your chances of answering any question correctly!

It is very important to realize that every question is different and every person is different: no single strategy will work on every question, and no single strategy will work for every person. That's why we've included all of them here, so you can try them out and determine which ones work best for different types of questions and which ones work best for you.

Question Strategies

Read Carefully

Read the question and answer choices carefully. Don't miss the question because you misread the terms. You have plenty of time to read each question thoroughly and make sure you understand what is being asked. Yet a happy medium must be attained, so don't waste too much time. You must read carefully, but efficiently.

Contextual Clues

Look for contextual clues. If the question includes a word you are not familiar with, look at the immediate context for some indication of what the word might mean. Contextual clues can often give you all the information you need to decipher the meaning of an unfamiliar word. Even if you can't determine the meaning, you may be able to narrow down the possibilities enough to make a solid guess at the answer to the question.

Prefixes

If you're having trouble with a word in the question or answer choices, try dissecting it. Take advantage of every clue that the word might include. Prefixes and suffixes can be a huge help. Usually they allow you to determine a basic meaning. Pre- means before, post- means after, pro - is positive, de- is negative. From prefixes and suffixes, you can get an idea of the general meaning of the word and try to put it into context.

Hedge Words

Watch out for critical hedge words, such as *likely, may, can, sometimes, often, almost, mostly, usually, generally, rarely,* and *sometimes.* Question writers insert these hedge phrases to cover every possibility. Often an answer choice will be wrong simply because it leaves no room for exception. Be on guard for answer choices that have definitive words such as *exactly* and *always.*

Switchback Words

Stay alert for *switchbacks.* These are the words and phrases frequently used to alert you to shifts in thought. The most common switchback words are *but, although,* and *however.* Others include *nevertheless, on the other hand, even though, while, in spite of, despite, regardless of.* Switchback words are important to catch because they can change the direction of the question or an answer choice.

Face Value

When in doubt, use common sense. Accept the situation in the problem at face value. Don't read too much into it. These problems will not require you to make wild assumptions. If you have to go beyond creativity and warp time or space in order to have an answer choice fit the question, then you should move on and consider the other answer choices. These are normal problems rooted in reality. The applicable relationship or explanation may not be readily apparent, but it is there for you to figure out. Use your common sense to interpret anything that isn't clear.

Answer Choice Strategies

Answer Selection

The most thorough way to pick an answer choice is to identify and eliminate wrong answers until only one is left, then confirm it is the correct answer. Sometimes an answer choice may immediately seem right, but be careful. The test writers will usually put more than one reasonable answer choice on each question, so take a second to read all of them and make sure that the other choices are not equally obvious. As long as you have time left, it is better to read every answer choice than to pick the first one that looks right without checking the others.

Answer Choice Families

An answer choice family consists of two (in rare cases, three) answer choices that are very similar in construction and cannot all be true at the same time. If you see two answer choices that are direct opposites or parallels, one of them is usually the correct answer. For instance, if one answer choice says that quantity *x* increases and another either says that quantity *x* decreases (opposite) or says that quantity *y* increases (parallel), then those answer choices would fall into the same family. An answer choice that doesn't match the construction of the answer choice family is more likely to be incorrect. Most questions will not have answer choice families, but when they do appear, you should be prepared to recognize them.

Eliminate Answers

Eliminate answer choices as soon as you realize they are wrong, but make sure you consider all possibilities. If you are eliminating answer choices and realize that the last one you are left with is also wrong, don't panic. Start over and consider each choice again. There may be something you missed the first time that you will realize on the second pass.

Avoid Fact Traps

Don't be distracted by an answer choice that is factually true but doesn't answer the question. You are looking for the choice that answers the question. Stay focused on what the question is asking for so you don't accidentally pick an answer that is true but incorrect. Always go back to the question and make sure the answer choice you've selected actually answers the question and is not merely a true statement.

Extreme Statements

In general, you should avoid answers that put forth extreme actions as standard practice or proclaim controversial ideas as established fact. An answer choice that states the "process should be used in certain situations, if…" is much more likely to be correct than one that states the "process should be discontinued completely." The first is a calm rational statement and doesn't even make a definitive, uncompromising stance, using a hedge word *if* to provide wiggle room, whereas the second choice is a radical idea and far more extreme.

Benchmark

As you read through the answer choices and you come across one that seems to answer the question well, mentally select that answer choice. This is not your final answer, but it's the one that will help you evaluate the other answer choices. The one that you selected is your benchmark or standard for judging each of the other answer choices. Every other answer choice must be compared to your benchmark. That choice is correct until proven otherwise by another answer choice beating it. If you find a better answer, then that one becomes your new benchmark. Once you've decided that no other choice answers the question as well as your benchmark, you have your final answer.

Predict the Answer

Before you even start looking at the answer choices, it is often best to try to predict the answer. When you come up with the answer on your own, it is easier to avoid distractions and traps because you will know exactly what to look for. The right answer choice is unlikely to be word-for-word what you came up with, but it should be a close match. Even if you are confident that you have the right answer, you should still take the time to read each option before moving on.

General Strategies

Tough Questions

If you are stumped on a problem or it appears too hard or too difficult, don't waste time. Move on! Remember though, if you can quickly check for obviously incorrect answer choices, your chances of guessing correctly are greatly improved. Before you completely give up, at least try to knock out a couple of possible answers. Eliminate what you can and then guess at the remaining answer choices before moving on.

Check Your Work

Since you will probably not know every term listed and the answer to every question, it is important that you get credit for the ones that you do know. Don't miss any questions through careless mistakes. If at all possible, try to take a second to look back over your answer selection and make sure you've selected the correct answer choice and haven't made a costly careless mistake (such as marking an answer choice that you didn't mean to mark). This quick double check should more than pay for itself in caught mistakes for the time it costs.

Pace Yourself

It's easy to be overwhelmed when you're looking at a page full of questions; your mind is confused and full of random thoughts, and the clock is ticking down faster than you would like. Calm down and maintain the pace that you have set for yourself. Especially as you get down to the last few minutes of the test, don't let the small numbers on the clock make you panic. As long as you are on track by monitoring your pace, you are guaranteed to have time for each question.

Don't Rush

It is very easy to make errors when you are in a hurry. Maintaining a fast pace in answering questions is pointless if it makes you miss questions that you would have gotten right otherwise. Test writers like to include distracting information and wrong answers that seem right. Taking a little extra time to avoid careless mistakes can make all the difference in your test score. Find a pace that allows you to be confident in the answers that you select.

KEEP MOVING

Panicking will not help you pass the test, so do your best to stay calm and keep moving. Taking deep breaths and going through the answer elimination steps you practiced can help to break through a stress barrier and keep your pace.

Final Notes

The combination of a solid foundation of content knowledge and the confidence that comes from practicing your plan for applying that knowledge is the key to maximizing your performance on test day. As your foundation of content knowledge is built up and strengthened, you'll find that the strategies included in this chapter become more and more effective in helping you quickly sift through the distractions and traps of the test to isolate the correct answer.

Now it's time to move on to the test content chapters of this book, but be sure to keep your goal in mind. As you read, think about how you will be able to apply this information on the test. If you've already seen sample questions for the test and you have an idea of the question format and style, try to come up with questions of your own that you can answer based on what you're reading. This will give you valuable practice applying your knowledge in the same ways you can expect to on test day.

Good luck and good studying!

Reading Test

The reading portion of the PSAT consists of one 60-minute section. It will contain 5 single passages or passage pairs. There will be a total of 47 questions relating to these passages. The breakdown of passages and questions is in the table below.

U.S and World Literature	1 passage; 9 questions	20%
History/Social Studies	2 passages, or 1 passage and 1 pair; 9-10 questions each	40%
Science	2 passages, or 1 passage and 1 pair; 9-10 questions each	40%

The PSAT Reading Test will contain a range of text complexities from grades 9-10 and post-secondary entry. The passages will cover U.S. and World Literature, History/Social Studies, and Science. The test will also contain 1-2 graphical representations. These may include tables, graphs, and charts. They will vary in level of difficulty as well as data density, and number of variables.

Information and Ideas

The questions tested in this section will focus on the informational content contained in the text.

Reading Closely

These questions will focus on the student's ability to read a passage and extrapolate beyond the information presented. They will look at both the explicit and implicit meanings of the text.

Explicitly Stated Information

Identifying information stated explicitly in text means locating facts or opinions stated outright in the text and not requiring reader inference or interpretation. For example, when including factual information, an author might give specific names of people, places, or events; specific numbers; specific days of the week, names of months, or dates including the month, date, and year. In informational text, the author might state numerical measurements, (e.g., the size of a room or object; the distance between places; how many people live in a certain locality; how many people die annually from a certain cause; or the date, time, and/or place a certain event occurred). Abraham Lincoln began his Gettysburg Address, "Four score and seven years ago," which today is archaic language but does not require inference or interpretation; even a reader unfamiliar with the meaning of *score* can easily look up and find it. In a fictional novel, the author might state how many people are invited to, or were in attendance at, a party or other event.

Drawing Inferences from Text

Some meanings in text are implicit rather than explicit; in other words, they are not directly stated (explicit), but implied (implicit). This means the reader needs to assume or draw an inference based on what is stated. Inferring meaning is often described by the saying *reading between the lines*, (i.e., determining what is unsaid through carefully observing what is said). For example, if an author writes, "Considering recent economic changes, what were once necessities are now luxuries for many businesses," the reader can infer that the "recent economic changes" the author refers to are economic decline, not economic prosperity. Describing things formerly viewed as necessary but now as unnecessary implies worse, not better changes. Or a novelist might write, "Trembling and flushing, she asked breathlessly, 'You saw him? How is he? Did he ask how I was? Did he mention me at all?'" From the author's description of the character, the reader can infer she feels love/attraction for the person being referenced.

Determining Explicit Meanings

These questions will require the student to identify information explicitly stated in the text.

Explicit Descriptors

Writers explicitly state not only factual information in their texts; they also explicitly state other kinds of information. For example, authors use description to give readers a better idea of the characteristics of whatever they are describing. If an author writes, "This sarcophagus is decorated with a vivid color illustration," the word *vivid* is more descriptive than factual. It communicates to the reader that the color illustration described is especially bright, vibrant, or intense visually. This is very helpful when there are no visual images of the object being described to accompany the text. Explicit descriptive words also apply to abstract concepts. For example, the author might write that the vivid color illustration depicts a famous figure's "brave actions." The word *brave* describes the actions of the person using an abstract concept. It communicates to the reader that the person's actions are considered brave or courageous by the author, and usually by other people as well.

Explicitly Stated Opinions

An essayist might state an opinion; for example, "These people were not treated fairly." Since readers are expected to be able to distinguish opinion from fact, the essayist need not write, "*In my opinion*, these people were not treated fairly." It is a common practice of authors, especially those writing argumentative or persuasive types of text, to state opinions in the same way as facts. Even though not proven factual, opinions are stated just as explicitly as facts in these instances. Writers state ideas explicitly in text as well. For example, an author might write about how people historically believed that the Earth was flat, or that the Sun revolved around the Earth. These are not factual, but not simply opinions either; they were the prevailing beliefs at the time, (i.e., commonly held ideas). When an author explicitly states a *main idea*, he or she typically makes it the topic sentence of the paragraph, chapter, or piece. Topic sentences are also examples of explicitly stating ideas, (i.e., expressing them directly in text rather than implying them).

Determining Implicit Meanings

The questions in this section will require the student to read the text and then draw inferences from the text and form logical conclusions.

Inferences

Inferences are educated guesses that can be drawn from the facts and information available to a reader. Inferences are usually based upon a reader's own assumptions and beliefs. The ability to make inferences is often called reading between the lines. There are three basic types of inference: deductive reasoning, abductive reasoning, and inductive reasoning. Deductive reasoning is the ability to find an effect when given a cause and a rule. Abductive reasoning is the ability to find a cause when given a rule and an effect. Inductive reasoning is the ability to find a rule when given the cause and effect. Each type of reasoning can be used to make logical inferences from a piece of writing.

Review Video: Inference
Visit mometrix.com/academy and enter code: 379203

Drawing Conclusions

Drawing logical conclusions is a way, along with making reasonable inferences, of determining implicit meanings, (i.e., meanings not directly or explicitly stated in the text but indirectly implied). For example, if an author of a fictional work has described a character who is emotionally distraught and hysterical running headlong toward a cliff without looking, without reading any further the reader can logically conclude that unless something happens in the interim—like another character appearing out of nowhere and stopping the first one—the character who is running will probably fall over the cliff. If a character in a novel talks about fighting and how they should all support their soldiers, the reader can logically conclude that the novel takes place during a war, even though the author does not explicitly state that a war is going on during the time period in which the author has set the novel's events.

Ways That Drawing Inferences Are Tested

One way a test might ask you to draw inferences or conclusions is asking what a character in text would likely react to a given event/circumstance based on a text passage. You would need to read closely for clues on which to base your inference. You might see a description of an earlier incident wherein this character reacted a certain way. For example, the author wrote, "The last time somebody hit her, she ran away." Based on this, you could infer she would do the same thing. Or one character says, "If he finds out what you did, he'll kill you," and the passage includes explicit description of the referenced character having killed people. You could then conclude if the third character finds out what the second character did, he will kill him or her. Some works, rather than providing a neat conclusion, seem to end in mid-action; yet readers can predict much from it.

Using Analogical Reasoning

The student will be required to extrapolate information and idea from the text to answer these questions. They will also need to be able to this information and ideas to new, analogous situations.

Using analogical reasoning as described above involves thinking about situations that are comparable to one in the text and applying information from the text to those other parallel situations. For example, suppose a student reads that colonial Americans, dissatisfied with British laws and influenced by Enlightenment philosophy, wanted freedom to govern themselves instead of being ruled by the British monarchy, so they started the American Revolution to fight for their freedom and won, forming a democratic government. Suppose the student then further reads that the French, strongly influenced both by the same Enlightenment philosophy and by the Americans' success, started the French Revolution, also fighting for their freedom from an unfair monarchy, winning, and forming a democratic government. Then suppose the same student reads about people in other countries being ruled unfairly by a tyrannical monarchy. The student could reasonably apply the information about America and France to these other countries and expect revolutionary wars to break out in some of these other countries.

Extrapolate from Text

Even fictional text can be applied to analogous situations, particularly when the author's knowledge of human nature is sound and some of the text elements can be applied across settings. For example, reading William Shakespeare's tragedy *Romeo and Juliet,* one might first observe differences from today's real world: It is set centuries ago, in another country, and involves a family feud, which is rare today. However, one could then observe similarities: The main characters are teenagers; they fall madly in love; their families prohibit their seeing each other; and their families dislike each other, which is commoner today than actual feuds. Teen suicide and teen suicide pacts occur today. Thus, the student could extrapolate from this play, albeit fictional, that two teens today as fervently in love as Romeo and Juliet whose parents kept them apart, feeling there were no better options, might take the same actions. Despite today's technology, the chance/accidental element (lack of timely information) causing the double tragedy could equally occur today.

EXAMPLE

Consider that a student reads in a biology text that mitosis is an asexual type of reproduction in which cells divide to produce more identical cells. The student reads further that mitosis takes place in all living organisms. From this information, the student can extrapolate that since mitosis occurs in all living organisms, mitosis must therefore occur in human beings. Since mitosis is an asexual type of reproduction, the student can further infer that mitosis is not the way in which humans reproduce sexually. By process of elimination, the student can then deduce that mitosis in humans must involve only the reproduction of cells within each individual human body. The student can further deduce that sexual reproduction in human beings must not be mitosis. The student cannot know that human sexual reproduction involves meiosis, or how this differs from mitosis, without reading about meiosis; however, he or she can determine all the aforementioned things just from reading about mitosis alone.

CITING TEXTUAL EVIDENCE

These questions will ask the student to support their answer with evidence from the text. The student should be able to specifically identify the information in the text and properly cite it.

CITING SUPPORTING EVIDENCE

Citing evidence from text that supports a point or claim in that text involves identifying which information is most directly related to that point or claim. As an example, if a writer makes the claim that the world population is increasing, that author might provide evidence to support this claim, such as census statistics from the past several consecutive years, decades, or centuries that give world population numbers larger than they were previously. In the same text, the author may also provide figures measuring poverty, hunger, and other ills related to overpopulation in certain parts of the world to make a case for the argument that population growth is bad and should be controlled. However, the student would be mistaken to cite those figures as evidence supporting the claim that the population is increasing; they are, rather, evidence supporting the claim that population growth is bad and should be controlled.

Review Video: Text Evidence
Visit mometrix.com/academy and enter code: 486236

CITING INFORMATION

Whereas informational and argumentative text may often use facts and/or figures as evidence to support various points or claims, fictional narration or description may use more descriptive details as supporting evidence. Moreover, the points or claims in such works may not be stated explicitly in words, but instead may be demonstrated through the actions or responses of characters. For example, an author of a play or novel may establish that a character is highly emotional by portraying or describing behaviors demonstrating this—flying into a rage, crying easily, becoming overjoyed readily, etc. The playwright or novelist need not write in another character's dialogue that this character is passionate or has mood swings; it is demonstrated through actions/behaviors. Subsequently in the play or novel, the character may do something which is not surprising but expected based on this established character trait. The character's previous actions are evidence supporting the credibility of the later action, (i.e., it was *in character*).

Steps to Cite Textual Evidence

To cite evidence explicitly stated in text to support what they think about the text, students can take several steps. First, students should state their idea regarding the text. When answering a test question, students should also ensure his or her idea is or includes a restatement of the question. Then, to cite textual evidence supporting that idea, students can either paraphrase the evidence (i.e., restate or describe it in their own words) or quote part of the text directly, enclosing it in quotation marks and introducing it by referencing the paragraph or portion where it appears. Then students need to explain how the evidence they cited supports their idea about the text. For example, students might write that the evidence illustrates a similarity or difference between things, gives a reason for something, demonstrates a cause-and-effect relationship, explains what something means or how something works, etc. Students should also identify how the evidence cited contributed to their formulation of the idea answering the question. Students should cite at least two pieces of textual evidence per idea/question.

Determining Central Ideas and Themes

For these questions the student should be able to identify central ideas and themes that are explicitly stated in the text. They will also need to be able to determine implicit central ideas and themes from the text.

Central Ideas

Central ideas are what a passage is mainly about. They are why the passage is written. The main idea is often found in a topic sentence or even a concluding sentence, and there are supporting details found in the passage that expand upon the main idea. There can, however, be more than one central idea, and these main ideas can be related and intertwined. For instance, the main or central idea of a passage may be that rainforests are drying out. A related main idea might be that the result of rainforest destruction is a loss of wildlife. These two central ideas are obviously related, and the passage may present both by focusing on one in one part of the passage and the other in another part of the passage. Another way they could be related is in a cause and effect relationship, with the loss of rainforests being the reason for losses of wildlife. It is important to always check to see if there is more than one central idea in a passage.

Read the excerpt below. Identify and discuss the main idea.

> Students who have jobs while attending high school tend not to have as much time to complete their homework as other students. They also do not have time for other activities. We should try to persuade our young people to concentrate on doing well in school, not to concentrate on making money. Having a job while you are a student is harmful.

The main idea of the excerpt is actually the last sentence: "Having a job while you are a student is harmful." This is what the excerpt is mostly about. The other sentences contain supporting information: students who have jobs don't have as much time for homework; students with jobs don't have time for as many activities. These are both supporting details that tell more about the main idea. The third sentence deals with a persuasive argument; it is another kind of detail. Only the last sentence tells what the excerpt is mostly about. Main ideas are sometimes found in a topic sentence at the start of a text or in the concluding sentence, which is the case in this excerpt.

Theme

As opposed to a main idea, themes are seldom expressed directly in a text, so they can be difficult to identify. A theme is an issue, an idea, or a question raised by the text. For instance, a theme of William Shakespeare's *Hamlet* is indecision, as the title character explores his own psyche and the results of his failure to make bold choices. A great work of literature may have many themes, and the reader is justified in identifying any for which he or she can find support. One common characteristic of themes is that they raise more questions than they answer. In a good piece of fiction, the author is not always trying to convince the reader, but is instead trying to elevate the reader's perspective and encourage him to consider the themes more deeply.

Review Video: Theme
Visit mometrix.com/academy and enter code: 732074

5 Steps to Take

As with all learning and development, reading should begin with concrete and gradually progress to abstract. Students must identify and understand literal information before they can make inferences. The first step is to identify the most important nouns and verbs in a sentence and define what the sentence is about. The second step is to identify the most important nouns, verbs, and adjectives in a whole paragraph, and define what that paragraph is about. The third step is to read brief passages, all of which use topic sentences with literal meanings. Students should be able to identify topic sentences not only at the beginning, but also anywhere else in a paragraph. In the fourth step, students can begin to make inferences by reading a single paragraph and then determining and articulating what the main idea is that the paragraph implies. The fifth step involves reading passages with more than one paragraph, gradually and slowly increasing the length of passages and identifying the implicit main idea each time. Students should be able to infer the main idea in shorter texts before proceeding to longer ones.

Summarizing

These questions will test the student's ability to identify a summary of a text after reading the text. The student should be able to identify a reasonable summary of the text or of key information presented in the text.

It is also helpful to summarize the information you have read in a paragraph or passage format. This process is like creating an effective outline. To begin with, a summary should accurately define the main idea of the passage, though it does not need to explain this main idea in exhaustive detail. It should continue by laying out the most important supporting details or arguments from the passage. All the significant supporting details should be included, and none of the details included should be irrelevant or insignificant. Also, the summary should accurately report all of these details. Too often, the desire for brevity in a summary leads to the sacrifice of clarity or veracity. Summaries are often difficult to read, because they omit all graceful language, digressions, and asides that distinguish great writing. However, if the summary is effective, it should contain much the same message as the original text.

Review Video: Summarizing Text
Visit mometrix.com/academy and enter code: 172903

Improving Summarization Skills

For students to be able to identify good summaries of text or its key information, it will help if they learn how to summarize these themselves. Although they will find recognizing good summaries easier than making their own summaries, both processes require identifying subject matter through locating representative words and recalling significant information. One activity in which students can practice summarizing skills and teachers can provide scaffolding and guidance is using an ABC Chart. This is a simple square grid containing smaller squares, each labeled A, B, C, etc. through Z. Students read a passage; the teacher guides them to recall important phrases and words in the text, write each one on a Post-it Note, and attach it to the square labeled with the first letter of the phrase/word. Students should try to recall as many details, facts, etc. as possible. Then they remove the Post-it Notes from the chart and stick them randomly on the board. The teacher helps them arrange the notes in some pattern, (e.g., into a web by ideas, chronologically along a timeline). This helps students organize their thoughts.

Understanding Relationships

Texts will contain many different relationships between individuals, events, and ideas. These questions will test the student's ability to identify explicitly stated relationships as well as determine implicit ones.

Review Video: Relationships in a Story
Visit mometrix.com/academy and enter code: 929925

Textual Features

Authors use various relationships as ways of organizing, presenting, and explaining information. For example, describing cause-and-effect relationships is a common technique in expository/informational text. The author describes some event(s), and then either explicitly states or implicitly establishes factors causing them. When authors use comparison-contrast, they typically compare similarities between/among ideas/things using similes (stated comparisons), metaphors (implied comparisons), and analogies (comparisons of similarities in two unrelated things). Authors identify contrasts by describing opposing qualities/characteristics in things/ideas. One example of using sequence or order is arranging events chronologically, beginning to end. Students can recognize sequential organization by observing specific dates, times, and signal words including *first, before, next, then, following, after, subsequently, finally*, etc. Sequence can also be spatial or by order of importance. Authors introduce some problem, describe its characteristics, and then offer solutions in problem-solution relationships. Descriptive writing provides sensory details to make information realer and easier for readers to imagine. How-to/instructional texts use serial directions to provide information.

Compare and Contrast

Authors will use different stylistic and writing devices to make their meaning more clearly understood. One of those devices is comparison and contrast. When an author describes the ways in which two things are alike, he or she is comparing them. When the author describes the ways in which two things are different, he or she is contrasting them. The *compare and contrast* essay is one of the most common forms in nonfiction. It is often signaled with certain words: a comparison may be indicated with such words as *both, same, like, too*, and *as well*; while a contrast may be indicated by words like *but, however, on the other hand, instead*, and *yet*. Of course, comparisons and contrasts may be implicit without using any such signaling language. A single sentence may both compare and contrast. Consider the sentence *Brian and Sheila love ice cream, but Brian prefers vanilla and Sheila prefers strawberry*. In one sentence, the author has described both a similarity (love of ice cream) and a difference (favorite flavor).

Review Video: Compare and Contrast
Visit mometrix.com/academy and enter code: 171799

Cause and Effect

One of the most common text structures is cause and effect. A cause is an act or event that makes something happen, and an effect is the thing that happens because of that cause. A cause-and-effect relationship is not always explicit, but there are some words in English that signal causality, such as *since, because*, and *as a result*. As an example, consider the sentence *Because the sky was clear, Ron did not bring an umbrella*. The cause is the clear sky, and the effect is that Ron did not bring an umbrella. However, sometimes the cause-and-effect relationship will not be clearly noted. For instance, the sentence *He was late and missed the meeting* does not contain any signaling words, but it still contains a cause (he was late) and an effect (he missed the meeting). It is possible for a single cause to have multiple effects, or for a single effect to have multiple causes. Also, an effect can in turn be the cause of another effect, in what is known as a cause-and-effect chain.

Review Video: Cause and Effect
Visit mometrix.com/academy and enter code: 428037

Text Sequence

A reader must be able to identify a text's sequence, or the order in which things happen. Often, and especially when the sequence is very important to the author, it is indicated with signal words like first, then, next, and last. However, sometimes a sequence is merely implied and must be noted by the reader. Consider the sentence He walked in the front door and switched on the hall lamp. Clearly, the man did not turn the lamp on before he walked in the door, so the implied sequence is that he first walked in the door and then turned on the lamp. Texts do not always proceed in an orderly sequence from first to last: sometimes, they begin at the end and then start over at the beginning. As a reader, it can be useful to make brief notes to clarify the sequence.

Review Video: Sequence
Visit mometrix.com/academy and enter code: 489027

Interpreting Words and Phrases in Context

These questions will ask the student to determine the meaning of words and phrases from the text. The student must use context clues to help determine the meaning of these words and phrases.

Contextual Clues

Look for contextual clues. An answer can be right but not correct. The contextual clues will help you find the answer that is most right and is correct. Understand the context in which a phrase is stated.

When asked for the implied meaning of a statement made in the passage, immediately go find the statement and read the context. Also, look for an answer choice that has a similar phrase to the statement in question.

Example:

> In the passage, what is implied by the phrase "Churches have become more or less part of the furniture"?

Find an answer choice that is similar or describes the phrase *part of the furniture* as that is the key phrase in the question. *Part of the furniture* is a saying that means something is fixed, immovable, or set in their ways. Those are all similar ways of saying *part of the furniture*. As such, the correct answer choice will probably include a similar rewording of the expression.

Example:

> Why was John described as "morally desperate"?

The answer will probably have some sort of definition of *morals* in it. *Morals* refers to a code of right and wrong behavior, so the correct answer choice will likely have words that mean something like that.

Review Video: Context
Visit mometrix.com/academy and enter code: 613660

Word Meaning

Paying attention to the phrase, sentence, paragraph, or larger context surrounding a word gives students two distinct advantages: One, it can help figure out the meaning of a new or unfamiliar vocabulary word by the information its context provides; and two, it can help distinguish between/among different meanings of the same word according to which meaning makes sense within context. For example, when reading words like *nickelback* and *bootleg*, if the surrounding context is football, these refer to an additional, fifth defensive back position played by a safety or cornerback and a play run by the quarterback, respectively; but if the surrounding context is rock music, *Nickelback* refers to a Canadian band, and *bootleg* to unofficial or unauthorized recordings of musical performances. Students can look for contextual synonyms for unknown words; for example, a reader unfamiliar with the meaning of *prudent* may observe the words *careful*, *cautious*, *judicious*, etc. Antonyms also help; for example, if a text says, "Smug? On the contrary, he's the most self-critical person I know." This informs defining *smug* as self-congratulatory or overly self-satisfied.

Rhetoric

The questions in this section will focus on the rhetorical analysis of a text.

Analyzing Word Choice

Authors use specific words, phrases, and patterns of words in their writing. The student will be asked to determine how these help shape the meaning and tone in the text.

Rhetorical Analysis

When analyzing a text's rhetoric, students should aim to reveal the purpose of the text or the author's purpose in writing it; who the author's intended audience was; the decisions that the author made, and how these decisions may have influenced the final result of the text. Identifying the intended purpose and audience of a text is identifying two main components of its rhetorical situation, (i.e., the circumstances wherein communication occurs), which serves as a major basis for rhetorical analysis. The third main component is the context. Context can include many factors, such as the occasion of the work; the exigency (i.e., what motivated the author to write the text); the media and/or venue of its original appearance; the historical background and even the state of the world relative to the text's topic. As an example, texts written respectively before and after 9/11/2001 on the topic of air travel would have some marked differences.

Word Choice or Diction in Rhetoric

Word choice or diction affects the tone of a text and how readers perceive its meaning. Writers inform their diction in part by considering their intended audience and selecting words that will be understood by and appeal to this audience. For instance, language with more denotative meanings (i.e., straightforward dictionary definitions) is more suitable for informational texts, whereas language with more connotative meanings (i.e., words that carry implied associated meanings) is more suitable for descriptive and narrative texts to evoke images and emotions. As examples, describing a sound or noise as *extremely loud* or *at a volume of 100 dB* is more factual and denotative; describing it as *thunderous, deafening*, or in specific reference to a speaker's voice, *stentorian*, is more descriptive, connotative, and evocative. Audience also influences the relative formality of diction. For example, more formal text appropriate for an adult professional academic audience might describe size as *massive*, whereas more informal language appropriate for high school and younger students might use the blending neologism *ginormous*.

Influence on Meaning and Understanding

When writers use good judgment in word choice, they communicate their messages more effectively for readers to understand. Poor word choice, as well as not considering the intended audience in one's diction, can distract readers to the point that they miss the message. Readers can consider the denotations (dictionary definition meanings) and connotations (implied associated meanings) of words used in text, as well as the rhythm and force of words and whether the author uses words concisely, includes verbiage, or appears to have logorrhea. When analyzing word choice in a text, students can consider whether the author has selected words that are comprehensible to the identified reading audience; whether words are chosen with precision and specificity; whether the author selected strong words to express meaning; whether the author placed more emphasis on positive than negative words in text; whether/how often the author included words that are overused, making the language cliché or trite; and whether the text incorporates words that are obsolete today, which readers may not recognize or understand.

Analyzing Text Structure

For these questions, students will be asked to answer questions about why the author structured the text a certain way. They will also be asked about the relationship between a part of the text and the whole text.

Elements to Consider

Text structure is how a text is organized. In analyzing the overall structure of a text, the reader can consider its order, (e.g., what is written first, what follows, and how it ends) and how its sections and chapters are divided. The genre or type of text is another consideration. For example, consider whether the text is fictional or nonfictional; prose, poetry, drama, or oratory; in fictional prose, whether a novel is a romantic, adventure, action, graphic, historical, fantasy, science fiction novel, etc.; in nonfiction, whether it is an essay; research article, journalistic article, opinion-editorial article; how-to manual; travelogue, etc. The relationship or pattern organizing the text may be a timeline sequence, logical sequence, a priority sequence, or spatial sequence; an analysis of the balance of forces; an analysis of similarities and differences/comparison-contrast; a process of problem, solution, and resolution; simply a list of items; or a piece that seems to jump around without order. Consider also what tone the language establishes; vocabulary and imagery used; and the accuracy of text mechanics (grammar, punctuation, spelling, etc.).

Organizational Methods

Authors organize their writing based on the purpose of their text. Common organizational methods that authors use include: cause and effect, compare and contrast, inductive presentation of ideas, deductive presentation of ideas, and chronological order. Cause and effect is used to present the reasons that something happened. Compare and contrast is used to discuss the similarities and differences between two things. Inductive presentation of ideas starts with specific examples and moves to a general conclusion. Deductive presentation of ideas starts with a conclusion and then explains the examples used to arrive at the conclusion. Chronological order presents information in the order that it occurred.

Review Video: Organizational Methods to Structure Text
Visit mometrix.com/academy and enter code: 606263

Authors should organize information logically so the reader can follow what is being said and locate information in the text. Two common organizational structures are cause and effect and chronological order. In cause and effect, an author presents one thing that makes something else happen. For example, if you go to bed very late, you will be tired. The cause is going to bed late. The effect is being tired the next day. When using chronological order, the author presents information in the order that it happened. Biographies are written in chronological order. The subject's birth and childhood are presented first, followed by adult life, and then by events leading up to the person's death.

Example 1

Read the following thesis statement and discuss the organizational pattern that the author will most likely use:

> Among people who are current on the latest technologies, there is a debate over whether DVD or Blu-ray Disc is a better choice for watching and recording video.

From the thesis statement the reader can assume that the author is most likely going to use a compare and contrast organizational structure. The compare and contrast structure is best used to discuss the similarities and differences of two things. The author mentions two options for watching and recording video: DVD and Blu-ray Disc. During the rest of the essay, the author will most likely describe the two technologies, giving specific examples of how they are similar and different. The author may discuss the pros and cons of each technology.

EXAMPLE 2

Read the following thesis statement and discuss the organizational pattern that the author will most likely use:

> Throughout his life, Thomas Edison used his questioning and creative mind to become one of America's greatest inventors.

Based on the thesis statement, the reader can assume that the author is most likely going to use chronological order to organize the information in the rest of the essay. Chronological order presents information in the order that it occurred. It is often used as the organizational structure in biographies to logically present the important events in a person's life. The words "throughout his life" clue in the reader to the chronological organizational structure. The author will probably discuss Edison's childhood and initial inventions first and then move on to his later queries and inventions.

EXAMPLE 3

Read the following thesis statement and discuss the organizational pattern that the author will most likely use:

> Todd is writing an editorial on the need for more bus stops in his town. Discuss the type of organization he should use for his editorial and what each might look like.

Todd could organize the information in his editorial in a few different ways. An editorial is a persuasive text so Todd will want to keep that in mind. First, he could organize the information by making his most important points first, following with his lesser points towards the end. Alternatively, Todd could use a cause and effect structure. He could discuss the reasons that his town needs more bus stops and the effects they would have for the people living there. Finally, Todd could discuss the pros and cons of adding the bus stops, using a compare and contrast structure. The organizational structure Todd chooses will depend on the information he wants to write and the method he thinks will be most persuasive.

PART-WHOLE RELATIONSHIPS

Students should be able to recognize and explain how a portion of a text is related to the overall text to demonstrate they understand part-to-whole relationships when analyzing text. Every part of a text must serve essential purposes, including setting up/establishing the text at the beginning; fitting together logically with all other parts of the text; remaining focused on the point; supporting the overall text through introducing its topic, establishing evidence, supporting or countering a claim, outlining subtopics, aspects, or components, describing a characteristic or feature, etc.; and informing the reader—about the setting of the text, a character in it, a relationship between/among characters, a research study, an opinion, or something else relevant to the text. Test questions may ask about how words function within sentences, as these examples address; or sentence-to-paragraph relationships, which also include setup or setting the tone, logic, focus or point, including shifts in focus, and evidence supporting claims as functions; or paragraph-to-whole-text relationships, wherein paragraphs should establish a claim/situation; support or refute a claim; maintain focus; and/or inform readers.

Analyzing Point of View

These questions will ask the student to determine the author's point of view. They will also need to determine the influence that that this point of view has on the content and style of the text.

In expository text, authors apply various strategies for communicating their points of view about specific topics. As readers, students can identify author point of view readily in some texts; however, they will have to analyze other texts closely to determine point of view. To discern author viewpoint, students can ask themselves four questions: (1) The author is writing to persuade readers to agree with what main idea? (2) How does the author's word choice influence the reader perceptions about the topic? (3) How does the author's selection of examples and/or facts as supporting evidence influence reader thinking about the topic? And (4) What purpose does the author wish to achieve through the text? Students may find the main idea stated directly, as in a topic sentence found in the text, often somewhere in the first paragraph; or they may need to infer it by carefully reading to identify sentences or paragraphs implying it. Students can assess influences of word choice by identifying words/phrases with positive or negative connotations rather than only objective denotations, emphasis through repetition, etc. Examples/facts should illustrate the main idea/point. Author purpose coincides with point of view.

Analyzing Purpose

These questions will ask the student to determine the purpose of a text or a piece of a text. The pieces of text are typically one paragraph of the text.

An author writes with four main purposes: to inform, to entertain, to describe, or to persuade. These purposes play into an author's motivation to create a text. If the author wants to entertain, he or she may write a novel or short story that has humorous elements and/or dramatic elements. Remember, entertainment does not have to mean comedy or humor; it can just as easily be drama. To determine an author's motives, think about the author's purpose. If the text is fiction, the author's purpose is most likely to entertain or describe. If the text is nonfiction, the author's purpose is most likely to inform. If the text is an editorial or advertisement, the author's purpose is most likely to persuade. Once you identify the author's purpose, you can determine the author's motives.

Review Video: Author's Main Point or Purpose
Visit mometrix.com/academy and enter code: 734339

Using Context Clues

To determine the author's purpose in writing text, students can look for certain words as clues to various purposes. For example, if the author's purpose was to compare similarities between/among ideas, look for *clue words* including *like, similar(ly), same, in the same way*, and *just as*. If the author's purpose was to contrast differences between/among ideas, clue words include *but, however, on the other hand, dissimilar(ly)*, and *in contrast/contrastingly*. If the author's purpose was to criticize an idea, clue words connoting judgment/negative opinion include *poor, bad, inadequate, insufficient, lacking, excessive, wasteful, harmful, deleterious, disservice, unfair*, etc. If the purpose was to paint a picture illustrating an idea, descriptive clue words include *morose, crestfallen, lusty, glittering, exuberant*, etc. Explanatory purposes involve using simpler words to describe or explain more complex/abstract ideas. Identification purposes entail listing series of ideas without much accompanying opinion or description. To intensify an idea, authors add superlative (*-est*) adjectives, more specific details; and enlarge concepts. To suggest or propose an idea, authors typically express positive opinions and provide supporting evidence for points to convince readers to agree.

Analyzing Arguments

Students will need to be able to analyze arguments in a text for their structure and content.

The best way to introduce an argument in a persuasive passage and to structure it is to begin by organizing your thoughts and researching the evidence carefully. You should write everything down in outline format to start. Make sure you put the claim at the beginning of the passage. Then, list the reasons and the evidence that you have to support the claim. It is important that you provide enough evidence. Reasons and evidence should follow each other in a logical order. Write the passage so that you hold the reader's attention; use a strong tone and choose words carefully for maximum effect. If you can get the reader to understand your claim, he or she will be more likely to agree with your argument. Restate your claim in the concluding paragraph to maximize the impact on the reader.

Analyzing Claims and Counterclaims

These questions will ask the student to identify explicitly stated claims and counter claims made in a text. They will also need to be able determine implicit claims and counterclaims made in a text.

Defining and Supporting Claims

A claim/argument/proposition/thesis is anything a writer asserts in that is not a known/proven/accepted fact. As such, it is the author's opinion or at least includes an element of opinion. The writer usually will, or should, provide evidence to back up this claim. Some writers make claims without supporting them, but these are not as effective in convincing readers to believe or agree with them. Some may attempt to provide evidence but choose it poorly; if they cite evidence that is not related directly enough to the claim, or the *evidence* is information from untrustworthy sources or not verified as accurate, this is also less effective. Writers sometimes state their claims directly and clearly; in other instances, they may discuss a number of related topics from which the reader must infer the claims implied in the discussion. For example, suppose two writers take opposing positions, one that immigration to the USA is bad and the other that it is good. Rather than explicitly stating these claims, both may present information supporting negative/positive aspects/views of immigration. Critical readers can infer these claims from the information's negativity/positivity.

Making Claims

A persuasive essay will likely focus on one central argument, but it may make many smaller claims along the way. These are subordinate arguments with which the reader must agree if he or she is going to agree with the central argument. The central argument will only be as strong as the subordinate claims. These claims should be rooted in fact and observation, rather than subjective judgment. The best persuasive essays provide enough supporting detail to justify claims without overwhelming the reader. Remember that a fact must be susceptible to independent verification: that is, it must be something the reader could confirm. Also, statistics are only effective when they take into account possible objections. For instance, a statistic on the number of foreclosed houses would only be useful if it was taken over a defined interval and in a defined area. Most readers are wary of statistics, because they are so often misleading. If possible, a persuasive essay should always include references so that the reader can obtain more information. Of course, this means that the writer's accuracy and fairness may be judged by the inquiring reader.

Counterclaims

Whereas a claim represents a text's main argument, a counterclaim represents an argument that opposes that claim. Writers actually use counterclaims to support their claims. They do this by presenting their claim; introducing a counterclaim to it; and then definitively refuting the counterclaim. Rather than only promoting and supporting the claim, which leaves the text open to being refuted or attacked by other writers who present their own counterclaims, authors who present both claim and counterclaim have anticipated opposing arguments before others can raise them; have given a voice to the opposition to their claim, and then discredited that voice; and, when they do this effectively, show that their ability to do so indicates how familiar and competent they are with respect to the topic they are discussing in their text. Words such as *but, yet, however, nevertheless, nonetheless, notwithstanding, despite, in spite of, on the contrary, contrastingly*, etc. indicating contrast/difference/disagreement signal counterclaims. If readers/students cannot locate a claim in text, they may identify a counterclaim by signal words and work backwards to discover what claim the counterclaim opposes.

Discrediting a Counterclaim

When writers present a claim, (i.e., a central argument in text), they may also introduce a counterclaim opposing that claim. When journalists do this, by presenting the other side to their argument they can demonstrate their objectivity. In a different use, writers of argumentative/persuasive text may find that furnishing evidence to support a claim, appealing to various reader responses, and other rhetorical devices may still not lend their claim as much strength as they would like. In such cases, another rhetorical technique they may use is presenting a counterclaim. This enables writers not only to anticipate opposing arguments to their claim, but also to rebut these opposing arguments, which in turn lends additional strength to their original claim. As an example, one might claim that using a dentist-approved mouthwash regularly can prevent gingivitis. A counterclaim might be that in a recent survey, dentists questioned the effectiveness of mouthwash. When the next sentence states that this survey included only three dentists, all of whose dental studies were incomplete, the writer has effectively discredited the counterclaim and opposition, reinforcing the original claim.

Assessing Reasoning

Assessing Soundness

In addition to identifying claims and counterclaims that authors present in their texts, students must be able to evaluate whether those claims and counterclaims are sound. The PSAT, SAT, and other standardized tests ask questions that require students to assess the soundness of an author's reasoning in text. A valid argument is logical, (i.e., each premise or statement follows upon the previous one). However, test questions are not limited to requiring students to assess text logic/validity; they moreover require students to assess soundness, meaning whether the argument is true. Students will likely not have thorough knowledge of all text content on tests. They should assume the content of unfamiliar text is true, since the test will not try to trick students by providing false material. To assess a text argument, the student must first identify its central claim. The remainder of the argument should both answer why the central claim is true, and also prove or support that claim.

Approach for Test Questions

Some text-based test questions may ask students not only what central claim or argument an author makes in a passage, but also what the author's reasoning behind that claim is. To help select the correct answer from among multiple choices on such questions, the student will need to follow the reasoning that the author uses in the text and relate it to the answer choices. The student can do this by reading each answer choice and then asking himself/herself whether this choice answers the question of why the author's central claim is true. For the student to be able to assess the author's reasoning for soundness, he or she must have the ability to cite evidence with accuracy to support that assessment of reasoning and its soundness or lack thereof. The best and easiest way of justifying one's assessment of reasoning and its relative soundness by citing evidence is to ask oneself whether why the author makes the claim; how the author justifies the claim; and whether evidence supports the claim and answers the question of why.

Levels of Critical Reading

Experts (cf. Elder and Paul, 2004) identify four levels of critical reading. The first level is paraphrasing the text one sentence at a time, which develops and demonstrates understanding. The second level is identifying and explicating a text paragraph's main idea. The third level is analyzing the author's logic and reasoning, including the main purpose, question, information, inferences, concepts, assumptions, implications, and viewpoints. The fourth level is assessing logic or reasoning. Since text quality varies among authors and texts, readers must assess author reasoning. Paraphrasing author meaning accurately on the first level is a prerequisite. To assess reasoning, consider whether the author states his or her meaning clearly; whether the author's claims are accurate; whether he or she offers specifics and/or details with enough precision when these are relevant; whether the author strays from his or her purpose by introducing irrelevant information; whether the text is written superficially or addresses the topic's inherent complexities; whether the author's perspective is narrow or considers other pertinent perspectives; whether the text has internal contradictions or is consistent; whether the text addresses the topic in a trivial or significant way; and whether the author's attitude is narrow/unilateral or fair.

Analyzing Evidence

For these questions the student will be asked to determine how the author uses evidence to support his claims and counterclaims.

Presenting Evidence

When in a focused discussion, be prepared to present your claims, findings, and supporting evidence in a clear and distinct manner. This means being prepared. When compiling your data, make sure to create an outline that has the main ideas and then the supporting evidence, including graphics that you want to present. Attention to details will result in a successful presentation, one in which the diverse individuals in the group will come away with a feeling of having been part of something meaningful. Facts and examples should be stressed. Repetition creates retention. It is important for the speaker to choose the right words, and to build momentum by gradually building up to the strongest argument(s). Graphics are important, because participants will be more convinced if they can see evidence as well as hear it. By breaking up the flow of the discussion and introducing pauses before and after pertinent arguments, the speaker will make the presentation of facts more interesting.

Identifying Evidence

To assess claims an author makes in text, the reader must be able to analyze the evidence the author supplies to support those claims and evaluate whether the evidence is convincing or not. Students should ask themselves why the author makes a given claim; how the author justifies that claim; and whether the evidence the author uses to justify the claim convincingly and thoroughly answers the *why* question, which means the evidence is effective. If the student can easily come up with counterclaims to the author's claims, the author's reasoning and/or evidence used to support it may not be as convincing as they could be. When answering text-based multiple-choice questions asking them to identify evidence supporting a central claim, students can determine the correct choice by identifying and eliminating choices citing text that extends the argument rather than supporting it because it does not answer why; and text that is related but not the main source of support, in addition to completely incorrect choices.

Supporting Evidence

Test questions will not only ask students to identify what evidence an author uses in text to support his or her claims; they will also ask students to evaluate an author's strategy for using evidence to support his or her argument. For example, a passage of text might be an author's review of a book, film, or other work. A review most commonly makes the main point that the work is either good or bad, or sometimes a combination of both. A review might also make, argue, and support the point that a movie or book demonstrates a particular central trait (e.g., that a movie identified in the romantic comedy genre is actually *anti-romantic*). In order to support his or her main point, the reviewer could use various tactics, such as comparing the work to others as evidence supporting the claim; stating and then effectively addressing a counterclaim to support the claim; or giving a number of examples from the work which can all be used to serve as support for the claim. Some reviewers combine all of these strategies, which when done well can be most effective.

Essential Considerations

When analyzing the evidence that an author presents in a text to organize and back up his or her argument, as he or she reads, the student should remember to focus not only on what the author's central claim or point is, but also on what the actual content of that evidence is; how the author uses the evidence to prove the point or claim that he or she is making; and whether or not the evidence that the author provides is effective in supporting that central claim or point. A good way to evaluate whether a piece of evidence that an author uses is supportive of that author's central claim is whether that evidence answers the question of why the author is making that claim. The reader should also consider the questions of how the author justifies this claim and whether the evidence the author has presented to justify the claim is convincing or not.

Synthesis

The questions in this section will focus on synthesizing across multiple sources of information.

Analyzing Multiple Texts

The student will be required to synthesize information and ideas across multiple texts. This means that they will need to apply all the other skills above to analyze paired passages.

Synthesizing, (i.e., understanding and integrating), information from multiple texts can at times be among the most challenging skills for some students to succeed with on tests and in school, and yet it is also among the most important. Students who read at the highest cognitive levels can select related material from different text sources and construct coherent arguments that account for these varied information sources. Synthesizing ideas and information from multiple texts actually combines other reading skills that students should have mastered previously in reading one text at a time, and applies them in the context of reading more than one text. For example, students are required to read texts closely, including identifying explicit and implicit meanings; use critical thinking and reading; draw inferences; assess author reasoning; analyze supporting evidence; and formulate opinions they can justify, based on more passages than one. When two paired texts represent opposing sides of the same argument, students can find analyzing them easier; but this is not always the case.

Review Video: Synthesizing Text
Visit mometrix.com/academy and enter code: 187664

Similarities

When students are called upon to compare things two texts share, the most obvious commonality might be the same subject matter or specific topic. However, two texts need not be about the same thing to compare them. Some other features texts can share include structural characteristics. For example, they may both be written using a sequential format, such as narrating events or giving instructions in chronological order; listing and/or discussing subtopics by order of importance; or describing a place spatially in sequence from each point to the next. They may both use a comparison-contrast structure, identifying similarities and differences between, among, or within topics. They might both organize information by identifying cause-and-effect relationships. Texts can be similar in type, (e.g., description, narration, persuasion, or exposition). They can be similar in using technical vocabulary or using formal or informal language. They may share similar tones and/or styles, (e.g., humorous, satirical, serious). They can share similar purposes, (e.g., to alarm audiences, incite them to action, reassure them, inspire them, provoke strong emotional responses).

Contrasts

When analyzing paired or multiple texts, students might observe differences in tone; for example, one text might take a serious approach while another uses a humorous one. Even within approaches or treatments, style can differ: one text may be humorous in a witty, sophisticated, clever way while another may exercise broad, low-brow humor; another may employ mordant sarcasm; another may use satire, couching outrageous suggestions in a deadpan logical voice to lampoon social attitudes and behaviors as Jonathan Swift did in *A Modest Proposal.* Serious writing can range from darkly pessimistic to alarmist to objective and unemotional. Texts might have similar information, yet organize it using different structures. One text may support points or ideas using logical arguments, while another may seek to persuade its audience by appealing to their emotions. A very obvious difference in text is genre: for example, the same mythological or traditional stories have been told as oral folk tales, written dramas, written novels, etc.; and/or set in different times and places (e.g., Shakespeare's *Romeo and Juliet* vs. Laurents, Bernstein, and Sondheim's *West Side Story*).

Analyzing Quantitative Information

These questions will test the student's ability to analyze quantitative information. This information may be presented in graphs, tables, and charts and may relate to other information presented in the text.

When students read text, particularly informational text, authors may include graphs, charts, and/or tables to illustrate the written information under discussion. Students need to be able to understand these representations and how they are related to the text they supplement. For example, a line graph can show how some numerical value—like number or percentage of items, people, groups, dollars, births, deaths, cases of specific illnesses, etc. or amount of rainfall, products, waste matter, etc.—has increased, decreased, or stayed the same over designated periods of time. A bar graph may be used like a line graph to show the same chronological change; or to compare different numbers or proportions of things side by side without reference to time. A pie chart visualizes distribution and proportion by depicting percentages or fractions of a whole occupied by different categories, (e.g., how much money is allocated or spent for each division among services or products, what percentages or proportions of a population has certain characteristics). Tables and charts often list numbers by category; students must be able to identify largest and smallest quantities, order by quantity, etc.

Interpreting Graphics

An author may organize information in a chart, a graph, in paragraph format, or as a list. Information may also be presented in a picture or a diagram. The information may be arranged according to the order in which it occurred over time, placed in categories, or it may be arranged in a cause-and-effect relationship. Information can also be presented according to where it occurs in a given space (spatial order), or organized through description. The way an author chooses to organize information is often based on the purpose of information that is being presented, the best way to present given information, and the audience that the information is meant to reach.

It is important to be able to interpret information presented in graphics and be able to translate it to text. These graphics can include maps, charts, illustrations, graphs, timelines, and tables. Each of these different graphics is used to present a different type of quantitative or technical information. Maps show a visual representation of a certain area. A map may contain a legend which helps to identify certain geographic features on the map. A graph or chart will usually contain two axes that show the relationship between two variables. A table can also be like this but may show the relationship between any number of variables. So, no matter how the information is presented it is important to be able to interpret it and explain what it means.

Review Video: Drawing Conclusions from Graphic Organizers
Visit mometrix.com/academy and enter code: 363785

Reading Passages

Some questions will be concerning sentence insertions. In those cases, do not look for the ones that simply restate what was in the previous sentence. New sentences should contain new information and new insights into the subject of the text. If asked for the paragraph to which a sentence would most naturally be added, find a key noun or word in that new sentence. Then find the paragraph containing exactly or another word closely related to that key noun or word. That is the paragraph that should include the new sentence.

Some questions will ask what purpose a phrase fulfilled in a text. It depends upon the subject of the text. If the text is dramatic, then the phrase was probably used to show drama. If the text is comedic, then the phrase was probably to show comedy.

In related cases, you may be asked to provide a sentence that summarizes the text, or to reorganize a paragraph. Simple sentences, without wordy phrases, are usually best. If asked for a succinct answer, then the shorter the answer, the more likely it is correct.

Skimming

Your first task when you begin reading is to answer the question "What is the topic of the selection?" This can best be answered by quickly skimming the passage for the general idea, stopping to read only the first sentence of each paragraph. A paragraph's first is usually the main topic sentence, and it gives you a summary of the content of the paragraph.

Once you've skimmed the passage, stopping to read only the first sentences, you will have a general idea about what it is about, as well as what is the expected topic in each paragraph.

Each question will contain clues as to where to find the answer in the passage. Do not just randomly search through the passage for the correct answer to each question. Search scientifically. Find key word(s) or ideas in the question that are going to either contain or be near the correct answer. These are typically nouns, verbs, numbers, or phrases in the question that will probably be duplicated in the passage. Once you have identified those key word(s) or idea, skim the passage quickly to find where those key word(s) or idea appears. The correct answer choice will be nearby.

EXAMPLE:

> What caused Martin to suddenly return to Paris?

The key word is Paris. Skim the passage quickly to find where this word appears. The answer will be close by that word.

However, sometimes key words in the question are not repeated in the passage. In those cases, search for the general idea of the question.

Example:

> Which of the following was the psychological impact of the author's childhood upon the remainder of his life?

Key words are *childhood* or *psychology*. While searching for those words, be alert for other words or phrases that have similar meaning, such as *emotional effect* or *mentally* which could be used in the passage, rather than the exact word *psychology*.

Numbers or years can be particularly good key words to skim for, as they stand out from the rest of the text.

Example:

Which of the following best describes the influence of Monet's work in the 20th century?

20th contains numbers and will easily stand out from the rest of the text. Use *20th* as the key word to skim for in the passage.

Other good key word(s) may be in quotation marks. These identify a word or phrase that is copied directly from the passage. In those cases, the word(s) in quotation marks are exactly duplicated in the passage.

EXAMPLE:

In her college years, what was meant by Margaret's "drive for excellence"?

Drive for excellence is a direct quote from the passage and should be easy to find.

DIRECTLY QUOTED ANSWERS

Once you've quickly found the correct section of the passage to find the answer, focus upon the answer choices. Sometimes a choice will repeat word for word a portion of the passage near the answer. However, beware of such duplication – it may be a trap! More than likely, the correct choice will paraphrase or summarize the related portion of the passage, rather than being exactly the same wording.

TRUE DOES NOT EQUAL CORRECT

For the answers that you think are correct, read them carefully and make sure that they answer the question. An answer can be factually correct, but it MUST answer the question asked. Additionally, two answers can both be seemingly correct, so be sure to read all of the answer choices, and make sure that you get the one that BEST answers the question.

NO KEY WORD?

Some questions will not have a key word.

EXAMPLE:

Which of the following would the author of this passage likely agree with?

In these cases, look for key words in the answer choices. Then skim the passage to find where the answer choice occurs. By skimming to find where to look, you can minimize the time required.

Sometimes it may be difficult to identify a good key word in the question to skim for in the passage. In those cases, look for a key word in one of the answer choices to skim for. Often the answer choices can all be found in the same paragraph, which can quickly narrow your search.

Review Video: When There's No Keyword
Visit mometrix.com/academy and enter code: 312791

PARAGRAPH FOCUS

Focus upon the first sentence of each paragraph, which is the most important. The main topic of the paragraph is usually there.

Once you've read the first sentence in the paragraph, you have a general idea about what each paragraph will be about. As you read the questions, try to determine which paragraph will have the answer. Paragraphs have a concise topic. The answer should either obviously be there or obviously not. It will save time if you can jump straight to the paragraph, so try to remember what you learned from the first sentences.

Example: The first paragraph is about poets; the second is about poetry. If a question asks about poetry, where will the answer be? The second paragraph.

The main idea of a passage is typically spread across all or most of its paragraphs. Whereas the main idea of a paragraph may be completely different than the main idea of the very next paragraph, a main idea for a passage affects all of the paragraphs in one form or another.

EXAMPLE:

> What is the main idea of the passage?

For each answer choice, try to see how many paragraphs are related. It can help to count how many sentences are affected by each choice, but it is best to see how many paragraphs are affected by the choice. Typically, the answer choices will include incorrect choices that are main ideas of individual paragraphs, but not the entire passage. That is why it is crucial to choose ideas that are supported by the most paragraphs possible.

ELIMINATE CHOICES

Some choices can quickly be eliminated. "Andy Warhol lived there." Is Andy Warhol even mentioned in the article? If not, quickly eliminate it.

When trying to answer a question such as "the passage indicates all of the following EXCEPT" quickly skim the paragraph searching for references to each choice. If the reference exists, scratch it off as a choice. Similar choices may be crossed off simultaneously if they are close enough.

Watch for answers that are similarly worded. Since only one answer can be correct, if there are two answers that appear to mean the same thing, they must BOTH be incorrect, and can be eliminated.

EXAMPLE ANSWER CHOICES:

> a. changing values and attitudes
> b. a large population of mobile or uprooted people

These answer choices are similar; they both describe a fluid culture. Because of their similarity, they can be linked together. Since the answer can have only one choice, they can also be eliminated together.

FACT OR OPINION?

Remember that answer choices that are facts will typically have no ambiguous words. For example, how long is a long time? What defines an ordinary person? These ambiguous words of *long* and *ordinary* should not be in a factual statement. However, if all of the choices have ambiguous words, go to the context of the passage. Often a factual statement may be set out as a research finding.

Review Video: Fact or Opinion
Visit mometrix.com/academy and enter code: 870899

EXAMPLE:

"The scientist found that the eye reacts quickly to change in light."

Opinions may be set out in the context of words like thought, believed, understood, or wished.

EXAMPLE:

"He thought the Yankees should win the World Series."

TIME MANAGEMENT

Depending on your personal preference, try reading the questions before reading the passage. Doing so will help you be aware of what to look for while reading a passage and may even help with comprehension.

In technical passages, do not get lost on the technical terms. Skip them and move on. You want a general understanding of what is going on, not a mastery of the passage.

When you encounter material in the selection that seems difficult to understand, bracket it. It often may not be necessary and can be skipped. Only spend time trying to understand it if it is going to be relevant for a question. Understand difficult phrases only as a last resort.

Answer general questions before detail questions. A reader with a good understanding of the whole passage can often answer general questions without rereading a word. Get the easier questions out of the way before tackling the more time-consuming ones.

Identify each question by type. Usually the wording of a question will tell you whether you can find the answer by referring directly to the passage or by using your reasoning powers. You alone know which question types you customarily handle with ease and which give you trouble and will require more time. Save the difficult questions for last.

Final Warnings

Hedge Phrases

Once again, watch out for critical hedge phrases, such as likely, may, can, will often, mostly, usually, generally, rarely, sometimes, etc. Question writers insert these hedge phrases, to cover every possibility. Often an answer will be wrong simply because it leaves no room for exception.

Example:

> Animals live longer in cold places than animals in warm places.

This answer choice is wrong, because there are exceptions in which certain warm climate animals live longer. This answer choice leaves no possibility of exception. It states that every animal species in cold places live longer than animal species in warm places. Correct answer choices will typically have a key hedge word to leave room for exceptions.

Example:

> In severe cold, a polar bear cub is likely to survive longer than an adult polar bear.

This answer choice is correct, because not only does the passage imply that younger animals survive better in the cold, it also allows for exceptions to exist. The use of the word *likely* leaves room for cases in which a polar bear cub might not survive longer than the adult polar bear.

Word Usage

When asked how a word is used in the passage, don't use your existing knowledge of the word. The question is being asked precisely because there is some strange or unusual usage of the word in the passage. Go to the passage and use contextual clues to determine the answer. Don't simply use the popular definition you already know.

Review Video: Word Usage
Visit mometrix.com/academy and enter code: 197863

Switchback Words

Stay alert for *switchbacks*. These are the words and phrases frequently used to alert you to shifts in thought. The most common switchback word is *but*. Others include although, however, nevertheless, on the other hand, even though, while, in spite of, despite, regardless of.

Fact Traps

Once you know which paragraph the answer will be in, focus on that paragraph. However, don't get distracted by a choice that is factually true about the paragraph. Your search is for the answer that answers the question, which may be about a tiny aspect in the paragraph. Stay focused and don't fall for an answer that describes the larger picture of the paragraph. Always go back to the question and make sure you're choosing an answer that actually answers the question and is not just a true statement.

Writing and Language Test

The writing and language portion of the PSAT consists of one 35-minute section. It will contain 4 passages and there will be a total of 44 questions relating to these passages. The breakdown of passages and questions is shown in the table below.

Careers	1 passage; 11 questions	25%
History/Social Studies	1 passage; 11 questions	25%
Humanities	1 passage; 11 questions	25%
Science	1 passage; 11 questions	25%

The PSAT Writing and Language Test will contain a range of text complexities from grades 9-10 to post-secondary entry. The passages will cover the subjects from the table above. The test will also contain one or more graphics in one or more sets of questions. These may include tables, graphs, and charts. They will vary in level of difficulty as well as data density, and number of variables.

The questions on the Writing and Language portion of the test are divided into two categories. The first category, called **Expression of Ideas**, is essentially testing whether students understand how to effectively communicate ideas in writing. The second category, called **Standard English Conventions**, is essentially testing whether students are able to practically apply their knowledge of the conventions of standard written English. Both types of questions are set in the context of revising a sample written passage. Students are asked to modify specific portions of the passage by selecting the best words, phrases, concepts, order, and structure to ensure that the final version of the passage adheres to the conventions of writing, is consistent with the author's style and purpose, and effectively conveys the message the author intends.

Expression of Ideas

The questions in this section will focus on the revision of text. They will ask the student to revise for topic development, accuracy, logic, cohesion, and rhetorically effective use of language. Many of the skills needed for these questions are the same skills as are needed for the Reading Test, or are built upon those skills.

Development

Proposition and Support

Proposition questions will require the student to add, retain, or revise central ideas, main claims, counterclaims, and topic sentences. These revisions should be made to convey arguments, information, and ideas more clearly and effectively. *Support* questions will ask the student to add, revise, or retain information and ideas with the intention of supporting claims in the text.

Topics and Main Ideas

The topic is the **subject** of a text (i.e., what the text is all about). The main idea, on the other hand, is the **most important point** being made by the author. The topic is usually expressed in a few words at the most while the main idea often needs a full sentence to be completely defined. As an example, a short passage might have the topic of penguins and the main idea could be written as: *Penguins are different from other birds in many ways.* In most nonfiction writing, the topic and the main idea will be stated directly and often appear in a sentence at the very **beginning** or **end** of the text. When being tested on an understanding of the author's topic, you may be able to **skim** the passage for the general idea, by reading only the first sentence of each paragraph. A body paragraph's first sentence is often—but not always—the main topic sentence which gives you a summary of the content in the paragraph. However, there are cases in which the reader must figure out an **unstated** topic or main idea. In these instances, you must read every sentence of the text and try to come up with an overarching idea that is supported by each of those sentences.

Be aware though that identifying the main idea is only the first step. Once you've determined what it is, you have to decide how to express it in the most effective way.

Review Video: Topics and Main Ideas
Visit mometrix.com/academy and enter code: 407801

Supporting Details

Effective supporting details provide **evidence** and backing for the main point. In order to show that a main idea is correct, or valid, authors add details that prove their point. All texts contain details, but they are only classified as **supporting details** when they serve to reinforce some larger point. Supporting details are most commonly found in **informative** and **persuasive** texts. In some cases, they will be clearly indicated with terms like *for example* or *for instance*, or they will be enumerated with terms like *first*, *second*, and *last*. However, you need to be prepared for texts that do not contain those indicators. In considering which supporting details to include, you should consider whether the details *effectively* support the main point. **Ineffective supporting details** can be factual and correct, yet they may not be relevant to the author's point. Conversely, ineffective supporting details can seem pertinent, but may be ineffective because they are based on opinion or unprovable assertions.

Review Video: Supporting Details
Visit mometrix.com/academy and enter code: 396297

Topic and Summary Sentences

Topic and summary sentences are a convenient way to encapsulate the **main idea** of a text. In some textbooks and academic articles, the author will place a **topic** or **summary sentence** at the beginning of each section as a means of preparing the reader for what is to come. A good topic sentence will be **clear** and not contain any **jargon**. When topic or summary sentences are not provided, good readers can jot down their own so that they can find their place in a text and refresh their memory.

Focus

For these questions, students will be asked to add, revise, retain, or delete information for the sake of relevance. These revisions should make the text more relevant and focused.

These questions are generally straightforward and do not require any special skills to answer. The correct answer will be the one that best stays on topic and coherently contributes to the author's main point in the paragraph or passage.

Quantitative Information

These questions will ask the student to relate information presented quantitatively to information presented in the text. The quantitative information may be in the form of graphs, charts, and tables.

The only particular skill needed for these questions is the ability to read and understand the information contained within a graphic. Questions will typically require you to select the choice that accurately reflects the quantitative information conveyed by the graphic. Answer choices for this type of question are often long, so reading through them can be time-consuming. However, you should be able to scan the answer choices for numbers, and quickly determine which ones match the quantities with their correct values. In general, there should be only one choice that uses the correct values (i.e., a single question won't ask you to both determine the correct quantitative information and decide how to state it in the most concise way).

Organization

Logical Sequence

For these questions the student should revise the text with the intention of improving the logical order that the information is presented in.

These questions generally come at the end of a paragraph (or the whole passage) and ask you to decide whether a sentence (or a paragraph) should be moved to a different location. Since these questions come at the end of the paragraph, you will already have read the paragraph when you get to them, so start by mentally relocating the sentence into each of the suggested positions to see what makes the most sense. In some cases, the sentence may fit into a logical progression within the paragraph that will give you a clue about where it ought to go. Does the sentence refer back to anything that has already been said? At other times, there may be grammatical clues within the sentence that offer hints. Do the verb tenses transition from past to present or present to future over the course of the paragraph? Even if you can't determine exactly which choice would be considered the best, you can usually use these techniques to rule out some of them.

Introductions, Conclusions, and Transitions

These questions require the student to revise the beginning or ending of passages, paragraphs, and sentences. Students will ensure that transition words, phrases, or sentences are used effectively to connect the information and ideas being presented in the passage.

This is often the largest single category of questions on the Writing and Language test. There will usually be 5-7 of these questions on each test.

Introductions and Conclusions

An ideal introduction to a paragraph or passage sets up the reader to understand what is coming. In some cases, you may have to read the entire paragraph to see where the author is going before you can knowledgeably select the best way to introduce it.

The conclusion of a text is typically found in the last one or two paragraphs of the text. A conclusion wraps-up the text and reminds the reader of the main point of the text. The conclusion is the author's way of leaving the reader with a final note to remember about the paper and comes after all the supporting points of the text have been presented. For example, a paper about the importance of avoiding too much sunlight may have a conclusion that reads: By limiting sun exposure to 15 minutes a day and wearing sunscreen of at least SPF 15, a person can reduce their risk of getting skin cancer later in life.

Transitions

Appropriate transition words help clarify the relationships between sentences and paragraphs, and they create a much more cohesive passage. Below are listed several categories of transitions that you will need to be familiar with along with the associated transition words:

- **Logical Continuation**: therefore, as such, for this reason, thus, consequently, as a result
- **Extended Argument**: moreover, furthermore, also
- **Example or Illustration**: for instance, for example
- **Comparison**: similarly, likewise, in like manner

- **Contrast**: however, nevertheless, by contrast
- **Restatement or Clarification**: in other words, to put it another way
- **Generalization or General Application**: in broad terms, broadly speaking, in general

EFFECTIVE LANGUAGE USE

PRECISION

For these questions, students will revise the text to improve the exactness or context-appropriateness of word choice.

This is as close as the Writing and Language test gets to testing your vocabulary directly. As with everything on the test, these questions are asked within the context of the passage, but you will have to select the word from among the answer choices that most closely means what the author intends. Connotation and tone will play some role here, but rarely will you be presented with more than one choice whose dictionary definition fits the situation.

CONCISION

For these questions, students will revise the text to improve the economy of word choice. This means they should cut out wordiness and redundancy.

In general, these questions can be solved by feel. The incorrect choices on these questions tend to be rambling or awkward. If you pick the answer that uses a simple construction, does not repeat itself, and carries a reasonable meaning, you'll get it right just about every time.

EXAMPLE

Edit the following sentence so that it expresses ideas precisely and concisely, and wordiness and redundancy are eliminated.

> If you go to the library on Sunday, you will find that the library doors are locked and that the facility is closed on Sunday.

Here is one possible revision:

> If you go to the library on Sunday, you will find the doors locked and the facility closed.

STYLE AND TONE

These questions require the student to revise the style and tone of the text. These revisions are made primarily to ensure consistency of style and tone throughout the passage but also to improve the appropriateness of the style and tone to the author's purpose.

If the author has been using formal words and tone throughout, maintain that pattern. If the author has been writing relatively informally, don't suddenly transition to formal language. Most passages on the test will be on the formal side, but you should be able to distinguish between slightly formal and overly formal. Don't choose fancy words just because they're fancy. If there are simpler more precise words available, go with those.

SYNTAX

These questions will require the student to use varied sentence structure to achieve the desired rhetorical purpose.

Syntax is the order of the words in a sentence. When writing, it is important to make sure not only that the syntax is correct, but also that it is not repetitive. There is nothing worse than reading a passage that has sentences that are all alike: noun, verb, object. These need to be interspersed with sentences that use a variety of clause constructions. This will lend a musicality to the writing, and will allow for greater flow of language and ideas.

EXAMPLE:

Rewrite the following sentences by varying their syntax.

> Marilyn and Rosemary worked together. They were having a party. They had to get all the food done first. They cleaned the house and decorated. They invited about 20 people. The people were all work associates. They were having the party in Marilyn's backyard. This is where she had many similar parties. They were always fun.

This is one way to rewrite the sentences so that the syntax is varied:

> Marilyn and Rosemary were coworkers who decided to throw a party. To prepare, they had to get all the food ready, as well as clean and decorate the house. They invited about 20 people, all work associates, and held the party in Marilyn's backyard, where they had hosted many fun parties before.

The rewritten sentences provide a greater variety of syntax, and consequently, greater rhythm. The language is more engaging as a result.

Standard English Conventions

The questions in this section focus on editing the text to make sure that it conforms to the conventions of standard written English. This includes the editing of sentences, usage, and punctuation. While this part of the test does not specifically require a detailed knowledge of technical grammar, it would be next to impossible to excel on these questions without it. We will therefore be reviewing the basics of grammar and using that vocabulary as we discuss what to do on the test.

The Eight Parts of Speech

Nouns

When you talk about a person, place, thing, or idea, you are talking about **nouns**. The two main types of nouns are **common** and **proper** nouns. Also, nouns can be abstract (i.e., general) or concrete (i.e., specific).

Common nouns are the class or group of people, places, and things (Note: Do not capitalize common nouns). Examples of common nouns:

People: boy, girl, worker, manager

Places: school, bank, library, home

Things: dog, cat, truck, car

Proper nouns are the names of a specific person, place, or thing (Note: Capitalize all proper nouns). Examples of proper nouns:

People: Abraham Lincoln, George Washington, Martin Luther King, Jr.

Places: Los Angeles, California / New York / Asia

Things: Statue of Liberty, Earth*, Lincoln Memorial

*Note: When you talk about the planet that we live on, you capitalize *Earth*. When you mean the dirt, rocks, or land, you lowercase *earth*.

General nouns are the names of conditions or ideas. **Specific nouns** name people, places, and things that are understood by using your senses.

General nouns:

Condition: beauty, strength

Idea: truth, peace

Specific nouns:

People: baby, friend, father

Places: town, park, city hall

Things: rainbow, cough, apple, silk, gasoline

Collective nouns are the names for a person, place, or thing that may act as a whole. The following are examples of collective nouns: *class, company, dozen, group, herd, team,* and *public.*

PRONOUNS

Pronouns are words that are used to stand in for a noun. A pronoun may be classified as personal, intensive, relative, interrogative, demonstrative, indefinite, and reciprocal.

Personal: *Nominative* is the case for nouns and pronouns that are the subject of a sentence. *Objective* is the case for nouns and pronouns that are an object in a sentence. *Possessive* is the case for nouns and pronouns that show possession or ownership.

SINGULAR

	Nominative	Objective	Possessive
First Person	I	me	my, mine
Second Person	you	you	your, yours
Third Person	he, she, it	him, her, it	his, her, hers, its

PLURAL

	Nominative	Objective	Possessive
First Person	we	us	our, ours
Second Person	you	you	your, yours
Third Person	they	them	their, theirs

Intensive: I myself, you yourself, he himself, she herself, the (thing) itself, we ourselves, you yourselves, they themselves

Relative: which, who, whom, whose

Interrogative: what, which, who, whom, whose

Demonstrative: this, that, these, those

Indefinite: all, any, each, everyone, either/neither, one, some, several

Reciprocal: each other, one another

Review Video: Nouns and Pronouns
Visit mometrix.com/academy and enter code: 312073

VERBS

If you want to write a sentence, then you need a verb in your sentence. Without a verb, you have no sentence. The verb of a sentence explains action or being. In other words, the verb shows the subject's movement or the movement that has been done to the subject.

Transitive and Intransitive Verbs

A transitive verb is a verb whose action (e.g., drive, run, jump) points to a receiver (e.g., car, dog, kangaroo). Intransitive verbs do not point to a receiver of an action. In other words, the action of the verb does not point to a subject or object.

> **Transitive**: He plays the piano. | The piano was played by him.

> **Intransitive**: He plays. | John writes well.

A dictionary will let you know whether a verb is transitive or intransitive. Some verbs can be transitive and intransitive.

Action Verbs and Linking Verbs

An action verb is a verb that shows what the subject is doing in a sentence. In other words, an action verb shows action. A sentence can be complete with one word: an action verb. Linking verbs are intransitive verbs that show a condition (i.e., the subject is described but does no action).

Linking verbs link the subject of a sentence to a noun or pronoun, or they link a subject with an adjective. You always need a verb if you want a complete sentence. However, linking verbs are not able to complete a sentence.

Common linking verbs include *appear, be, become, feel, grow, look, seem, smell, sound,* and *taste*. However, any verb that shows a condition and has a noun, pronoun, or adjective that describes the subject of a sentence is a linking verb.

Action: He sings. | Run! | Go! | I talk with him every day. | She reads.

Linking:

> Incorrect: I am.

> Correct: I am John. | I smell roses. | I feel tired.

Note: Some verbs are followed by words that look like prepositions, but they are a part of the verb and a part of the verb's meaning. These are known as phrasal verbs and examples include *call off*, *look up*, and *drop off*.

Voice

Transitive verbs come in active or passive voice. If the subject does an action or receives the action of the verb, then you will know whether a verb is active or passive. When the subject of the sentence is doing the action, the verb is **active voice**. When the subject receives the action, the verb is **passive voice**.

> **Active**: Jon drew the picture. (The subject *Jon* is doing the action of *drawing a picture*.)

> **Passive**: The picture is drawn by Jon. (The subject *picture* is receiving the action from Jon.)

Verb Tenses

A verb tense shows the different form of a verb to point to the time of an action. The present and past tense are shown by changing the verb's form. An action in the present *I talk* can change form for the past: *I talked*. However, for the other tenses, an auxiliary (i.e., helping) verb is needed to show the change in form. These helping verbs include *am, are, is* | *have, has, had* | *was, were, will* (or *shall*).

Present: I talk	Present perfect: I have talked
Past: I talked	Past perfect: I had talked
Future: I will talk	Future perfect: I will have talked

Present: The action happens at the current time.

Example: He *walks* to the store every morning.

To show that something is happening right now, use the progressive present tense: I *am walking*.

Past: The action happened in the past.

Example: He *walked* to the store an hour ago.

Future: The action is going to happen later.

Example: I *will walk* to the store tomorrow.

Present perfect: The action started in the past and continues into the present.

Example: I *have walked* to the store three times today.

Past perfect: The second action happened in the past. The first action came before the second.

Example: Before I walked to the store (Action 2), I *had walked* to the library (Action 1).

Future perfect: An action that uses the past and the future. In other words, the action is complete before a future moment.

Example: When she comes for the supplies (future moment), I *will have walked* to the store (action completed in the past).

Review Video: Present Perfect, Past Perfect, and Future Perfect Verb Tenses
Visit mometrix.com/academy and enter code: 269472

Conjugating Verbs

When you need to change the form of a verb, you are **conjugating** a verb. The key parts of a verb are first person singular, present tense (dream); first person singular, past tense (dreamed); and the past participle (dreamed). Note: the past participle needs a helping verb to make a verb tense. For example, I *have dreamed* of this day. | I *am dreaming* of this day.

Present Tense: Active Voice

	Singular	**Plural**
First Person	I dream	We dream
Second Person	You dream	You dream
Third Person	He, she, it dreams	They dream

Mood

There are three moods in English: the indicative, the imperative, and the subjunctive.

The **indicative mood** is used for facts, opinions, and questions.

> Fact: You can do this.
>
> Opinion: I think that you can do this.
>
> Question: Do you know that you can do this?

The **imperative** is used for orders or requests.

> Order: You are going to do this!
>
> Request: Will you do this for me?

The **subjunctive mood** is for wishes and statements that go against fact.

> Wish: I wish that I were going to do this.
>
> Statement against fact: If I were you, I would do this. (This goes against fact because I am not you. You have the chance to do this, and I do not have the chance.)

The mood that causes trouble for most people is the subjunctive mood. If you have trouble with any of the moods, then be sure to practice.

Adjectives

An adjective is a word that is used to modify a noun or pronoun. An adjective answers a question: *Which one? What kind of?* or *How many?* Usually, adjectives come before the words that they modify, but they may also come after a linking verb.

> Which one? The *third* suit is my favorite.
>
> What kind? This suit is *navy blue*.
>
> How many? Can I look over the *four* neckties for the suit?

Articles

Articles are adjectives that are used to mark nouns. There are only three: the **definite** (i.e., limited or fixed amount) article *the*, and the **indefinite** (i.e., no limit or fixed amount) articles *a* and *an*. Note: *An* comes before words that start with a vowel sound (i.e., vowels include *a*, *e*, *i*, *o*, *u*, and *y*). For example, "Are you going to get an **u**mbrella?"

> **Definite**: I lost *the* bottle that belongs to me.
>
> **Indefinite**: Does anyone have *a* bottle to share?

Comparison with Adjectives

Some adjectives are relative and other adjectives are absolute. Adjectives that are **relative** can show the comparison between things. Adjectives that are **absolute** can show comparison. However, they show comparison in a different way. Let's say that you are reading two books. You think that one book is perfect, and the other book is not exactly perfect. It is not possible for the book to be more perfect than the other. Either you think that the book is perfect, or you think that the book is not perfect.

The adjectives that are relative will show the different **degrees** of something or someone to something else or someone else. The three degrees of adjectives include positive, comparative, and superlative.

The **positive** degree is the normal form of an adjective.

> Example: This work is *difficult*. | She is *smart*.

The **comparative** degree compares one person or thing to another person or thing.

> Example: This work is *more difficult* than your work. | She is *smarter* than me.

The **superlative** degree compares more than two people or things.

> Example: This is the *most difficult* work of my life. | She is the *smartest* lady in school.

Review Video: What is an Adjective?
Visit mometrix.com/academy and enter code: 470154

Adverbs

An adverb is a word that is used to **modify** a verb, adjective, or another adverb. Usually, adverbs answer one of these questions: *When?*, *Where?*, *How?*, and *Why?* . The negatives *not* and *never* are known as adverbs. Adverbs that modify adjectives or other adverbs **strengthen** or **weaken** the words that they modify.

Examples:

> He walks quickly through the crowd.
>
> The water flows smoothly on the rocks.

Note: While many adverbs end in *-ly*, you need to remember that not all adverbs end in *-ly*. Also, some words that end in *-ly* are adjectives, not adverbs. Some examples include: *early, friendly, holy, lonely, silly*, and *ugly*. To know if a word that ends in *-ly* is an adjective or adverb, you need to check your dictionary.

Examples:

> He is *never* angry.
>
> You talk *too* loudly.

Comparison with Adverbs

The rules for comparing adverbs are the same as the rules for adjectives.

The **positive** degree is the standard form of an adverb.

> Example: He arrives soon. | She speaks softly to her friends.

The **comparative** degree compares one person or thing to another person or thing.

> Example: He arrives sooner than Sarah. | She speaks more softly than him.

The **superlative** degree compares more than two people or things.

> Example: He arrives soonest of the group. | She speaks most softly of any of her friends.

Review Video: Adverbs
Visit mometrix.com/academy and enter code: 713951

Prepositions

A preposition is a word placed before a noun or pronoun that shows the relationship between an object and another word in the sentence.

Common prepositions:

about	before	during	on	under
after	beneath	for	over	until
against	between	from	past	up
among	beyond	in	through	with
around	by	of	to	within
at	down	off	toward	without

Examples:

> The napkin is *in* the drawer.
>
> The Earth rotates *around* the Sun.
>
> The needle is *beneath* the haystack.
>
> Can you find me *among* the words?

Review Video: What is a Preposition?
Visit mometrix.com/academy and enter code: 946763

Conjunctions

Conjunctions join words, phrases, or clauses, and they show the connection between the joined pieces. **Coordinating** conjunctions connect equal parts of sentences. **Correlative** conjunctions show the connection between pairs. **Subordinating** conjunctions join subordinate (i.e., dependent) clauses with independent clauses.

Coordinating Conjunctions

The coordinating conjunctions include: *and, but, yet, or, nor, for,* and *so*

Examples:

> The rock was small, but it was heavy.
>
> She drove in the night, and he drove in the day.

Correlative Conjunctions

The correlative conjunctions are: *either...or* | *neither...nor* | *not only...but also*

Examples:

Either you are coming *or* you are staying.

He ran *not only* three miles *but also* swam 200 yards.

Review Video: Coordinating and Correlative Conjunctions
Visit mometrix.com/academy and enter code: 390329

Subordinating Conjunctions

Common subordinating conjunctions include:

after	since	whenever
although	so that	where
because	unless	wherever
before	until	whether
in order that	when	while

Examples:

I am hungry *because* I did not eat breakfast.

He went home *when* everyone left.

Review Video: Subordinating Conjunctions
Visit mometrix.com/academy and enter code: 958913

Interjections

An interjection is a word for **exclamation** (i.e., great amount of feeling) that is used alone or as a piece to a sentence. Often, they are used at the beginning of a sentence for an **introduction**. Sometimes, they can be used in the middle of a sentence to show a **change** in thought or attitude.

Common Interjections: Hey! | Oh, | Ouch! | Please! | Wow!

Agreement and Sentence Structure

Subjects and Predicates

Subjects

Every sentence has two things: a subject and a verb. The **subject** of a sentence names who or what the sentence is all about. The subject may be directly stated in a sentence, or the subject may be the implied *you.*

The **complete subject** includes the simple subject and all of its modifiers. To find the complete subject, ask *Who* or *What* and insert the verb to complete the question. The answer is the complete subject. To find the **simple subject**, remove all of the modifiers (adjectives, prepositional phrases, etc.) in the complete subject. Being able to locate the subject of a sentence helps with many problems, such as those involving sentence fragments and subject-verb agreement.

Examples:

> The small red car is the one that he wants for Christmas.
>
> (The complete subject is *the small red car.*)
>
> The young artist is coming over for dinner.
>
> (The complete subject is *the young artist.*)

Review Video: Subjects
Visit mometrix.com/academy and enter code: 444771

In **imperative** sentences, the verb's subject is understood (e.g., [You] Run to the store), but not actually present in the sentence. Normally, the subject comes before the verb. However, the subject comes after the verb in sentences that begin with *There are* or *There was.*

Direct:

> John knows the way to the park.
>
> (Who knows the way to the park? Answer: John)
>
> The cookies need ten more minutes.
>
> (What needs ten minutes? Answer: The cookies)
>
> By five o' clock, Bill will need to leave.
>
> (Who needs to leave? Answer: Bill)

Remember: The subject can come after the verb.

> There are five letters on the table for him.
>
> (What is on the table? Answer: Five letters)
>
> There were coffee and doughnuts in the house.
>
> (What was in the house? Answer: Coffee and doughnuts)

Implied:

Go to the post office for me.

(Who is going to the post office? Answer: You are.)

Come and sit with me, please?

(Who needs to come and sit? Answer: You do.)

PREDICATES

In a sentence, you always have a predicate and a subject. The subject tells what the sentence is about, and the **predicate** explains or describes the subject.

Think about the sentence: *He sings*. In this sentence, we have a subject (He) and a predicate (sings). This is all that is needed for a sentence to be complete. Would we like more information? Of course, we would like to know more. However, if this all the information that you are given, you have a complete sentence.

Now, let's look at another sentence:

John and Jane sing on Tuesday nights at the dance hall.

What is the subject of this sentence?

Answer: John and Jane.

What is the predicate of this sentence?

Answer: Everything else in the sentence (sing on Tuesday nights at the dance hall).

SUBJECT-VERB AGREEMENT

Verbs **agree** with their subjects in number. In other words, *singular* subjects need *singular* verbs. *Plural* subjects need *plural* verbs. Singular is for one person, place, or thing. Plural is for more than one person, place, or thing. Subjects and verbs must also agree in person: first, second, or third. The present tense ending *-s* is used on a verb if its subject is third person singular; otherwise, the verb takes no ending.

Review Video: Subject Verb Agreement
Visit mometrix.com/academy and enter code: 479190

NUMBER AGREEMENT EXAMPLES:

Single Subject and Verb: *Dan calls home.*

(Dan is one person. So, the singular verb *calls* is needed.)

Plural Subject and Verb: *Dan and Bob call home.*

(More than one person needs the plural verb *call.*)

Person Agreement Examples:

First Person: I *am* walking.

Second Person: You *are* walking.

Third Person: He *is* walking.

Complications with Subject-Verb Agreement

Words Between Subject and Verb

Words that come between the simple subject and the verb may serve as an effective distraction, but they have no bearing on subject-verb agreement.

Examples:

The joy of my life returns home tonight.

(**Singular Subject**: joy. **Singular Verb**: returns)

The phrase *of my life* does not influence the verb *returns*.

The question that still remains unanswered is "Who are you?"

(**Singular Subject**: question. **Singular Verb**: is)

Don't let the phrase "*that still remains…*" trouble you. The subject *question* goes with *is*.

Compound Subjects

A compound subject is formed when two or more nouns joined by *and*, *or*, or *nor* jointly act as the subject of the sentence.

Joined by And

When a compound subject is joined by *and*, it is treated as a plural subject and requires a plural verb.

Examples:

You and Jon are invited to come to my house.

(**Plural Subject**: You and Jon. **Plural Verb**: are)

The pencil and paper belong to me.

(**Plural Subject**: pencil and paper. **Plural Verb**: belong)

Joined by Or/Nor

For a compound subject joined by *or* or *nor*, the verb must agree in number with the part of the subject that is closest to the verb (italicized in the examples below).

Examples:

Today or *tomorrow is* the day.

(**Subject**: Today / tomorrow. **Verb**: is)

Stan or *Phil wants* to read the book.

(**Subject**: Stan / Phil. **Verb**: wants)

Neither the books nor the *pen is* on the desk.

(**Subject**: Books / Pen. **Verb**: is)

Either the blanket or *pillows arrive* this afternoon.

(**Subject**: Blanket / Pillows. **Verb**: arrive)

Indefinite Pronouns as Subject

An indefinite pronoun is a pronoun that does not refer to a specific noun. Indefinite pronouns may be only singular, be only plural, or change depending on how they are used.

Always Singular

Pronouns such as *each*, *either*, *everybody*, *anybody*, *somebody*, and *nobody* are always singular.

Examples:

Each of the runners *has* a different bib number.

(**Singular Subject**: Each. **Singular Verb**: has)

Is either of you ready for the game?

(**Singular Subject**: Either. **Singular Verb**: is)

Note: The words *each* and *either* can also be used as adjectives (e.g., *each* person is unique). When one of these adjectives modifies the subject of a sentence, it is always a singular subject.

Everybody grows a day older every day.

(**Singular Subject**: Everybody. **Singular Verb**: grows)

Anybody is welcome to bring a tent.

(**Singular Subject**: Anybody. **Singular Verb**: is)

Always Plural

Pronouns such as *both*, *several*, and *many* are always plural.

Examples:

Both of the siblings *were* too tired to argue.

(**Plural Subject**: Both. **Plural Verb**: were)

Many have tried, but none have succeeded.

(**Plural Subject**: Many. **Plural Verb**: have tried)

DEPEND ON CONTEXT

Pronouns such as *some, any, all, none, more,* and *most* can be either singular or plural depending on what they are representing in the context of the sentence.

Examples:

All of my dog's food *was* still there in his bowl

(**Singular Subject**: All. **Singular Verb**: was)

By the end of the night, *all* of my guests *were* already excited about coming to my next party.

(**Plural Subject**: All. **Plural Verb**: were)

OTHER CASES INVOLVING PLURAL OR IRREGULAR FORM

Some nouns are **singular in meaning but plural in form**: news, mathematics, physics, and economics.

The *news is* coming on now.

Mathematics is my favorite class.

Some nouns are plural in form and meaning, and have **no singular equivalent**: scissors and pants.

Do these *pants come* with a shirt?

The *scissors are* for my project.

Mathematical operations are **irregular** in their construction, but are normally considered to be **singular in meaning**.

One plus one is two.

Three times three is nine.

Note: Look to your **dictionary** for help when you aren't sure whether a noun with a plural form has a singular or plural meaning.

COMPLEMENTS

A complement is a noun, pronoun, or adjective that is used to give more information about the subject or verb in the sentence.

DIRECT OBJECTS

A direct object is a noun or pronoun that takes or receives the **action** of a verb. (Remember: a complete sentence does not need a direct object, so not all sentences will have them. A sentence needs only a subject and a verb.) When you are looking for a direct object, find the verb and ask *who* or *what.*

Examples:

I took the blanket. (Who or what did I take? *The blanket*)

Jane read books. (Who or what does Jane read? *Books*)

Indirect Objects

An indirect object is a word or group of words that show how an action had an **influence** on someone or something. If there is an indirect object in a sentence, then you always have a direct object in the sentence. When you are looking for the indirect object, find the verb and ask *to/for whom or what.*

Examples:

We taught the old dog a new trick.

(To/For Whom or What was taught? *The old dog*)

I gave them a math lesson.

(To/For Whom or What was given? *Them*)

Predicate Nominatives and Predicate Adjectives

As we looked at previously, verbs may be classified as either action verbs or linking verbs. A linking verb is so named because it links the subject to words in the predicate that describe or define the subject. These words are called predicate nominatives (if nouns or pronouns) or predicate adjectives (if adjectives).

Examples:

My father is a *lawyer.*

(Father is the **subject**. Lawyer is the **predicate nominative**.)

Your mother is *patient.*

(Mother is the **subject**. Patient is the **predicate adjective**.)

Pronoun Usage

The **antecedent** is the noun that has been replaced by a pronoun. A pronoun and its antecedent **agree** when they have the same number (singular or plural) and gender (male, female, or neuter).

Examples:

Singular agreement: *John* came into town, and *he* played for us.

(The word *he* replaces *John.*)

Plural agreement: *John and Rick* came into town, and *they* played for us.

(The word *they* replaces *John and Rick.*)

To determine which is the correct pronoun to use in a compound subject or object, try each pronoun **alone** in place of the compound in the sentence. Your knowledge of pronouns will tell you which one is correct.

Example:

> Bob and (I, me) will be going.
>
> Test: (1) *I will be going* or (2) *Me will be going*. The second choice cannot be correct because *me* cannot be used as the subject of a sentence. Instead, *me* is used as an object.
>
> **Answer**: Bob and I will be going.

When a pronoun is used with a noun immediately following (as in "we boys"), try the sentence **without the added noun**.

Example:

> (We/Us) boys played football last year.
>
> Test: (1) *We played football last ye*ar or (2) *Us played football last year*. Again, the second choice cannot be correct because *us* cannot be used as a subject of a sentence. Instead, *us* is used as an object.
>
> **Answer**: We boys played football last year.

Review Video: Pronoun Usage
Visit mometrix.com/academy and enter code: 666500

A pronoun should point clearly to the **antecedent**. Here is how a pronoun reference can be unhelpful if it is not directly stated or puzzling.

> **Unhelpful**: Ron and Jim went to the store, and *he* bought soda.
>
> (Who bought soda? Ron or Jim?)
>
> **Helpful**: Jim went to the store, and *he* bought soda.
>
> (The sentence is clear. Jim bought the soda.)

Some pronouns change their form by their placement in a sentence. A pronoun that is a subject in a sentence comes in the **subjective case**. Pronouns that serve as objects appear in the **objective case**. Finally, the pronouns that are used as possessives appear in the **possessive case**.

Examples:

> **Subjective case**: *He* is coming to the show.
>
> (The pronoun *He* is the subject of the sentence.)
>
> **Objective case**: Josh drove *him* to the airport.
>
> (The pronoun *him* is the object of the sentence.)

Possessive case: The flowers are *mine*.

(The pronoun *mine* shows ownership of the flowers.)

The word *who* is a subjective-case pronoun that can be used as a **subject**. The word *whom* is an objective-case pronoun that can be used as an **object**. The words *who* and *whom* are common in subordinate clauses or in questions.

Examples:

Subject: He knows who wants to come.

(*Who* is the subject of the verb *wants*.)

Object: He knows the man whom we want at the party.

(*Whom* is the object of *we want*.)

CLAUSES

A clause is a group of words that contains both a subject and a predicate (verb). There are two types of clauses: independent and dependent. An **independent clause** contains a complete thought, while a **dependent (or subordinate) clause** does not. A dependent clause includes a subject and a verb, and may also contain objects or complements, but it cannot stand as a complete thought without being joined to an independent clause. Dependent clauses function within sentences as adjectives, adverbs, or nouns.

Example:

Independent Clause: I am running

Dependent Clause: because I want to stay in shape

The clause *I am running* is an independent clause: it has a subject and a verb, and it gives a complete thought. The clause *because I want to stay in shape* is a dependent clause: it has a subject and a verb, but it does not express a complete thought. It adds detail to the independent clause to which it is attached.

Combined: I am running because I want to stay in shape.

Review Video: Clauses
Visit mometrix.com/academy and enter code: 940170

TYPES OF DEPENDENT CLAUSES

ADJECTIVE CLAUSES

An **adjective clause** is a dependent clause that modifies a noun or a pronoun. Adjective clauses begin with a relative pronoun (*who, whose, whom, which,* and *that*) or a relative adverb (*where, when,* and *why*).

Also, adjective clauses come after the noun that the clause needs to explain or rename. This is done to have a clear connection to the independent clause.

Examples:

> I learned the reason *why I won the award.*
>
> This is the place *where I started my first job.*

An adjective clause can be an essential or nonessential clause. An essential clause is very important to the sentence. **Essential clauses** explain or define a person or thing. **Nonessential clauses** give more information about a person or thing but are not necessary to define them. Nonessential clauses are set off with commas while essential clauses are not.

Examples:

> **Essential**: A person *who works hard at first* can often rest later in life.
>
> **Nonessential**: Neil Armstrong, *who walked on the moon*, is my hero.

Adverb Clauses

An **adverb clause** is a dependent clause that modifies a verb, adjective, or adverb. In sentences with multiple dependent clauses, adverb clauses are usually placed immediately before or after the independent clause. An adverb clause is introduced with words such as *after, although, as, before, because, if, since, so, unless, when, where*, and *while*.

Examples:

> *When you walked outside*, I called the manager.
>
> I will go with you *unless you want to stay*.

Noun Clauses

A **noun clause** is a dependent clause that can be used as a subject, object, or complement. Noun clauses begin with words such as *how, that, what, whether, which, who,* and *why*. These words can also come with an adjective clause. Unless the noun clause is being used as the subject of the sentence, it should come after the verb of the independent clause.

Examples:

> The real mystery is *how you avoided serious injury*.
>
> *What you learn from each other* depends on your honesty with others.

Subordination

When two related ideas are not of equal importance, the ideal way to combine them is to make the more important idea an independent clause, and the less important idea a dependent or subordinate clause. This is called **subordination**.

Example:

> **Separate ideas**: The team had a perfect regular season. The team lost the championship.
>
> **Subordinated**: Despite having a perfect regular season, *the team lost the championship*.

PHRASES

A phrase is a group of words that functions as a single part of speech, usually a noun, adjective, or adverb. A phrase is not a complete thought, but it adds **detail** or **explanation** to a sentence, or **renames** something within the sentence.

PREPOSITIONAL PHRASES

One of the most common types of phrases is the prepositional phrase. A **prepositional phrase** begins with a preposition and ends with a noun or pronoun that is the object of the preposition. Normally, the prepositional phrase functions as an **adjective** or an **adverb** within the sentence.

Examples:

The picnic is *on the blanket.*

I am sick *with a fever* today.

Among the many flowers, John found a four-leaf clover.

VERBAL PHRASES

A verbal is a word or phrase that is formed from a verb but does not function as a verb. Depending on its particular form, it may be used as a noun, adjective, or adverb. A verbal does **not** replace a verb in a sentence.

Examples:

Correct: *Walk* a mile daily.

(*Walk* is the verb of this sentence. The subject is the implied *you.*)

Incorrect: *To walk* a mile.

(*To walk* is a type of verbal. This is not a sentence since there is no functional verb)

There are three types of verbals: **participles**, **gerunds**, and **infinitives**. Each type of verbal has a corresponding **phrase** that consists of the verbal itself along with any complements or modifiers.

PARTICIPLES

A **participle** is a type of verbal that always functions as an adjective. The present participle always ends with *-ing*. Past participles end with *-d, -ed, -n,* or *-t.*

Examples: Verb: *dance* | Present Participle: *dancing* | Past Participle: *danced*

Participial phrases most often come right before or right after the noun or pronoun that they modify.

Examples:

Shipwrecked on an island, the boys started to fish for food.

Having been seated for five hours, we got out of the car to stretch our legs.

Praised for their work, the group accepted the first-place trophy.

Gerunds

A **gerund** is a type of verbal that always functions as a noun. Like present participles, gerunds always end with *-ing*, but they can be easily distinguished from one another by the part of speech they represent (participles always function as adjectives). Since a gerund or gerund phrase always functions as a noun, it can be used as the subject of a sentence, the predicate nominative, or the object of a verb or preposition.

Examples:

> We want to be known for *teaching the poor.* (Object of preposition)
>
> *Coaching this team* is the best job of my life. (Subject)
>
> We like *practicing our songs* in the basement. (Object of verb)

Infinitives

An **infinitive** is a type of verbal that can function as a noun, an adjective, or an adverb. An infinitive is made of the word *to* + the basic form of the verb. As with all other types of verbal phrases, an infinitive phrase includes the verbal itself and all of its complements or modifiers.

Examples:

> *To join the team* is my goal in life. (Noun)
>
> The animals have enough food *to eat for the night.* (Adjective)
>
> People lift weights *to exercise their muscles.* (Adverb)

Appositive Phrases

An **appositive** is a word or phrase that is used to explain or rename nouns or pronouns. Noun phrases, gerund phrases, and infinitive phrases can all be used as appositives.

Examples:

> Terriers, *hunters at heart*, have been dressed up to look like lap dogs.
>
> (The noun phrase *hunters at heart* renames the noun *terriers.*)
>
> His plan, *to save and invest his money*, was proven as a safe approach.
>
> (The infinitive phrase explains what the plan is.)

Appositive phrases can be **essential** or **nonessential**. An appositive phrase is essential if the person, place, or thing being described or renamed is too general for its meaning to be understood without the appositive.

Examples:

> **Essential**: Two Founding Fathers George Washington and Thomas Jefferson served as presidents.
>
> **Nonessential**: George Washington and Thomas Jefferson, two Founding Fathers, served as presidents.

Absolute Phrases

An absolute phrase is a phrase that consists of **a noun followed by a participle**. An absolute phrase provides **context** to what is being described in the sentence, but it does not modify or explain any particular word; it is essentially independent.

Examples:

The alarm ringing, he pushed the snooze button.

The music paused, she continued to dance through the crowd.

Note: Absolute phrases can be confusing, so don't be discouraged if you have a difficult time with them.

Parallelism

When multiple items or ideas are presented in a sentence in series, such as in a list, the items or ideas must be stated in grammatically equivalent ways. In other words, if one idea is stated in gerund form, the second cannot be stated in infinitive form. For example, to write, *I enjoy reading and to study* would be incorrect. An infinitive and a gerund are not equivalent. Instead, you should write *I enjoy reading and studying*. In lists of more than two, it can be harder to keep straight, but all items in a list must be parallel.

Example:

Incorrect: He stopped at the office, grocery store, and the pharmacy before heading home.

The first and third items in the list of places include the article *the*, so the second item needs it as well.

Correct: He stopped at the office, *the* grocery store, and the pharmacy before heading home.

Example:

Incorrect: While vacationing in Europe, she went biking, skiing, and climbed mountains.

The first and second items in the list are gerunds, so the third item must be as well.

Correct: While vacationing in Europe, she went biking, skiing, and *mountain climbing*.

Sentence Purpose

There are four types of sentences: declarative, imperative, interrogative, and exclamatory.

A **declarative** sentence states a fact and ends with a period.

Example: *The football game starts at seven o'clock.*

An **imperative** sentence tells someone to do something and generally ends with a period. (An urgent command might end with an exclamation point instead.)

Example: *Don't forget to buy your ticket.*

An **interrogative** sentence asks a question and ends with a question mark.

Example: *Are you going to the game on Friday?*

An **exclamatory** sentence shows strong emotion and ends with an exclamation point.

Example: *I can't believe we won the game!*

SENTENCE STRUCTURE

Sentences are classified by structure based on the type and number of clauses present. The four classifications of sentence structure are the following:

Simple: A simple sentence has one independent clause with no dependent clauses. A simple sentence may have **compound elements** (i.e., compound subject or verb).

Examples:

Judy *watered* the lawn. (single subject, single *verb*)

Judy and Alan *watered* the lawn. (compound subject, single *verb*)

Judy *watered* the lawn and *pulled* weeds. (single subject, compound *verb*)

Judy and Alan *watered* the lawn and *pulled* weeds. (compound subject, compound *verb*)

Compound: A compound sentence has two or more independent clauses with no dependent clauses. Usually, the independent clauses are joined with a comma and a coordinating conjunction or with a semicolon.

Examples:

The time has come, and we are ready.

I woke up at dawn; the sun was just coming up.

Complex: A complex sentence has one independent clause and at least one *dependent clause.*

Examples:

Although he had the flu, Harry went to work.

Marcia got married *after she finished college.*

Compound-Complex: A compound-complex sentence has at least two independent clauses and at least one *dependent clause.*

Examples:

John is my friend *who went to India*, and he brought back souvenirs.

You may not realize this, but we heard the music *that you played last night.*

Review Video: Sentence Structure
Visit mometrix.com/academy and enter code: 700478

SENTENCE FRAGMENTS

Usually when the term *sentence fragment* comes up, it is because you have to decide whether or not a group of words is a complete sentence, and if it's not a complete sentence, you're about to have to fix it. Recall that a group of words must contain at least one **independent clause** in order to be considered a sentence. If it doesn't contain even one independent clause, it would be called a **sentence fragment**. (If it contains two or more independent clauses that are not joined correctly, it would be called a run-on sentence.)

The process to use for **repairing** a sentence fragment depends on what type of fragment it is. If the fragment is a dependent clause, it can sometimes be as simple as removing a subordinating word (e.g., when, because, if) from the beginning of the fragment. Alternatively, a dependent clause can be incorporated into a closely related neighboring sentence. If the fragment is missing some required part, like a subject or a verb, the fix might be as simple as adding it in.

Examples:

> **Fragment**: Because he wanted to sail the Mediterranean.
>
> **Removed subordinating word**: He wanted to sail the Mediterranean.
>
> **Combined with another sentence**: Because he wanted to sail the Mediterranean, he booked a Greek island cruise.

Run-on Sentences

Run-on sentences consist of multiple independent clauses that have not been joined together properly. Run-on sentences can be corrected in several different ways:

Join clauses properly: This can be done with a comma and coordinating conjunction, with a semicolon, or with a colon or dash if the second clause is explaining something in the first.

Example:

> **Incorrect**: I went on the trip, we visited lots of castles.
>
> **Corrected**: I went on the trip, and we visited lots of castles.

Split into separate sentences: This correction is most effective when the independent clauses are very long or when they are not closely related.

Example:

> **Incorrect**: The drive to New York takes ten hours, my uncle lives in Boston.
>
> **Corrected**: The drive to New York takes ten hours. My uncle lives in Boston.

Make one clause dependent: This is the easiest way to make the sentence correct and more interesting at the same time. It's often as simple as adding a subordinating word between the two clauses

Example:

> **Incorrect**: I finally made it to the store and I bought some eggs.
>
> **Corrected**: When I finally made it to the store, I bought some eggs.

Reduce to one clause with a compound verb: If both clauses have the same subject, remove the subject from the second clause, and you now have just one clause with a compound verb.

Example:

Incorrect: The drive to New York takes ten hours, it makes me very tired.

Corrected: The drive to New York takes ten hours and makes me very tired.

Note: While these are the simplest ways to correct a run-on sentence, often the best way is to completely reorganize the thoughts in the sentence and rewrite it.

Review Video: Fragments and Run-on Sentences
Visit mometrix.com/academy and enter code: 541989

Dangling and Misplaced Modifiers

Dangling Modifiers

A dangling modifier is a dependent clause or verbal phrase that does not have a **clear logical connection** to a word in the sentence.

Example:

Dangling: *Reading each magazine article*, the stories caught my attention.

The word *stories* cannot be modified by *Reading each magazine article*. People can read, but stories cannot read. Therefore, the subject of the sentence must be a person.

Corrected: Reading each magazine article, *I* was entertained by the stories.

Example:

Dangling: Ever since childhood, my grandparents have visited me for Christmas.

The speaker in this sentence can't have been visited by her grandparents when *they* were children, since she wouldn't have been born yet. Either the modifier should be **clarified** or the sentence should be **rearranged** to specify whose childhood is being referenced.

Clarified: Ever since I was a child, my grandparents have visited for Christmas.

Rearranged: Ever since childhood, I have enjoyed my grandparents visiting for Christmas.

Misplaced Modifiers

Because modifiers are grammatically versatile, they can be put in many different places within the structure of a sentence. The danger of this versatility is that a modifier can accidentally be placed where it is modifying the wrong word or where it is not clear which word it is modifying.

Example:

Misplaced: She read the book to a crowd *that was filled with beautiful pictures*.

The book was filled with beautiful pictures, not the crowd.

Corrected: She read the book *that was filled with beautiful pictures* to a crowd.

Example:

Ambiguous: Derek saw a bus nearly hit a man *on his way to work.*

Was Derek on his way to work? Or was the other man?

Derek: *On his way to work*, Derek saw a bus nearly hit a man.

The other man: Derek saw a bus nearly hit a man *who was on his way to work.*

SPLIT INFINITIVES

A split infinitive occurs when a modifying word comes between the word *to* and the verb that pairs with *to*.

Example: To *clearly* explain vs. *To explain* clearly | To *softly* sing vs. *To sing* softly

Though considered improper by some, split infinitives may provide better clarity and simplicity in some cases than the alternatives. As such, avoiding them should not be considered a universal rule.

DOUBLE NEGATIVES

Standard English allows **two negatives** only when a **positive** meaning is intended. For example, *The team was not displeased with their performance*. Double negatives to emphasize negation are not used in standard English.

Negative modifiers (e.g., never, no, and not) should not be paired with other negative modifiers or negative words (e.g., none, nobody, nothing, or neither). The modifiers *hardly, barely*, and *scarcely* are considered negatives in standard English, so they should not be used with other negatives.

Punctuation

End Punctuation

Periods

Use a period to end all sentences except direct questions, exclamations.

Declarative Sentence

A declarative sentence gives information or makes a statement.

Examples: I can fly a kite. | The plane left two hours ago.

Imperative Sentence

An imperative sentence gives an order or command.

Examples: You are coming with me. | Bring me that note.

Periods for Abbreviations

Examples: 3 P.M. | 2 A.M. | Mr. Jones | Mrs. Stevens | Dr. Smith | Bill Jr. | Pennsylvania Ave.

Note: an abbreviation is a shortened form of a word or phrase.

Question Marks

Question marks should be used following a direct question. A polite request can be followed by a period instead of a question mark.

Direct Question: What is for lunch today? | How are you? | Why is that the answer?

Polite Requests: Can you please send me the item tomorrow. | Will you please walk with me on the track.

Exclamation Marks

Exclamation marks are used after a word group or sentence that shows much feeling or has special importance. Exclamation marks should not be overused. They are saved for proper **exclamatory interjections**.

Example: We're going to the finals! | You have a beautiful car! | That's crazy!

Commas

The comma is a punctuation mark that can help you understand connections in a sentence. Not every sentence needs a comma. However, if a sentence needs a comma, you need to put it in the right place. A comma in the wrong place (or an absent comma) will make a sentence's meaning unclear. These are some of the rules for commas:

1. Use a comma **before a coordinating conjunction** joining independent clauses
   Example: Bob caught three fish, and I caught two fish.

2. Use a comma after an introductory phrase or an adverbial clause
   Examples:
   After the final out, we went to a restaurant to celebrate.
   Studying the stars, I was surprised at the beauty of the sky.

3. Use a comma between items in a series.

   Example: I will bring the turkey, the pie, and the coffee.

4. Use a comma **between coordinate adjectives** not joined with *and*

   Incorrect: The kind, brown dog followed me home.
   Correct: The *kind, loyal* dog followed me home.
   Not all adjectives are **coordinate** (i.e., equal or parallel). There are two simple ways to know if your adjectives are coordinate. One, you can join the adjectives with *and*: *The kind and loyal dog*. Two, you can change the order of the adjectives: *The loyal, kind dog*.

5. Use commas for **interjections** and **after *yes* and *no*** responses

   Examples:

   Interjection: Oh, I had no idea. | Wow, you know how to play this game.
   Yes and No: *Yes,* I heard you. | *No,* I cannot come tomorrow.

6. Use commas to separate nonessential modifiers and nonessential appositives

   Examples:

   Nonessential Modifier: John Frank, who is coaching the team, was promoted today.
   Nonessential Appositive: Thomas Edison, an American inventor, was born in Ohio.

7. Use commas to set off nouns of direct address, interrogative tags, and contrast

   Examples:

   Direct Address: You, *John,* are my only hope in this moment.
   Interrogative Tag: This is the last time, *correct*?
   Contrast: You are my friend, *not my enemy.*

8. Use commas with dates, addresses, geographical names, and titles

   Examples:

   Date: *July 4, 1776,* is an important date to remember.
   Address: He is meeting me at *456 Delaware Avenue, Washington, D.C.,* tomorrow morning.
   Geographical Name: *Paris, France,* is my favorite city.
   Title: John Smith, *Ph. D.,* will be visiting your class today.

9. Use commas to **separate expressions like *he said*** and ***she said*** if they come between a sentence of a quote

   Examples:

   "I want you to know," he began, "that I always wanted the best for you."
   "You can start," Jane said, "with an apology."

Review Video: Commas
Visit mometrix.com/academy and enter code: 786797

Semicolons

The semicolon is used to connect major sentence pieces of equal value. Some rules for semicolons include:

1. Use a semicolon **between closely connected independent clauses** that are not connected with a coordinating conjunction.

   Examples:

   She is outside; we are inside.
   You are right; we should go with your plan.

2. Use a semicolon **between independent clauses linked with a transitional word.**

   Examples:

   I think that we can agree on this*; however,* I am not sure about my friends.
   You are looking in the wrong places*; therefore,* you will not find what you need.

3. Use a semicolon **between items in a series that has internal punctuation.**

   Example: I have visited New York, New York; Augusta, Maine; and Baltimore, Maryland.

Review Video: Semicolon Usage
Visit mometrix.com/academy and enter code: 370605

Colons

The colon is used to call attention to the words that follow it. A colon must come after a **complete independent clause**. The rules for colons are as follows:

1. Use a colon after an independent clause to **make a list**

   Example: I want to learn many languages: Spanish, German, and Italian.

2. Use a colon for **explanations** or to **give a quote**

   Examples:

   Quote: He started with an idea: "We are able to do more than we imagine."
   Explanation: There is one thing that stands out on your resume: responsibility.

3. Use a colon **after the greeting in a formal letter**, to **show hours and minutes**, and to **separate a title and subtitle**

   Examples:

   Greeting in a formal letter: Dear Sir: | To Whom It May Concern:
   Time: It is 3:14 P.M.
   Title: The essay is titled "America: A Short Introduction to a Modern Country"

Parentheses

Parentheses are used for additional information. Also, they can be used to put labels for letters or numbers in a series. Parentheses should be not be used very often. If they are overused, parentheses can be a distraction instead of a help.

Examples:

Extra Information: The rattlesnake (see Image 2) is a dangerous snake of North and South America.

Series: Include in the email (1) your name, (2) your address, and (3) your question for the author.

Quotation Marks

Use quotation marks to close off **direct quotations** of a person's spoken or written words. Do not use quotation marks around indirect quotations. An indirect quotation gives someone's message without using the person's exact words. Use **single quotation marks** to close off a quotation inside a quotation.

Direct Quote: Nancy said, "I am waiting for Henry to arrive."

Indirect Quote: Henry said that he is going to be late to the meeting.

Quote inside a Quote: The teacher asked, "Has everyone read 'The Gift of the Magi'?"

Quotation marks should be used around the titles of **short works**: newspaper and magazine articles, poems, short stories, songs, television episodes, radio programs, and subdivisions of books or web sites.

Examples:

"Rip van Winkle" (short story by Washington Irving)

"O Captain! My Captain!" (poem by Walt Whitman)

Although it is not standard usage, quotation marks are sometimes used to highlight **irony**, or the use of words to mean something other than their dictionary definition. This type of usage should be employed sparingly, if at all.

Examples:

The boss warned Frank that he was walking on "thin ice."

(Frank is not walking on real ice. Instead, Frank is being warned to avoid mistakes.)

The teacher thanked the young man for his "honesty."

(In this example, the quotation marks around *honesty* show that the teacher does not believe the young man's explanation.)

Review Video: Quotation Marks
Visit mometrix.com/academy and enter code: 884918

Periods and commas are put **inside** quotation marks. Colons and semicolons are put **outside** the quotation marks. Question marks and exclamation points are placed inside quotation marks when they are part of a quote. When the question or exclamation mark goes with the whole sentence, the mark is left outside of the quotation marks.

Examples:

Period and comma: We read "The Gift of the Magi," "The Skylight Room," and "The Cactus."

Semicolon: They watched "The Nutcracker"; then, they went home.

Exclamation mark that is a part of a quote: The crowd cheered, "Victory!"

Question mark that goes with the whole sentence: Is your favorite short story "The Tell-Tale Heart"?

Apostrophes

An apostrophe is used to show **possession** or the **deletion of letters in contractions**. An apostrophe is not needed with the possessive pronouns *his, hers, its, ours, theirs, whose*, and *yours*.

Singular Nouns: David's car | a book's theme | my brother's board game

Plural Nouns with ***-s***: the scissors' handle | boys' basketball

Plural Nouns without ***-s***: Men's department | the people's adventure

Review Video: Apostrophes
Visit mometrix.com/academy and enter code: 213068

Review Video: Punctuation Errors in Possessive Pronouns
Visit mometrix.com/academy and enter code: 221438

Hyphens

Hyphens are used to **separate compound words**. Use hyphens in the following cases:

1. **Compound numbers** between 21 and 99 when written out in words
   Example: This team needs *twenty-five* points to win the game.

2. **Written-out fractions** that are used as **adjectives**
   Correct: The recipe says that we need a *three-fourths* cup of butter.
   Incorrect: *One-fourth* of the road is under construction.

3. Compound words used as **adjectives that come before a noun**
   Correct: The *well-fed* dog took a nap.
   Incorrect: The dog was *well-fed* for his nap.

4. Compound words that would be **hard to read** or **easily confused with other words**
   Examples: Semi-irresponsible | Anti-itch | Re-sort

Note: This is not a complete set of the rules for hyphens. A dictionary is the best tool for knowing if a compound word needs a hyphen.

Dashes

Dashes are used to show a **break** or a **change in thought** in a sentence or to act as parentheses in a sentence. When typing, use two hyphens to make a dash. Do not put a space before or after the dash. The following are the rules for dashes:

1. To set off **parenthetical statements** or an **appositive with internal punctuation**
   Example: The three trees—oak, pine, and magnolia—are coming on a truck tomorrow.
2. To show a **break or change in tone or thought**
   Example: The first question—how silly of me—does not have a correct answer.

Ellipsis Marks

The ellipsis mark has three periods (...) to show when **words have been removed** from a quotation. If a full sentence or more is removed from a quoted passage, you need to use four periods to show the removed text and the end punctuation mark. The ellipsis mark should not be used at the beginning of a quotation. The ellipsis mark should also not be used at the end of a quotation unless some words have been deleted from the end of the final sentence.

Example:

> "Then he picked up the groceries...paid for them...later he went home."

Brackets

There are two main reasons to use brackets:

1. When **placing parentheses inside of parentheses**
   Example: The hero of this story, Paul Revere (a silversmith and industrialist [see Ch. 4]), rode through towns of Massachusetts to warn of advancing British troops.
2. When adding **clarification or detail** to a quotation that is **not part of the quotation**
   Example:
   > The father explained, "My children are planning to attend my alma mater [State University]."

Common Errors

Word Confusion

Which, That, and Who

Which is used for things only.

Example: John's dog, *which was called Max,* is large and fierce.

That is used for people or things.

Example: Is this the only book *that Louis L'Amour wrote?*

Example: Is Louis L'Amour the author *that wrote Western novels?*

Who is used for people only.

Example: Mozart was the composer *who wrote those operas.*

Homophones

Homophones are words that sound alike (or similar), but they have different **spellings** and **definitions**.

To, Too, and Two

To can be an adverb or a preposition for showing direction, purpose, and relationship. See your dictionary for the many other ways use *to* in a sentence.

Examples: I went to the store. | I want to go with you.

Too is an adverb that means *also, as well, very, or more than enough*.

Examples: I can walk a mile too. | You have eaten too much.

Two is the second number in the series of numbers (e.g., one (1), two, (2), three (3)...)

Example: You have two minutes left.

There, Their, and They're

There can be an adjective, adverb, or pronoun. Often, *there* is used to show a place or to start a sentence.

Examples: I went there yesterday. | There is something in his pocket.

Their is a pronoun that is used to show ownership.

Examples: He is their father. | This is their fourth apology this week.

They're is a contraction of *they are*.

Example: Did you know that they're in town?

Knew and New

Knew is the past tense of *know*.

Example: I knew the answer.

New is an adjective that means something is current, has not been used, or modern.

Example: This is my new phone.

Then and Than

Then is an adverb that indicates sequence or order:

Example: I'm going to run to the library and then come home.

Than is special-purpose word used only for comparisons:

Example: Susie likes chips better than candy.

Its and It's

Its is a pronoun that shows ownership.

Example: The guitar is in its case.

It's is a contraction of *it is*.

Example: It's an honor and a privilege to meet you.

Note: The *h* in honor is silent, so the sound of the vowel *o* must have the article *an*.

Your and You're

Your is a pronoun that shows ownership.

Example: This is your moment to shine.

You're is a contraction of *you are*.

Example: Yes, you're correct.

Affect and Effect

There are two main reasons that **affect** and **effect** are so often confused: 1) both words can be used as either a noun or a verb, and 2) unlike most homophones, their usage and meanings are closely related to each other. Here is a quick rundown of the four usage options:

Affect (n): feeling, emotion, or mood that is displayed

Example: The patient had a flat *affect*. (i.e., his face showed little or no emotion)

Affect (v): to alter, to change, to influence

Example: The sunshine *affects* the plant's growth.

Effect (n): a result, a consequence

Example: What *effect* will this weather have on our schedule?

Effect (v): to bring about, to cause to be

Example: These new rules will *effect* order in the office.

The noun form of *affect* is rarely used outside of technical medical descriptions, so if a noun form is needed on the test, you can safely select *effect*. The verb form of *effect* is not as rare as the noun form of *affect*, but it's still not all that likely to show up on your test. If you need a verb and you can't decide which to use based on the definitions, choosing *affect* is your best bet.

HOMOGRAPHS

Homographs are words that share the same spelling, and they have multiple meanings. To figure out which meaning is being used, you should be looking for context clues. The context clues give hints to the meaning of the word. For example, the word *spot* has many meanings. It can mean "a place" or "a stain or blot." In the sentence "After my lunch, I saw a spot on my shirt," the word *spot* means "a stain or blot." The context clues of "After my lunch…" and "on my shirt" guide you to this decision.

BANK

(noun): an establishment where money is held for savings or lending

(verb): to collect or pile up

CONTENT

(noun): the topics that will be addressed within a book

(adjective): pleased or satisfied

FINE

(noun): an amount of money that acts a penalty for an offense

(adjective): very small or thin

INCENSE

(noun): a material that is burned in religious settings and makes a pleasant aroma

(verb): to frustrate or anger

LEAD

(noun): the first or highest position

(verb): to direct a person or group of followers

OBJECT

(noun): a lifeless item that can be held and observed

(verb): to disagree

PRODUCE

(noun): fruits and vegetables

(verb): to make or create something

Refuse

(noun): garbage or debris that has been thrown away

(verb): to not allow

Subject

(noun): an area of study

(verb): to force or subdue

Tear

(noun): a fluid secreted by the eyes

(verb): to separate or pull apart

Mathematics Test

The math portion of the PSAT consists of a 45-minute section in which a calculator may be used and a 25-minute section in which no calculator may be used. The calculator portion contains 31 questions and the no-calculator portion contains 17 questions.

Concepts Covered

PSAT questions fall into four categories:

- Heart of Algebra
- Problem Solving and Data Analysis
- Passport to Advanced Math
- Additional Topics in Math

The table below gives a complete breakdown of questions:

Calculator Portion	**Number of Questions**	**% of Test**
Total Questions	*31*	*100%*
Multiple Choice	27	87%
Student-Produced Response	4	13%
Content Categories		
Heart of Algebra	8	26%
Problem Solving and Data Analysis	16	52%
Passport to Advanced Math	6	19%
Additional Math Topics	1	3%
No-Calculator Portion	**Number of Questions**	**% of Test**
Total Questions	*17*	*100%*
Multiple Choice	13	76%
Student-Produced Response	4	24%
Content Categories		
Heart of Algebra	8	47%
Passport to Advanced Math	8	47%
Additional Math Topics	1	6%

Use the Practice Tests

The best thing you can do to prepare for the PSAT is to take several practice tests and review all your wrong answers very carefully. Work back through those problems until you understand how the answer was derived and you're confident you could answer a similar problem on your own.

This guide includes a practice test with an answer key and explanations. Examples are also available on the College Board website. If you feel uncertain on a particular concept or problem type, use these tests to practice.

How to Approach the Math Questions

Take an Approved Calculator You're Familiar with. Check Its Batteries

If you normally use a scientific or graphic calculator, check the PSAT website to make sure it's one you'll be allowed to use. Use that calculator as you work through the practice tests.

Remember That the Test Provides All the Information You Need

There's even a handy chart of "reference information" in the test booklet with geometry formulas you might need, including the Pythagorean Theorem and special right triangles. The chart even tells you that the sum of angles in a triangle equals 180. Don't worry about cramming to memorize the formula for calculating the area of a circle. All you need to know is that A = area, C = circumference, and r = radius.

Read Carefully

Yes, it's a math test, but these questions require careful reading. Look for key words such as "is" (equals), "more than," "less than," "of" (percentage, ratio, or multiplication), and so forth. Ask yourself:

- "What do I know?"
- "What information does the problem provide?"
- "What is the question asking, exactly?"

Remember That You Don't Always Have to Solve the Whole Problem to Answer the Question

Especially with algebra problems, answering the question may not actually require solving the entire equation or finding all the variables. This is another example of "read carefully"—be sure you understand what the question is asking for.

Look at the Answers Before You Begin Calculating

What form do the possible answers take? If they're fractions, then work in fractions rather than decimals. Do they include negative numbers? (Negative numbers are an often-forgotten option for many problems involving exponents, roots, and absolute values.)

Take It One Step at a Time

If a problem seems overwhelming at first, just look for the first step. Write down what information you know. Break it down. And remember that by just using logic and basic techniques, you can work through even the most complex multi-step problems.

Draw a Picture or Write down Expressions as You Read

Many of the problems require more logic than raw mathematical knowledge. As you read a problem, make a sketch in the margin, draw on the figure in the test book, or write out the mathematical expression described. (For example, if you read "The area of Circle A is twice the area of Circle B," write down "A = 2B.")

Substitute Numbers for Variables

Sometimes the easiest thing to do is pick a value for *x*, *n*, or another variable, and work through the problem using that number. It may be easier to work through that way, especially for geometry problems. (Just remember that the value isn't "true," merely convenient.)

Use Elimination

As with all PSAT questions, the first thing to do is eliminate obviously wrong answers. Are there choices that are clearly too big or too small? In an impossible form? Based on a common error, such as a sign or exponent error?

Check Your Answers

When you solve a problem, plug the answer back in to confirm it makes sense. Make sure you haven't made careless mistakes such as skipping a step or making an arithmetic error.

Fill in All the Circles, Then Double-Check

For the "student-produced" responses, where you have to supply the actual number instead of selecting from multiple choices, make sure to fill in all the circles. You get no credit for the number written at the top — those boxes are only there to help you mark the circles accurately. Make sure you've filled in the right spots.

Give an Educated Guess

The PSAT no longer penalizes students for wrong answers. This means that you should always narrow down your answer choices by eliminating anything you know is wrong and then give an educated guess at the answer.

Don't Get Mired down on Any One Question

The first, easiest problem on the test is worth the same points as the last, hardest question. If one problem is taking a long time, move on. You can come back to it later if you have time.

Foundational Math Concepts

NUMBERS

CLASSIFICATIONS OF NUMBERS

Numbers are the basic building blocks of mathematics. Specific features of numbers are identified by the following terms:

Integer – any positive or negative whole number, including zero. Integers do not include fractions $\left(\frac{1}{3}\right)$, decimals (0.56), or mixed numbers $\left(7\frac{3}{4}\right)$.

Prime number – any whole number greater than 1 that has only two factors, itself and 1; that is, a number that can be divided evenly only by 1 and itself.

Composite number – any whole number greater than 1 that has more than two different factors; in other words, any whole number that is not a prime number. For example: The composite number 8 has the factors of 1, 2, 4, and 8.

Even number – any integer that can be divided by 2 without leaving a remainder. For example: 2, 4, 6, 8, and so on.

Odd number – any integer that cannot be divided evenly by 2. For example: 3, 5, 7, 9, and so on.

Decimal number – any number that uses a decimal point to show the part of the number that is less than one. Example: 1.234.

Decimal point – a symbol used to separate the ones place from the tenths place in decimals or dollars from cents in currency.

Decimal place – the position of a number to the right of the decimal point. In the decimal 0.123, the 1 is in the first place to the right of the decimal point, indicating tenths; the 2 is in the second place, indicating hundredths; and the 3 is in the third place, indicating thousandths.

The **decimal**, or base 10, system is a number system that uses ten different digits (0, 1, 2, 3, 4, 5, 6, 7, 8, 9). An example of a number system that uses something other than ten digits is the **binary**, or base 2, number system, used by computers, which uses only the numbers 0 and 1. It is thought that the decimal system originated because people had only their 10 fingers for counting.

Rational numbers include all integers, decimals, and fractions. Any terminating or repeating decimal number is a rational number.

Irrational numbers cannot be written as fractions or decimals because the number of decimal places is infinite and there is no recurring pattern of digits within the number. For example, pi (π) begins with 3.141592 and continues without terminating or repeating, so pi is an irrational number.

Real numbers are the set of all rational and irrational numbers.

Review Video: Numbers and Their Classifications
Visit mometrix.com/academy and enter code: 461071

Review Video: Rational and Irrational Numbers
Visit mometrix.com/academy and enter code: 280645

The Number Line

A number line is a graph to see the distance between numbers. Basically, this graph shows the relationship between numbers. So, a number line may have a point for zero and may show negative numbers on the left side of the line. Also, any positive numbers are placed on the right side of the line. For example, consider the points labeled on the following number line:

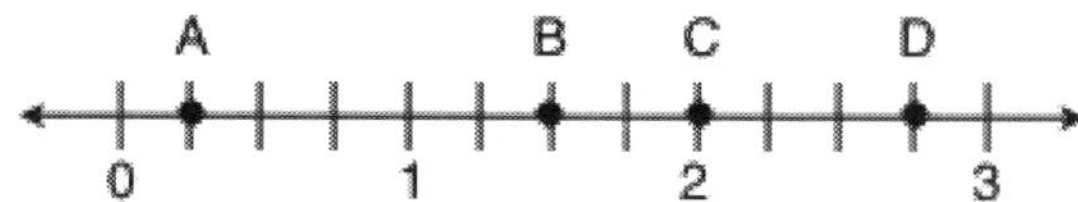

We can use the dashed lines on the number line to identify each point. Each dashed line between two whole numbers is $\frac{1}{4}$. The line halfway between two numbers is $\frac{1}{2}$.

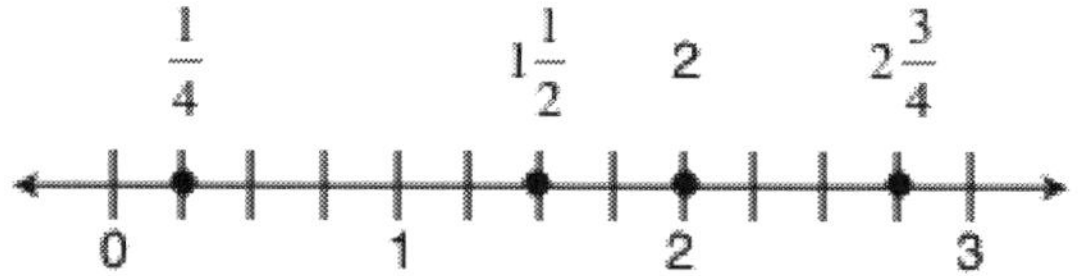

Review Video: Negative and Positive Number Line
Visit mometrix.com/academy and enter code: 816439

Numbers in Word Form and Place Value

When writing numbers out in word form or translating word form to numbers, it is essential to understand how a place value system works. In the decimal or base-10 system, each digit of a number represents how many of the corresponding place value – a specific factor of 10 – are contained in the number being represented. To make reading numbers easier, every three digits to the left of the decimal place is preceded by a comma. The following table demonstrates some of the place values:

Power of 10	10^3	10^2	10^1	10^0	10^{-1}	10^{-2}	10^{-3}
Value	1,000	100	10	1	0.1	0.01	0.001
Place	thousands	hundreds	tens	ones	tenths	hundredths	thousandths

For example, consider the number 4,546.09, which can be separated into each place value like this:

4: thousands
5: hundreds
4: tens
6: ones
0: tenths
9: hundredths

This number in word form would be *four thousand five hundred forty-six and nine hundredths.*

Review Video: Number Place Value
Visit mometrix.com/academy and enter code: 205433

Absolute Value

A precursor to working with negative numbers is understanding what **absolute values** are. A number's absolute value is simply the distance away from zero a number is on the number line. The absolute value of a number is always positive and is written $|x|$. For example, the absolute value of 3, written as $|3|$, is 3 because the distance between 0 and 3 on a number line is three units. Likewise, the absolute value of –3, written as $|-3|$, is 3 because the distance between 0 and –3 on a number line is three units. So, $|3| = |-3|$.

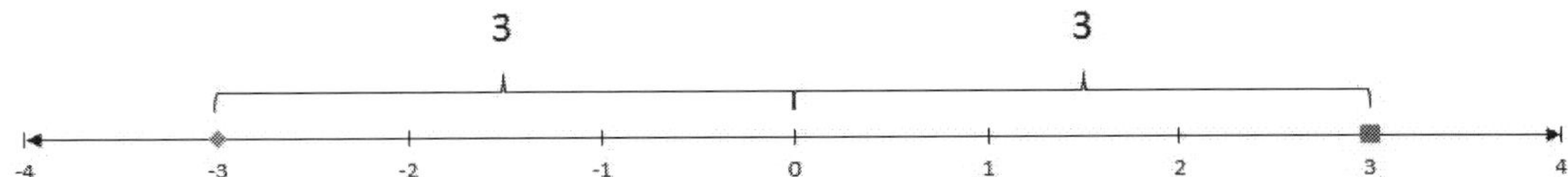

Review Video: Absolute Value
Visit mometrix.com/academy and enter code: 314669

Practice

P1. Write the place value of each digit in 14,059.826

P2. Write out each of the following in words:

(a) 29
(b) 478
(c) 98,542
(d) 0.06
(e) 13.113

P3. Write each of the following in numbers:

(a) nine thousand four hundred thirty-five
(b) three hundred two thousand eight hundred seventy-six
(c) nine hundred one thousandths
(d) nineteen thousandths
(e) seven thousand one hundred forty-two and eighty-five hundredths

Practice Solutions

P1. The place value for each digit would be as follows:

Digit	Place Value
1	ten-thousands
4	thousands
0	hundreds
5	tens
9	ones
8	tenths
2	hundredths
6	thousandths

P2. Each written out in words would be:

(a) twenty-nine
(b) four hundred seventy-eight
(c) ninety-eight thousand five hundred forty-two
(d) six hundredths
(e) thirteen and one hundred thirteen thousandths

P3. Each in numeric form would be:

(a) 9,435
(b) 302, 876
(c) 0.901
(d) 0.019
(e) 7,142.85

Operations

Operations

An **operation** is simply a mathematical process that takes some value(s) as input(s) and produces an output. Elementary operations are often written in the following form: *value operation value*. For instance, in the expression $1 + 2$ the values are 1 and 2 and the operation is addition. Performing the operation gives the output of 3. In this way we can say that $1 + 2$ and 3 are equal, or $1 + 2 = 3$.

Addition

Addition increases the value of one quantity by the value of another quantity (both called **addends**). For example, $2 + 4 = 6; 8 + 9 = 17$. The result is called the **sum**. With addition, the order does not matter, $4 + 2 = 2 + 4$.

When adding signed numbers, if the signs are the same simply add the absolute values of the addends and apply the original sign to the sum. For example, $(+4) + (+8) = +12$ and $(-4) +$

$(-8) = -12$. When the original signs are different, take the absolute values of the addends and subtract the smaller value from the larger value, then apply the original sign of the larger value to the difference. For instance, $(+4) + (-8) = -4$ and $(-4) + (+8) = +4$.

SUBTRACTION

Subtraction is the opposite operation to addition; it decreases the value of one quantity (the **minuend**) by the value of another quantity (the **subtrahend**). For example, $6 - 4 = 2$; $17 - 8 = 9$. The result is called the **difference**. Note that with subtraction, the order does matter, $6 - 4 \neq 4 - 6$.

For subtracting signed numbers, change the sign of the subtrahend and then follow the same rules used for addition. For example, $(+4) - (+8) = (+4) + (-8) = -4$.

Review Video: Addition and Subtraction
Visit mometrix.com/academy and enter code: 521157

MULTIPLICATION

Multiplication can be thought of as repeated addition. One number (the **multiplier**) indicates how many times to add the other number (the **multiplicand**) to itself. For example, 3×2 (three times two) $= 2 + 2 + 2 = 6$. With multiplication, the order does not matter: $2 \times 3 = 3 \times 2$ or $3 + 3 = 2 + 2 + 2$, either way the result (the **product**) is the same.

If the signs are the same the product is positive when multiplying signed numbers. For example, $(+4) \times (+8) = +32$ and $(-4) \times (-8) = +32$. If the signs are opposite, the product is negative. For example, $(+4) \times (-8) = -32$ and $(-4) \times (+8) = -32$. When more than two factors are multiplied together, the sign of the product is determined by how many negative factors are present. If there are an odd number of negative factors then the product is negative, whereas an even number of negative factors indicates a positive product. For instance, $(+4) \times (-8) \times (-2) = +64$ and $(-4) \times (-8) \times (-2) = -64$.

DIVISION

Division is the opposite operation to multiplication; one number (the **divisor**) tells us how many parts to divide the other number (the **dividend**) into. The result of division is called the **quotient**. For example, $20 \div 4 = 5$; if 20 is split into 4 equal parts, each part is 5. With division, the order of the numbers does matter, $20 \div 4 \neq 4 \div 20$.

The rules for dividing signed numbers are similar to multiplying signed numbers. If the dividend and divisor have the same sign, the quotient is positive. If the dividend and divisor have opposite signs, the quotient is negative. For example, $(-4) \div (+8) = -0.5$.

Review Video: Multiplication and Division
Visit mometrix.com/academy and enter code: 643326

PARENTHESES

Parentheses are used to designate which operations should be done first when there are multiple operations. Example: $4 - (2 + 1) = 1$; the parentheses tell us that we must add 2 and 1, and then subtract the sum from 4, rather than subtracting 2 from 4 and then adding 1 (this would give us an answer of 3).

Review Video: Mathematical Parentheses
Visit mometrix.com/academy and enter code: 978600

EXPONENTS

An **exponent** is a superscript number placed next to another number at the top right. It indicates how many times the base number is to be multiplied by itself. Exponents provide a shorthand way to write what would be a longer mathematical expression, for example: $2^4 = 2 \times 2 \times 2 \times 2$. A number with an exponent of 2 is said to be "squared," while a number with an exponent of 3 is said to be "cubed." The value of a number raised to an exponent is called its power. So, 8^4 is read as "8 to the 4th power," or "8 raised to the power of 4."

The properties of exponents are as follows:

Property	Description
$a^1 = a$	Any number to the power of 1 is equal to itself
$1^n = 1$	The number 1 raised to any power is equal to 1
$a^0 = 1$	Any number raised to the power of 0 is equal to 1
$a^n \times a^m = a^{n+m}$	Add exponents to multiply powers of the same base number
$a^n \div a^m = a^{n-m}$	Subtract exponents to divide powers of the same base number
$(a^n)^m = a^{n\times m}$	When a power is raised to a power, the exponents are multiplied
$(a \times b)^n = a^n \times b^n$ $(a \div b)^n = a^n \div b^n$	Multiplication and division operations inside parentheses can be raised to a power. This is the same as each term being raised to that power.
$a^{-n} = \frac{1}{a^n}$	A negative exponent is the same as the reciprocal of a positive exponent

Note that exponents do not have to be integers. Fractional or decimal exponents follow all the rules above as well. Example: $5^{\frac{1}{4}} \times 5^{\frac{3}{4}} = 5^{\frac{1}{4}+\frac{3}{4}} = 5^1 = 5$.

Review Video: Exponents
Visit mometrix.com/academy and enter code: 600998

Review Video: Laws of Exponents
Visit mometrix.com/academy and enter code: 532558

ROOTS

A **root**, such as a square root, is another way of writing a fractional exponent. Instead of using a superscript, roots use the radical symbol ($\sqrt{\ }$) to indicate the operation. A radical will have a number underneath the bar, and may sometimes have a number in the upper left: $\sqrt[n]{a}$, read as "the nth root of a." The relationship between radical notation and exponent notation can be described by this equation: $\sqrt[n]{a} = a^{\frac{1}{n}}$. The two special cases of $n = 2$ and $n = 3$ are called square roots and cube roots. If there is no number to the upper left, it is understood to be a square root ($n = 2$). Nearly all of the roots you encounter will be square roots. A square root is the same as a number raised to the one-half power. When we say that a is the square root of b ($a = \sqrt{b}$), we mean that a multiplied by itself equals b: ($a \times a = b$).

A **perfect square** is a number that has an integer for its square root. There are 10 perfect squares from 1 to 100: 1, 4, 9, 16, 25, 36, 49, 64, 81, 100 (the squares of integers 1 through 10).

Review Video: Roots
Visit mometrix.com/academy and enter code: 795655

Review Video: Square Root and Perfect Square
Visit mometrix.com/academy and enter code: 648063

MATHEMATICAL SYMBOLS

You must be able to translate verbal expressions or "math words" into math symbols. This chart contains several "math words" and their appropriate symbols:

equal, is, was, will be, has, costs, gets to, is the same as, becomes	=
time, of, multiplied by, product of, twice, doubles, halves, triples	×
divided by, per, ratio of/to, out of	÷
plus, added to, sum, combined, and, more than, totals of	+
subtracted from, less than, decreased by, minus, difference between	-
what, how much, original value, how many, a number, a variable	x, n, etc.

For example, the phrase *four more than twice a number* can be written algebraically as $2x + 4$. The phrase *half a number decreased by six* can be written algebraically as $\frac{1}{2}x - 6$. The phrase *the sum of a number and the product of five and that number* can be written algebraically as $x + 5x$. You may see a test question that says, "Olivia is constructing a bookcase from seven boards. Two of them are for vertical supports and five are for shelves. The height of the bookcase is twice the width of the bookcase. If the seven boards total 36 feet in length, what will be the height of Olivia's bookcase?" You would need to make a sketch and then create the equation to determine the width of the shelves. The height can be represented as double the width. (If x represents the width of the shelves in feet, then the height of the book shelf is $2x$. Since the seven boards total 36 feet, $2x + 2x + x + x + x + x + x = 36$; $9x = 36$; $x = 4$. The height is twice the width, or 8 feet.)

ORDER OF OPERATIONS

Order of operations is a set of rules that dictates the order in which we must perform each operation in an expression so that we will evaluate it accurately. If we have an expression that includes multiple different operations, order of operations tells us which operations to do first. The most common mnemonic for order of operations is **PEMDAS**, or "Please Excuse My Dear Aunt Sally." PEMDAS stands for parentheses, exponents, multiplication, division, addition, and subtraction. It is important to understand that multiplication and division have equal precedence, as do addition and subtraction, so those pairs of operations are simply worked from left to right in order.

For example, evaluating the expression $5 + 20 \div 4 \times (2 + 3) - 6$ using the correct order of operations would be done like this:

- **P:** Perform the operations inside the parentheses: $(2 + 3) = 5$
- **E:** Simplify the exponents.
  - The equation now looks like this: $5 + 20 \div 4 \times 5 - 6$

- **MD:** Perform multiplication and division from left to right: $20 \div 4 = 5$; then $5 \times 5 = 25$
  - The equation now looks like this: $5 + 25 - 6$
- **AS:** Perform addition and subtraction from left to right: $5 + 25 = 30$; then $30 - 6 = 24$

Review Video: Order of Operations
Visit mometrix.com/academy and enter code: 259675

Subtraction with Regrouping

A great way to make use of some of the features built into the decimal system would be regrouping when attempting longform subtraction operations. When subtracting within a place value, sometimes the minuend is smaller than the subtrahend, **regrouping** enables you to 'borrow' a unit from a place value to the left in order to get a positive difference. For example, consider subtracting 189 from 525 with regrouping.

Review Video: Subtracting Large Numbers
Visit mometrix.com/academy and enter code: 603350

First, set up the subtraction problem in vertical form:

$$\begin{array}{r} 525 \\ -\ 189 \\ \hline \end{array}$$

Notice that the numbers in the ones and tens columns of 525 are smaller than the numbers in the ones and tens columns of 189. This means you will need to use regrouping to perform subtraction:

$$\begin{array}{rrrr} & 5 & 2 & 5 \\ - & 1 & 8 & 9 \\ \hline \end{array}$$

To subtract 9 from 5 in the ones column you will need to borrow from the 2 in the tens columns:

$$\begin{array}{rrrr} & 5 & 1 & 15 \\ - & 1 & 8 & 9 \\ \hline & & & 6 \end{array}$$

Next, to subtract 8 from 1 in the tens column you will need to borrow from the 5 in the hundreds column:

$$\begin{array}{rrrr} & 4 & 11 & 15 \\ - & 1 & 8 & 9 \\ \hline & & 3 & 6 \end{array}$$

Last, subtract the 1 from the 4 in the hundreds column:

$$\begin{array}{rrrr} & 4 & 11 & 15 \\ - & 1 & 8 & 9 \\ \hline & 3 & 3 & 6 \end{array}$$

Practice

P1. Demonstrate how to subtract 477 from 620 using regrouping.

P2. Simplify the following expressions with exponents:

(a) 37^0
(b) 1^{30}
(c) $2^3 \times 2^4 \times 2^x$
(d) $(3^x)^3$
(e) $(12 \div 3)^2$

Practice Solutions

P1. First, set up the subtraction problem in vertical form:

$$\begin{array}{rrrr} & 6 & 2 & 0 \\ - & 4 & 7 & 7 \\ \hline \end{array}$$

To subtract 7 from 0 in the ones column you will need to borrow from the 2 in the tens column:

$$\begin{array}{rrrr} & 6 & 1 & 10 \\ - & 4 & 7 & 7 \\ \hline & & & 3 \end{array}$$

Next, to subtract 7 from the 1 that's still in the tens column you will need to borrow from the 6 in the hundreds column:

$$\begin{array}{rrrr} & 5 & 11 & 10 \\ - & 4 & 7 & 7 \\ \hline & & 4 & 3 \end{array}$$

Lastly, subtract 4 from the 5 remaining in the hundreds column:

$$\begin{array}{rrrr} & 5 & 11 & 10 \\ - & 4 & 7 & 7 \\ \hline & 1 & 4 & 3 \end{array}$$

P2. Using the properties of exponents and the proper order of operations:

(a) Any number raised to the power of 0 is equal to 1: $37^0 = 1$
(b) The number 1 raised to any power is equal to 1: $1^{30} = 1$
(c) Add exponents to multiply powers of the same base: $2^3 \times 2^4 \times 2^x = 2^{(3+4+x)} = 2^{(7+x)}$
(d) When a power is raised to a power, the exponents are multiplied: $(3^x)^3 = 3^{3x}$
(e) Perform the operation inside the parentheses first: $(12 \div 3)^2 = 4^2 = 16$

Factoring

Factors and Greatest Common Factor

Factors are numbers that are multiplied together to obtain a **product**. For example, in the equation $2 \times 3 = 6$, the numbers 2 and 3 are factors. A **prime number** has only two factors (1 and itself), but other numbers can have many factors.

A **common factor** is a number that divides exactly into two or more other numbers. For example, the factors of 12 are 1, 2, 3, 4, 6, and 12, while the factors of 15 are 1, 3, 5, and 15. The common factors of 12 and 15 are 1 and 3.

A **prime factor** is also a prime number. Therefore, the prime factors of 12 are 2 and 3. For 15, the prime factors are 3 and 5.

The **greatest common factor** (GCF) is the largest number that is a factor of two or more numbers. For example, the factors of 15 are 1, 3, 5, and 15; the factors of 35 are 1, 5, 7, and 35. Therefore, the greatest common factor of 15 and 35 is 5.

Review Video: Factors
Visit mometrix.com/academy and enter code: 920086

Review Video: Greatest Common Factor (GCF)
Visit mometrix.com/academy and enter code: 838699

Multiples and Least Common Multiple

Often listed out in multiplication tables, **multiples** are integer increments of a given factor. In other words, dividing a multiple by the factor number will result in an integer. For example, the multiples of 7 include: $1 \times 7 = 7,\ 2 \times 7 = 14,\ 3 \times 7 = 21,\ 4 \times 7 = 28,\ 5 \times 7 = 35$. Dividing 7, 14, 21, 28, or 35 by 7 will result in the integers 1, 2, 3, 4, and 5, respectively.

The least common multiple (**LCM**) is the smallest number that is a multiple of two or more numbers. For example, the multiples of 3 include 3, 6, 9, 12, 15, etc.; the multiples of 5 include 5, 10, 15, 20, etc. Therefore, the least common multiple of 3 and 5 is 15.

Review Video: Multiples
Visit mometrix.com/academy and enter code: 626738

Review Video: Multiples and Least Common Multiple (LCM)
Visit mometrix.com/academy and enter code: 520269

Rational Numbers

Fractions

A **fraction** is a number that is expressed as one integer written above another integer, with a dividing line between them $\left(\frac{x}{y}\right)$. It represents the **quotient** of the two numbers "x divided by y." It can also be thought of as x out of y equal parts.

The top number of a fraction is called the **numerator**, and it represents the number of parts under consideration. The 1 in $\frac{1}{4}$ means that 1 part out of the whole is being considered in the calculation. The bottom number of a fraction is called the **denominator**, and it represents the total number of equal parts. The 4 in $\frac{1}{4}$ means that the whole consists of 4 equal parts. A fraction cannot have a denominator of zero; this is referred to as "*undefined*."

Fractions can be manipulated, without changing the value of the fraction, by multiplying or dividing (but not adding or subtracting) both the numerator and denominator by the same number. If you divide both numbers by a common factor, you are **reducing** or simplifying the fraction. Two fractions that have the same value but are expressed differently are known as **equivalent fractions**. For example, $\frac{2}{10}, \frac{3}{15}, \frac{4}{20}$, and $\frac{5}{25}$ are all equivalent fractions. They can also all be reduced or simplified to $\frac{1}{5}$.

When two fractions are manipulated so that they have the same denominator, this is known as finding a **common denominator**. The number chosen to be that common denominator should be the least common multiple of the two original denominators. Example: $\frac{3}{4}$ and $\frac{5}{6}$; the least common multiple of 4 and 6 is 12. Manipulating to achieve the common denominator: $\frac{3}{4} = \frac{9}{12}$; $\frac{5}{6} = \frac{10}{12}$.

Proper Fractions and Mixed Numbers

A fraction whose denominator is greater than its numerator is known as a **proper fraction**, while a fraction whose numerator is greater than its denominator is known as an **improper fraction**. Proper fractions have values *less than one* and improper fractions have values *greater than one*.

A **mixed number** is a number that contains both an integer and a fraction. Any improper fraction can be rewritten as a mixed number. Example: $\frac{8}{3} = \frac{6}{3} + \frac{2}{3} = 2 + \frac{2}{3} = 2\frac{2}{3}$. Similarly, any mixed number can be rewritten as an improper fraction. Example: $1\frac{3}{5} = 1 + \frac{3}{5} = \frac{5}{5} + \frac{3}{5} = \frac{8}{5}$.

Review Video: Proper and Improper Fractions and Mixed Numbers
Visit mometrix.com/academy and enter code: 211077

Review Video: Fractions
Visit mometrix.com/academy and enter code: 262335

Adding and Subtracting Fractions

If two fractions have a common denominator, they can be added or subtracted simply by adding or subtracting the two numerators and retaining the same denominator. If the two fractions do not already have the same denominator, one or both of them must be manipulated to achieve a common denominator before they can be added or subtracted. Example: $\frac{1}{2} + \frac{1}{4} = \frac{2}{4} + \frac{1}{4} = \frac{3}{4}$.

Review Video: Adding and Subtracting Fractions
Visit mometrix.com/academy and enter code: 378080

Multiplying Fractions

Two fractions can be multiplied by multiplying the two numerators to find the new numerator and the two denominators to find the new denominator. Example: $\frac{1}{3} \times \frac{2}{3} = \frac{1\times2}{3\times3} = \frac{2}{9}$.

Review Video: Multiplying Fractions
Visit mometrix.com/academy and enter code: 638849

Dividing Fractions

Two fractions can be divided by flipping the numerator and denominator of the second fraction and then proceeding as though it were a multiplication. Example: $\frac{2}{3} \div \frac{3}{4} = \frac{2}{3} \times \frac{4}{3} = \frac{8}{9}$.

Review Video: Dividing Fractions
Visit mometrix.com/academy and enter code: 300874

Multiplying a Mixed Number by a Whole Number or a Decimal

When multiplying a mixed number by something, it is usually best to convert it to an improper fraction first. Additionally, if the multiplicand is a decimal, it is most often simplest to convert it to a fraction. For instance, to multiply $4\frac{3}{8}$ by 3.5, begin by rewriting each quantity as a whole number plus a proper fraction. Remember, a mixed number is a fraction added to a whole number and a decimal is a representation of the sum of fractions, specifically tenths, hundredths, thousandths, and so on:

$$4\frac{3}{8} \times 3.5 = \left(4 + \frac{3}{8}\right) \times \left(3 + \frac{1}{2}\right)$$

Next, the quantities being added need to be expressed with the same denominator. This is achieved by multiplying and dividing the whole number by the denominator of the fraction. Recall that a whole number is equivalent to that number divided by 1:

$$= \left(\frac{4}{1} \times \frac{8}{8} + \frac{3}{8}\right) \times \left(\frac{3}{1} \times \frac{2}{2} + \frac{1}{2}\right)$$

When multiplying fractions, remember to multiply the numerators and denominators separately:

$$= \left(\frac{4 \times 8}{1 \times 8} + \frac{3}{8}\right) \times \left(\frac{3 \times 2}{1 \times 2} + \frac{1}{2}\right)$$
$$= \left(\frac{32}{8} + \frac{3}{8}\right) \times \left(\frac{6}{2} + \frac{1}{2}\right)$$

Now that the fractions have the same denominators, they can be added:

$$= \frac{35}{8} \times \frac{7}{2}$$

Finally, perform the last multiplication and then simplify:

$$= \frac{35 \times 7}{8 \times 2} = \frac{245}{16} = \frac{240}{16} + \frac{5}{16} = 15\frac{5}{16}$$

DECIMALS

Decimals are one way to represent parts of a whole. Using the place value system, each digit to the right of a decimal point denotes the number of units of a corresponding *negative* power of ten. For example, consider the decimal 0.24. We can use a model to represent the decimal. Since a dime is worth one-tenth of a dollar and a penny is worth one-hundredth of a dollar, one possible model to represent this fraction is to have 2 dimes representing the 2 in the tenths place and 4 pennies representing the 4 in the hundredths place:

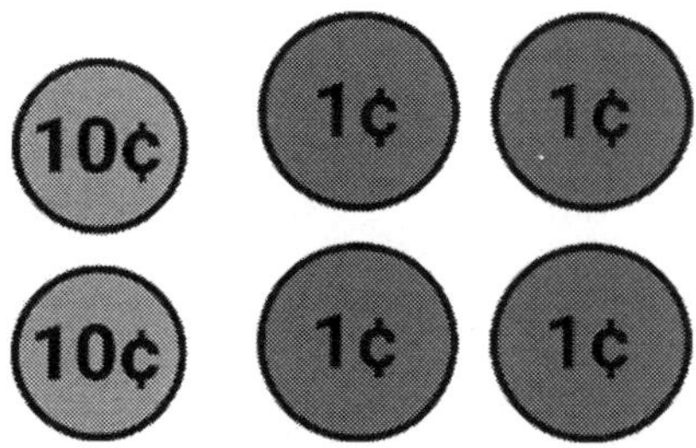

To write the decimal as a fraction, put the decimal in the numerator with 1 in the denominator. Multiply the numerator and denominator by tens until there are no more decimal places. Then simplify the fraction to lowest terms. For example, converting 0.24 to a fraction:

$$0.24 = \frac{0.24}{1} = \frac{0.24 \times 100}{1 \times 100} = \frac{24}{100} = \frac{6}{25}$$

Review Video: Decimals
Visit mometrix.com/academy and enter code: 837268

Adding and Subtracting Decimals

When adding and subtracting decimals, the decimal points must always be aligned. Adding decimals is just like adding regular whole numbers. Example: $4.5 + 2 = 6.5$.

If the problem-solver does not properly align the decimal points, an incorrect answer of 4.7 may result. An easy way to add decimals is to align all of the decimal points in a vertical column visually. This will allow one to see exactly where the decimal should be placed in the final answer. Begin adding from right to left. Add each column in turn, making sure to carry the number to the left if a column adds up to more than 9. The same rules apply to the subtraction of decimals.

Review Video: Adding and Subtracting Decimals
Visit mometrix.com/academy and enter code: 381101

Multiplying Decimals

A simple multiplication problem has two components: a **multiplicand** and a **multiplier**. When multiplying decimals, work as though the numbers were whole rather than decimals. Once the final product is calculated, count the number of places to the right of the decimal in both the multiplicand and the multiplier. Then, count that number of places from the right of the product and place the decimal in that position.

For example, 12.3×2.56 has a total of three places to the right of the respective decimals. Multiply 123×256 to get 31488. Now, beginning on the right, count three places to the left and insert the decimal. The final product will be 31.488.

Review Video: Multiplying Decimals
Visit mometrix.com/academy and enter code: 731574

Dividing Decimals

Every division problem has a **divisor** and a **dividend**. The dividend is the number that is being divided. In the problem $14 \div 7$, 14 is the dividend and 7 is the divisor. In a division problem with decimals, the divisor must be converted into a whole number. Begin by moving the decimal in the divisor to the right until a whole number is created. Next, move the decimal in the dividend the same number of spaces to the right. For example, 4.9 into 24.5 would become 49 into 245. The decimal was moved one space to the right to create a whole number in the divisor, and then the same was done for the dividend. Once the whole numbers are created, the problem is carried out normally: $245 \div 49 = 5$.

Review Video: Dividing Decimals
Visit mometrix.com/academy and enter code: 560690

PERCENTAGES

Percentages can be thought of as fractions that are based on a whole of 100; that is, one whole is equal to 100%. The word **percent** means "per hundred." Percentage problems are often presented in three main ways:

- Find what percentage of some number another number is.
  - Example: What percentage of 40 is 8?
- Find what number is some percentage of a given number.
  - Example: What number is 20% of 40?
- Find what number another number is a given percentage of.
  - Example: What number is 8 20% of?

There are three components in each of these cases: a **whole** (W), a **part** (P), and a **percentage** (%). These are related by the equation: $P = W \times \%$. This can easily be rearranged into other forms that may suit different questions better: $\% = \frac{P}{W}$ and $W = \frac{P}{\%}$. Percentage problems are often also word problems. As such, a large part of solving them is figuring out which quantities are what. For example, consider the following word problem:

In a school cafeteria, 7 students choose pizza, 9 choose hamburgers, and 4 choose tacos. What percentage of student choose tacos?

To find the whole, you must first add all of the parts: $7 + 9 + 4 = 20$. The percentage can then be found by dividing the part by the whole ($\% = \frac{P}{W}$): $\frac{4}{20} = \frac{20}{100} = 20\%$.

Review Video: Percentages
Visit mometrix.com/academy and enter code: 141911

Review Video: Finding Percentage of Number Given Whole
Visit mometrix.com/academy and enter code: 932623

CONVERTING BETWEEN PERCENTAGES, FRACTIONS, AND DECIMALS

Converting decimals to percentages and percentages to decimals is as simple as moving the decimal point. To *convert from a decimal to a percentage*, move the decimal point **two places to the right**. To *convert from a percentage to a decimal*, move it **two places to the left**. It may be helpful to remember that the percentage number will always be larger than the equivalent decimal number. For example:

$$0.23 = 23\% \quad 5.34 = 534\% \quad 0.007 = 0.7\%$$
$$700\% = 7.00 \quad 86\% = 0.86 \quad 0.15\% = 0.0015$$

To convert a fraction to a decimal, simply divide the numerator by the denominator in the fraction. To convert a decimal to a fraction, put the decimal in the numerator with 1 in the denominator. Multiply the numerator and denominator by tens until there are no more decimal places. Then simplify the fraction to lowest terms. For example, converting 0.24 to a fraction:

$$0.24 = \frac{0.24}{1} = \frac{0.24 \times 100}{1 \times 100} = \frac{24}{100} = \frac{6}{25}$$

Fractions can be converted to a percentage by finding equivalent fractions with a denominator of 100. For example,

$$\frac{7}{10} = \frac{70}{100} = 70\% \quad \frac{1}{4} = \frac{25}{100} = 25\%$$

To convert a percentage to a fraction, divide the percentage number by 100 and reduce the fraction to its simplest possible terms. For example,

$$60\% = \frac{60}{100} = \frac{3}{5} \quad 96\% = \frac{96}{100} = \frac{24}{25}$$

Review Video: Converting Decimals to Fractions and Percentages
Visit mometrix.com/academy and enter code: 986765

Review Video: Converting Fractions to Percentages and Decimals
Visit mometrix.com/academy and enter code: 306233

Review Video: Converting Percentages to Decimals and Fractions
Visit mometrix.com/academy and enter code: 287297

Rational Numbers

The term **rational** means that the number can be expressed as a ratio or fraction. That is, a number, r, is rational if and only if it can be represented by a fraction $\frac{a}{b}$ where a and b are integers and b does not equal 0. The set of rational numbers includes integers and decimals. If there is no finite way to represent a value with a fraction of integers, then the number is **irrational**. Common examples of irrational numbers include: $\sqrt{5}, (1 + \sqrt{2})$, and π.

Review Video: Rational Numbers
Visit mometrix.com/academy and enter code: 280645

Practice

P1. What is 30% of 120?

P2. What is 150% of 20?

P3. What is 14.5% of 96?

P4. Simplify the following expressions:

(a) $\left(\frac{2}{5}\right)/\left(\frac{4}{7}\right)$
(b) $\frac{7}{8} - \frac{8}{16}$
(c) $\frac{1}{2} + \left(3\left(\frac{3}{4}\right) - 2\right) + 4$
(d) $0.22 + 0.5 - (5.5 + 3.3 \div 3)$
(e) $\frac{3}{2} + (4(0.5) - 0.75) + 2$

P5. Convert the following to a fraction and to a decimal: **(a)** 15%; **(b)** 24.36%

P6. Convert the following to a decimal and to a percentage. **(a)** 4/5; **(b)** $3\frac{2}{5}$

P7. A woman's age is thirteen more than half of 60. How old is the woman?

P8. A patient was given pain medicine at a dosage of 0.22 grams. The patient's dosage was then increased to 0.80 grams. By how much was the patient's dosage increased?

P9. At a hotel, $\frac{3}{4}$ of the 100 rooms are occupied today. Yesterday, $\frac{4}{5}$ of the 100 rooms were occupied. On which day were more of the rooms occupied and by how much more?

P10. At a school, 40% of the teachers teach English. If 20 teachers teach English, how many teachers work at the school?

P11. A patient was given blood pressure medicine at a dosage of 2 grams. The patient's dosage was then decreased to 0.45 grams. By how much was the patient's dosage decreased?

P12. Two weeks ago, $\frac{2}{3}$ of the 60 customers at a skate shop were male. Last week, $\frac{3}{6}$ of the 80 customers were male. During which week were there more male customers?

P13. Jane ate lunch at a local restaurant. She ordered a $4.99 appetizer, a $12.50 entrée, and a $1.25 soda. If she wants to tip her server 20%, how much money will she spend in all?

P14. According to a survey, about 82% of engineers were highly satisfied with their job. If 145 engineers were surveyed, how many reported that they were highly satisfied?

P15. A patient was given 40 mg of a certain medicine. Later, the patient's dosage was increased to 45 mg. What was the percent increase in his medication?

P16. Order the following rational numbers from least to greatest: 0.55, 17%, $\sqrt{25}$, $\frac{64}{4}$, $\frac{25}{50}$, 3.

P17. Order the following rational numbers from greatest to least: 0.3, 27%, $\sqrt{100}$, $\frac{72}{9}$, $\frac{1}{9}$, 4.5

P18. Perform the following multiplication. Write each answer as a mixed number.

(a) $\left(1\frac{11}{16}\right) \times 4$
(b) $\left(12\frac{1}{3}\right) \times 1.1$
(c) $3.71 \times \left(6\frac{1}{5}\right)$

P19. Suppose you are making doughnuts and you want to triple the recipe you have. If the following list is the original amounts for the ingredients, what would be the amounts for the tripled recipe?

$1\,^{3}/_{4}$	cup	Flour
$1\,^{1}/_{4}$	tsp	Baking powder
$^{3}/_{4}$	tsp	Salt
$^{3}/_{8}$	cup	Sugar
$1\,^{1}/_{2}$	Tbsp	Butter
2	large	Eggs
$^{3}/_{4}$	tsp	Vanilla extract
$^{3}/_{8}$	cup	Sour cream

Practice Solutions

P1. The word *of* indicates multiplication, so 30% of 120 is found by multiplying 120 by 30%. Change 30% to a decimal, then multiply: $120 \times 0.3 = 36$

P2. The word *of* indicates multiplication, so 150% of 20 is found by multiplying 20 by 150%. Change 150% to a decimal, then multiply: $20 \times 1.5 = 30$

P3. Change 14.5% to a decimal before multiplying. $0.145 \times 96 = 13.92$.

P4. Follow the order of operations and utilize properties of fractions to solve each:

(a) Rewrite the problem as a multiplication problem: $\frac{2}{5} \times \frac{7}{4} = \frac{2\times7}{5\times4} = \frac{14}{20}$. Make sure the fraction is reduced to lowest terms. Both 14 and 20 can be divided by 2.

$$\frac{14}{20} = \frac{14 \div 2}{20 \div 2} = \frac{7}{10}$$

(b) The denominators of $\frac{7}{8}$ and $\frac{8}{16}$ are 8 and 16, respectively. The lowest common denominator of 8 and 16 is 16 because 16 is the least common multiple of 8 and 16. Convert the first fraction to its equivalent with the newly found common denominator of 16: $\frac{7 \times 2}{8 \times 2} = \frac{14}{16}$. Now that the fractions have the same denominator, you can subtract them.

$$\frac{14}{16} - \frac{8}{16} = \frac{6}{16} = \frac{3}{8}$$

(c) When simplifying expressions, first perform operations within groups. Within the set of parentheses are multiplication and subtraction operations. Perform the multiplication first to get $\frac{1}{2} + \left(\frac{9}{4} - 2\right) + 4$. Then, subtract two to obtain $\frac{1}{2} + \frac{1}{4} + 4$. Finally, perform addition from left to right:

$$\frac{1}{2} + \frac{1}{4} + 4 = \frac{2}{4} + \frac{1}{4} + \frac{16}{4} = \frac{19}{4} = 4\frac{3}{4}$$

(d) First, evaluate the terms in the parentheses $(5.5 + 3.3 \div 3)$ using order of operations. $3.3 \div 3 = 1.1$, and $5.5 + 1.1 = 6.6$. Next, rewrite the problem: $0.22 + 0.5 - 6.6$. Finally, add and subtract from left to right: $0.22 + 0.5 = 0.72$; $0.72 - 6.6 = -5.88$. The answer is -5.88.

(e) First, simplify within the parentheses, then change the fraction to a decimal and perform addition from left to right:

$$\frac{3}{2} + (2 - 0.75) + 2 =$$
$$\frac{3}{2} + 1.25 + 2 =$$
$$1.5 + 1.25 + 2 = 4.75$$

P5. (a) 15% can be written as $\frac{15}{100}$. Both 15 and 100 can be divided by 5: $\frac{15 \div 5}{100 \div 5} = \frac{3}{20}$

When converting from a percentage to a decimal, drop the percent sign and move the decimal point two places to the left: 15% = 0.15

(b) 24.36% written as a fraction is $\frac{24.36}{100}$, or $\frac{2436}{10{,}000}$, which reduces to $\frac{609}{2500}$. 24.36% written as a decimal is 0.2436. Recall that dividing by 100 moves the decimal two places to the left.

P6. (a) Recall that in the decimal system the first decimal place is one tenth: $\frac{4 \times 2}{5 \times 2} = \frac{8}{10} = 0.8$

Percent means "per hundred." $\frac{4 \times 20}{5 \times 20} = \frac{80}{100} = 80\%$

(b) The mixed number $3\frac{2}{5}$ has a whole number and a fractional part. The fractional part $\frac{2}{5}$ can be written as a decimal by dividing 5 into 2, which gives 0.4. Adding the whole to the part gives 3.4.

To find the equivalent percentage, multiply the decimal by 100. 3.4(100) = 340%. Notice that this percentage is greater than 100%. This makes sense because the original mixed number $3\frac{2}{5}$ is greater than 1.

P7. "More than" indicates addition, and "of" indicates multiplication. The expression can be written as $\frac{1}{2}(60) + 13$. So, the woman's age is equal to $\frac{1}{2}(60) + 13 = 30 + 13 = 43$. The woman is 43 years old.

P8. The first step is to determine what operation (addition, subtraction, multiplication, or division) the problem requires. Notice the keywords and phrases "by how much" and "increased." "Increased" means that you go from a smaller amount to a larger amount. This change can be found by subtracting the smaller amount from the larger amount: 0.80 grams– 0.22 grams = 0.58 grams.

Remember to line up the decimal when subtracting:

$$\begin{array}{r} 0.80 \\ -\ 0.22 \\ \hline 0.58 \end{array}$$

P9. First, find the number of rooms occupied each day. To do so, multiply the fraction of rooms occupied by the number of rooms available:

$$\text{Number occupied} = \text{Fraction occupied} \times \text{Total number}$$

$$\text{Number of rooms occupied today} = \frac{3}{4} \times 100 = 75$$

$$\text{Number of rooms occupied} = \frac{4}{5} \times 100 = 80$$

The difference in the number of rooms occupied is: $80 - 75 = 5$ rooms

P10. To answer this problem, first think about the number of teachers that work at the school. Will it be more or less than the number of teachers who work in a specific department such as English? More teachers work at the school, so the number you find to answer this question will be greater than 20.

40% of the teachers are English teachers. "Of" indicates multiplication, and words like "is" and "are" indicate equivalence. Translating the problem into a mathematical sentence gives $40\% \times t = 20$, where t represents the total number of teachers. Solving for t gives $t = \frac{20}{40\%} = \frac{20}{0.40} = 50$. Fifty teachers work at the school.

P11. The decrease is represented by the difference between the two amounts:

$$2 \text{ grams} - 0.45 \text{ grams} = 1.55 \text{ grams}.$$

Remember to line up the decimal point before subtracting.

$$\begin{array}{r} 2.00 \\ -\ 0.45 \\ \hline 1.55 \end{array}$$

P12. First, you need to find the number of male customers that were in the skate shop each week. You are given this amount in terms of fractions. To find the actual number of male customers, multiply the fraction of male customers by the number of customers in the store.

$$\text{Actual number of male customers} = \text{fraction of male customers} \times \text{total customers}$$

$$\text{Number of male customers two weeks ago} = \frac{2}{3} \times 60 = \frac{120}{3} = 40$$

$$\text{Number of male customers last week} = \frac{3}{6} \times 80 = \frac{1}{2} \times 80 = \frac{80}{2} = 40$$

The number of male customers was the same both weeks.

P13. To find total amount, first find the sum of the items she ordered from the menu and then add 20% of this sum to the total.

$$\$4.99 + \$12.50 + \$1.25 = \$18.74$$

$$\$18.74 \times 20\% = (0.20)(\$18.74) = \$3.748 \approx \$3.75$$

$$\text{Total} = \$18.74 + \$3.75 = \$22.49$$

P14. 82% of 145 is $0.82 \times 145 = 118.9$. Because you can't have 0.9 of a person, we must round up to say that 119 engineers reported that they were highly satisfied with their jobs.

P15. To find the percent increase, first compare the original and increased amounts. The original amount was 40 mg, and the increased amount is 45 mg, so the dosage of medication was increased by 5 mg ($45-40=5$). Note, however, that the question asks not by how much the dosage increased but by what percentage it increased.

$$\begin{aligned}\text{Percent increase} &= \frac{\text{new amount} - \text{original amount}}{\text{original amount}} \times 100\% \\ &= \frac{45\text{ mg} - 40\text{ mg}}{40\text{ mg}} \times 100\% = \frac{5}{40} \times 100\% = 0.125 \times 100\% = 12.5\%\end{aligned}$$

P16. Recall that the term rational simply means that the number can be expressed as a ratio or fraction. Notice that each of the numbers in the problem can be written as a decimal or integer:

$$\begin{aligned}17\% &= 0.1717 \\ \sqrt{25} &= 5 \\ \frac{64}{4} &= 16 \\ \frac{25}{50} &= \frac{1}{2} = 0.5\end{aligned}$$

So, the answer is 17%, $\frac{25}{50}$, 0.55, 3, $\sqrt{25}$, $\frac{64}{4}$.

P17. Converting all the numbers to integers and decimals makes it easier to compare the values:

$$\begin{aligned}27\% &= 0.27 \\ \sqrt{100} &= 10 \\ \frac{72}{9} &= 8 \\ \frac{1}{9} &\approx 0.11\end{aligned}$$

So, the answer is $\sqrt{100}$, $\frac{72}{9}$, 4.5, 0.3, 27%, $\frac{1}{9}$.

Review Video: Ordering Rational Numbers
Visit mometrix.com/academy and enter code: 419578

P18. For each, convert improper fractions, adjust to a common denominator, perform the operations, and then simplify:

(a) Sometimes, you can skip converting the denominator and just distribute the multiplication.

$$\begin{aligned}\left(1\frac{11}{16}\right)\times 4 &= \left(1+\frac{11}{16}\right)\times 4\\ &= 1\times 4+\frac{11}{16}\times 4\\ &= 4+\frac{11}{16}\times\frac{4}{1}\\ &= 4+\frac{44}{16} = 4+\frac{11}{4} = 4+2\frac{3}{4} = 6\frac{3}{4}\end{aligned}$$

(b)

$$\begin{aligned}\left(12\frac{1}{3}\right)\times 1.1 &= \left(12+\frac{1}{3}\right)\times\left(1+\frac{1}{10}\right)\\ &= \left(\frac{12}{1}\times\frac{3}{3}+\frac{1}{3}\right)\times\left(\frac{10}{10}+\frac{1}{10}\right)\\ &= \left(\frac{36}{3}+\frac{1}{3}\right)\times\frac{11}{10}\\ &= \frac{37}{3}\times\frac{11}{10}\\ &= \frac{407}{30} = \frac{390}{30}+\frac{17}{30} = 13\frac{17}{30}\end{aligned}$$

(c)

$$\begin{aligned}3.71\times\left(6\frac{1}{5}\right) &= \left(3+\frac{71}{100}\right)\times\left(6+\frac{1}{5}\right)\\ &= \left(\frac{300}{100}+\frac{71}{100}\right)\times\left(\frac{6}{1}\times\frac{5}{5}+\frac{1}{5}\right)\\ &= \frac{371}{100}\times\left(\frac{30}{5}+\frac{1}{5}\right)\\ &= \frac{371}{100}\times\frac{31}{5}\\ &= \frac{11501}{500} = \frac{11500}{500}+\frac{1}{500} = 23\frac{1}{500}\end{aligned}$$

P19. Fortunately, some of the amounts are duplicated, so we do not need to figure out every amount.

$$\begin{aligned}1\frac{3}{4}\times 3 &= (1\times 3)+\left(\frac{3}{4}\times 3\right)\\ &= 3+\frac{9}{4}\\ &= 3+2\frac{1}{4}\\ &= 5\frac{1}{4}\end{aligned}$$

$$\begin{aligned}1\frac{1}{4}\times 3 &= (1\times 3)+\left(\frac{1}{4}\times 3\right)\\ &= 3+\frac{3}{4}\\ &= 3\frac{3}{4}\end{aligned}$$

$$\begin{aligned}\frac{3}{4}\times 3 &= \frac{3}{4}\times 3\\ &= \frac{9}{4}\\ &= 2\frac{1}{4}\end{aligned}$$

$$\frac{3}{8} \times 3 = \frac{3}{8} \times 3$$
$$= \frac{9}{8}$$
$$= 1\frac{1}{8}$$

$$1\frac{1}{2} \times 3 = 1 \times 3 + \frac{1}{2} \times 3$$
$$= 3 + \frac{3}{2}$$
$$= 3 + 1\frac{1}{2}$$
$$= 4\frac{1}{2}$$

$$2 \times 3 = 6$$

So, the result for the triple recipe is:

$5\,^1/_4$	cup	Flour
$3\,^3/_4$	tsp	Baking powder
$2\,^1/_4$	tsp	Salt
$1\,^1/_8$	cup	Sugar
$4\,^1/_2$	Tbsp	Butter
6	large	Eggs
$2\,^1/_4$	tsp	Vanilla extract
$1\,^1/_8$	cup	Sour cream

Heart of Algebra

The questions in this section will cover a range of topics in algebra. Students will be tested on their ability to analyze and solve linear equations and systems of equations. They will also need to be able to create these equations to represent a relationship between two or more quantities and solve problems. Along with linear equations, students will need to be able to create and solve linear inequalities. Some questions will also require the student to interpret formulas and rearrange them to solve the problem.

Expressions

You must be able to translate verbal expressions into mathematical language. These may be simple or complex algebraic expressions (linear, quadratic, or exponential); you must be able to simplify these expressions using order of operations. You may be asked to determine an algebraic model involving costs or interest and then use that model to perform a calculation. You may be given a geometric situation involving area or perimeter in which you have to write and simplify an expression. These problems may be complex and require sketches in order to choose or produce a correct answer.

Terms and Coefficients

Mathematical expressions consist of a combination of one or more values arranged in terms that are added together. As such, an expression could be just a single number, including zero. A **variable term** is the product of a real number, also called a **coefficient**, and one or more variables, each of which may be raised to an exponent. Expressions may also include numbers without a variable, called **constants** or **constant terms**. The expression $6s^2$, for example, is a single term where the coefficient is the real number 6 and the variable is s^2. Note that if a term is written as simply a variable to some exponent, like t^2, then the coefficient is 1, because $t^2 = 1t^2$.

LINEAR EXPRESSIONS

You should expect to create, solve, or interpret a linear equation in one variable. These equations will have rational coefficients and may require multiple steps to simplify or solve. Linear equations in one variable have just one unknown variable. That variable has an exponent of one. For example, $2m + 3 = 3m + 7$ and $1.2(2.5x + 3.2) = 6.7x$ are linear equations in one variable. Typically, a question asks you to translate a verbal expression into an algebraic expression or a word problem into an equation. Then, you may need to solve the equation or answer another question related to that equation. The problems may include questions about any topic that lends itself to a linear expression or equation in one variable. For instance, you may see a question that says, "Jacob rents a car during his vacation. The rental agency's daily charge is $49.95, which is taxed at a rate of 7%. Jacob is also charged a one-time nonrefundable rental fee of $50. Which of the following represents Jacob's total car rental expenses, in dollars, for use of the car for *x* days?" You would then need to create the expression that computes the total cost for *x* days.

A **single variable linear expression** is the sum of a single variable term, where the variable has no exponent, and a constant, which may be zero. For instance, the expression $2w + 7$ has $2w$ as the variable term and 7 as the constant term. It is important to realize that terms are separated by addition or subtraction. Since an expression is a sum of terms, expressions such as $5x - 3$ can be written as $5x + (-3)$ to emphasize that the constant term is negative. A real-world example of a single variable linear expression is the perimeter of a square, four times the side length, often expressed: $4s$.

In general, a **linear expression** is the sum of any number of variable terms so long as none of the variables have an exponent. For example, $3m + 8n - \frac{1}{4}p + 5.5q - 1$ is a linear expression, but $3y^3$ is not. In the same way, the expression for the perimeter of a general triangle, the sum of the side lengths: $a + b + c$, is considered to be linear, but the expression for the area of square, the side length squared: s^2, is not.

EQUATIONS

LINEAR EQUATIONS

Equations that can be written as $ax + b = 0$, where $a \neq 0$, are referred to as **one variable linear equations.** A solution to such an equation is called a **root**. In the case where we have the equation $5x + 10 = 0$, if we solve for x we get a solution of $x = -2$. In other words, the root of the equation is -2. This is found by first subtracting 10 from both sides, which gives $5x = -10$. Next, simply divide both sides by the coefficient of the variable, in this case 5, to get $x = -2$. This can be checked by plugging -2 back into the original equation $(5)(-2) + 10 = -10 + 10 = 0$.

The **solution set** is the set of all solutions of an equation. In our example, the solution set would simply be -2. If there were more solutions (there usually are in multivariable equations) then they would also be included in the solution set. When an equation has no true solutions, this is referred to as an **empty set**. Equations with identical solution sets are **equivalent equations**. An **identity** is a term whose value or determinant is equal to 1.

Linear equations can be written many ways. Below is a list of some forms linear equations can take:

- **Standard Form**: $Ax + By = C$; the slope is $\frac{-A}{B}$ and the y-intercept is $\frac{C}{B}$
- **Slope Intercept Form**: $y = mx + b$, where m is the slope and b is the y-intercept
- **Point-Slope Form**: $y - y_1 = m(x - x_1)$, where m is the slope and (x_1, y_1) is a point on the line

- **Two-Point Form**: $\frac{y-y_1}{x-x_1} = \frac{y_2-y_1}{x_2-x_1}$, where (x_1, y_1) and (x_2, y_2) are two points on the given line
- **Intercept Form**: $\frac{x}{x_1} + \frac{y}{y_1} = 1$, where $(x_1, 0)$ is the point at which a line intersects the *x*-axis, and $(0, y_1)$ is the point at which the same line intersects the *y*-axis

Review Video: Slope-Intercept and Point-Slope Forms
Visit mometrix.com/academy and enter code: 113216

Solving One-Variable Linear Equations

Multiply all terms by the lowest common denominator to eliminate any fractions. Look for addition or subtraction to undo so you can isolate the variable on one side of the equal sign. Divide both sides by the coefficient of the variable. When you have a value for the variable, substitute this value into the original equation to make sure you have a true equation. Consider the following example:

Kim's savings are represented by the table below. Represent her savings, using an equation.

X (Months)	Y (Total Savings)
2	\$1300
5	\$2050
9	\$3050
11	\$3550
16	\$4800

The table shows a function with a constant rate of change, or slope, of 250. Given the points on the table, the slopes can be calculated as $(2050 - 1300)/(5 - 2)$, $(3050 - 2050)/(9 - 5)$, $(3550 - 3050)/(11 - 9)$, and $(4800 - 3550)/(16 - 11)$, each of which equals 250. Thus, the table shows a constant rate of change, indicating a linear function. The slope-intercept form of a linear equation is written as $y = mx + b$, where m represents the slope and b represents the y-intercept. Substituting the slope into this form gives $y = 250x + b$. Substituting corresponding x- and y-values from any point into this equation will give the y-intercept, or b. Using the point, (2, 1300), gives $1300 = 250(2) + b$, which simplifies as b = 800. Thus, her savings may be represented by the equation, $y = 250x + 800$.

You should expect to be given a real-world scenario and the linear function associated with that scenario. You may be asked to identify variable terms or constant terms from the given function as well as interpret their meanings in the given real-world situation. You may see a test question like "The school van begins a field trip with 14 gallons of gasoline. After travelling 120 miles, the van has 8 gallons of gasoline. If this relationship is modeled by the linear function $f(x) = -20x + 280$, what does the *x* represent?" Or you might be asked what -20 and 280 represent in the given function.

Rules for Manipulating Equations

Like Terms

Like terms are terms in an equation that have the same variable, regardless of whether or not they also have the same coefficient. This includes terms that *lack* a variable; all constants (i.e. numbers without variables) are considered like terms. If the equation involves terms with a variable raised to different powers, the like terms are those that have the variable raised to the same power.

For example, consider the equation $x^2 + 3x + 2 = 2x^2 + x - 7 + 2x$. In this equation, 2 and -7 are like terms; they are both constants. $3x$, x, and $2x$ are like terms: they all include the variable x raised to the first power. x^2 and $2x^2$ are like terms; they both include the variable x, raised to the second power. $2x$ and $2x^2$ are not like terms; although they both involve the variable x, the variable is not raised to the same power in both terms. The fact that they have the same coefficient, 2, is not relevant.

CARRYING OUT THE SAME OPERATION ON BOTH SIDES OF AN EQUATION

When solving an equation, the general procedure is to carry out a series of operations on both sides of an equation, choosing operations that will tend to simplify the equation when doing so. The reason why the same operation must be carried out on both sides of the equation is because that leaves the meaning of the equation unchanged, and yields a result that is equivalent to the original equation. This would not be the case if we carried out an operation on one side of an equation and not the other. Consider what an equation means: it is a statement that two values or expressions are equal. If we carry out the same operation on both sides of the equation—add 3 to both sides, for example—then the two sides of the equation are changed in the same way, and so remain equal. If we do that to only one side of the equation—add 3 to one side but not the other—then that wouldn't be true; if we change one side of the equation but not the other then the two sides are no longer equal.

ADVANTAGE OF COMBINING LIKE TERMS

Combining like terms refers to adding or subtracting like terms—terms with the same variable—and therefore reducing sets of like terms to a single term. The main advantage of doing this is that it simplifies the equation. Often combining like terms can be done as the first step in solving an equation, though it can also be done later, such as after distributing terms in a product.

For example, consider the equation $2(x + 3) + 3(2 + x + 3) = -4$. The 2 and the 3 in the second set of parentheses are like terms, and we can combine them, yielding $2(x + 3) + 3(x + 5) = -4$. Now we can carry out the multiplications implied by the parentheses, distributing outer 2 and 3 accordingly: $2x + 6 + 3x + 15 = -4$. The $2x$ and the $3x$ are like terms, and we can add them together: $5x + 6 + 15 = -4$. Now, the constants 6, 15, and -4 are also like terms, and we can combine them as well: subtracting 6 and 15 from both sides of the equation, we get $5x = -4 - 6 - 15$, or $5x = -25$, which simplifies further to $x = -5$.

CANCELING TERMS ON OPPOSITE SIDES OF AN EQUATION

Two terms on opposite sides of an equation can be canceled if and only if they *exactly* match each other. They must have the same variable raised to the same power and the same coefficient. For example, in the equation $3x + 2x^2 + 6 = 2x^2 - 6$, $2x^2$ appears on both sides of the equation, and can be canceled, leaving $3x + 6 = -6$. The 6 on each side of the equation can*not* be canceled, because it is added on one side of the equation and subtracted on the other. While they cannot be canceled, however, the 6 and -6 are like terms and can be combined, yielding $3x = -12$, which simplifies further to $x = -4$.

It's also important to note that the terms to be canceled must be independent terms and cannot be part of a larger term. For example, consider the equation $2(x + 6) = 3(x + 4) + 1$. We cannot cancel the xs, because even though they match each other they are part of the larger terms $2(x + 6)$ and $3(x + 4)$. We must first distribute the 2 and 3, yielding $2x + 12 = 3x + 12 + 1$. Now we see that the terms with the x's do not match, but the 12's do, and can be canceled, leaving $2x = 3x + 1$, which simplifies to $x = -1$.

Determining If Two Equations Are Equivalent

One way to check for equivalence is to evaluate each expression at a chosen value, say $x = 0$ or $x = 1$, and see if the results agree. If the expressions do not yield the same result, then they are not equivalent, but it is important to note that yielding the same result does not necessarily mean the expressions are equivalent. This is only a method to eliminate incorrect answers; as the choices are narrowed, you may continue to try other values until all but the correct choice have been eliminated. Another way to determine whether two algebraic expressions are equivalent is to choose the most complex expression and simplify it algebraically to see if you can produce the second expression. This may involve factoring and canceling like factors or distributing and combining like terms.

Process for Manipulating Equations

Isolating Variables

To **isolate a variable** means to manipulate the equation so that the variable appears by itself on one side of the equation, and does not appear at all on the other side. Generally, an equation or inequality is considered to be solved once the variable is isolated and the other side of the equation or inequality is simplified as much as possible. In the case of a two-variable equation or inequality, only one variable need be isolated; it will not usually be possible to simultaneously isolate both variables.

For a linear equation—an equation in which the variable only appears raised to the first power—isolating a variable can be done by first moving all the terms with the variable to one side of the equation and all other terms to the other side. (*Moving* a term really means adding the inverse of the term to both sides; when a term is *moved* to the other side of the equation its sign is flipped.) Then combine like terms on each side. Finally, divide both sides by the coefficient of the variable, if applicable. The steps need not necessarily be done in this order, but this order will always work.

Equations with More Than One Solution

Some types of non-linear equation, such as equations involving squares of variables, may have more than one solution. For example, the equation $x^2 = 4$ has two solutions: 2 and –2. Equations with absolute values can also have multiple solutions: $|x| = 1$ has the solutions $x = 1$ and $x = -1$.

It is also possible for a linear equation to have more than one solution, but only if the equation is true regardless of the value of the variable. In this case, the equation is considered to have infinitely many solutions, because any possible value of the variable is a solution. We know a linear equation has infinitely many solutions if when we combine like terms the variables cancel, leaving a true statement. For example, consider the equation $2(3x + 5) = x + 5(x + 2)$. Distributing, we get $6x + 10 = x + 5x + 10$; combining like terms gives $6x + 10 = 6x + 10$, and the $6x$ terms cancel to leave $10 = 10$. This is clearly true, so the original equation is true for any value of x. We could also have canceled the 10s leaving $0 = 0$, but again this is clearly true—in general if both sides of the equation match exactly, it has infinitely many solutions.

Equations with No Solution

Some types of non-linear equations, such as equations involving squares of variables, may have no solution. For example, the equation $x^2 = -2$ has no solutions in the real numbers, because the square of any real number must be positive. Similarly, $|x| = -1$ has no solution, because the absolute value of a number is always positive.

It is also possible for an equation to have no solution even if does not involve any powers greater than one or absolute values or other special functions. For example, the equation $2(x + 3) + x = 3x$ has no solution. We can see that if we try to solve it: first we distribute, leaving $2x + 6 + x = 3x$.

But now if we try to combine all the terms with the variable, we find that they cancel: we have $3x$ on the left and $3x$ on the right, canceling to leave us with $6 = 0$. This is clearly false. In general, whenever the variable terms in an equation cancel leaving different constants on both sides, it means that the equation has no solution. (If we are left with the *same* constant on both sides, the equation has infinitely many solutions instead.)

Features of Equations That Require Special Treatment

Linear Equations

A linear equation is an equation in which variables only appear by themselves: not multiplied together, not with exponents other than one, and not inside absolute value signs or any other functions. For example, the equation $x + 1 - 3x = 5 - x$ is a linear equation: while x appears multiple times, it never appears with an exponent other than one, or inside any function. The two-variable equation $2x - 3y = 5 + 2x$ is also a linear equation. In contrast, the equation $x^2 - 5 = 3x$ is *not* a linear equation, because it involves the term x^2. $\sqrt{x} = 5$ is not a linear equation, because it involves a square root. $(x - 1)^2 = 4$ is not a linear equation because even though there's no exponent on the x directly, it appears as part of an expression that is squared. The two-variable equation $x + xy - y = 5$ is not a linear equation because it includes the term xy, where two variables are multiplied together.

Linear equations can always be solved (or shown to have no solution) by combining like terms and performing simple operations on both sides of the equation. Some non-linear equations can also be solved by similar methods, but others may require more advanced methods of solution, if they can be solved analytically at all.

Solving Equations Involving Roots

In an equation involving roots, the first step is to isolate the term with the root, if possible, and then raise both sides of the equation to the appropriate power to eliminate it. Consider an example equation, $2\sqrt{x+1} - 1 = 3$. In this case, begin by adding 1 to both sides, yielding $2\sqrt{x+1} = 4$, and then dividing both sides by 2, yielding $\sqrt{x+1} = 2$. Now square both sides, yielding $x + 1 = 4$. Finally, subtracting 1 from both sides yields $x = 3$.

Squaring both sides of an equation may, however, yield a spurious solution—a solution to the squared equation that is *not* a solution of the original equation. It's therefore necessary to plug the solution back into the original equation to make sure it works. In this case, it does: $2\sqrt{3+1} - 1 = 2\sqrt{4} - 1 = 2(2) - 1 = 4 - 1 = 3$.

The same procedure applies for roots other than square roots. For example, given the equation $3 + \sqrt[3]{2x} = 5$, we can first subtract 3 from both sides, yielding $\sqrt[3]{2x} = 2$ and isolating the root. Raising both sides to the third power yields $2x = 2^3$, i.e. $2x = 8$. We can now divide both sides by 2 to get $x = 4$.

Solving Equations with Exponents

To solve an equation involving an exponent, the first step is to isolate the variable with the exponent. We can then take the appropriate root of both sides to eliminate the exponent. For instance, for the equation $2x^3 + 17 = 5x^3 - 7$, we can subtract $5x^3$ from both sides to get $-3x^3 + 17 = -7$, and then subtract 17 from both sides to get $-3x^3 = -24$. Finally, we can divide both sides by -3 to get $x^3 = 8$. Finally, we can take the cube root of both sides to get $x = \sqrt[3]{8} = 2$.

One important but often overlooked point is that equations with an exponent greater than 1 may have more than one answer. The solution to $x^2 = 9$ isn't simply $x = 3$; it's $x = \pm 3$: that is, $x = 3$ or

$x = -3$. For a slightly more complicated example, consider the equation $(x - 1)^2 - 1 = 3$. Adding one to both sides yields $(x - 1)^2 = 4$; taking the square root of both sides yields $x - 1 = 2$. We can then add 1 to both sides to get $x = 3$. However, there's a second solution: we also have the possibility that $x - 1 = -2$, in which case $x = -1$. Both $x = 3$ and $x = -1$ are valid solutions, as can be verified by substituting them both into the original equation.

Solving Equations with Absolute Values

When solving an equation with an absolute value, the first step is to isolate the absolute value term. We then consider the two possibilities: when the expression inside the absolute value is positive or when it is negative. In the former case, the expression in the absolute value equals the expression on the other side of the equation; in the latter, it equals the additive inverse of that expression—the expression times negative one. We consider each case separately, and finally check for spurious solutions.

For instance, consider solving $|2x - 1| + x = 5$ for x. We can first isolate the absolute value by moving the x to the other side: $|2x - 1| = -x + 5$. Now, we have two possibilities. First, that $2x - 1$ is positive, and hence $2x - 1 = -x + 5$. Rearranging and combining like terms yields $3x = 6$, and hence $x = 2$. The other possibility is that $2x - 1$ is negative, and hence $2x - 1 = -(-x + 5) = x - 5$. In this case, rearranging and combining like terms yields $x = -4$. Substituting $x = 2$ and $x = -4$ back into the original equation, we see that they are both valid solutions.

Note that the absolute value of a sum or difference applies to the sum or difference as a whole, not to the individual terms: in general, $|2x - 1|$ is not equal to $|2x + 1|$ or to $|2x| - 1$.

Review Video: Solving Absolute Value Inequalities
Visit mometrix.com/academy and enter code: 997008

Spurious Solutions

A **spurious solution** may arise when we square both sides of an equation as a step in solving it, or under certain other operations on the equation. It is a solution to the squared or otherwise modified equation that is *not* a solution of the original equation. To identify a spurious solution, it's useful when you solve an equation involving roots or absolute values to plug the solution back into the original equation to make sure it's valid.

Choosing Which Variable to Isolate in Two-Variable Equations

Similar to methods for a one-variable equation, solving a two-variable equation involves isolating a variable: manipulating the equation so that a variable appears by itself on one side of the equation, and not at all on the other side. However, in a two-variable equation, you will usually only be able to isolate one of the variables; the other variable may appear on the other side along with constant terms, or with exponents or other functions.

Often one variable will be much more easily isolated than the other, and therefore that's the variable you should choose. If one variable appears with various exponents, and the other only raised it to the first power, the latter variable is the one to isolate: given the equation $a^2 + 2b = a^3 + b + 3$, the b only appears to the first power, whereas a appears squared and cubed, so b is the variable that can be solved for: combining like terms and isolating the b on the left side of the equation, we get $b = a^3 - a^2 + 3$. If both variables are equally easy to isolate, then it's best to isolate the independent variable, if one is defined; if the two variables are x and y, the convention is that y is the independent variable.

Modeling Linear Relationships in Two Variables

The key idea when modeling linear relationships in two variables is to determine which quantity is the independent variable and which quantity is the dependent variable. For example, you might be asked to build a function to model the pressure at the bottom of a lake in terms of the depth of the lake. Since pressure depends on depth, depth is the independent variable, and pressure is the dependent variable. Your function would have the form of $p(d) = (rate)d + constant$. It helps to recognize that these functions typically fall into the slope-intercept form of a linear equation $y = mx + b$, where y represents the dependent variable, m represents the rate, x represents the independent variable, and b represents the constant. You may need to determine if the independent variable and dependent variable are directly or inversely related. Ask yourself, "As the dependent variable increases, does the dependent variable increase or decrease?" This will determine if the sign associated with your rate is positive or negative.

Practice

P1. Seeing the equation $2x + 4 = 4x + 7$, a student divides the first terms on each side by 2, yielding $x + 4 = 2x + 7$, and then combines like terms to get $x = -3$. However, this is incorrect, as can be seen by substituting -3 into the original equation. Explain what is wrong with the student's reasoning.

P2. Describe the steps necessary to solve the equation $2x + 1 - x = 4 + 3x + 7$.

P3. Describe the steps necessary to solve the equation $2(x + 5) = 7(4 - x)$.

P4. Find all real solutions to the equation $1 - \sqrt{x} = 2$.

P5. Find all real solutions to the equation $|x + 1| = 2x + 5$.

P6. Solve for x: $-x + 2\sqrt{x + 5} + 1 = 3$.

P7. Ray earns $10 an hour at his job. Write an equation for his earnings as a function of time spent working. Determine how long Ray has to work in order to earn $360.

P8. Simplify the following: $3x + 2 + 2y = 5y - 7 + |2x - 1|$

Practice Solutions

P1. As stated, it's easy to verify that the student's solution is incorrect: $2(-3) + 4 = -2$ and $4(-3) + 7 = -5$; clearly $-2 \neq -5$. The mistake was in the first step, which illustrates a common type of error in solving equations. The student tried to simplify the two variable terms by dividing them by 2. However, it's not valid to multiply or divide only one term on each side of an equation by a number; when multiplying or dividing, the operation must be applied to *every* term in the equation. So, dividing by 2 would yield not $x + 4 = 2x + 7$, but $x + 2 = 2x + \frac{7}{2}$. While this is now valid, that fraction is inconvenient to work with, so this may not be the best first step in solving the equation. Rather, it may have been better to first combine like terms: subtracting $4x$ from both sides yields $-2x + 4 = 7$; subtracting 4 from both sides yields $-2x = 3$; and *now* we can divide both sides by -2 to get $x = -\frac{3}{2}$.

P2. Our ultimate goal is to isolate the variable, x. To that end we first move all the terms containing x to the left side of the equation, and all the constant terms to the right side. Note that when we move a term to the other side of the equation its sign changes. We are therefore now left with $2x - x - 3x = 4 + 7 - 1$.

Next, we combine the like terms on each side of the equation, adding and subtracting the terms as appropriate. This leaves us with $-2x = 10$.

At this point, we're almost done; all that remains is to divide both sides by -2 to leave the x by itself. We now have our solution, $x = -5$. We can verify that this is a correct solution by substituting it back into the original equation.

P3. Generally, in equations that have a sum or difference of terms multiplied by another value or expression, the first step is to multiply those terms, distributing as necessary: $2(x + 5) = 2(x) + 2(5) = 2x + 10$, and $7(4 - x) = 7(4) - 7(x) = 28 - 7x$. So, the equation becomes $2x + 10 = 28 - 7x$. We can now add $7x$ to both sides to eliminate the variable from the right-hand side: $9x + 10 = 28$. Similarly, we can subtract 10 from both sides to move all the constants to the right: $9x = 18$. Finally, we can divide both sides by 9, yielding the final answer, $x = 2$.

P4. It's not hard to isolate the root: subtract one from both sides, yielding $-\sqrt{x} = 1$. Finally, multiply both sides by –1, yielding $\sqrt{x} = -1$. Squaring both sides of the equation yields $x = 1$. However, if we plug this back into the original equation, we get $1 - \sqrt{1} = 2$, which is false. Therefore $x = 1$ is a spurious solution, and the equation has no real solutions.

P5. This equation has two possibilities: $x + 1 = 2x + 5$, which simplifies to $x = -4$; or $x + 1 = -(2x + 5) = -2x - 5$, which simplifies to $x = -2$. However, if we try substituting both values back into the original equation, we see that only $x = -2$ yields a true statement. $x = -4$ is a spurious solution; $x = -2$ is the only valid solution to the equation.

P6. Start by isolating the term with the root. We can do that by moving the $-x$ and the 1 to the other side, yielding $2\sqrt{x + 5} = 3 + x - 1$, or $2\sqrt{x + 5} = x + 2$. Dividing both sides of the equation by 2 would give us a fractional term that could be messy to deal with, so we won't do that for now. Instead, we square both sides of the equation; note that on the left-hand side the 2 is outside the square root sign, so we have to square it. As a result, we get $4(x + 5) = (x + 2)^2$. Expanding both sides gives us $4x + 20 = x^2 + 4x + 4$. In this case, we see that we have $4x$ on both sides, so we can cancel the $4x$ (which is what allows us to solve this equation despite the different powers of x). We now have $20 = x^2 + 4$, or $x^2 = 16$. Since the variable is raised to an even power, we need to take the positive and negative roots, so $x = \pm 4$: that is, $x = 4$ or $x = -4$. Substituting both values into the original equation, we see that $x = 4$ satisfies the equation but $x = -4$ does not; hence $x = -4$ is a spurious solution, and the only solution to the equation is $x = 4$.

P7. The number of dollars that Ray earns is dependent on the number of hours he works, so earnings will be represented by the dependent variable y and hours worked will be represented by the independent variable x. He earns 10 dollars per hour worked, so his earnings can be calculated as $y = 10x$. To calculate the number of hours Ray must work in order to earn \$360, plug in 360 for y and solve for x:

$$360 = 10x$$
$$x = \frac{360}{10} = 36$$

P8. To simplify this equation, we must isolate one of its variables on one side of the equation. In this case, the x appears under an absolute value sign, which makes it difficult to isolate. The y, on the other hand, only appears without an exponent—the equation is linear in y. We will therefore choose to isolate the y. The first step, then, is to move all the terms with y to the left side of the equation, which we can do by subtracting $5y$ from both sides:

$$3x + 2 - 3y = -7 + |2x - 1|$$

We can then move all the terms that do *not* include y to the right side of the equation, by subtracting $3x$ and 2 from both sides of the equation:

$$-3y = -3x - 9 + |2x - 1|$$

Finally, we can isolate the y by dividing both sides by –3.

$$y = x + 3 - \frac{1}{3}|2x - 1|$$

This is as far as we can simplify the equation; we cannot combine the terms inside and outside the absolute value sign. We can therefore consider the equation to be solved.

INEQUALITIES

Commonly in algebra and other upper-level fields of math you find yourself working with mathematical expressions that do not equal each other. The statement comparing such expressions with symbols such as $<$ (less than) or $>$ (greater than) is called an *inequality*. An example of an inequality is $7x > 5$. To solve for x, simply divide both sides by 7 and the solution is shown to be $x > \frac{5}{7}$. Graphs of the solution set of inequalities are represented on a number line. Open circles are used to show that an expression approaches a number but is never quite equal to that number.

Review Video: Inequalities
Visit mometrix.com/academy and enter code: 347842

Conditional inequalities are those with certain values for the variable that will make the condition true and other values for the variable where the condition will be false. **Absolute inequalities** can have any real number as the value for the variable to make the condition true, while there is no real number value for the variable that will make the condition false. Solving inequalities is done by following the same rules as for solving equations with the exception that when multiplying or dividing by a negative number the direction of the inequality sign must be flipped or reversed. **Double inequalities** are situations where two inequality statements apply to the same variable expression. An example of this is $-c < ax + b < c$.

You should expect to create, solve, or interpret a linear inequality in one variable. Linear inequalities in one variable are inequalities with just one unknown variable. That variable has an exponent of one. For example, $4x + 2 > 10$ and $100 - 2x \geq 27$ are both linear equalities in one variable. Typically, the questions ask you to translate verbal expressions or word problems into algebraic inequalities. Then, you may be expected to solve the inequality or answer another question related to that inequality. Examples of key words and phrases indicating an inequality include *at least* (≥), *no more than* (≤), *more than* (>) and *less than* (<). You may see a test question that says, "Emily and Madison sold tickets to the school play. Emily sold 70 more tickets than Madison, but together they sold fewer than 200 tickets. Which of the following represents the number of tickets Madison sold?" You would then need to create an inequality from the given information and simplify that inequality using correct algebraic procedures; afterwards, when solving, remember to flip the inequality symbol if dividing or multiplying both sides by negative numbers.

Determining Solutions to Inequalities

To determine whether a coordinate is a solution of an inequality, you can substitute the values of the coordinate into the inequality, simplify, and check whether the resulting statement holds true. For instance, to determine whether $(-2, 4)$ is a solution of the inequality $y \geq -2x + 3$, substitute the values into the inequality, $4 \geq -2(-2) + 3$. Simplify the right side of the inequality and the result is $4 \geq 7$, which is a false statement. Therefore, the coordinate is not a solution of the inequality. You can also use this method to determine which part of the graph of an inequality is shaded. The graph of $y \geq -2x + 3$ includes the solid line $y = -2x + 3$ and, since it excludes the point $(-2, 4)$ to the left of the line, it is shaded to the right of the line.

Flipping Inequality Signs

When given an inequality, we can always turn the entire inequality around, swapping the two sides of the inequality and changing the inequality sign. For instance, $x + 2 > 2x - 3$ is equivalent to $2x - 3 < x + 2$. Aside from that, normally the inequality does not change if we carry out the same operation on both sides of the inequality. There is, however, one principal exception: if we *multiply* or *divide* both sides of the inequality by a *negative number*, the inequality is flipped. For example, if we take the inequality $-2x < 6$ and divide both sides by -2, the inequality flips and we are left with $x > -3$. This *only* applies to multiplication and division, and only with negative numbers. Multiplying or dividing both sides by a positive number, or adding or subtracting any number regardless of sign, does not flip the inequality.

Compound Inequalities

A **compound inequality** is an equality that consists of two inequalities combined with *and* or *or*. The two components of a proper compound inequality must be of opposite type: that is, one must be greater than (or greater than or equal to), the other less than (or less than or equal to). For instance, "$x + 1 < 2$ or $x + 1 > 3$" is a compound inequality, as is "$2x \geq 4$ and $2x \leq 6$." An *and* inequality can be written more compactly by having one inequality on each side of the common part: "$2x \geq 1$ and $2x \leq 6$," can also be written as $1 \leq 2x \leq 6$.

In order for the compound inequality to be meaningful, the two parts of an *and* inequality must overlap; otherwise no numbers satisfy the inequality. On the other hand, if the two parts of an *or* inequality overlap, then *all* numbers satisfy the inequality and as such is usually not meaningful.

Solving a compound inequality requires solving each part separately. For example, given the compound inequality "$x + 1 < 2$ or $x + 1 > 3$," the first inequality, $x + 1 < 2$, reduces to $x < 1$, and the second part, $x + 1 > 3$, reduces to $x > 2$, so the whole compound inequality can be written as "$x < 1$ or $x > 2$." Similarly, $1 \leq 2x \leq 6$ can be solved by dividing each term by 2, yielding $\frac{1}{2} \leq x \leq 3$.

Solving Inequalities Involving Absolute Values

To solve an inequality involving an absolute value, first isolate the term with the absolute value. Then proceed to treat the two cases separately as with an absolute value equation, but flipping the inequality in the case where the expression in the absolute value is negative (since that essentially involves multiplying both sides by -1.) The two cases are then combined into a compound inequality; if the absolute value is on the greater side of the inequality, then it is an *or* compound inequality, if on the lesser side, then it's an *and*.

Consider the inequality $2 + |x - 1| \geq 3$. We can isolate the absolute value term by subtracting 2 from both sides: $|x - 1| \geq 1$. Now, we're left with the two cases $x - 1 \geq 1$ or $x - 1 \leq -1$: note that in the latter, negative case, the inequality is flipped. $x - 1 \geq 1$ reduces to $x \geq 2$, and $x - 1 \leq -1$ reduces to $x \leq 0$. Since in the inequality $|x - 1| \geq 1$ the absolute value is on the greater side, the two cases combine into an *or* compound inequality, so the final, solved inequality is "$x \leq 0$ or $x \geq 2$."

Review Video: Solving Absolute Value Inequalities
Visit mometrix.com/academy and enter code: 997008

Solving Inequalities Involving Square Roots

Solving an inequality with a square root involves two parts. First, we solve the inequality as if it were an equation, isolating the square root and then squaring both sides of the equation. Second, we restrict the solution to the set of values of x for which the value inside the square root sign is non-negative.

For example, in the inequality, $\sqrt{x-2}+1<5$, we can isolate the square root by subtracting 1 from both sides, yielding $\sqrt{x-2}<4$. Squaring both sides of the inequality yields $x-2<16$, so $x<18$. Since we can't take the square root of a negative number, we also require the part inside the square root to be non-negative. In this case, that means $x-2\geq 0$. Adding 2 to both sides of the inequality yields $x\geq 2$. Our final answer is a compound inequality combining the two simple inequalities: $x\geq 2$ and $x<18$, or $2\leq x<18$.

Note that we only get a compound inequality if the two simple inequalities are in opposite directions; otherwise we take the one that is more restrictive.

The same technique can be used for other even roots, such as fourth roots. It is *not*, however, used for cube roots or other odd roots—negative numbers *do* have cube roots, so the condition that the quantity inside the root sign cannot be negative does not apply.

Special Circumstances

Sometimes an inequality involving an absolute value or an even exponent is true for all values of x, and we don't need to do any further work to solve it. This is true if the inequality, once the absolute value or exponent term is isolated, says that term is greater than a negative number (or greater than or equal to zero). Since an absolute value or a number raised to an even exponent is *always* non-negative, this inequality is always true.

Graphical Solutions to Equations and Inequalities

When equations are shown graphically, they are usually shown on a **Cartesian coordinate plane**. The Cartesian coordinate plane consists of two number lines placed perpendicular to each other, and intersecting at the zero point, also known as the origin. The horizontal number line is known as the x-axis, with positive values to the right of the origin, and negative values to the left of the origin. The vertical number line is known as the y-axis, with positive values above the origin, and negative values below the origin. Any point on the plane can be identified by an ordered pair in the form (x, y), called coordinates. The x-value of the coordinate is called the abscissa, and the y-value of the coordinate is called the ordinate. The two number lines divide the plane into **four quadrants**: I, II, III, and IV.

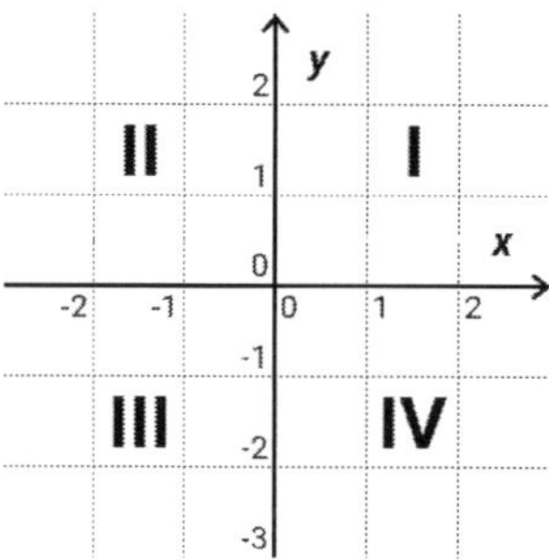

Note that in quadrant I $x > 0$ and $y > 0$, in quadrant II $x < 0$ and $y > 0$, in quadrant III $x < 0$ and $y < 0$, and in quadrant IV $x > 0$ and $y < 0$.

Recall that if the value of the slope of a line is positive, the line slopes upward from left to right. If the value of the slope is negative, the line slopes downward from left to right. If the y-coordinates are the same for two points on a line, the slope is 0 and the line is a **horizontal line**. If the x-coordinates are the same for two points on a line, there is no slope and the line is a **vertical line**. Two or more lines that have equivalent slopes are **parallel lines**. **Perpendicular lines** have slopes that are negative reciprocals of each other, such as $\frac{a}{b}$ and $\frac{-b}{a}$.

Graphing Simple Inequalities

To graph a simple inequality, we first mark on the number line the value that signifies the end point of the inequality. If the inequality is strict (involves a less than or greater than), we use a hollow circle; if it is not strict (less than or equal to or greater than or equal to), we use a solid circle. We then fill in the part of the number line that satisfies the inequality: to the left of the marked point for less than (or less than or equal to), to the right for greater than (or greater than or equal to).

For example, we would graph the inequality $x < 5$ by putting a hollow circle at 5 and filling in the part of the line to the left:

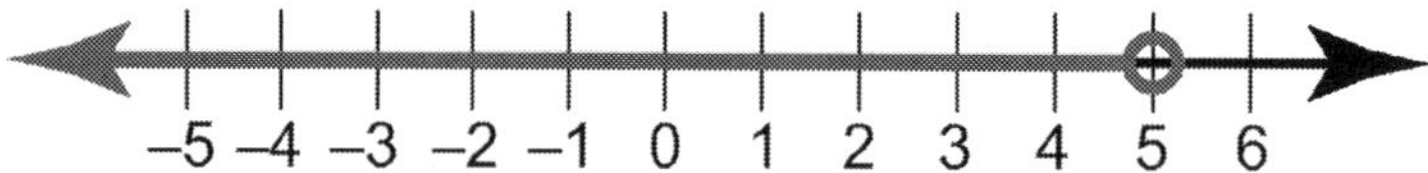

Graphing Compound Inequalities

To graph a compound inequality, we fill in both parts of the inequality for an *or* inequality, or the overlap between them for an *and* inequality. More specifically, we start by plotting the endpoints of each inequality on the number line. For an *or* inequality, we then fill in the appropriate side of the line for each inequality. Typically, the two component inequalities do not overlap, that means the shaded part is *outside* the two points. For an *and* inequality, we instead fill in the part of the line that meets both inequalities.

For the inequality "$x \leq -3$ or $x > 4$," we first put a solid circle at –3 and a hollow circle at 4. We then fill the parts of the line *outside* these circles:

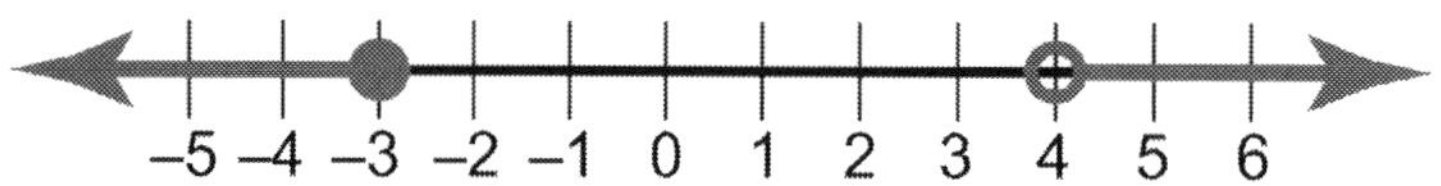

GRAPHING INEQUALITIES INCLUDING ABSOLUTE VALUES

An inequality with an absolute value can be converted to a compound inequality. To graph the inequality, first convert it to a compound inequality, and then graph that normally. If the absolute value is on the greater side of the inequality, we end up with an *or* inequality; we plot the endpoints of the inequality on the number line and fill in the part of the line *outside* those points. If the absolute value is on the smaller side of the inequality, we end up with an *and* inequality; we plot the endpoints of the inequality on the number line and fill in the part of the line *between* those points.

For example, the inequality $|x + 1| \geq 4$ can be rewritten as $x \geq 3$ or $x \leq -5$. We place solid circles at the points 3 and -5 and fill in the part of the line *outside* them:

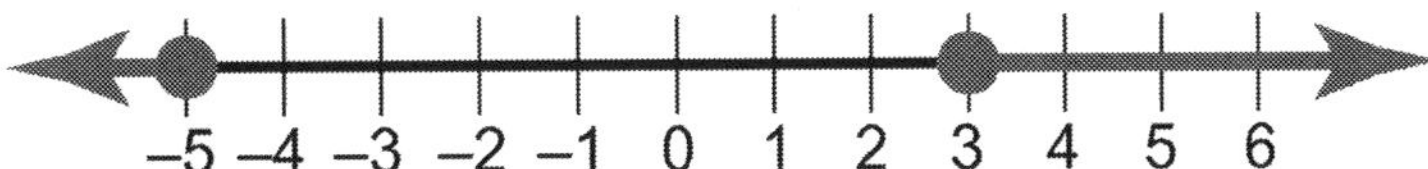

GRAPHING EQUATIONS IN TWO VARIABLES

One way of graphing an equation in two variables is to plot enough points to get an idea for its shape, and then draw the appropriate curve through those points. A point can be plotted by substituting in a value for one variable and solving for the other. If the equation is linear, we only need two points, and can then draw a straight line between them.

For example, consider the equation $y = 2x - 1$. This is a linear equation—both variables only appear raised to the first power—so we only need two points. When $x = 0$, $y = 2(0) - 1 = -1$. When $x = 2$, $y = 2(2) - 1 = 3$. We can therefore choose the points $(0, -1)$ and $(2, 3)$, and draw a line between them:

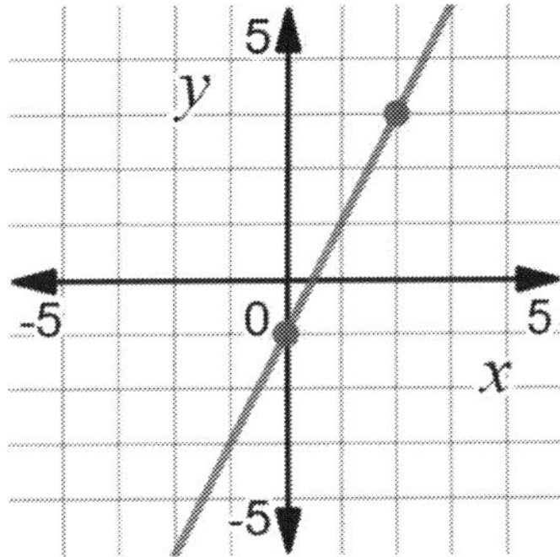

GRAPHING INEQUALITIES IN TWO VARIABLES

To graph an inequality in two variables, we first graph the border of the inequality. This means graphing the equation that we get if we replace the inequality sign with an equals sign. If the inequality is strict (> or <), we graph the border with a dashed or dotted line; if it is not strict (≥ or ≤), we use a solid line. We can then test any point not on the border to see if it satisfies the inequality. If it does, we shade in that side of the border; if not, we shade in the other side. As an example, consider $y > 2x + 2$. To graph this inequality, we first graph the border, $y = 2x + 2$. Since it is a strict inequality, we use a dashed line. Then, we choose a test point. This can be any point not on the border; in this case, we will choose the origin, $(0, 0)$. (This makes the calculation easy and is generally a good choice unless the border passes through the origin.) Putting this into the original inequality, we get $0 > 2(0) + 2$, i.e. $0 > 2$. This is *not* true, so we shade in the side of the border that does *not* include the point $(0, 0)$:

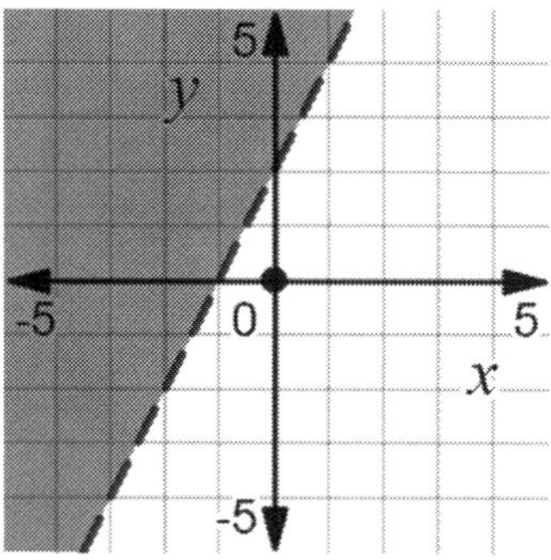

Graphing Compound Inequalities in Two Variables

One way to graph a compound inequality in two variables is to first graph each of the component inequalities. For an *and* inequality, we then shade in only the parts where the two graphs overlap; for an *or* inequality, we shade in any region that pertains to either of the individual inequalities.

Consider the graph of "$y \geq x - 1$ *and* $y \leq -x$":

We first shade in the individual inequalities:

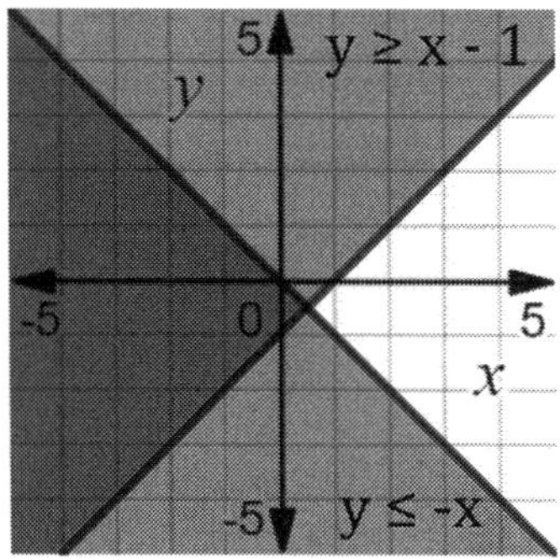

Now, since the compound inequality has an *and*, we only leave shaded the overlap—the part that pertains to *both* inequalities:

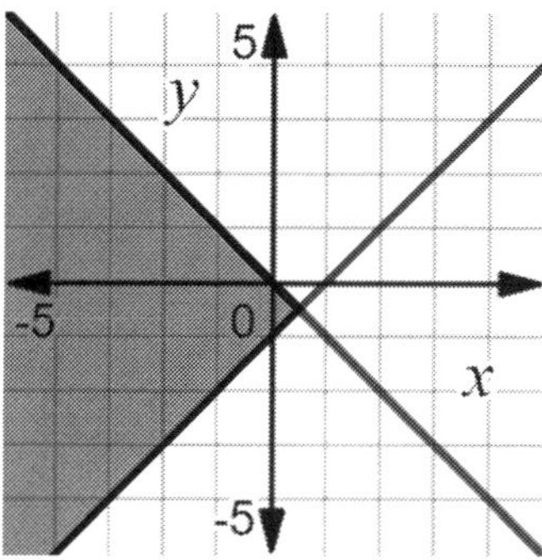

If instead the inequality had been "$y \geq x - 1$ *or* $y \leq -x$," our final graph would involve the *total* shaded area:

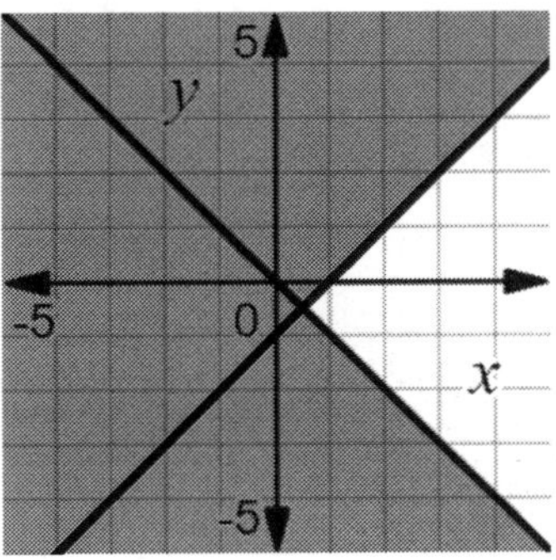

Practice

P1. Analyze the following inequalities:

(a) $2 - |x + 1| < 3$
(b) $2(x - 1)^2 + 7 \leq 1$

P2. Graph the following on a number line:

(a) $x \geq 3$
(b) $-2 \leq x \leq 6$
(c) $|x| < 2$

Practice Solutions

P1. (a) Subtracting 2 from both sides yields $-|x + 1| < 1$; multiplying by -1—and flipping the inequality, since we're multiplying by a negative number—yields $|x + 1| > -1$. But since the absolute value cannot be negative, it's *always* greater than –1, so this inequality is true for all values of x.

(b) Subtracting 7 from both sides yields $2(x - 1)^2 \leq -6$; dividing by 2 yields $(x - 1)^2 \leq -3$. But $(x - 1)^2$ must be nonnegative, and hence cannot be less than or equal to –3; this inequality has no solution.

P2. (a) We would graph the inequality $x \geq 3$ by putting a solid circle at 3 and filling in the part of the line to the right:

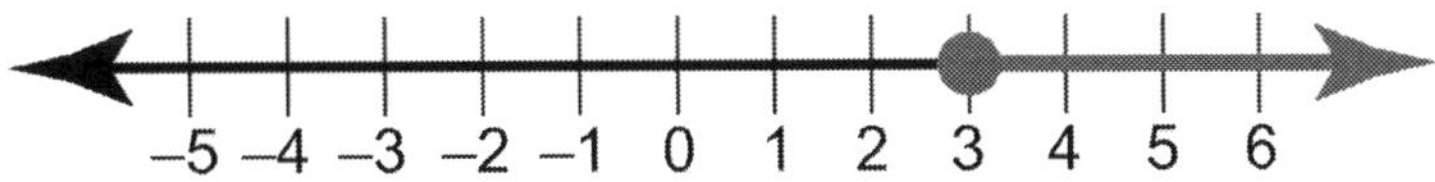

(b) The inequality $-2 \leq x \leq 6$ is equivalent to "$x \geq -2$ and $x \leq 6$." To plot this compound inequality, we first put solid circles at –2 and 6, and then fill in the part of the line *between* these circles:

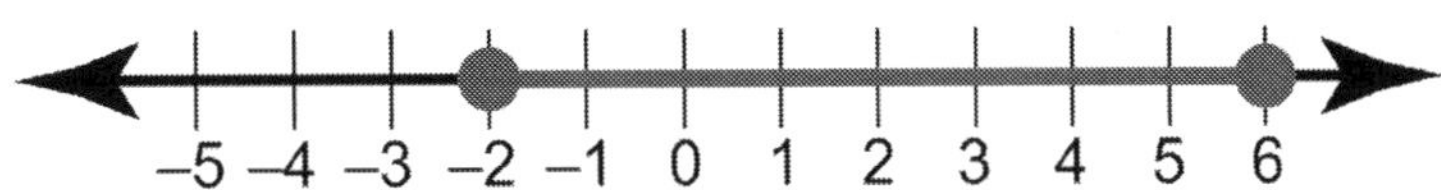

(c) The inequality $|x| < 2$ can be rewritten as "$x > -2$ and $x < 2$." We place hollow circles at the points –2 and 2 and fill in the part of the line between them:

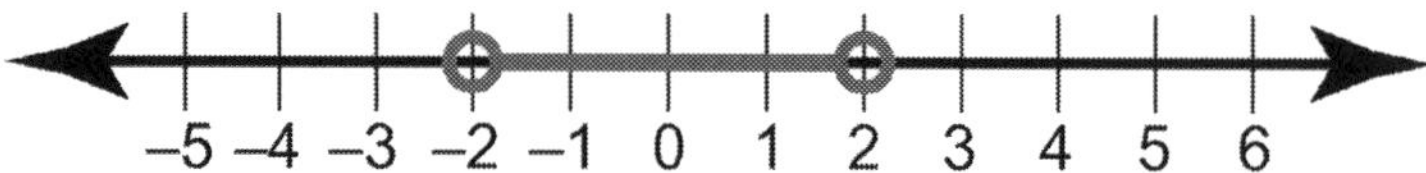

Systems of Equations

Systems of equations are a set of simultaneous equations that all use the same variables. A solution to a system of equations must be true for each equation in the system. **Consistent systems** are those with at least one solution. **Inconsistent systems** are systems of equations that have no solution.

Review Video: Systems of Equations
Visit mometrix.com/academy and enter code: 658153

You should expect to be asked to write and solve a system of linear equations from a word problem. You may see a test question that says, "Alyssa's scout troop is selling tickets for the community fun fair. Adult tickets cost \$8.50 each, and child tickets cost \$5.50 each. The troop sells a total of 375 tickets and collects \$2,512.50 in revenue. Solving which of these systems of equations yields the number of adult tickets, x, and the number of child tickets, y, sold by Alyssa's scout troop? How many of each ticket type are sold?" First, write an equation for the number of tickets sold ($x + y = 375$) and a second equation for revenue generated ($8.50x + 5.50y = 2512.50$). Then, solve the system of equations and answer the question that is asked. The methods used in solving systems of linear equations include elimination (addition), substitution, and graphing.

Often, complex geometry problems involve writing a system of equations. For example, if the problem gives the area and perimeter of a rectangular garden and asks for its length and width, you can use the formulas $A = lw$ and $p = 2l + 2w$ to write a system of equations. Sometimes, geometry problems involve two shapes, one of which is inside another. For example, you may be given the inner dimensions of a picture frame and asked to find the outer dimensions; in this case, if you designate the length and width of frame's inner rectangle as l and w, respectively, then the length and width of the outer rectangle are respectively represented by $l + 2x$ and $w + 2x$, where x is the width of the picture frame.

You may see a question with a graph of a line intersecting a circle or parabola. The question may ask about the number of solutions (which would be the number of times the line and circle or parabola intersect) or about the actual solutions (which would be the points of those intersections).

You may see a question with the equation of a line and the equation of a circle or parabola. In this case, you need to solve the linear equation for one variable and then substitute for that variable in the quadratic equation. If the question simply asks for the number of solutions, you may choose to make a quick sketch of the line and circle or parabola to see if you can see if they intersect and, if so, how many times.

Systems of Equations vs. Systems of Inequalities

Solving systems of inequalities is very similar to solving systems of equations in that you are looking for a solution or a range of solutions that satisfy all of the equations in the system. Since solutions to inequalities are within a certain interval, it is best to solve this type of system by graphing. Follow the same steps to graph an inequality as you would an equation, but in addition, shade the portion of the graph that represents the solution. Recall that when graphing an inequality on the coordinate plane, you replace the inequality symbol with an equal sign and draw a solid line if the points are included (greater than or equal to or less than or equal to) or a dashed line if the points are not included (greater than or less than). Then replace the inequality symbol and shade the portion of the graph that is included in the solution. Choose a point that is not on the line and test it in the inequality to see if it is makes sense. In a system, you repeat this process for all of the equations and the solution is the region in which the graphs overlap. This is unlike solving a system of equations, in which the solution is a single point where the lines intersect.

You should expect to create, solve, or interpret systems of linear inequalities in two variables. Linear inequalities in two variables resemble systems of equations except the equal signs are replaced with inequality symbols ($<, >, \leq, \geq$). You may be asked to solve a system of linear inequalities. To solve a system of linear inequalities, each inequality must be graphed on the same coordinate plane. If both inequalities are written in slope intercept form, they can be graphed using the slope-intercept method. A dotted line is used when the inequality includes a $<$ or $>$ symbol. A solid line is used when the inequality includes a $\leq$ or $\geq$ symbol. Shade above the line if $y <$ or $\leq mx + b$ and above if $y >$ or $\geq mx + b$. The region where the two shaded areas overlap is the solution to the original system of inequalities; if there is no overlap, there is no solution. You may be asked to determine whether a given point is in the solution set of a system of linear inequalities. If a graph is provided, simply check to see if the given point is located in the region where the regions of the inequalities overlap. If you are not given a graph, see if the point satisfies each of the given inequalities. If the given point satisfies both inequalities, it is in the solution set for the system of inequalities.

Solving Systems of Equations

Substitution

To solve a system of linear equations by **substitution**, start with the easier equation and solve for one of the variables. Express this variable in terms of the other variable. Substitute this expression in the other equation, and solve for the other variable. The solution should be expressed in the form (x, y). Substitute the values into both of the original equations to check your answer. Consider the following system of equations:

$$\begin{aligned} x + 6y &= 15 \\ 3x - 12y &= 18 \end{aligned}$$

Solving the first equation for x: $x = 15 - 6y$

Substitute this value in place of x in the second equation, and solve for y:

$$\begin{aligned} 3(15 - 6y) - 12y &= 18 \\ 45 - 18y - 12y &= 18 \\ 30y &= 27 \\ y &= \frac{27}{30} = \frac{9}{10} = 0.9 \end{aligned}$$

Plug this value for y back into the first equation to solve for x:

$$x = 15 - 6(0.9) = 15 - 5.4 = 9.6$$

Check both equations if you have time:

$$\begin{aligned} 9.6 + 6(0.9) &= 15 \\ 9.6 + 5.4 &= 15 \\ 15 &= 15 \end{aligned} \qquad \begin{aligned} 3(9.6) - 12(0.9) &= 18 \\ 28.8 - 10.8 &= 18 \\ 18 &= 18 \end{aligned}$$

Therefore, the solution is (9.6, 0.9).

Elimination

To solve a system of equations using **elimination**, begin by rewriting both equations in standard form $Ax + By = C$. Check to see if the coefficients of one pair of like variables add to zero. If not, multiply one or both of the equations by a non-zero number to make one set of like variables add to zero. Add the two equations to solve for one of the variables. Substitute this value into one of the original equations to solve for the other variable. Check your work by substituting into the other equation. Now, let's look at solving the following system using the elimination method:

$$\begin{aligned} 5x + 6y &= 4 \\ x + 2y &= 4 \end{aligned}$$

If we multiply the second equation by -3, we can eliminate the y terms:

$$\begin{aligned} 5x + 6y &= 4 \\ -3x - 6y &= -12 \end{aligned}$$

Add the equations together and solve for x:

$$\begin{aligned} 2x &= -8 \\ x &= \frac{-8}{2} = -4 \end{aligned}$$

Plug the value for x back in to either of the original equations and solve for y:

$$\begin{aligned} -4 + 2y &= 4 \\ y &= \frac{4 + 4}{2} = 4 \end{aligned}$$

Check both equations if you have time:

$$\begin{aligned} 5(-4) + 6(4) &= 4 \\ -20 + 24 &= 4 \\ 4 &= 4 \end{aligned} \qquad \begin{aligned} -4 + 2(4) &= 4 \\ -4 + 8 &= 4 \\ 4 &= 4 \end{aligned}$$

Therefore, the solution is (-4, 4).

Review Video: Substitution and Elimination for Solving Linear Systems
Visit mometrix.com/academy and enter code: 958611

GRAPHICALLY

To solve a system of linear equations **graphically**, plot both equations on the same graph. The solution of the equations is the point where both lines cross. If the lines do not cross (are parallel), then there is **no solution**.

For example, consider the following system of equations:

$$y = 2x + 7$$
$$y = -x + 1$$

Since these equations are given in slope-intercept form, they are easy to graph; the y intercepts of the lines are $(0, 7)$ and $(0, 1)$. The respective slopes are 2 and –1, thus the graphs look like this:

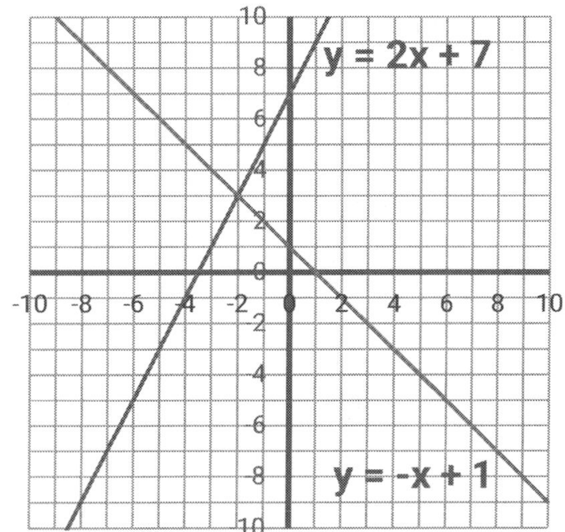

The two lines intersect at the point $(-2, 3)$, thus this is the solution to the system of equations.

Solving a system graphically is generally only practical if both coordinates of the solution are integers; otherwise the intersection will lie between gridlines on the graph and the coordinates will be difficult or impossible to determine exactly. It also helps if, as in this example, the equations are in slope-intercept form or some other form that makes them easy to graph. Otherwise, another method of solution (by substitution or elimination) is likely to be more useful.

SOLVING SYSTEMS OF EQUATIONS USING THE TRACE FEATURE

Using the **trace feature** on a calculator requires that you rewrite each equation, isolating the y-variable on one side of the equal sign. Enter both equations in the graphing calculator and plot the graphs simultaneously. Use the trace cursor to find where the two lines cross. Use the zoom feature if necessary to obtain more accurate results. Always check your answer by substituting into the original equations. The trace method is likely to be less accurate than other methods due to the resolution of graphing calculators, but is a useful tool to provide an approximate answer.

SYSTEMS OF THREE EQUATIONS

This test typically has one problem with a system of three equations. Usually the graphs as well as the equations are given. The key point is that the only solutions to this graph are the points at which all three graphs coincide or intersect. For example, the graph might include a circle, a parabola, and a line. There are no solutions to the given system if all three graphs do not intersect at one or more points. If the three graphs intersect at one point, then there is one solution to the given system, and that solution is the point of intersection. If the line intersects the circle at two points, and the line also intersects the parabola at the same exact two points, there are two solutions to the given system, and those solutions are the points of intersection. This system has at most two solutions.

Consistent, Inconsistent, or Dependent Systems

If a system of equations set up to represent a real-world problem turns out to be consistent (having exactly one solution), that solution is thc solution to the problem.

If the system turns out to be dependent (having infinitely many solutions), that means that the original information given was redundant, and was therefore not enough information to solve the problem. Practically speaking, this may mean that any of that infinite set of solutions will do, or it may mean that more information is needed.

If the system turns out to be inconsistent (having no solutions), that means the real-world situation described cannot be true. If the situation described was a hypothetical desired outcome, we now know that it is not possible to achieve that outcome; if the situation described was supposed to have really occurred, we can only conclude that it must have been described inaccurately.

Calculations Using Points

Sometimes you need to perform calculations using only points on a graph as input data. Using points, you can determine what the **midpoint** and **distance** are. If you know the equation for a line you can calculate the distance between the line and the point.

To find the **midpoint** of two points (x_1, y_1) and (x_2, y_2), average the x-coordinates to get the x-coordinate of the midpoint, and average the y-coordinates to get the y-coordinate of the midpoint. The formula is: $\left(\frac{x_1+x_2}{2}, \frac{y_1+y_2}{2}\right)$.

The **distance** between two points is the same as the length of the hypotenuse of a right triangle with the two given points as endpoints, and the two sides of the right triangle parallel to the x-axis and y-axis, respectively. The length of the segment parallel to the x-axis is the difference between the x-coordinates of the two points. The length of the segment parallel to the y-axis is the difference between the y-coordinates of the two points. Use the Pythagorean theorem $a^2 + b^2 = c^2$ or $c = \sqrt{a^2 + b^2}$ to find the distance. The formula is $\mathrm{d} = \sqrt{(x_2 - x_1)^2 + (y_2 - y_1)^2}$.

When a line is in the format $Ax + By + C = 0$, where A, B, and C are coefficients, you can use a point (x_1, y_1) not on the line and apply the formula $d = \frac{|Ax_1+By_1+C|}{\sqrt{A^2+B^2}}$ to find the distance between the line and the point (x_1, y_1).

Review Video: Calculations Using Points on a Graph
Visit mometrix.com/academy and enter code: 883228

Practice

P1. Solve the following systems of equations:

(a) $3x + 4y = 9$
$-12x + 7y = 10$

(b) $-3x + 2y = -1$
$4x - 5y = 6$

P2. Find the distance and midpoint between points (2, 4) and (8,6).

PRACTICE SOLUTIONS

P1. (a) If we multiply the first equation by 4, we can eliminate the x terms:

$$\begin{aligned} 12x + 16y &= 36 \\ -12x + 7y &= 10 \end{aligned}$$

Add the equations together and solve for y:

$$\begin{aligned} 23y &= 46 \\ y &= 2 \end{aligned}$$

Plug the value for y back in to either of the original equations and solve for x:

$$\begin{aligned} 3x + 4(2) &= 9 \\ x &= \frac{9-8}{3} = \frac{1}{3} \end{aligned}$$

The solution is $\left(\frac{1}{3}, 2\right)$

(b) Solving the first equation for y:

$$\begin{aligned} -3x + 2y &= -1 \\ 2y &= 3x - 1 \\ y &= \frac{3x-1}{2} \end{aligned}$$

Substitute this expression in place of y in the second equation, and solve for x:

$$\begin{aligned} 4x - 5\left(\frac{3x-1}{2}\right) &= 6 \\ 4x - \frac{15x}{2} + \frac{5}{2} &= 6 \\ 8x - 15x + 5 &= 12 \\ -7x &= 7 \\ x &= -1 \end{aligned}$$

Plug the value for x back in to either of the original equations and solve for y:

$$\begin{aligned} -3(-1) + 2y &= -1 \\ 3 + 2y &= -1 \\ 2y &= -4 \\ y &= -2 \end{aligned}$$

The solution is $(-1, -2)$

P2. Use the formulas for distance and midpoint:

$$\text{Distance} = \sqrt{(x_2 - x_1)^2 + (y_2 - y_1)^2}$$
$$= \sqrt{(8-2)^2 + (6-4)^2}$$
$$= \sqrt{(6)^2 + (2)^2}$$
$$= \sqrt{36+4}$$
$$= \sqrt{40} \text{ or } 2\sqrt{10}$$

$$\text{Midpoint} = \left(\frac{x_1 + x_2}{2}, \frac{y_1 + y_2}{2}\right)$$
$$= \left(\frac{2+8}{2}, \frac{4+6}{2}\right)$$
$$= \left(\frac{10}{2}, \frac{10}{2}\right)$$
$$= (5,5)$$

Problem Solving and Data Analysis

The questions in this section will require students to create and analyze relationships. They will solve single- and multistep problems using ratios, rates, proportions, and percentages. Some questions will also require students to describe relationships that are presented graphically. In addition, students should be able to analyze and summarize both qualitative and quantitative data.

Proportions and Ratios

You should expect three types of questions in this category. First, you may be asked to use a proportional relationship between two quantities to solve a multistep problem or to find a ratio or rate. Proportional relationships can be direct relationships (as x increases, y increases) or inverse relationships (as x increases, y decreases). Remember, units can be cancelled just like factors. You may be expected to use some basic knowledge such as *distance = rate × time*. Second, you might be asked to calculate a ratio or rate and to use that rate or ratio to solve a multistep problem. Third, you might be given a ratio or rate and be expected to solve a multistep problem. You may see a test question that says, "The ratio of boys to girls in the children's choir is 2:3. If there are eight boys in the choir, how many total children are in the choir?" You may be given a mixture problem in the form of a ratio and be expected to determine how much of a component is needed. You may be asked to determine a ratio associated with a geometric relationship, such as the ratio of a circle's circumference to its radius. You may be given a scale drawing and be expected to find a ratio associated with that drawing.

Proportions

A proportion is a relationship between two quantities that dictates how one changes when the other changes. A **direct proportion** describes a relationship in which a quantity increases by a set amount for every increase in the other quantity, or decreases by that same amount for every decrease in the other quantity. Example: Assuming a constant driving speed, the time required for a car trip increases as the distance of the trip increases. The distance to be traveled and the time required to travel are directly proportional.

Inverse proportion is a relationship in which an increase in one quantity is accompanied by a decrease in the other, or vice versa. Example: the time required for a car trip decreases as the speed increases, and increases as the speed decreases, so the time required is inversely proportional to the speed of the car.

Review Video: Proportions
Visit mometrix.com/academy and enter code: 505355

RATIOS

A **ratio** is a comparison of two quantities in a particular order. Example: If there are 14 computers in a lab, and the class has 20 students, there is a student to computer ratio of 20 to 14, commonly written as 20:14. Ratios are normally reduced to their smallest whole number representation, so 20:14 would be reduced to 10:7 by dividing both sides by 2.

Review Video: Ratios
Visit mometrix.com/academy and enter code: 996914

CONSTANT OF PROPORTIONALITY

When two quantities have a proportional relationship, there exists a **constant of proportionality** between the quantities; the product of this constant and one of the quantities is equal to the other quantity. For example, if one lemon costs \$0.25, two lemons cost \$0.50, and three lemons cost \$0.75, there is a proportional relationship between the total cost of lemons and the number of lemons purchased. The constant of proportionality is the **unit price**, namely \$0.25/lemon. Notice that the total price of lemons, t, can be found by multiplying the unit price of lemons, p, and the number of lemons, n: $t = pn$.

WORK/UNIT RATE

Unit rate expresses a quantity of one thing in terms of one unit of another. For example, if you travel 30 miles every two hours, a unit rate expresses this comparison in terms of one hour: in one hour you travel 15 miles, so your unit rate is 15 miles per hour. Other examples are how much one ounce of food costs (price per ounce) or figuring out how much one egg costs out of the dozen (price per 1 egg, instead of price per 12 eggs). The denominator of a unit rate is always 1. Unit rates are used to compare different situations to solve problems. For example, to make sure you get the best deal when deciding which kind of soda to buy, you can find the unit rate of each. If soda #1 costs \$1.50 for a 1-liter bottle, and soda #2 costs \$2.75 for a 2-liter bottle, it would be a better deal to buy soda #2, because its unit rate is only \$1.375 per 1-liter, which is cheaper than soda #1. Unit rates can also help determine the length of time a given event will take. For example, if you can paint 2 rooms in 4.5 hours, you can determine how long it will take you to paint 5 rooms by solving for the unit rate per room and then multiplying that by 5.

Review Video: Rates and Unit Rates
Visit mometrix.com/academy and enter code: 185363

You should expect to be asked to determine a unit rate and then use that rate to solve another problem. You may see a question that gives a conversion rate for an unfamiliar quantity to a familiar quantity, such as from a foreign currency to US dollars. You may be asked to solve a multistep unit problem using unfamiliar conversion rates along with other concepts, such as finding percentages. You may be asked to solve multistep problems to determine an item's density, or you may be asked to apply the concept of density. You may see a problem that says, "A bar of gold has dimensions of 5.0 cm by 5.0 cm by 10.0 cm. If gold has a density of 19,300 kg/m^3, what is the mass of the gold bar in grams?"

SLOPE

On a graph with two points, (x_1, y_1) and (x_2, y_2), the **slope** is found with the formula $m = \frac{y_2 - y_1}{x_2 - x_1}$; where $x_1 \neq x_2$ and m stands for slope. If the value of the slope is **positive**, the line has an *upward direction* from left to right. If the value of the slope is **negative**, the line has a *downward direction* from left to right. Consider the following example:

A new book goes on sale in bookstores and online stores. In the first month, 5,000 copies of the book are sold. Over time, the book continues to grow in popularity. The data for the number of copies sold is in the table below.

# of Months on Sale	1	2	3	4	5
# of Copies Sold (In Thousands)	5	10	15	20	25

So, the number of copies that are sold and the time that the book is on sale is a proportional relationship. In this example, an equation can be used to show the data: $y = 5x$, where x is the number of months that the book is on sale. Also, y is the number of copies sold. So, the slope of the corresponding line is $\frac{\text{rise}}{\text{run}} = \frac{5}{1} = 5$.

Review Video: Finding the Slope of a Line
Visit mometrix.com/academy and enter code: 766664

Finding an Unknown in Equivalent Expressions

It is often necessary to apply information given about a rate or proportion to a new scenario. For example, if you know that Jedha can run a marathon (26 miles) in 3 hours, how long would it take her to run 10 miles at the same pace? Start by setting up equivalent expressions:

$$\frac{26\text{ mi}}{3\text{ hr}} = \frac{10\text{ mi}}{x\text{ hr}}$$

Now, cross multiply and, solve for x:

$$26x = 30$$
$$x = \frac{30}{26} = \frac{15}{13}$$
$$x \cong 1.15\text{ hrs } or \text{ 1 hr 9 min}$$

So, at this pace, Jedha could run 10 miles in about 1.15 hours or about 1 hour and 9 minutes.

Review Video: Cross Multiply Fractions
Visit mometrix.com/academy and enter code: 893904

Practice

P1. Solve the following for x.

(a) $\frac{45}{12} = \frac{15}{x}$

(b) $\frac{0.50}{2} = \frac{1.50}{x}$

(c) $\frac{40}{8} = \frac{x}{24}$

P2. At a school, for every 20 female students there are 15 male students. This same student ratio happens to exist at another school. If there are 100 female students at the second school, how many male students are there?

P3. In a hospital emergency room, there are 4 nurses for every 12 patients. What is the ratio of nurses to patients? If the nurse-to-patient ratio remains constant, how many nurses must be present to care for 24 patients?

P4. In a bank, the banker-to-customer ratio is 1:2. If seven bankers are on duty, how many customers are currently in the bank?

P5. Janice made $40 during the first 5 hours she spent babysitting. She will continue to earn money at this rate until she finishes babysitting in 3 more hours. Find how much money Janice earns per hour and the total she earned babysitting.

P6. The McDonalds are taking a family road trip, driving 300 miles to their cabin. It took them 2 hours to drive the first 120 miles. They will drive at the same speed all the way to their cabin. Find the speed at which the McDonalds are driving and how much longer it will take them to get to their cabin.

P7. It takes Andy 10 minutes to read 6 pages of his book. He has already read 150 pages in his book that is 210 pages long. Find how long it takes Andy to read 1 page and also find how long it will take him to finish his book if he continues to read at the same speed.

Practice Solutions

P1. First, cross multiply; then, solve for x:

(a) $45x = 12 \times 15$
$45x = 180$
$x = \frac{180}{45} = 4$

(b) $0.5x = 1.5 \times 2$
$0.5x = 3$
$x = \frac{3}{0.5} = 6$

(c) $8x = 40 \times 24$
$8x = 960$
$x = \frac{960}{8} = 120$

P2. One way to find the number of male students is to set up and solve a proportion.

$$\frac{\text{number of female students}}{\text{number of male students}} = \frac{20}{15} = \frac{100}{\text{number of male students}}$$

Represent the unknown number of male students as the variable x: $\frac{20}{15} = \frac{100}{x}$

Cross multiply and then solve for x:

$$20x = 15 \times 100$$
$$x = \frac{1500}{20}$$
$$x = 75$$

P3. The ratio of nurses to patients can be written as 4 to 12, 4:12, or $\frac{4}{12}$. Because four and twelve have a common factor of four, the ratio should be reduced to 1:3, which means that there is one nurse present for every three patients. If this ratio remains constant, there must be eight nurses present to care for 24 patients.

P4. Use proportional reasoning or set up a proportion to solve. Because there are twice as many customers as bankers, there must be fourteen customers when seven bankers are on duty. Setting up and solving a proportion gives the same result:

$$\frac{\text{number of bankers}}{\text{number of customers}} = \frac{1}{2} = \frac{7}{\text{number of customers}}$$

Represent the unknown number of patients as the variable x: $\frac{1}{2} = \frac{7}{x}$.

To solve for x, cross multiply: $1 \times x = 7 \times 2$, so $x = 14$.

P5. Janice earns \$8 per hour. This can be found by taking her initial amount earned, \$40, and dividing it by the number of hours worked, 5. Since $\frac{40}{5} = 8$, Janice makes \$8 in one hour. This can also be found by finding the unit rate, money earned per hour: $\frac{40}{5} = \frac{x}{1}$. Since cross multiplying yields $5x = 40$, and division by 5 shows that $x = 8$, Janice earns \$8 per hour.

Janice will earn \$64 babysitting in her 8 total hours (adding the first 5 hours to the remaining 3 gives the 8-hour total). Since Janice earns \$8 per hour and she worked 8 hours, $\frac{\$8}{\text{hr}} \times 8 \text{ hrs} = \$64$. This can also be found by setting up a proportion comparing money earned to babysitting hours. Since she earns \$40 for 5 hours and since the rate is constant, she will earn a proportional amount in 8 hours: $\frac{40}{5} = \frac{x}{8}$. Cross multiplying will yield $5x = 320$, and division by 5 shows that $x = 64$.

P6. The McDonalds are driving 60 miles per hour. This can be found by setting up a proportion to find the unit rate, the number of miles they drive per one hour: $\frac{120}{2} = \frac{x}{1}$. Cross multiplying yields $2x = 120$ and division by 2 shows that $x = 60$.

Since the McDonalds will drive this same speed, it will take them another 3 hours to get to their cabin. This can be found by first finding how many miles the McDonalds have left to drive, which is $300 - 120 = 180$. The McDonalds are driving at 60 miles per hour, so a proportion can be set up to determine how many hours it will take them to drive 180 miles: $\frac{180}{x} = \frac{60}{1}$. Cross multiplying yields $60x = 180$, and division by 60 shows that $x = 3$. This can also be found by using the formula $D = r \times t$ (or distance = rate × time), where $180 = 60 \times t$, and division by 60 shows that $t = 3$.

P7. It takes Andy 10 minutes to read 6 pages, $\frac{10}{6} = 1\frac{2}{3}$ minutes, which is 1 minute and 40 seconds.

Next, determine how many pages Andy has left to read, $210 - 150 = 60$. Since it is now known that it takes him $1\frac{2}{3}$ minutes to read each page, then that rate must be multiplied by however many pages he has left to read (60) to find the time he'll need: $60 \times 1\frac{2}{3} = 100$, so it will take him 100 minutes, or 1 hour and 40 minutes, to read the rest of his book.

Review Video: Proportions in the Real World
Visit mometrix.com/academy and enter code: 221143

Units of Measurement

Metric Measurement Prefixes

Giga-: one billion (1 *giga*watt is one billion watts)
Mega-: one million (1 *mega*hertz is one million hertz)
Kilo-: one thousand (1 *kilo*gram is one thousand grams)
Deci-: one tenth (1 *deci*meter is one tenth of a meter)
Centi-: one hundredth (1 *centi*meter is one hundredth of a meter)
Milli-: one thousandth (1 *milli*liter is one thousandth of a liter)
Micro-: one millionth (1 *micro*gram is one millionth of a gram)

Measurement Conversion

When converting between units, the goal is to maintain the same meaning but change the way it is displayed. In order to go from a larger unit to a smaller unit, multiply the number of the known amount by the equivalent amount. When going from a smaller unit to a larger unit, divide the number of the known amount by the equivalent amount.

For complicated conversions, it may be helpful to set up conversion fractions. In these fractions, one fraction is the **conversion factor**. The other fraction has the unknown amount in the numerator. So, the known value is placed in the denominator. Sometimes the second fraction has the known value from the problem in the numerator, and the unknown in the denominator. Multiply the two fractions to get the converted measurement. Note that since the numerator and the denominator of the factor are equivalent, the value of the fraction is 1. That is why we can say that the result in the new units is equal to the result in the old units even though they have different numbers.

It can often be necessary to chain known conversion factors together. As an example, consider converting 512 square inches to square meters. We know that there are 2.54 centimeters in an inch and 100 centimeters in a meter, and that we will need to square each of these factors to achieve the conversion we are looking for.

$$\frac{512\text{ in}^2}{1}\times\left(\frac{2.54\text{ cm}}{1\text{ in}}\right)^2\times\left(\frac{1\text{ m}}{100\text{ cm}}\right)^2=\frac{512\,\cancel{\text{in}^2}}{1}\times\left(\frac{6.4516\,\cancel{\text{cm}^2}}{1\,\cancel{\text{in}^2}}\right)\times\left(\frac{1\text{ m}^2}{10000\,\cancel{\text{cm}^2}}\right)=0.330\text{ m}^2$$

Common Units and Equivalents

Metric Equivalents

1000 μg (microgram)	1 mg
1000 mg (milligram)	1 g
1000 g (gram)	1 kg
1000 kg (kilogram)	1 metric ton
1000 mL (milliliter)	1 L
1000 μm (micrometer)	1 mm
1000 mm (millimeter)	1 m
100 cm (centimeter)	1 m
1000 m (meter)	1 km

DISTANCE AND AREA MEASUREMENT

Unit	Abbreviation	U.S. equivalent	Metric equivalent
Inch	in	1 inch	2.54 centimeters
Foot	ft	12 inches	0.305 meters
Yard	yd	3 feet	0.914 meters
Mile	mi	5280 feet	1.609 kilometers
Acre	ac	4840 square yards	0.405 hectares
Square Mile	mi^2	640 acres	2.590 square kilometers

CAPACITY MEASUREMENTS

Unit	Abbreviation	U.S. equivalent	Metric equivalent
Fluid Ounce	fl oz	8 fluid drams	29.573 milliliters
Cup	cp	8 fluid ounces	0.237 liter
Pint	pt	16 fluid ounces	0.473 liter
Quart	qt	2 pints	0.946 liter
Gallon	gal	4 quarts	3.785 liters
Teaspoon	t or tsp	1 fluid dram	5 milliliters
Tablespoon	T or tbsp	4 fluid drams	15 or 16 milliliters
Cubic Centimeter	cc or cm^3	0.271 drams	1 milliliter

WEIGHT MEASUREMENTS

Unit	Abbreviation	U.S. equivalent	Metric equivalent
Ounce	oz	16 drams	28.35 grams
Pound	lb	16 ounces	453.6 grams
Ton	t	2,000 pounds	907.2 kilograms

VOLUME AND WEIGHT MEASUREMENT CLARIFICATIONS

Always be careful when using ounces and fluid ounces. They are not equivalent.

$$1 \text{ pint} = 16 \text{ fluid ounces} \qquad 1 \text{ fluid ounce} \neq 1 \text{ ounce}$$
$$1 \text{ pound} = 16 \text{ ounces} \qquad 1 \text{ pint} \neq 1 \text{ pound}$$

Having one pint of something does not mean you have one pound of it. In the same way, just because something weighs one pound does not mean that its volume is one pint.

In the United States, the word "ton" by itself refers to a short ton or a net ton. Do not confuse this with a long ton (also called a gross ton) or a metric ton (also spelled *tonne*), which have different measurement equivalents.

$$1 \text{ U.S. ton} = 2000 \text{ pounds} \quad \neq \quad 1 \text{ metric ton} = 1000 \text{ kilograms}$$

Practice

P1. Perform the following conversions:

(a) 1.4 meters to centimeters

(b) 218 centimeters to meters

(c) 42 inches to feet

(d) 15 kilograms to pounds

(e) 80 ounces to pounds

(f) 2 miles to kilometers

(g) 5 feet to centimeters

(h) 15.14 liters to gallons

(i) 8 quarts to liters

(j) 13.2 pounds to grams

Practice Solutions

P1. (a) $\frac{100\text{ cm}}{1\text{ m}} = \frac{x\text{ cm}}{1.4\text{ m}}$ Cross multiply to get $x = 140$

(b) $\frac{100\text{ cm}}{1\text{ m}} = \frac{218\text{ cm}}{x\text{ m}}$ Cross multiply to get $100x = 218$, or $x = 2.18$

(c) $\frac{12\text{ in}}{1\text{ ft}} = \frac{42\text{ in}}{x\text{ ft}}$ Cross multiply to get $12x = 42$, or $x = 3.5$

(d) 15 kilograms $\times \frac{2.2\text{ pounds}}{1\text{ kilogram}} = 33$ pounds

(e) 80 ounces $\times \frac{1\text{ pound}}{16\text{ ounces}} = 5$ pounds

(f) 2 miles $\times \frac{1.609\text{ kilometers}}{1\text{ mile}} = 3.218$ kilometers

(g) 5 feet $\times \frac{12\text{ inches}}{1\text{ foot}} \times \frac{2.54\text{ centimeters}}{1\text{ inch}} = 152.4$ centimeters

(h) 15.14 liters $\times \frac{1\text{ gallon}}{3.785\text{ liters}} = 4$ gallons

(i) 8 quarts $\times \frac{1\text{ gallon}}{4\text{ quarts}} \times \frac{3.785\text{ liters}}{1\text{ gallon}} = 7.57$ liters

(j) 13.2 pounds $\times \frac{1\text{ kilogram}}{2.2\text{ pounds}} \times \frac{1000\text{ grams}}{1\text{ kilogram}} = 6000$ grams

Displaying Information

Frequency Tables

Frequency tables show how frequently each unique value appears in the set. A **relative frequency table** is one that shows the proportions of each unique value compared to the entire set. Relative frequencies are given as percentages; however, the total percent for a relative frequency table will not necessarily equal 100 percent due to rounding. An example of a frequency table with relative frequencies is below.

Favorite Color	Frequency	Relative Frequency
Blue	4	13%
Red	7	22%
Green		9%
Purple	6	19%
Cyan	12	38%

Review Video: Data Interpretation of Graphs
Visit mometrix.com/academy and enter code: 200439

Circle Graphs

Circle graphs, also known as *pie charts*, provide a visual depiction of the relationship of each type of data compared to the whole set of data. The circle graph is divided into sections by drawing radii to create central angles whose percentage of the circle is equal to the individual data's percentage of the whole set. Each 1% of data is equal to 3.6° in the circle graph. Therefore, data represented by a 90° section of the circle graph makes up 25% of the whole. When complete, a circle graph often looks like a pie cut into uneven wedges. The pie chart below shows the data from the frequency table referenced earlier where people were asked their favorite color.

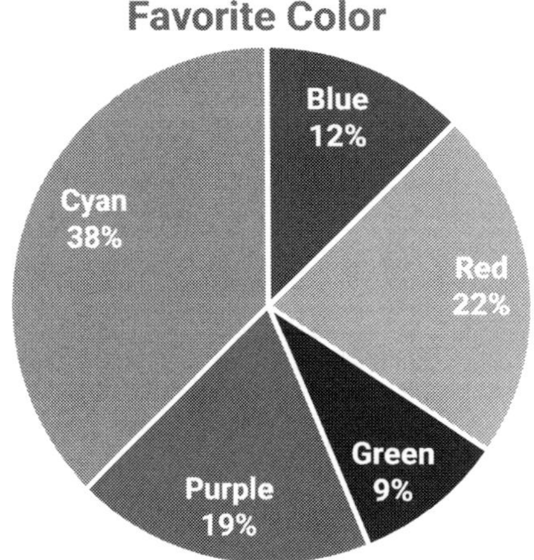

Review Video: Pie Chart
Visit mometrix.com/academy and enter code: 895285

Pictographs

A **pictograph** is a graph, generally in the horizontal orientation, that uses pictures or symbols to represent the data. Each pictograph must have a key that defines the picture or symbol and gives the quantity each picture or symbol represents. Pictures or symbols on a pictograph are not always shown as whole elements. In this case, the fraction of the picture or symbol shown represents the same fraction of the quantity a whole picture or symbol stands for. For example, a row with $3\frac{1}{2}$ ears of corn, where each ear of corn represents 100 stalks of corn in a field, would equal $3\frac{1}{2} \times 100 = 350$ stalks of corn in the field.

LINE GRAPHS

Line graphs have one or more lines of varying styles (solid or broken) to show the different values for a set of data. The individual data are represented as ordered pairs, much like on a Cartesian plane. In this case, the *x*- and *y*-axes are defined in terms of their units, such as dollars or time. The individual plotted points are joined by line segments to show whether the value of the data is increasing (line sloping upward), decreasing (line sloping downward) or staying the same (horizontal line). Multiple sets of data can be graphed on the same line graph to give an easy visual comparison. An example of this would be graphing achievement test scores for different groups of students over the same time period to see which group had the greatest increase or decrease in performance from year-to-year (as shown below).

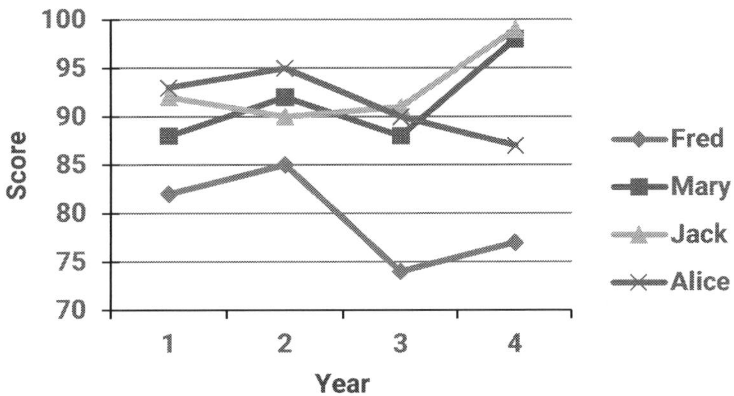

Review Video: Line Graphs
Visit mometrix.com/academy and enter code: 480147

LINE PLOTS

A **line plot**, also known as a *dot plot*, has plotted points that are not connected by line segments. In this graph, the horizontal axis lists the different possible values for the data, and the vertical axis lists the number of times the individual value occurs. A single dot is graphed for each value to show the number of times it occurs. This graph is more closely related to a bar graph than a line graph. Do not connect the dots in a line plot or it will misrepresent the data.

Review Video: Line Plot
Visit mometrix.com/academy and enter code: 754610

STEM AND LEAF PLOTS

A **stem and leaf plot** is useful for depicting groups of data that fall into a range of values. Each piece of data is separated into two parts: the first, or left, part is called the stem; the second, or right, part is called the leaf. Each stem is listed in a column from smallest to largest. Each leaf that has the common stem is listed in that stem's row from smallest to largest. For example, in a set of two-digit numbers, the digit in the tens place is the stem, and the digit in the ones place is the leaf. With a stem and leaf plot, you can easily see which subset of numbers (10s, 20s, 30s, etc.) is the largest. This information is also readily available by looking at a histogram, but a stem and leaf plot also allows you to look closer and see exactly which values fall in that range. Using all of the test scores from above, we can assemble a stem and leaf plot like the one below.

Test Scores

7	4 8
8	2 5 7 8 8
9	0 0 1 2 2 3 5 8 9

Bar Graphs

A **bar graph** is one of the few graphs that can be drawn correctly in two different configurations – both horizontally and vertically. A bar graph is similar to a line plot in the way the data is organized on the graph. Both axes must have their categories defined for the graph to be useful. Rather than placing a single dot to mark the point of the data's value, a bar, or thick line, is drawn from zero to the exact value of the data, whether it is a number, percentage, or other numerical value. Longer bar lengths correspond to greater data values. To read a bar graph, read the labels for the axes to find the units being reported. Then look where the bars end in relation to the scale given on the corresponding axis and determine the associated value.

The bar chart below represents the responses from our favorite color survey.

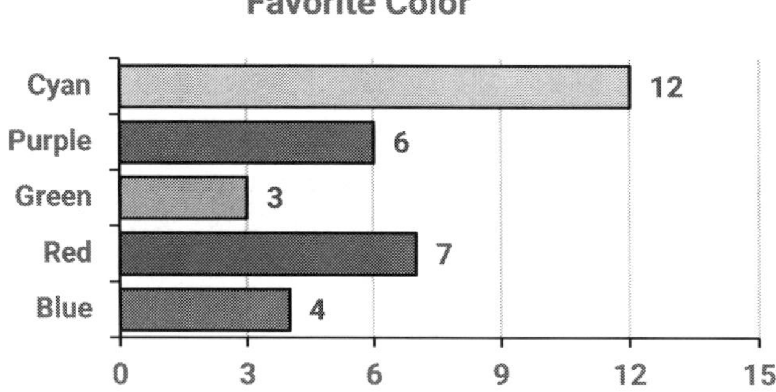

Review Video: Bar Graph
Visit mometrix.com/academy and enter code: 226729

Histograms

At first glance, a **histogram** looks like a vertical bar graph. The difference is that a bar graph has a separate bar for each piece of data and a histogram has one continuous bar for each *range* of data. For example, a histogram may have one bar for the range 0–9, one bar for 10–19, etc. While a bar graph has numerical values on one axis, a histogram has numerical values on both axes. Each range is of equal size, and they are ordered left to right from lowest to highest. The height of each column on a histogram represents the number of data values within that range. Like a stem and leaf plot, a histogram makes it easy to glance at the graph and quickly determine which range has the greatest quantity of values. A simple example of a histogram is below.

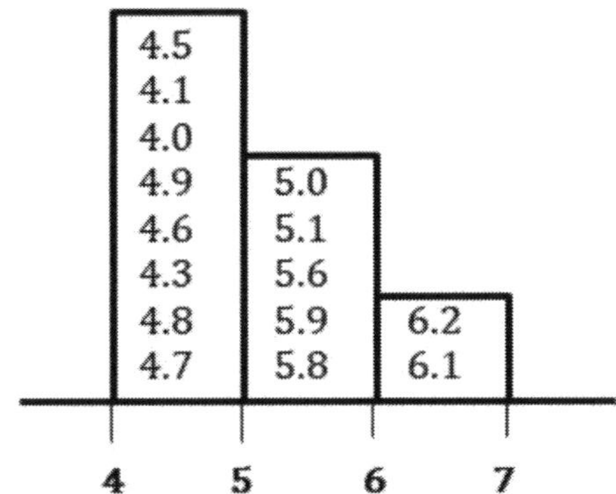

Review Video: Histogram
Visit mometrix.com/academy and enter code: 735897

Bivariate Data

Bivariate data is simply data from two different variables. (The prefix *bi-* means *two.*) In a *scatter plot,* each value in the set of data is plotted on a grid similar to a Cartesian plane, where each axis represents one of the two variables. By looking at the pattern formed by the points on the grid, you can often determine whether or not there is a relationship between the two variables, and what that relationship is, if it exists. The variables may be directly proportionate, inversely proportionate, or show no proportion at all. It may also be possible to determine if the data is linear, and if so, to find an equation to relate the two variables. The following scatter plot shows the relationship between preference for brand "A" and the age of the consumers surveyed.

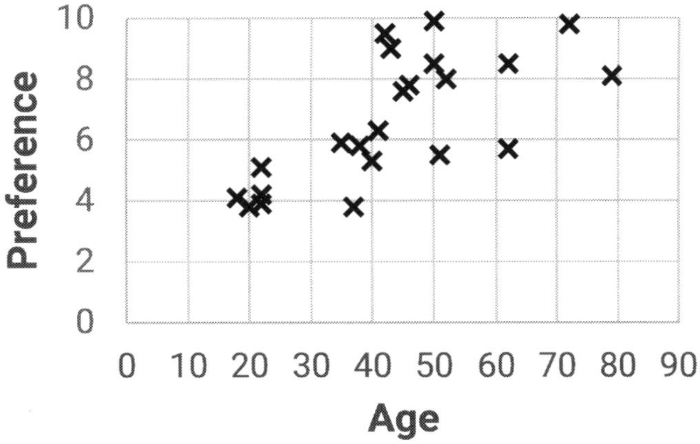

Scatter Plots

Scatter plots are also useful in determining the type of function represented by the data and finding the simple regression. Linear scatter plots may be positive or negative. Nonlinear scatter plots are generally exponential or quadratic. Below are some common types of scatter plots:

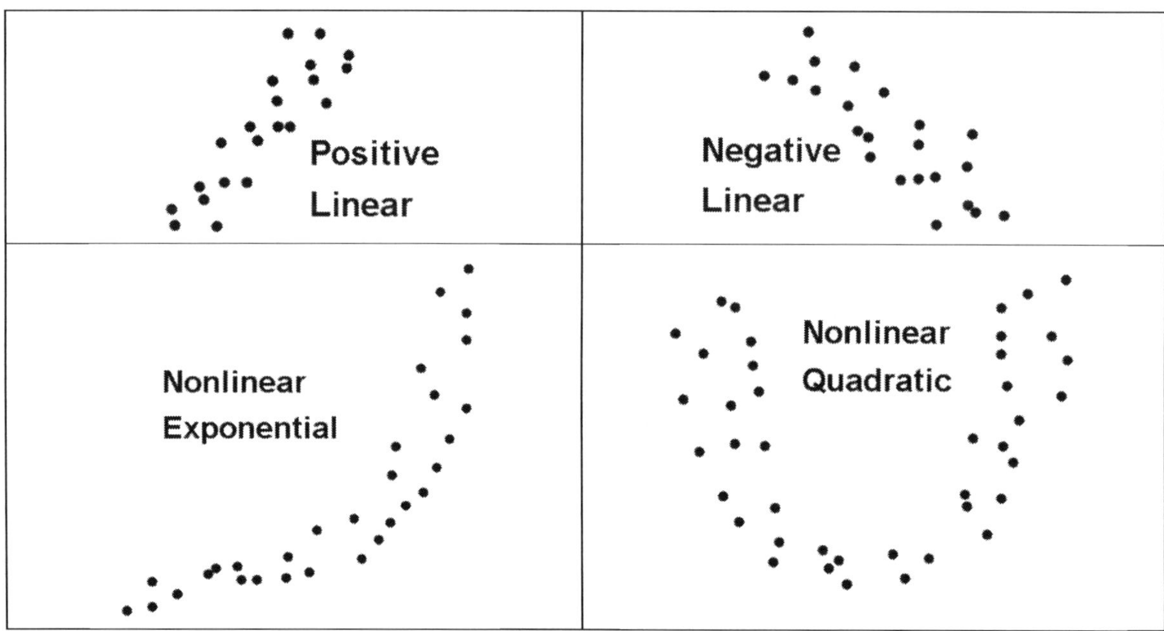

Review Video: Scatter Plot
Visit mometrix.com/academy and enter code: 596526

You should expect to be given a scatterplot in a real-world context. The scatterplot may already include a line of best fit, or you may be expected to select the equation of a line or curve of best fit. You may be expected to interpret the relationship between two variables based on the scatterplot. This relationship may be linear, quadratic, or exponential. You may be expected to use the line or curve of best fit to make a prediction about the situation. You may be given a scatter plot and asked, "Based on the line of best fit to the data shown, which of the following values is closest to the average yearly increase?" You must determine the slope of the line of best fit to answer the question. It is important to understand correlations shown by scatterplots. Make sure you do not try to apply a line of best fit to data that show no correlation. Make sure you do not try to apply a line to a curvilinear model. You probably will not have to actually find the equation of the line of best fit. You just need to be able to interpret the information that is given.

5-Number Summary

The **5-number summary** of a set of data gives a very informative picture of the set. The five numbers in the summary include the minimum value, maximum value, and the three quartiles. This information gives the reader the range and median of the set, as well as an indication of how the data is spread about the median.

Box and Whisker Plots

A **box-and-whisker plot** is a graphical representation of the 5-number summary. To draw a box-and-whiskers plot, plot the points of the 5-number summary on a number line. Draw a box whose ends are through the points for the first and third quartiles. Draw a vertical line in the box through the median to divide the box in half. Draw a line segment from the first quartile point to the minimum value, and from the third quartile point to the maximum value.

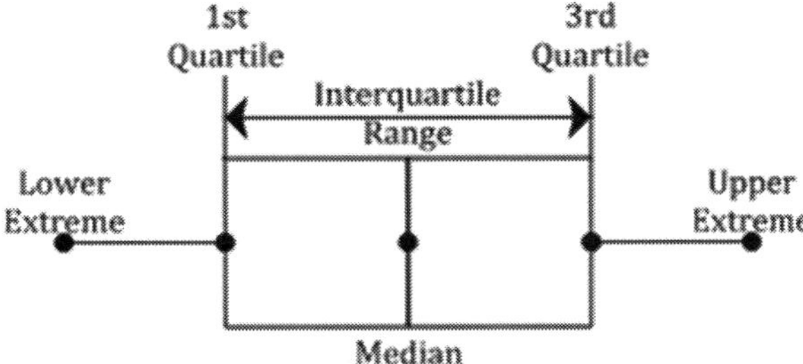

68-95-99.7 Rule

The **68–95–99.7 rule** describes how a normal distribution of data should appear when compared to the mean. This is also a description of a normal bell curve. According to this rule, 68 percent of the data values in a normally distributed set should fall within one standard deviation of the mean (34 percent above and 34 percent below the mean), 95 percent of the data values should fall within two standard deviations of the mean (47.5 percent above and 47.5 percent below the mean), and 99.7 percent of the data values should fall within three standard deviations of the mean, again, equally distributed on either side of the mean. This means that only 0.3 percent of all data values should fall more than three standard deviations from the mean. On the graph below, the normal curve is centered on the y-axis. The x-axis labels are how many standard deviations away from the center you are. Therefore, it is easy to see how the 68-95-99.7 rule can apply.

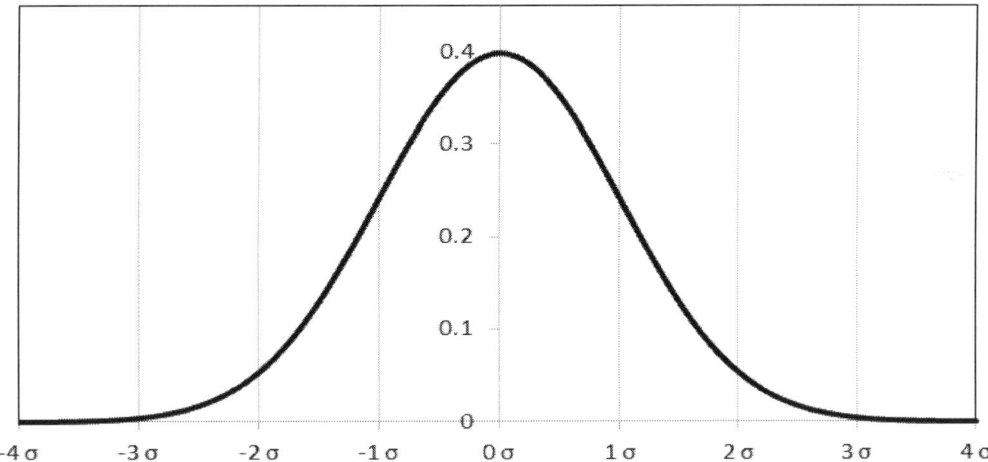

Statistical Analysis

Measures of Central Tendency

A **measure of central tendency** is a statistical value that gives a reasonable estimate for the center of a group of data. There are several different ways of describing the measure of central tendency. Each one has a unique way it is calculated, and each one gives a slightly different perspective on the data set. Whenever you give a measure of central tendency, always make sure the units are the same. If the data has different units, such as hours, minutes, and seconds, convert all the data to the same unit, and use the same unit in the measure of central tendency. If no units are given in the data, do not give units for the measure of central tendency.

Mean

The **statistical mean** of a group of data is the same as the arithmetic average of that group. To find the mean of a set of data, first convert each value to the same units, if necessary. Then find the sum of all the values, and count the total number of data values, making sure you take into consideration each individual value. If a value appears more than once, count it more than once. Divide the sum of the values by the total number of values and apply the units, if any. Note that the mean does not have to be one of the data values in the set, and may not divide evenly.

$$\text{mean} = \frac{\text{sum of the data values}}{\text{quantity of data values}}$$

For instance, the mean of the data set {88, 72, 61, 90, 97, 68, 88, 79, 86, 93, 97, 71, 80, 84, 89} would be the sum of the fifteen numbers divided by 15:

$$\frac{88 + 72 + 61 + 90 + 97 + 68 + 88 + 79 + 86 + 93 + 97 + 71 + 80 + 84 + 88}{15} = \frac{1242}{15} = 82.8$$

While the mean is relatively easy to calculate and averages are understood by most people, the mean can be very misleading if used as the sole measure of central tendency. If the data set has outliers (data values that are unusually high or unusually low compared to the rest of the data values), the mean can be very distorted, especially if the data set has a small number of values. If unusually high values are countered with unusually low values, the mean is not affected as much. For example, if five of twenty students in a class get a 100 on a test, but the other 15 students have an average of 60 on the same test, the class average would appear as 70. Whenever the mean is skewed by outliers, it is always a good idea to include the median as an alternate measure of central tendency.

A **weighted mean**, or weighted average, is a mean that uses "weighted" values. The formula is weighted mean $= \frac{w_1x_1+w_2x_2+w_3x_3 ...+w_nx_n}{w_1+w_2+w_3+\cdots+w_n}$. Weighted values, such as $w_1, w_2, w_3, ... w_n$ are assigned to each member of the set $x_1, x_2, x_3, ... x_n$. If calculating weighted mean, make sure a weight value for each member of the set is used.

Median

The **statistical median** is the value in the middle of the set of data. To find the median, list all data values in order from smallest to largest or from largest to smallest. Any value that is repeated in the set must be listed the number of times it appears. If there are an odd number of data values, the median is the value in the middle of the list. If there is an even number of data values, the median is the arithmetic mean of the two middle values.

For example, the median of the data set {88, 72, 61, 90, 97, 68, 88, 79, 86, 93, 97, 71, 80, 84, 88} is 86 since the ordered set is {61, 68, 71, 72, 79, 80, 84, **86**, 88, 88, 88, 90, 93, 97, 97}.

The big disadvantage of using the median as a measure of central tendency is that is relies solely on a value's relative size as compared to the other values in the set. When the individual values in a set of data are evenly dispersed, the median can be an accurate tool. However, if there is a group of rather large values or a group of rather small values that are not offset by a different group of values, the information that can be inferred from the median may not be accurate because the distribution of values is skewed.

Mode

The **statistical mode** is the data value that occurs the greatest number of times in the data set. It is possible to have exactly one mode, more than one mode, or no mode. To find the mode of a set of data, arrange the data like you do to find the median (all values in order, listing all multiples of data values). Count the number of times each value appears in the data set. If all values appear an equal number of times, there is no mode. If one value appears more than any other value, that value is the mode. If two or more values appear the same number of times, but there are other values that appear fewer times and no values that appear more times, all of those values are the modes.

For example, the mode of the data set {**88**, 72, 61, 90, 97, 68, **88**, 79, 86, 93, 97, 71, 80, 84, **88**} is 88.

The main disadvantage of the mode is that the values of the other data in the set have no bearing on the mode. The mode may be the largest value, the smallest value, or a value anywhere in between in the set. The mode only tells which value or values, if any, occurred the greatest number of times. It does not give any suggestions about the remaining values in the set.

Review Video: Mean, Median, and Mode
Visit mometrix.com/academy and enter code: 286207

Dispersion

A **measure of dispersion** is a single value that helps to "interpret" the measure of central tendency by providing more information about how the data values in the set are distributed about the measure of central tendency. The measure of dispersion helps to eliminate or reduce the disadvantages of using the mean, median, or mode as a single measure of central tendency, and give a more accurate picture of the dataset as a whole. To have a measure of dispersion, you must know or calculate the range, standard deviation, or variance of the data set.

Range

The **range** of a set of data is the difference between the greatest and lowest values of the data in the set. To calculate the range, you must first make sure the units for all data values are the same, and then identify the greatest and lowest values. If there are multiple data values that are equal for the highest or lowest, just use one of the values in the formula. Write the answer with the same units as the data values you used to do the calculations.

Standard Deviation

Standard deviation is a measure of dispersion that compares all the data values in the set to the mean of the set to give a more accurate picture. To find the standard deviation of a sample, use the formula

$$s = \sqrt{\frac{\sum_{i=1}^{n}(x_i - \bar{x})^2}{n-1}}$$

Note that s is the standard deviation of a sample, x represents the individual values in the data set, $\bar{x}$ is the mean of the data values in the set, and n is the number of data values in the set. The higher the value of the standard deviation is, the greater the variance of the data values from the mean. The units associated with the standard deviation are the same as the units of the data values.

Review Video: Standard Deviation
Visit mometrix.com/academy and enter code: 419469

VARIANCE

The **variance** of a sample, or just variance, is the square of the standard deviation of that sample. While the mean of a set of data gives the average of the set and gives information about where a specific data value lies in relation to the average, the variance of the sample gives information about the degree to which the data values are spread out and tell you how close an individual value is to the average compared to the other values. The units associated with variance are the same as the units of the data values squared.

PERCENTILE

Percentiles and quartiles are other methods of describing data within a set. **Percentiles** tell what percentage of the data in the set fall below a specific point. For example, achievement test scores are often given in percentiles. A score at the 80th percentile is one which is equal to or higher than 80 percent of the scores in the set. In other words, 80 percent of the scores were lower than that score.

Quartiles are percentile groups that make up quarter sections of the data set. The first quartile is the 25th percentile. The second quartile is the 50th percentile; this is also the median of the dataset. The third quartile is the 75th percentile.

UNIMODAL VS. BIMODAL

If a distribution has a single peak, it would be considered **unimodal**. If it has two discernible peaks it would be considered **bimodal**. Bimodal distributions may be an indication that the set of data being considered is actually the combination of two sets of data with significant differences. A **uniform distribution** is a distribution in which there is *no distinct peak or variation* in the data. No values or ranges are particularly more common than any other values or ranges.

OUTLIER

An outlier is an extremely high or extremely low value in the data set. It may be the result of measurement error, in which case, the outlier is not a valid member of the data set. However, it may also be a valid member of the distribution. Unless a measurement error is identified, the experimenter cannot know for certain if an outlier is or is not a member of the distribution. There are arbitrary methods that can be employed to designate an extreme value as an outlier. One method designates an outlier (or possible outlier) to be any value less than $Q_1 - 1.5(IQR)$ or any value greater than $Q_3 + 1.5(IQR)$.

DATA ANALYSIS

SIMPLE REGRESSION

In statistics, **simple regression** is using an equation to represent a relation between independent and a dependent variables. The independent variable is also referred to as the explanatory variable or the predictor, and is generally represented by the variable x in the equation. The dependent variable, usually represented by the variable y, is also referred to as the response variable. The equation may be any type of function – linear, quadratic, exponential, etc. The best way to handle this task is to use the regression feature of your graphing calculator. This will easily give you the curve of best fit and provide you with the coefficients and other information you need to derive an equation.

LINE OF BEST FIT

In a scatter plot, the **line of best fit** is the line that best shows the trends of the data. The line of best fit is given by the equation $\hat{y} = ax + b$, where a and b are the regression coefficients. The regression coefficient a is also the slope of the line of best fit, and b is also the y-coordinate of the point at which the line of best fit crosses the y-axis. Not every point on the scatter plot will be on the line of best fit. The differences between the y-values of the points in the scatter plot and the corresponding y-values according to the equation of the line of best fit are the residuals. The line of best fit is also called the least-squares regression line because it is also the line that has the lowest sum of the squares of the residuals.

CENTRAL LIMIT THEOREM

According to the **central limit theorem**, regardless of what the original distribution of a sample is, the distribution of the means tends to get closer and closer to a normal distribution as the sample size gets larger and larger (this is necessary because the sample is becoming more all-encompassing of the elements of the population). As the sample size gets larger, the distribution of the sample mean will approach a normal distribution with a mean of the population mean and a variance of the population variance divided by the sample size.

PRACTICE

P1. Given the following graph, determine the range of patient ages:

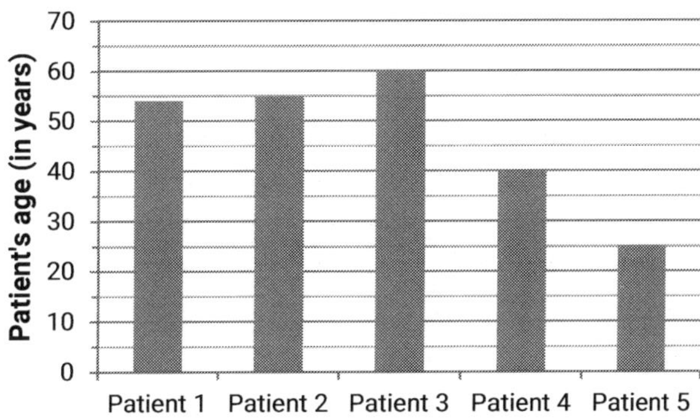

P2. Calculate the sample standard deviation for the dataset $\{10, 13, 11, 5, 8, 18\}$

PRACTICE SOLUTIONS

P1. Patient 1 is 54 years old; Patient 2 is 55 years old; Patient 3 is 60 years old; Patient 4 is 40 years old; and Patient 5 is 25 years old. The range of patient ages is the age of the oldest patient minus the age of the youngest patient. In other words, $60 - 25 = 35$. The range of ages is 35 years.

P2. To find the standard deviation, first find the mean:

$$\frac{10 + 13 + 12 + 5 + 8 + 18}{6} = \frac{66}{6} = 11$$

Now, apply the formula for sample standard deviation:

$$s = \sqrt{\frac{\sum_{i=1}^{n}(x_i - \bar{x})^2}{n-1}} = \sqrt{\frac{\sum_{i=1}^{6}(x_i - 11)^2}{6-1}}$$
$$= \frac{\sqrt{(10-11)^2 + (13-11)^2 + (12-11)^2 + (5-11)^2 + (8-11)^2 + (18-11)^2}}{5}$$
$$= \frac{\sqrt{(-1)^2 + 2^2 + 1^2 + (-6)^2 + (-3)^2 + 7^2}}{5}$$
$$= \frac{\sqrt{1+4+1+36+9+49}}{5}$$
$$= \frac{\sqrt{100}}{5} = \frac{10}{5} = 2$$

STATISTICS

Statistics is the branch of mathematics that deals with collecting, recording, interpreting, illustrating, and analyzing large amounts of **data**. The following terms are often used in the discussion of data and **statistics**:

- **Data** – the collective name for pieces of information (singular is datum).
- **Quantitative data** – measurements (such as length, mass, and speed) that provide information about quantities in numbers
- **Qualitative data** – information (such as colors, scents, tastes, and shapes) that cannot be measured using numbers
- **Discrete data** – information that can be expressed only by a specific value, such as whole or half numbers. For example, since people can be counted only in whole numbers, a population count would be discrete data.
- **Continuous data** – information (such as time and temperature) that can be expressed by any value within a given range
- **Primary data** – information that has been collected directly from a survey, investigation, or experiment, such as a questionnaire or the recording of daily temperatures. Primary data that has not yet been organized or analyzed is called **raw data**.
- **Secondary data** – information that has been collected, sorted, and processed by the researcher
- **Ordinal data** – information that can be placed in numerical order, such as age or weight
- **Nominal data** – information that *cannot* be placed in numerical order, such as names or places.

DATA COLLECTION

You should expect to be given tables, graphs, and/or text summaries and to be asked to make inferences, justify conclusions, and determine the appropriateness of the data collection methods.

POPULATION

In statistics, the **population** is the entire collection of people, plants, etc., that data can be collected from. For example, a study to determine how well students in the area schools perform on a standardized test would have a population of all the students enrolled in those schools, although a study may include just a small sample of students from each school. A **parameter** is a numerical value that gives information about the population, such as the mean, median, mode, or standard deviation. Remember that the symbol for the mean of a population is μ and the symbol for the standard deviation of a population is σ.

You may be asked to estimate a population parameter given the results from a random sample of a population. A question might say, "In the survey of a random sample of 1,200 cell phone users aged 18-25 from a particular region, 420 used their phones exclusively to do their banking. If the region had 160,000 residents aged 18-25, approximately how many of those residents could be expected to use their cell phones exclusively to do their banking?" You are also expected to understand any confidence intervals and measurement errors included in the problem. You may see a question that says, "A researcher collected information from 1,000 randomly selected public high school science teachers in the United States and concluded that the median annual salary was between $52,400 and $63,800 with a 99% confidence level. Which of the following could represent the median annual salary for the same sample with a 95% confidence level?"

Sample

A **sample** is a portion of the entire population. Whereas a parameter helped describe the population, a **statistic** is a numerical value that gives information about the sample, such as mean, median, mode, or standard deviation. Keep in mind that the symbols for mean and standard deviation are different when they are referring to a sample rather than the entire population. For a sample, the symbol for mean is $\bar{x}$ and the symbol for standard deviation is s. The mean and standard deviation of a sample may or may not be identical to that of the entire population due to a sample only being a subset of the population. However, if the sample is random and large enough, statistically significant values can be attained. Samples are generally used when the population is too large to justify including every element or when acquiring data for the entire population is impossible.

Inferential Statistics

Inferential statistics is the branch of statistics that uses samples to make predictions about an entire population. This type of statistics is often seen in political polls, where a sample of the population is questioned about a particular topic or politician to gain an understanding about the attitudes of the entire population of the country. Often, exit polls are conducted on election days using this method. Inferential statistics can have a large margin of error if you do not have a valid sample.

Sampling Distribution

Statistical values calculated from various samples of the same size make up the **sampling distribution**. For example, if several samples of identical size are randomly selected from a large population and then the mean of each sample is calculated, the distribution of values of the means would be a sampling distribution.

The **sampling distribution of the mean** is the distribution of the sample mean, $\bar{x}$, derived from random samples of a given size. It has three important characteristics. First, the mean of the sampling distribution of the mean is equal to the mean of the population that was sampled. Second, assuming the standard deviation is non-zero, the standard deviation of the sampling distribution of the mean equals the standard deviation of the sampled population divided by the square root of the sample size. This is sometimes called the standard error. Finally, as the sample size gets larger, the sampling distribution of the mean gets closer to a normal distribution via the central limit theorem.

Survey Study

A **survey study** is a method of gathering information from a small group in an attempt to gain enough information to make accurate general assumptions about the population. Once a survey study is completed, the results are then put into a summary report.

Survey studies are generally in the format of surveys, interviews, or questionnaires as part of an effort to find opinions of a particular group or to find facts about a group.

It is important to note that the findings from a survey study are only as accurate as the sample chosen from the population.

Correlational Studies

Correlational studies seek to determine how much one variable is affected by changes in a second variable. For example, correlational studies may look for a relationship between the amount of time a student spends studying for a test and the grade that student earned on the test or between student scores on college admissions tests and student grades in college.

It is important to note that correlational studies cannot show a cause and effect, but rather can show only that two variables are or are not potentially correlated.

You will be asked to determine if there is a correlation between two variables, but you cannot conclude that a change in one variable causes a change in the other. Ask yourself questions like, "Do both variables increase or decrease?" or "Does one increase as the other decreases?" Then, find the answer choice that makes the best statement explaining that correlation. If there is no correlation, look for a statement that reflects that. Avoid answer choices that say, "The increase of ___ caused the increase of ____" or "The increase of _____ caused the decrease of ____." Again, correlation does not imply causation. You may simply have to choose between answer choices that say, "There is a correlation between ____," or "There is no correlation between ____."

Experimental Studies

Experimental studies take correlational studies one step farther, in that they attempt to prove or disprove a cause-and-effect relationship. These studies are performed by conducting a series of experiments to test the hypothesis. For a study to be scientifically accurate, it must have both an experimental group that receives the specified treatment and a control group that does not get the treatment. This is the type of study pharmaceutical companies do as part of drug trials for new medications. Experimental studies are only valid when proper scientific method has been followed. In other words, the experiment must be well-planned and executed without bias in the testing process, all subjects must be selected at random, and the process of determining which subject is in which of the two groups must also be completely random.

Observational Studies

Observational studies are the opposite of experimental studies. In observational studies, the tester cannot change or in any way control all of the variables in the test. For example, a study to determine which gender does better in math classes in school is strictly observational. You cannot change a person's gender, and you cannot change the subject being studied. The big downfall of observational studies is that you have no way of proving a cause-and-effect relationship because you cannot control outside influences. Events outside of school can influence a student's performance in school, and observational studies cannot take that into consideration.

RANDOM SAMPLES

For most studies, a **random sample** is necessary to produce valid results. Random samples should not have any particular influence to cause sampled subjects to behave one way or another. The goal is for the random sample to be a **representative sample**, or a sample whose characteristics give an accurate picture of the characteristics of the entire population. To accomplish this, you must make sure you have a proper **sample size**, or an appropriate number of elements in the sample.

BIASES

In statistical studies, biases must be avoided. **Bias** is an error that causes the study to favor one set of results over another. For example, if a survey to determine how the country views the president's job performance only speaks to registered voters in the president's party, the results will be skewed because a disproportionately large number of responders would tend to show approval, while a disproportionately large number of people in the opposite party would tend to express disapproval. **Extraneous variables** are, as the name implies, outside influences that can affect the outcome of a study. They are not always avoidable, but could trigger bias in the result.

PRACTICE

P1. Determine if the following statements are TRUE or FALSE:

(a) Just because a sample is random, does not guarantee that it is representative.

(b) Qualitative data cannot be statistically analyzed, since the data is non-numeric.

(c) Sample statistics are a useful tool to estimate population parameters.

PRACTICE SOLUTIONS

P1. (a). TRUE: A good representative sample will also be a random sample, but sampling 10 random people from a city of 4 million will not be a representative sample.

(b) FALSE: Even though qualitative data is often non-numeric, there are special methods designed to specifically tally and analyze qualitative data.

(c) TRUE: The entire field of statistics is built upon this, since it is almost always beyond the scope of researchers to survey or collect data on an entire population.

PROBABILITY

Probability is the likelihood of a certain outcome occurring for a given event. An **event** is a situation that produces a result; that could be something as simple as flipping a coin or as complex as launching a rocket. Determining the probability of an outcome for an event can be equally simple or complex. As such there are specific terms used in the study of probability that need to be understood:

- **Compound event** – event that involves two or more independent events (rolling a pair of dice and taking the sum)
- **Desired outcome** (or success) – an outcome that meets a particular set of criteria (a roll of 1 or 2 if we are looking for numbers less than 3)
- **Independent events** – two or more events whose outcomes do not affect one another (two coins tossed at the same time)
- **Dependent events** – two or more events whose outcomes affect one another (two cards drawn consecutively from the same deck)
- **Certain outcome** – probability of outcome is 100% or 1

- **Impossible outcome** – probability of outcome is 0% or 0
- **Mutually exclusive outcomes** – two or more outcomes whose criteria cannot all be satisfied in a single event (a coin coming up heads and tails on the same toss)
- **Random variable** – refers to all possible outcomes of a single event which may be discrete or continuous.

Review Video: Intro to Probability
Visit mometrix.com/academy and enter code: 212374

Theoretical and Experimental Probability

Theoretical probability can usually be determined without actually performing the event. The likelihood of a outcome occurring, or the probability of an outcome occurring, is given by the formula:

$$P(A) = \frac{\text{Number of acceptable outcomes}}{\text{Number of possible outcomes}}$$

Note that $P(A)$ is the probability of an outcome A occurring, and each outcome is just as likely to occur as any other outcome. If each outcome has the same probability of occurring as every other possible outcome, the outcomes are said to be equally likely to occur. The total number of acceptable outcomes must be less than or equal to the total number of possible outcomes. If the two are equal, then the outcome is certain to occur and the probability is 1. If the number of acceptable outcomes is zero, then the outcome is impossible and the probability is 0. For example, if there are 20 marbles in a bag and 5 are red, then the theoretical probability of randomly selecting a red marble is 5 out of 20, ($\frac{5}{20} = \frac{1}{4}$, 0.25, or 25%).

If the theoretical probability is unknown or too complicated to calculate, it can be estimated by an experimental probability. **Experimental probability**, also called empirical probability, is an estimate of the likelihood of a certain outcome based on repeated experiments or collected data. In other words, while theoretical probability is based on what *should* happen, experimental probability is based on what *has* happened. Experimental probability is calculated in the same way as theoretical, except that actual outcomes are used instead of possible outcomes. The more experiments performed or datapoints gathered, the better the estimate should be.

Theoretical and experimental probability do not always line up with one another. Theoretical probability says that out of 20 coin-tosses, 10 should be heads. However, if we were actually to toss 20 coins, we might record just 5 heads. This doesn't mean that our theoretical probability is incorrect; it just means that this particular experiment had results that were different from what was predicted. A practical application of empirical probability is the insurance industry. There are no set functions that define lifespan, health, or safety. Insurance companies look at factors from hundreds of thousands of individuals to find patterns that they then use to set the formulas for insurance premiums.

Review Video: Empirical Probability
Visit mometrix.com/academy and enter code: 513468

Objective and Subjective Probability

Objective probability is based on mathematical formulas and documented evidence. Examples of objective probability include raffles or lottery drawings where there is a pre-determined number of possible outcomes and a predetermined number of outcomes that correspond to an event. Other cases of objective probability include probabilities of rolling dice, flipping coins, or drawing cards. Most gambling games are based on objective probability.

In contrast, **subjective probability** is based on personal or professional feelings and judgments. Often, there is a lot of guesswork following extensive research. Areas where subjective probability is applicable include sales trends and business expenses. Attractions set admission prices based on subjective probabilities of attendance based on varying admission rates in an effort to maximize their profit.

Sample Space

The total set of all possible results of a test or experiment is called a **sample space**, or sometimes a universal sample space. The sample space, represented by one of the variables S, Ω, or U (for universal sample space) has individual elements called outcomes. Other terms for outcome that may be used interchangeably include elementary outcome, simple event, or sample point. The number of outcomes in a given sample space could be infinite or finite, and some tests may yield multiple unique sample sets. For example, tests conducted by drawing playing cards from a standard deck would have one sample space of the card values, another sample space of the card suits, and a third sample space of suit-denomination combinations. For most tests, the sample spaces considered will be finite.

An **event**, represented by the variable E, is a portion of a sample space. It may be one outcome or a group of outcomes from the same sample space. If an event occurs, then the test or experiment will generate an outcome that satisfies the requirement of that event. For example, given a standard deck of 52 playing cards as the sample space, and defining the event as the collection of face cards, then the event will occur if the card drawn is a J, Q, or K. If any other card is drawn, the event is said to have not occurred.

For every sample space, each possible outcome has a specific likelihood, or probability, that it will occur. The probability measure, also called the **distribution**, is a function that assigns a real number probability, from zero to one, to each outcome. For a probability measure to be accurate, every outcome must have a real number probability measure that is greater than or equal to zero and less than or equal to one. Also, the probability measure of the sample space must equal one, and the probability measure of the union of multiple outcomes must equal the sum of the individual probability measures.

Probabilities of events are expressed as real numbers from zero to one. They give a numerical value to the chance that a particular event will occur. The probability of an event occurring is the sum of the probabilities of the individual elements of that event. For example, in a standard deck of 52 playing cards as the sample space and the collection of face cards as the event, the probability of drawing a specific face card is $\frac{1}{52} = 0.019$, but the probability of drawing any one of the twelve face cards is $12(0.019) = 0.228$. Note that rounding of numbers can generate different results. If you multiplied 12 by the fraction $\frac{1}{52}$ before converting to a decimal, you would get the answer $\frac{12}{52} = 0.231$.

TREE DIAGRAM

For a simple sample space, possible outcomes may be determined by using a **tree diagram** or an organized chart. In either case, you can easily draw or list out the possible outcomes. For example, to determine all the possible ways three objects can be ordered, you can draw a tree diagram:

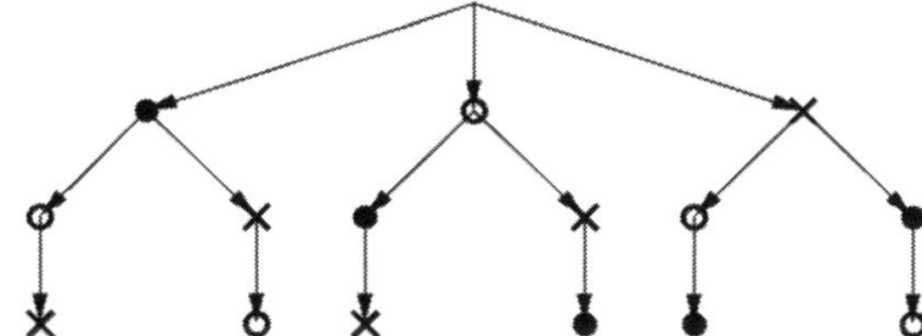

You can also make a chart to list all the possibilities:

First object	Second object	Third object
•	x	o
•	o	x
o	•	x
o	x	•
x	•	o
x	o	•

Either way, you can easily see there are six possible ways the three objects can be ordered.

If two events have no outcomes in common, they are said to be **mutually exclusive**. For example, in a standard deck of 52 playing cards, the event of all card suits is mutually exclusive to the event of all card values. If two events have no bearing on each other so that one event occurring has no influence on the probability of another event occurring, the two events are said to be independent. For example, rolling a standard six-sided die multiple times does not change that probability that a particular number will be rolled from one roll to the next. If the outcome of one event does affect the probability of the second event, the two events are said to be dependent. For example, if cards are drawn from a deck, the probability of drawing an ace after an ace has been drawn is different than the probability of drawing an ace if no ace (or no other card, for that matter) has been drawn.

In probability, the **odds in favor of an event** are the number of times the event will occur compared to the number of times the event will not occur. To calculate the odds in favor of an event, use the formula $\frac{P(A)}{1-P(A)}$, where $P(A)$ is the probability that the event will occur. Many times, odds in favor is given as a ratio in the form $\frac{a}{b}$ or $a:b$, where a is the probability of the event occurring and b is the complement of the event, the probability of the event not occurring. If the odds in favor are given as 2:5, that means that you can expect the event to occur two times for every 5 times that it does not occur. In other words, the probability that the event will occur is $\frac{2}{2+5} = \frac{2}{7}$.

In probability, the **odds against an event** are the number of times the event will not occur compared to the number of times the event will occur. To calculate the odds against an event, use the formula $\frac{1-P(A)}{P(A)}$, where $P(A)$ is the probability that the event will occur. Many times, odds against is given as a ratio in the form $\frac{b}{a}$ or $b:a$, where b is the probability the event will not occur (the complement of the event) and a is the probability the event will occur. If the odds against an event are given as 3:1, that means that you can expect the event to not occur 3 times for every one time it does occur. In other words, 3 out of every 4 trials will fail.

PERMUTATIONS AND COMBINATIONS

When trying to calculate the probability of an event using the $\frac{\text{desired outcomes}}{\text{total outcomes}}$ formula, you may frequently find that there are too many outcomes to individually count them. **Permutation** and **combination formulas** offer a shortcut to counting outcomes. A permutation is an arrangement of a specific number of a set of objects in a specific order. The number of **permutations** of *r* items given a set of *n* items can be calculated as ${}_nP_r = \frac{n!}{(n-r)!}$. Combinations are similar to permutations, except there are no restrictions regarding the order of the elements. While ABC is considered a different permutation than BCA, ABC and BCA are considered the same combination. The number of **combinations** of *r* items given a set of *n* items can be calculated as ${}_nC_r = \frac{n!}{r!(n-r)!}$ or ${}_nC_r = \frac{{}_nP_r}{r!}$.

Suppose you want to calculate how many different 5-card hands can be drawn from a deck of 52 cards. This is a combination since the order of the cards in a hand does not matter. There are 52 cards available, and 5 to be selected. Thus, the number of different hands is ${}_{52}C_5 = \frac{52!}{5!\times 47!} =$ 2,598,960.

Review Video: Probability - Permutation and Combination
Visit mometrix.com/academy and enter code: 907664

UNION AND INTERSECTION OF TWO SETS OF OUTCOMES

If A and B are each a set of elements or outcomes from an experiment, then the **union** (symbol $\cup$) of the two sets is the set of elements found in set A or set B. For example, if $A = \{2, 3, 4\}$ and $B = \{3, 4, 5\}$, $A \cup B = \{2, 3, 4, 5\}$. Note that the outcomes 3 and 4 appear only once in the union. For statistical events, the union is equivalent to "or"; $P(A \cup B)$ is the same thing as $P(A \text{ or } B)$. The **intersection** (symbol $\cap$) of two sets is the set of outcomes common to both sets. For the above sets A and B, $A \cap B = \{3, 4\}$. For statistical events, the intersection is equivalent to "and"; $P(A \cap B)$ is the same thing as $P(A \text{ and } B)$. It is important to note that union and intersection operations commute. That is:

$$A \cup B = B \cup A \text{ and } A \cap B = B \cap A$$

COMPLEMENT OF AN EVENT

Sometimes it may be easier to calculate the possibility of something not happening, or the **complement of an event**. Represented by the symbol $\bar{A}$, the complement of A is the probability that event A does not happen. When you know the probability of event A occurring, you can use the formula $P(\bar{A}) = 1 - P(A)$, where $P(\bar{A})$ is the probability of event A not occurring, and $P(A)$ is the probability of event A occurring.

ADDITION RULE

The **addition rule** for probability is used for finding the probability of a compound event. Use the formula $P(A \text{ or } B) = P(A) + P(B) - P(A \text{ and } B)$, where $P(A \text{ and } B)$ is the probability of both events occurring to find the probability of a compound event. The probability of both events occurring at the same time must be subtracted to eliminate any overlap in the first two probabilities.

CONDITIONAL PROBABILITY

Given two events A and B, the **conditional probability** $P(A|B)$ is the probability that event B will occur, given that event A has occurred. The conditional probability cannot be calculated simply from $P(A)$ and $P(B)$; these probabilities alone do not give sufficient information to determine the conditional probability. It can, however, be determined if you are also given the probability of the intersection of events A and B, $P(A \cap B)$, the probability that events A and B both occur. Specifically, $P(A|B) = \frac{P(A \cap B)}{P(B)}$. For instance, suppose you have a jar containing two red marbles and two blue marbles, and you draw two marbles at random. Consider event A being the event that the first marble drawn is red, and event B being the event that the second marble drawn is blue. $P(A)$ is $\frac{1}{2}$, and $P(A \cap B)$ is $\frac{1}{3}$. (The latter may not be obvious, but may be determined by finding the product of $\frac{1}{2}$ and $\frac{2}{3}$). Therefore $P(A|B) = \frac{1/3}{1/2} = \frac{2}{3}$.

CONDITIONAL PROBABILITY IN EVERYDAY SITUATIONS

Conditional probability often arises in everyday situations in, for example, estimating the risk or benefit of certain activities. The conditional probability of having a heart attack given that you exercise daily may be smaller than the overall probability of having a heart attack. The conditional probability of having lung cancer given that you are a smoker is larger than the overall probability of having lung cancer. Note that changing the order of the conditional probability changes the meaning: the conditional probability of having lung cancer given that you are a smoker is a very different thing from the probability of being a smoker given that you have lung cancer. In an extreme case, suppose that a certain rare disease is caused only by eating a certain food, but even then, it is unlikely. Then the conditional probability of having that disease given that you eat the dangerous food is nonzero but low, but the conditional probability of having eaten that food given that you have the disease is 100%!

Review Video: Conditional Probability
Visit mometrix.com/academy and enter code: 397924

INDEPENDENCE

The conditional probability $P(A|B)$ is the probability that event B will occur given that event A occurs. If the two events are independent, we do not expect that whether or not event A occurs should have any effect on whether or not event B occurs. In other words, we expect $P(A|B) = P(A)$.

This can be proven using the usual equations for conditional probability and the joint probability of independent events. The conditional probability $P(A|B) = \frac{P(A \cap B)}{P(B)}$. If A and B are independent, then $P(A \cap B) = P(A)P(B)$. So $P(A|B) = \frac{P(A)P(B)}{P(B)} = P(A)$. By similar reasoning, if A and B are independent then $P(B|A) = P(B)$.

TWO-WAY FREQUENCY TABLES

You should expect to see questions with categorical data summarized in two-way tables. You need to make comparisons among the data contained in the columns and rows of data. You may need to use proportions or calculate percentages. Two-way frequency tables typically include cells which total the data contained in the columns and rows, as well as an overall sum of data. These sums are used when calculating proportions and percentages. You may be asked to determine the relative frequencies of the data included in the rows or the columns. You may need to determine conditional probability, which is the probability of one event given the occurrence of another; additionally, you may be asked to compare conditional probabilities to determine the association between events.

If we have a two-way frequency table, it is generally a straightforward matter to read off the probabilities of any two events A and B, as well as the joint probability of both events occurring, $P(A \cap B)$. We can then find the conditional probability $P(A|B)$ by calculating $P(A|B) = \frac{P(A \cap B)}{P(B)}$. We could also check whether or not events are independent by verifying whether $P(A)P(B) = P(A \cap B)$.

For example, a certain store's recent T-shirt sales:

		Size			
		Small	**Medium**	**Large**	**Total**
Color	**Blue**	25	40	35	100
	White	27	25	22	74
	Black	8	23	15	46
	Total	60	88	72	220

Suppose we want to find the conditional probability that a customer buys a black shirt (event A), given that the shirt he buys is size small (event B). From the table, the probability $P(A)$ that a customer buys a small shirt is $\frac{60}{220} = \frac{3}{11}$. The probability $P(A \cap B)$ that he buys a small, black shirt is $\frac{8}{220} = \frac{2}{55}$. The conditional probability $P(A|B)$ that he buys a black shirt, given that he buys a small shirt, is therefore $P(A|B) = \frac{2/55}{3/11} = \frac{2}{15}$.

Similarly, if we want to check whether the event a customer buys a blue shirt, A, is independent of the event that a customer buys a medium shirt, B. From the table, $P(A) = \frac{100}{220} = \frac{5}{11}$ and $P(B) = \frac{88}{220} = \frac{4}{10}$. Also, $P(A \cap B) = \frac{40}{220} = \frac{2}{11}$. Since $\left(\frac{5}{11}\right)\left(\frac{4}{10}\right) = \frac{20}{220} = \frac{2}{11}$, $P(A)P(B) = P(A \cap B)$ and these two events are indeed independent.

Multiplication Rule

The **multiplication rule** can be used to find the probability of two independent events occurring using the formula $P(A \text{ and } B) = P(A) \times P(B)$, where $P(A \text{ and } B)$ is the probability of two independent events occurring, $P(A)$ is the probability of the first event occurring, and $P(B)$ is the probability of the second event occurring.

The multiplication rule can also be used to find the probability of two dependent events occurring using the formula $P(A \text{ and } B) = P(A) \times P(B|A)$, where $P(A \text{ and } B)$ is the probability of two dependent events occurring and $P(B|A)$ is the probability of the second event occurring after the first event has already occurred. Before using the multiplication rule, you MUST first determine whether the two events are *dependent* or *independent*.

Use a **combination of the multiplication** rule and the rule of complements to find the probability that at least one outcome of the element will occur. This given by the general formula $P(\text{at least one event occurring}) = 1 - P(\text{no outcomes occurring})$. For example, to find the probability that at least one even number will show when a pair of dice is rolled, find the probability that two odd numbers will be rolled (no even numbers) and subtract from one. You can always use a tree diagram or make a chart to list the possible outcomes when the sample space is small, such as in the dice-rolling example, but in most cases it will be much faster to use the multiplication and complement formulas.

Review Video: Multiplication Rule
Visit mometrix.com/academy and enter code: 782598

Expected Value

Expected value is a method of determining expected outcome in a random situation. It is really a sum of the weighted probabilities of the possible outcomes. Multiply the probability of an event occurring by the weight assigned to that probability (such as the amount of money won or lost). A practical application of the expected value is to determine whether a game of chance is really fair. If the sum of the weighted probabilities is equal to zero, the game is generally considered fair because the player has a fair chance to at least break even. If the expected value is less than zero, then players lose more than they win. For example, a lottery drawing might allow the player to choose any three-digit number, 000–999. The probability of choosing the winning number is 1:1000. If it costs $1 to play, and a winning number receives $500, the expected value is $\left(-\$1 \times \frac{999}{1{,}000}\right) + \left(\$499 \times \frac{1}{1{,}000}\right) = -\$0.50$. You can expect to lose on average 50 cents for every dollar you spend.

Review Video: Expected Value
Visit mometrix.com/academy and enter code: 643554

Expected Value and Simulators

A die roll simulator will show the results of *n* rolls of a die. The result of each die roll may be recorded. For example, suppose a die is rolled 100 times. All results may be recorded. The numbers of 1s, 2s, 3s, 4s, 5s, and 6s, may be counted. The experimental probability of rolling each number will equal the ratio of the frequency of the rolled number to the total number of rolls. As the number of rolls increases, or approaches infinity, the experimental probability will approach the theoretical probability of 1/6. Thus, the expected value for the roll of a die is shown to be $(1 \times 1/6) + (2 \times 1/6) + (3 \times 1/6) + (4 \times 1/6) + (5 \times 1/6) + (6 \times 1/6)$, or 3.5.

Practice

P1. Determine the theoretical probability of the following events:

(a) Rolling an even number on a regular 6-sided die.

(b) Not getting a red ball when selecting one from a bag of 3 red balls, 4 black balls, and 2 green balls.

(c) Rolling a standard die and then selecting a card from a standard deck that is less than the value rolled.

P2. There is a game of chance involving a standard deck of cards that has been shuffled and then laid on a table. The player wins $10 if they can turn over 2 cards of matching color (black or red),

$50 for 2 cards with matching value (A-K), and $100 for 2 cards with both matching color and value. What is the expected value of playing this game?

P3. Today, there were two food options for lunch at a local college cafeteria. Given the following survey data, what is the probability that a junior selected at random from the sample had a sandwich?

	Freshman	Sophomore	Junior	Senior
Salad	15	12	27	36
Sandwich	24	40	43	35
Nothing	42	23	23	30

Practice Solutions

P1. (a). The values on the faces of a regular die are 1, 2, 3, 4, 5, and 6. Since three of these are even numbers (2, 4, 6), The probability of rolling an even number is $\frac{3}{6} = \frac{1}{2} = 0.5 = 50\%$.

(b) The bag contains a total of 9 balls, 6 of which are not red, so the probability of selecting one non-red ball would be $\frac{6}{9} = \frac{2}{3} \cong 0.667 \cong 66.7\%$.

(c) In this scenario, we need to determine how many cards could satisfy the condition for each possible value of the die roll. If a one is rolled, there is no way to achieve the desired outcome, since no cards in a standard deck are less than 1. If a two is rolled, then any of the four aces would achieve the desired result. If a three is rolled, then either an ace or a two would satisfy the condition, and so on. Note that any value on the die is equally likely to occur, meaning that the probability of each roll is $\frac{1}{6}$. Putting all this in a table can help:

Roll	Cards < Roll	Probability of Card	Probability of Event
1	-	$\frac{0}{52} = 0$	$\frac{1}{6} \times 0 = 0$
2	1	$\frac{4}{52} = \frac{1}{13}$	$\frac{1}{6} \times \frac{1}{13} = \frac{1}{78}$
3	1,2	$\frac{8}{52} = \frac{2}{13}$	$\frac{1}{6} \times \frac{2}{13} = \frac{2}{78}$
4	1,2,3	$\frac{12}{52} = \frac{3}{13}$	$\frac{1}{6} \times \frac{3}{13} = \frac{3}{78}$
5	1,2,3,4	$\frac{16}{52} = \frac{4}{13}$	$\frac{1}{6} \times \frac{4}{13} = \frac{4}{78}$
6	1,2,3,4,5	$\frac{20}{52} = \frac{5}{13}$	$\frac{1}{6} \times \frac{5}{13} = \frac{5}{78}$

Assuming that each value of the die is equally likely, then the probability is the sum of the probabilities of each way to achieve the desired outcome: $\frac{0+1+2+3+4+5}{78} = \frac{15}{78} = \frac{5}{26} \cong 0.192 \cong$ 19.2%.

P2. First, determine the probability of each way of winning. In each case, the fist card simply determines which of the remaining 51 cards in the deck correspond to a win. For the color of the cards to match, there are 25 cards remaining in the deck that match the color of the first, but one of the 25 also matches the value, so only 24 are left in this category. For the value of the cards to match, there are 3 cards remaining cards in the deck that match the value of the first, but one of the three also matches the color, so only 2 are left in this category. For the cards to match both color and value, there is only one card in the deck that will work. Finally, there are 24 cards left that don't match at all.

Now we can find the expected value of playing the game, where we multiply the value of each event by the probability it will occur and sum over all of them:

$$\$10 \times \frac{24}{51} = \$4.71$$
$$\$50 \times \frac{2}{51} = \$1.96$$
$$\$100 \times \frac{1}{51} = \$1.96$$
$$\$0 \times \frac{24}{51} = \$0$$

$$\$4.71 + \$1.96 + \$1.96 = \$8.63$$

This game therefore has an expected value of $8.63 each time you play, which means if the cost to play is less than $8.63 then you would, on average, *gain* money. However, if the cost to play is more than $8.63, then you would, on average, *lose* money.

P3. With two-way tables it is often most helpful to start by totaling the rows and columns:

	Freshman	Sophomore	Junior	Senior	Total
Salad	15	12	27	36	90
Sandwich	24	40	43	35	142
Nothing	42	23	23	30	118
Total	81	75	93	101	350

Since the question is focused on juniors, we can focus on that column. There was a total of 93 juniors surveyed and 43 of them had a sandwich for lunch. Thus, the probability that a junior selected at random had a sandwich would be $\frac{43}{93} \cong 0.462 \cong 46.2\%$.

POLYNOMIAL ALGEBRA

POLYNOMIALS

Polynomials are made up of monomials and polynomials. A **monomial** is a single variable or product of constants and variables, such as x, $2x$, or $\frac{2}{x}$. There will never be addition or subtraction symbols in a monomial. Like monomials have like variables, but they may have different coefficients. **Polynomials** are algebraic expressions which use addition and subtraction to combine two or more monomials. Two terms make a **binomial**, three terms make a **trinomial**, etc. The

degree of a monomial is the sum of the exponents of the variables. The **degree of a polynomial** is the highest degree of any individual term.

Review Video: Polynomials
Visit mometrix.com/academy and enter code: 305005

You should expect to add, subtract, and multiply polynomial expressions and simplify the results. These expressions will have rational coefficients. You may see a question that says, "Add $(2x^2 + 4y + 5xy)$, $(3x^2 - 3xy - x)$, and $(xy + 1)$" or "Subtract $(6x^2 + 6y - xy + 1)$ from $(2x^2 + 3xy - 2)$." You may see a question that says, "If $p = 3x^3 - 2x^2 + 5x - 7$ and $q = 2x^3 - 7x^2 - x + 3$, what is $p - 2q$?" You may see a question that says, "Multiply$(x + 2y)(4x - 3y + 1)$" or "What is the product of $(2x + 1)$, $(2x - 1)$, and $(2x^2 + 1)$?" In each of these types of questions, you should perform the operation, collecting like terms to simplify the result.

SIMPLIFYING POLYNOMIALS

Simplifying polynomials requires combining like terms. The like terms in a polynomial expression are those that have the same variable raised to the same power. It is often helpful to connect the like terms with arrows or lines in order to separate them from the other monomials. Once you have determined the like terms, you can rearrange the polynomial by placing them together. Remember to include the sign that is in front of each term. Once the like terms are placed together, you can apply each operation and simplify. When adding and subtracting polynomials, only add and subtract the **coefficient**, or the number part; the variable and exponent stay the same.

Review Video: Adding and Subtracting Polynomials
Visit mometrix.com/academy and enter code: 124088

THE FOIL METHOD

In general, multiplying polynomials is done by multiplying each term in one polynomial by each term in the other and adding the results. In the specific case for multiplying binomials, there is useful acronym, FOIL, that can help you make sure to cover each combination of terms. The **FOIL method** for $(Ax + By)(Cx + Dy)$ would be:

F	Multiply the *first* terms of each binomial	$(\overbrace{Ax}^{first} + By)(\overbrace{Cx}^{first} + Dy)$	ACx^2
O	Multiply the *outer* terms	$(\overbrace{Ax}^{outer} + By)(Cx + \overbrace{Dy}^{outer})$	$ADxy$
I	Multiply the *inner* terms	$(Ax + \overbrace{By}^{inner})(\overbrace{Cx}^{inner} + Dy)$	$BCxy$
L	Multiply the *last* terms of each binomial	$(Ax + \overbrace{By}^{last})(Cx + \overbrace{Dy}^{last})$	BDy^2

Then add up the result of each and combine like terms: $ACx^2 + (AD + BC)xy + BDy^2$.

For example, using the FOIL method on binomials $(x + 2)$ and $(x - 3)$:

$$\begin{aligned}
\text{First:} \quad & (\boxed{x} + 2)(\boxed{x} + (-3)) \rightarrow (x)(x) = x^2 \\
\text{Outer:} \quad & (\boxed{x} + 2)(x + \boxed{(-3)}) \rightarrow (x)(-3) = -3x \\
\text{Inner:} \quad & (x + \boxed{2})(\boxed{x} + (-3)) \rightarrow (2)(x) = 2x \\
\text{Last:} \quad & (x + \boxed{2})(x + \boxed{(-3)}) \rightarrow (2)(-3) = -6
\end{aligned}$$

This results in: $(x^2) + (-3x) + (2x) + (-6)$

Combine like terms: $x^2 + (-3 + 2)x + (-6) = x^2 - x - 6$

Review Video: Multiplying Terms Using the FOIL Method
Visit mometrix.com/academy and enter code: 854792

Dividing Polynomials

To divide polynomials, set up a long division problem, dividing a polynomial by either a monomial or another polynomial of equal or lesser degree.

When **dividing by a monomial**, divide each term of the polynomial by the monomial.

When **dividing by a polynomial**, begin by arranging the terms of each polynomial in order of one variable. You may arrange in ascending or descending order, but be consistent with both polynomials. To get the first term of the quotient, divide the first term of the dividend by the first term of the divisor. Multiply the first term of the quotient by the entire divisor and subtract that product from the dividend. Repeat for the second and successive terms until you either get a remainder of zero or a remainder whose degree is less than the degree of the divisor. If the quotient has a remainder, write the answer as a mixed expression in the form:

$$\text{quotient} + \frac{\text{remainder}}{\text{divisor}}$$

For example, we can evaluate the following expression in the same way as long division:

$$\frac{x^3 - 3x^2 - 2x + 5}{x - 5}$$

$$\begin{array}{r} x^2 \;+2x\;+8 \\ x-5 \,\overline{)\, x^3 - 3x^2 - 2x + 5} \\ \underline{x^3 - 5x^2} \\ 2x^2 - 2x \\ \underline{2x^2 - 10x} \\ 8x + 5 \\ \underline{8x + 40} \\ 45 \end{array}$$

$$\frac{x^3 - 3x^2 - 2x + 5}{x - 5} = x^2 + 2x + 8 + \frac{45}{x - 5}$$

When **factoring** a polynomial, first check for a common monomial factor, that is look to see if each coefficient has a common factor or if each term has an x in it. If the factor is a trinomial but not a perfect trinomial square, look for a factorable form, such as one of these:

$$x^2 + (a + b)x + ab = (x + a)(x + b)$$
$$(ac)x^2 + (ad + bc)x + bd = (ax + b)(cx + d)$$

For factors with four terms, look for groups to factor. Once you have found the factors, write the original polynomial as the product of all the factors. Make sure all of the polynomial factors are prime. Monomial factors may be *prime* or *composite*. Check your work by multiplying the factors to make sure you get the original polynomial.

Below are patterns of some special products to remember to help make factoring easier:

- Perfect trinomial squares: $x^2 + 2xy + y^2 = (x + y)^2$ or $x^2 - 2xy + y^2 = (x - y)^2$
- Difference between two squares: $x^2 - y^2 = (x + y)(x - y)$
- Sum of two cubes: $x^3 + y^3 = (x + y)(x^2 - xy + y^2)$
  - Note: the second factor is *not* the same as a perfect trinomial square, so do not try to factor it further.
- Difference between two cubes: $x^3 - y^3 = (x - y)(x^2 + xy + y^2)$
  - Again, the second factor is *not* the same as a perfect trinomial square.
- Perfect cubes: $x^3 + 3x^2y + 3xy^2 + y^3 = (x + y)^3$ and $x^3 - 3x^2y + 3xy^2 - y^3 = (x - y)^3$

You may be expected to factor a polynomial, or you may be given the factored form of a polynomial and asked to select the appropriate graph from a set of given graphs. You may see a question that says, "Which of the following graphs represents the polynomial $f(x) = (x-1)(x+2)(x+5)$?" or "Which of the following graphs represents the quadratic equation $y = x^2 + 4x - 5$?" You may be given a polynomial function with the ordered pairs of its zeros and be asked to solve for a missing coefficient or a missing coordinate. You may be given a function such as $f(x) = 2x^4 + 3x^2 - 5x + 7$ and be expected to use the Factor Theorem to find zeros or verify zeros. You may be given the zeros of a quadratic or cubic function and asked to write the function. You might see a question that says, "If the zeros of a cubic function are -2, 3, and 5 and the graph of that function passes through (1, 8), what is the equation of the function?"

RATIONAL EXPRESSIONS

Rational expressions are fractions with polynomials in both the numerator and the denominator; the value of the polynomial in the denominator cannot be equal to zero. Be sure to keep track of values that make the denominator of the original expression zero as the final result inherits the same restrictions. For example, a denominator of $x - 3$ indicates that the expression is not defined when $x = 3$ and as such, regardless of any operations done to the expression, it remains undefined there.

To **add or subtract** rational expressions, first find the common denominator, then rewrite each fraction as an equivalent fraction with the common denominator. Finally, add or subtract the numerators to get the numerator of the answer, and keep the common denominator as the denominator of the answer.

When **multiplying** rational expressions factor each polynomial and cancel like factors (a factor which appears in both the numerator and the denominator). Then, multiply all remaining factors in the numerator to get the numerator of the product, and multiply the remaining factors in the denominator to get the denominator of the product. Remember: cancel entire factors, not individual terms.

To **divide** rational expressions, take the reciprocal of the divisor (the rational expression you are dividing by) and multiply by the dividend.

Review Video: Rational Expressions
Visit mometrix.com/academy and enter code: 415183

You should expect questions asking you to add or subtract rational expressions. You may see a question that says, "Add $\frac{2a+3}{3ab} + \frac{3a-2}{2bc}$," or "Subtract $\frac{m-2}{m-3} - \frac{m-1}{m-2}$." The questions may have more than two terms and may combine addition and subtraction, such as "Simplify $\frac{1}{x}+\frac{2}{y}-\frac{3}{z}$." In order to be able to add or subtract rational expressions, the expressions must have the same denominator. Find the least common denominator (LCD) of the terms in the expression. Then, multiply each term of the expression by the ratio $\frac{LCD}{LCD}$. Simplify where possible and present your answer as one term over the LCD. Since these are rational expressions, not equations, you cannot clear the fractions as you do in an equation.

You should also expect questions asking you to multiply or divide rational expressions. You may see a question that says, "Multiply $\frac{n^2+n-6}{4}\cdot\frac{8}{2n+6}$" or "Divide $\frac{m^2+6m+5}{m^2-2m-3}\div\frac{m^2+8m+15}{3m^2-9m}$." To multiply rational expressions, the numerators and the denominators of each expression must be factored. Always check for a common monomial factor first. Then, check for differences of squares or a perfect square trinomial. A difference of squares a^2-b^2 factors to $(a+b)(a-b)$. A perfect square trinomial factors to a binomial squared: $a^2+2ab+b^2$ factors to $(a+b)^2$, and $a^2-2ab+b^2$ factors to $(a-b)^2$. Also, check for other factorable trinomials. After factoring the numerators and denominators, cancel like factors and then multiply. To divide a rational expression, change the problem to a multiplication problem by multiplying the dividend by the reciprocal of the divisor, just like you would do if you were asked to divide two fractions containing no variables.

Simplifying Rational Expressions

To simplify a rational expression, factor the numerator and denominator completely. Factors that are the same and appear in the numerator and denominator have a ratio of 1. For example, look at the following expression:

$$\frac{x-1}{1-x^2}$$

The denominator, $(1-x^2)$, is a difference of squares. It can be factored as $(1-x)(1+x)$. The factor $1-x$ and the numerator $x-1$ are opposites and have a ratio of -1. Rewrite the numerator as $-1(1-x)$. So, the rational expression can be simplified as follows:

$$\frac{x-1}{1-x^2}=\frac{-1(1-x)}{(1-x)(1+x)}=\frac{-1}{1+x}$$

Note that since the original expression is only defined for $x \neq \{-1,1\}$, the simplified expression has the same restrictions.

Review Video: Reducing Rational Expressions
Visit mometrix.com/academy and enter code: 788868

Practice

P1. Expand the following polynomials:

(a) $(x+3)(x-7)(2x)$

(b) $(x+2)^2(x-2)^2$

(c) $(x^2+5x+5)(3x-1)$

P2. Evaluate the following rational expressions:

(a) $\frac{x^3-2x^2-5x+6}{3x+6}$

(b) $\frac{x^2+4x+4}{4-x^2}$

PRACTICE SOLUTIONS

P1. (a) Apply the FOIL method and the distributive property of multiplication:

$$\begin{aligned}(x+3)(x-7)(2x) &= (x^2-7x+3x-21)(2x)\\ &= (x^2-4x-21)(2x)\\ &= 2x^3-8x^2-42x\end{aligned}$$

(b) Note the difference of squares form:

$$\begin{aligned}(x+2)^2(x-2)^2 &= (x+2)(x+2)(x-2)(x-2)\\ &= [(x+2)(x-2)][(x+2)(x-2)]\\ &= (x^2-4)(x^2-4)\\ &= x^4-8x^2+16\end{aligned}$$

(c) Multiply each pair of monomials and combine like terms:

$$\begin{aligned}(x^2+5x+5)(3x-1) &= 3x^3+15x^2+15x-x^2-5x-5\\ &= 3x^3+14x^2+10x-5\end{aligned}$$

P2. (a) Rather than trying to factor the fourth-degree polynomial, we can use long division:

$$\frac{x^3-2x^2-5x+6}{3x+6} = \frac{x^3-2x^2-5x+6}{3(x+2)}$$

$$\begin{array}{r|l} & x^2 \quad -4x \quad +3 \\ x+2 & x^3 - 2x^2 - 5x + 6 \\ & \underline{x^3 + 2x^2} \\ & \quad -4x^2 - 5x \\ & \quad \underline{-4x^2 - 8x} \\ & \qquad 3x + 6 \\ & \qquad \underline{3x + 6} \\ & \qquad\quad 0 \end{array}$$

$$\frac{x^3-2x^2-5x+6}{3(x+2)} = \frac{x^2-4x+3}{3}$$

Note that since the original expression is only defined for $x \neq \{-2\}$, the simplified expression has the same restrictions.

(b) The denominator, $(4 - x^2)$, is a difference of squares. It can be factored as $(2 - x)(2 + x)$. The numerator, $(x^2 + 4x + 4)$, is a perfect square. It can be factored as $(x + 2)(x + 2)$. So, the rational expression can be simplified as follows:

$$\frac{x^2 + 4x + 4}{4 - x^2} = \frac{(x + 2)(x + 2)}{(2 - x)(2 + x)} = \frac{(x + 2)}{(2 - x)}$$

Note that since the original expression is only defined for $x \neq \{-2,2\}$, the simplified expression has the same restrictions.

QUADRATICS

SOLVING QUADRATIC EQUATIONS

Quadratic equations are a special set of trinomials of the form $y = ax^2 + bx + c$ that occur commonly in math and real world applications. The **roots** of a quadratic equation are the solutions that satisfy the equation when $y = 0$; in other words, where the graph touches the x-axis. There are several ways to determine these solutions including using the quadratic formula, factoring, completing the square, and graphing the function.

Review Video: Finding the Missing Roots
Visit mometrix.com/academy and enter code: 198376

Review Video: Changing Constants in Graphs of Functions: Quadratic Equations
Visit mometrix.com/academy and enter code: 476276

QUADRATIC FORMULA

The **quadratic formula** is used to solve quadratic equations when other methods are more difficult. To use the quadratic formula to solve a quadratic equation, begin by rewriting the equation in standard form $ax^2 + bx + c = 0$, where a, b, and c are coefficients. Once you have identified the values of the coefficients, substitute those values into the quadratic formula

$$x = \frac{-b \pm \sqrt{b^2 - 4ac}}{2a}$$

Evaluate the equation and simplify the expression. Again, check each root by substituting into the original equation. In the quadratic formula, the portion of the formula under the radical $(b^2 - 4ac)$ is called the **discriminant**. If the discriminant is zero, there is only one root: $-\frac{b}{2a}$. If the discriminant is positive, there are two different real roots. If the discriminant is negative, there are no real roots, you will instead find complex roots. Often these solutions don't make sense in context and are ignored.

Review Video: Using the Quadratic Formula
Visit mometrix.com/academy and enter code: 163102

FACTORING

To solve a quadratic equation by factoring, begin by rewriting the equation in standard form, $x^2 + bx + c = 0$. Remember that the goal of factoring is to find numbers f and g such that $(x + f)(x + g) = x^2 + (f + g)x + fg$, in other words $(f + g) = b$ and $fg = c$ or . This can be a really useful method when b and c are integers. Determine the factors of c and look for pairs that could sum to b.

For example, consider finding the roots of $x^2 + 6x - 16 = 0$. The factors of -16 include, -4 and 4, -8 and 2, -2 and 8, -1 and 16, and 1 and -16. The factors that sum to 6 are -2 and 8. Write these factors as the product of two binomials, $0 = (x - 2)(x + 8)$. Finally, since these binomials multiply together to equal zero, set them each equal to zero and solve each for x. This results in $x - 2 = 0$, which simplifies to $x = 2$ and $x + 8 = 0$, which simplifies to $x = -8$. Therefore, the roots of the equation are 2 and -8.

Review Video: Factoring Quadratic Equations
Visit mometrix.com/academy and enter code: 336566

Completing the Square

One way to find the roots of a quadratic equation is to find a way to manipulate it such that it follows the form of a perfect square $(x^2 + 2px + p^2)$ by adding and subtracting a constant. This process is called **completing the square**. In other words, if you are given a quadratic that is not a perfect square, $x^2 + bx + c = 0$, you can find a constant d that could be added in to make it a perfect square:

$$x^2 + bx + c + (d - d) = 0; \ \{\text{Let } b = 2p \text{ and } c + d = p^2\}$$
$$\text{then: } x^2 + 2px + p^2 - d = 0 \text{ and } d = \frac{b^2}{4} - c$$

Once you have completed the square you can find the roots of the resulting equation:

$$\begin{aligned} x^2 + 2px + p^2 - d &= 0 \\ (x + p)^2 &= d \\ x + p &= \pm\sqrt{d} \\ x &= -p \pm \sqrt{d} \end{aligned}$$

It is worth noting that substituting the original expressions into this solution gives the same result as the quadratic formula where $a = 1$:

$$x = -p \pm \sqrt{d} = -\frac{b}{2} \pm \sqrt{\frac{b^2}{4} - c} = -\frac{b}{2} \pm \frac{\sqrt{b^2 - 4c}}{2} = \frac{-b \pm \sqrt{b^2 - 4c}}{2}$$

Completing the square can be seen as arranging block representations of each of the terms to be as close to a square as possible and then filling in the gaps. For example, consider the quadratic expression $x^2 + 6x + 2$:

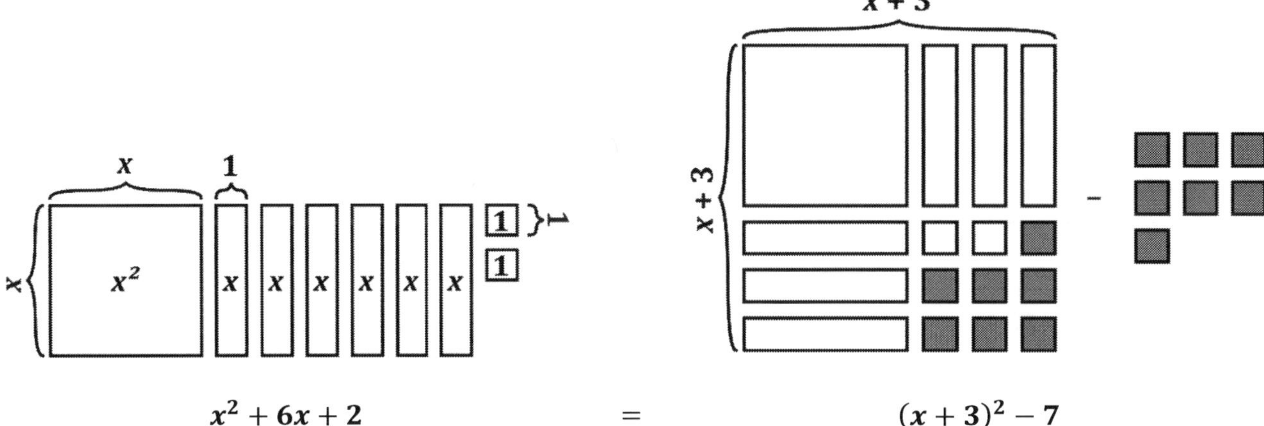

Using Given Roots to Find a Quadratic Equation

One way to find the roots of a quadratic equation is to factor the equation and use the **zero product property**, setting each factor of the equation equal to zero to find the corresponding root. We can use this technique in reverse to find an equation given its roots. Each root corresponds to a linear equation which in turn corresponds to a factor of the quadratic equation.

For example, we can find a quadratic equation whose roots are $x = 2$ and $x = -1$. The root $x = 2$ corresponds to the equation $x - 2 = 0$, and the root $x = -1$ corresponds to the equation $x + 1 = 0$.

These two equations correspond to the factors $(x - 2)$ and $(x + 1)$, from which we can derive the equation $(x - 2)(x + 1) = 0$, or $x^2 - x - 2 = 0$.

Any integer multiple of this entire equation will also yield the same roots, as the integer will simply cancel out when the equation is factored. For example, $2x^2 - 2x - 4 = 0$ factors as $2(x - 2)(x + 1) = 0$.

Solving a System of Equations Consisting of a Linear Equation and a Quadratic Equation

Algebraically

Generally, the simplest way to solve a system of equations consisting of a linear equation and a quadratic equation algebraically is through the method of substitution. One possible strategy is to solve the linear equation for y and then substitute that expression into the quadratic equation. After expansion and combining like terms, this will result in a new quadratic equation for x which, like all quadratic equations, may have zero, one, or two solutions. Plugging each solution for x back into one of the original equations will then produce the corresponding value of y.

For example, consider the following system of equations:

$$x + y = 1$$
$$y = (x + 3)^2 - 2$$

We can solve the linear equation for y to yield $y = -x + 1$. Substituting this expression into the quadratic equation produces $-x + 1 = (x + 3)^2 - 2$. We can simplify this equation:

$$-x + 1 = (x + 3)^2 - 2$$
$$-x + 1 = x^2 + 6x + 9 - 2$$
$$-x + 1 = x^2 + 6x + 7$$
$$0 = x^2 + 7x + 6$$

This quadratic equation can be factored as $(x + 1)(x + 6) = 0$. It therefore has two solutions: $x_1 = -1$ and $x_2 = -6$. Plugging each of these back into the original linear equation yields $y_1 = -x_1 + 1 = -(-1) + 1 = 2$ and $y_2 = -x_2 + 1 = -(-6) + 1 = 7$. Thus, this system of equations has two solutions, $(-1, 2)$ and $(-6, 7)$.

It may help to check your work by putting each x and y value back into the original equations and verifying that they do provide a solution.

GRAPHICALLY

To solve a system of equations consisting of a linear equation and a quadratic equation graphically, plot both equations on the same graph. The linear equation will of course produce a straight line, while the quadratic equation will produce a parabola. These two graphs will intersect at zero, one, or two points; each point of intersection is a solution of the system.

For example, consider the following system of equations:

$$y = -2x + 2$$
$$y = -2x^2 + 4x + 2$$

The linear equation describes a line with a y-intercept of $(0, 2)$ and a slope of -2.

To graph the quadratic equation, we can first find the vertex of the parabola: the x-coordinate of the vertex is $h = -\frac{b}{2a} = -\frac{4}{2(-2)} = 1$, and the y coordinate is $k = -2(1)^2 + 4(1) + 2 = 4$. Thus, the vertex lies at $(1, 4)$. To get a feel for the rest of the parabola, we can plug in a few more values of x to find more points; by putting in $x = 2$ and $x = 3$ in the quadratic equation, we find that the points $(2, 2)$ and $(3, -4)$ lie on the parabola; by symmetry thus do $(0, 2)$ and $(-1, -4)$. We can now plot both equations:

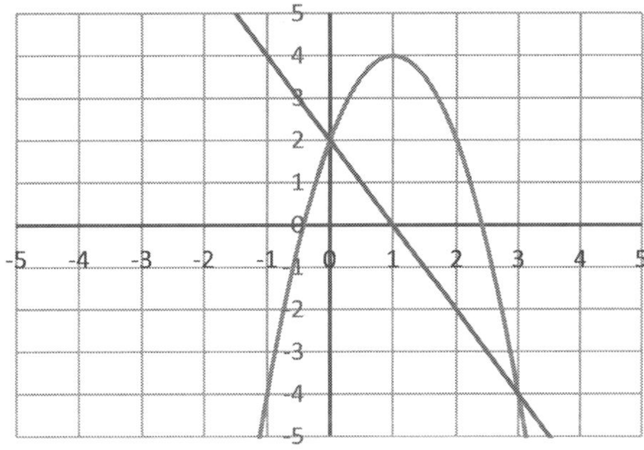

These two curves intersect at the points $(0, 2)$ and $(3, -4)$, thus these are the solutions of the equation.

STRATEGIES FOR COMPLETING QUESTIONS WITH QUADRATICS

Since these types of questions are in the no calculator section of the test, graphing is not your best choice due to time constraints. Set the equation equal to zero; if the quadratic expression is easily factored, factor it, and then solve the equation by setting each factor equal to zero. If the expression is not factorable and $a = 1$ when the equation is written in the general form $ax^2 + bx + c = 0$, you may choose to complete the square. Remember, if $a \neq 1$, you must divide the entire equation by a and work with resulting fractions. In these situations, it is easier to solve the equation using the quadratic formula $x = \frac{-b \pm \sqrt{b^2 - 4ac}}{2a}$. You may simply be asked to find the roots of a quadratic equation, or you may be asked to perform some operation with one of the roots once you have found the roots. Be careful to answer the question that is asked. For example, you may see a question that says, "If $3x^2 + 4x = 4$ and $x > 0$, what is the value of $x + \frac{1}{3}$?" First, you would write the equation in the form $3x^2 + 4x - 4 = 0$ and solve by factoring or by using the quadratic formula; then, you would use the positive root to find $x + \frac{1}{3}$.

MODELING A PROJECTILE'S TRAJECTORY

Since quadratic equations graph as parabolas, they are often used to model trajectories. To find the values of *x* for which a quadratic equation is equal to zero, you should set the equation equal to zero and then solve by factoring or by using the quadratic equation. For a trajectory problem, usually one zero is at $x = 0$, representing the launch of the projectile, and the other zero represents the landing. Inverse square relationships model scientific concepts, such as the relationship between gravitational force and the distance between two objects, the electric force between two charges, and the magnetic force between two poles. In each of these laws, the force increases as the distance between the objects decreases, and the force decreases as the distance between the objects increase. More specifically, if the distance is doubled, the force is reduced to one fourth of the original value; if the distance is halved, the force quadruples. When working with exponential relationships, a common mistake is to handle the exponent incorrectly. If you are given an equation and values to plug into that equation, be sure to apply the exponent to every factor inside the parenthesis under the exponent. Remember, when raising a power to a power, you should multiply exponents.

PRACTICE

P1. Find the roots of $y = 2x^2 + 8x + 4$.

P2. Find a quadratic equation with roots $x = 4$ and $x = -6$.

PRACTICE SOLUTIONS

P1. First, substitute 0 in for *y* in the quadratic equation: $0 = 2x^2 + 8x + 4$

Next, try to factor the quadratic equation. Since $a \neq 1$, list the factors of ac, or 8:

$$(1, 8), (-1, -8), (2, 4), (-2, -4)$$

Look for the factors of *ac* that add up to b, or 8. Since none do, the equation cannot be factored with whole numbers. Substitute the values of *a*, *b*, and *c* into the quadratic formula, $x = \frac{-b \pm \sqrt{b^2 - 4ac}}{2a}$:

$$x = \frac{-8 \pm \sqrt{8^2 - 4(2)(4)}}{2(2)}$$

Use the order of operations to simplify:

$$x = \frac{-8 \pm \sqrt{64 - 32}}{4}$$
$$x = \frac{-8 \pm \sqrt{32}}{4}$$

Reduce and simplify:

$$x = \frac{-8 \pm \sqrt{(16)(2)}}{4}$$
$$x = \frac{-8 \pm 4\sqrt{2}}{4}$$
$$x = -2 \pm \sqrt{2}$$
$$x = \left(-2 + \sqrt{2}\right) \text{ and } \left(-2 - \sqrt{2}\right)$$

P2. The root $x = 4$ corresponds to the equation $x - 4 = 0$, and the root $x = -6$ corresponds to the equation $x + 6 = 0$. These two equations correspond to the factors $(x - 4)$ and $(x + 6)$, from which we can derive the equation $(x - 4)(x + 6) = 0$, or $x^2 + 2x - 24 = 0$.

Passport to Advanced Math

In this section the questions will deal with more advanced equations and expressions. Students need to be able to create quadratic and exponential equations that model a context. They also need to be able to solve these equations. Students should also be able to create equivalent expressions that involve radicals and rational exponents. Like the Heart of Algebra section this section will test systems of equations. These systems however will involve one linear and one quadratic equation in two variables. Finally, students should be able to perform operations such as addition, subtraction, and multiplication on polynomials.

Equivalent Expressions

You might be given an algebraic expression and asked which, if any, of several other expressions is equivalent, or you might be given several pairs of algebraic expressions and be asked to determine which pairs are equivalent. For example, you may see a question that says, "Which of following pairs of algebraic expressions are equivalent" and an answer choice such as "$(2x + 3)(3x - 4)$ and $6x^2 + x + 12$." You would determine that is an incorrect choice since these are not equivalent expressions. You might see a question that says, "Which of the following rational expressions is equivalent to $\frac{x+3}{x-5}$?" You may be given choices in which the numerators and denominators can factored and some of the factors canceled.

Equivalent Expressions with Radical and Rational Exponents

You may see questions asking you to simplify a radical expression or perform operations with radicals. You may see a question that says, "Simplify $\sqrt[3]{-27x^6y^{15}}$," or "Simplify the expression $\sqrt{2}(3\sqrt{5} + \sqrt{20})$." You may see a question that says, "Which of the following expressions is equivalent to $\sqrt{(20)(4) + (12)(16)}$?" You should expect to be asked to simplify rational expressions. You may need to factor the numerator and the denominator and then cancel like factors, as in this example: "Simplify $\frac{x^2-4}{x^2-x-2}$." You may also be asked to change a rational expression from one form into another. For example, you may see a question that says, "If the expression $\frac{6x^2-5}{x-1}$

is written in the equivalent form $\frac{1}{x-1} + B$, what is B in terms of x?" You could equate the two expressions and solve for B, or you could use long division to simplify the first expression and compare the result to the equivalent expression to determine B.

REWRITING RADICAL EXPRESSIONS

Radical expressions can be rewritten as equivalent expressions with rational exponents. In general $\sqrt[b]{n^a}$ is equivalent to $n^{\frac{a}{b}}$ and $\sqrt[b]{m^c n^a}$ is equivalent to $m^{\frac{c}{b}} n^{\frac{a}{b}}$. For example, $\sqrt{x}$ is equivalent to $x^{\frac{1}{2}}$ and $\sqrt[3]{x^2}$ is equivalent to $x^{\frac{2}{3}}$. The radical $\sqrt[5]{x-1}$ is equivalent to $(x-1)^{\frac{1}{5}}$. Another point to remember is that, while $n^{\frac{a}{b}}$ can be rewritten as $\sqrt[b]{n^a}$, it can also be rewritten as $(\sqrt[b]{n})^a$. It is also important to understand the concept of negative exponents. A negative exponent basically flips a term from the numerator to the denominator or from the denominator to the numerator. You may see a question that says, "Rewrite the expression $2x^{-\frac{3}{4}}$ in radical form" or "Rewrite the expression $(\sqrt[3]{2xy})^2$ with rational exponents."

BASIC FUNCTIONS

You should expect to build or create a linear function or equation in two variables that models a context. Linear functions or equations in two variables are equations with two unknown variables. Both variables have an exponent of one. You might be required to express the relationship in functional notation. For example, $y = 3x + 12$ and $p = 0.5d + 14.7$ are both linear equations in two variables and can be expressed in functional notation as $f(x) = 3x + 12$ and $f(d) = 0.5d + 14.7$, respectively. You may be expected to simplify your equation or function. You may see a test question that says, "The pressure in a tank which contains an industrial chemical and which is open to the atmosphere increases linearly with the height of the chemical in the tank. The measured pressure is due to the combined hydrostatic pressure of the chemical and the atmospheric pressure. A pressure gauge at a depth of five feet beneath the surface reads 17.2 pounds per square inch (psi), and at a depth of ten feet reads 19.7 psi. Which of the following linear models best describes the pressure p in psi at a depth of d feet?" You must determine the relationship between pressure p and depth d. First, determine the rate at which the pressure changes with depth; then, consider the contribution of the atmospheric pressure to the total pressure.

FUNCTION AND RELATION

When expressing functional relationships, the **variables** x and y are typically used. These values are often written as the **coordinates** (x, y). The x-value is the independent variable and the y-value is the dependent variable. A **relation** is a set of data in which there is not a unique y-value for each x-value in the dataset. This means that there can be two of the same x-values assigned to different y-values. A relation is simply a relationship between the x and y-values in each coordinate but does not apply to the relationship between the values of x and y in the data set. A **function** is a relation where one quantity depends on the other. For example, the amount of money that you make depends on the number of hours that you work. In a function, each x-value in the data set has one unique y-value because the y-value depends on the x-value.

Review Video: Definition of a Function
Visit mometrix.com/academy and enter code: 784611

FUNCTIONS

A function has exactly one value of **output variable** (dependent variable) for each value of the **input variable** (independent variable). The set of all values for the input variable (here assumed to be x) is the domain of the function, and the set of all corresponding values of output variable (here assumed to be y) is the range of the function. When looking at a graph of an equation, the easiest way to determine if the equation is a function or not is to conduct the vertical line test. If a vertical line drawn through any value of x crosses the graph in more than one place, the equation is not a function.

A statement using function notation can model any situation in which one quantity depends uniquely on one or more other quantities. For example, the area of a rectangle can be expressed as a function of its width and height. The maximum vertical distance a projectile travels can be expressed as a function of its initial vertical speed. An object's position, the amount of money in a bank account, or any other quantity that changes over time can be expressed as a function of time.

A relationship cannot be modeled with a function, however, if it involves two quantities neither of which is uniquely determined by the other—that is, if each quantity may have multiple values corresponding to the same value of the other. For example, we could not write a function to represent the relationship between peoples' height in inches and their weight in pounds. There are people of the same height with different weights, and people of the same weight but different heights.

You may be asked to evaluate a given function. For example, you may see a question that says, "If $f(x) = x^3 - 4x^2 + 3x - 1$, find $f(2)$." You should expect to be given two functions such as $f(x)$ and $g(x)$ and be asked to find $f(g(x))$ or $g(f(x))$. For example, you may see a question that says, "Let $f(x) = x^2 - 1$ and $g(x) = x + 1$. Which of the following describes $f(g(x))$?" Or you may be asked to work a similar problem given $f(x)$ and $g(f(x))$ and be asked to find $g(x)$. For example, you may see a question that says, "Let $f(x) = x^2 - 3$. If $g(f(x)) = \sqrt{x^2 + 1}$, which of the following describes $g(x)$?" You may be asked to evaluate composite functions, as in this example: "Two functions are defined as $f(t) = 4t^2 - t$ and $g(x) = -3x^2 - 2x - 1$. Find the value of $g(f(2))$."

Finding the Domain and Range of a Function

The **domain** of a function $f(x)$ is the set of all input values for which the function is defined. The **range** of a function $f(x)$ is the set of all possible output values of the function—that is, of every possible value of $f(x)$, for any value of x in the function's domain. For a function expressed in a table, every input-output pair—is given explicitly. To find the domain, we just list all the x values and to find the range, we just list all the values of $f(x)$. Consider the following example:

x	-1	4	2	1	0	3	8	6
$f(x)$	3	0	3	−1	−1	2	4	6

In this case, the domain would be {-1, 4, 2, 1, 0, 3, 8, 6}, or, putting them in ascending order, {-1, 0, 1, 2, 3, 4, 6, 8}. (Putting the values in ascending order isn't strictly necessary, but generally makes the set easier to read.) The range would be {3, 0, 3, −1, −1, 2, 4, 6}. Note that some of these values appear more than once. This is entirely permissible for a function; while each value of x must be matched to a unique value of $f(x)$, the converse is not true. We don't need to list each value more than once, so eliminating duplicates, the range is {3, 0, −1, 2, 4, 6}, or, putting them in ascending order, {−1, 0, 2, 3, 4, 6}.

Note that by definition of a function, no input value can be matched to more than one output value. It is good to double check to make sure that the data given follows this and is therefore actually a function.

Review Video: Domain and Range
Visit mometrix.com/academy and enter code: 778133

Determining a Function

You can determine whether an equation is a **function** by substituting different values into the equation for x. These values are called input values. All possible input values are referred to as the **domain**. The result of substituting these values into the equation is called the output, or **range**. You can display and organize these numbers in a data table. A **data table** contains the values for x and y, which you can also list as coordinates. In order for a function to exist, the table cannot contain any repeating x-values that correspond with different y-values. If each x-coordinate has a unique y-coordinate, the table contains a function. However, there can be repeating y-values that correspond with different x-values. An example of this is when the function contains an exponent. For example, if $x^2 = y$, $2^2 = 4$, and $(-2)^2 = 4$.

Review Video: Basics of Functions
Visit mometrix.com/academy and enter code: 822500

Writing a Function Rule Using a Table

If given a set of data, place the corresponding x and y-values into a table and analyze the relationship between them. Consider what you can do to each x-value to obtain the corresponding y-value. Try adding or subtracting different numbers to and from x and then try multiplying or dividing different numbers to and from x. If none of these **operations** give you the y-value, try combining the operations. Once you find a rule that works for one pair, make sure to try it with each additional set of ordered pairs in the table. If the same operation or combination of operations satisfies each set of coordinates, then the table contains a function. The rule is then used to write the equation of the function in "$y =$" form.

Direct and Inverse Variations of Variables

Variables that vary directly are those that either both increase at the same rate or both decrease at the same rate. For example, in the functions $y = kx$ or $y = kx^n$, where k and n are positive, the value of y increases as the value of x increases and decreases as the value of x decreases.

Variables that vary inversely are those where one increases while the other decreases. For example, in the functions $y = \frac{k}{x}$ or $y = \frac{k}{x^n}$ where k and n are positive, the value of y increases as the value of x decreases, and decreases as the value of x increases.

In both cases, k is the constant of variation.

Properties of Functions

There are many different ways to classify functions based on their structure or behavior. Important features of functions include:

- **End behavior**: the behavior of the function at extreme values ($f(x)$ as $x \to \pm\infty$)
- ***y*-intercept**: the value of function at $f(0)$
- **Roots**: the values of x where the function equals zero ($f(x) = 0$)
- **Extrema**: minimum or maximum values of the function or where the function changes direction ($f(x) \geq k$ or $f(x) \leq k$)

Classification of Functions

An **invertible function** is defined as a function, $f(x)$, for which there is another function, $f^{-1}(x)$, such that $f^{-1}(f(x)) = x$. For example, if $f(x) = 3x - 2$ the inverse function, $f^{-1}(x)$, can be found:

$$x = 3(f^{-1}(x)) - 2$$
$$\frac{x+2}{3} = f^{-1}(x)$$

$$f^{-1}(f(x)) = \frac{3x - 2 + 2}{3} = \frac{3x}{3} = x$$

Note that $f^{-1}(x)$ is a valid function over all values of x.

In a **one-to-one function**, each value of x has exactly one value for y on the coordinate plane (this is the definition of a function) and each value of y has exactly one value for x. While the vertical line test will determine if a graph is that of a function, the horizontal line test will determine if a function is a one-to-one function. If a horizontal line drawn at any value of y intersects the graph in more than one place, the graph is not that of a one-to-one function. Do not make the mistake of using the horizontal line test exclusively in determining if a graph is that of a one-to-one function. A one-to-one function must pass both the vertical line test and the horizontal line test. As such, one-to-one functions are invertible functions.

A **many-to-one function** is a function whereby the relation is a function, but the inverse of the function is not a function. In other words, each element in the domain is mapped to one and only one element in the range. However, one or more elements in the range may be mapped to the same element in the domain. A graph of a many-to-one function would pass the vertical line test, but not the horizontal line test. One result of this is the fact that many-to-one functions are not invertible.

A **monotone function** is a function whose graph either constantly increases or constantly decreases. Examples include the functions $f(x) = x$, $f(x) = -x$, or $f(x) = x^3$.

An **even function** has a graph that is symmetric with respect to the y-axis and satisfies the equation $f(x) = f(-x)$. Examples include the functions $f(x) = x^2$ and $f(x) = ax^n$, where a is any real number and n is a positive even integer.

An **odd function** has a graph that is symmetric with respect to the origin and satisfies the equation $f(x) = -f(-x)$. Examples include the functions $f(x) = x^3$ and $f(x) = ax^n$, where a is any real number and n is a positive odd integer.

Constant functions are given by the equation $f(x) = b$, where b is a real number. There is no independent variable present in the equation, so the function has a constant value for all x. The graph of a constant function is a horizontal line of slope 0 that is positioned b units from the x-axis. If b is positive, the line is above the x-axis; if b is negative, the line is below the x-axis.

Identity functions are identified by the equation $f(x) = x$, where every value of the function is equal to its corresponding value of x. The only zero is the point $(0, 0)$. The graph is a line with slope of 1.

In **linear functions**, the value of the function changes in direct proportion to x. The rate of change,represented by the slope on its graph, is constant throughout. The standard form of a linear equation is $ax + cy = d$, where a, c, and d are real numbers. As a function, this equation is commonly in the form $y = mx + b$ or $f(x) = mx + b$ where $m = -\frac{a}{c}$ and $b = \frac{d}{c}$. This is known as the slope-intercept form, because the coefficients give the slope of the graphed function (m) and its y-intercept (b). Solve the equation $mx + b = 0$ for x to get $x = -\frac{b}{m}$, which is the only zero of the function. The domain and range are both the set of all real numbers.

Algebraic functions are those that exclusively use polynomials and roots. These would include polynomial functions, rational functions, square root functions, and all combinations of these functions, such as polynomials as the radicand. These combinations may be joined by addition, subtraction, multiplication, or division, but may not include variables as exponents.

ABSOLUTE VALUE FUNCTIONS

An **absolute value function** is in the format $f(x) = |ax + b|$. Like other functions, the domain is the set of all real numbers. However, because absolute value indicates positive numbers, the range is limited to positive real numbers. To find the zero of an absolute value function, set the portion inside the absolute value sign equal to zero and solve for x. An absolute value function is also known as a piecewise function because it must be solved in pieces – one for if the value inside the absolute value sign is positive, and one for if the value is negative. The function can be expressed as

$$f(x) = \begin{cases} ax + b \text{ if } ax + b \geq 0 \\ -(ax + b) \text{ if } ax + b < 0 \end{cases}$$

This will allow for an accurate statement of the range. The graph of an example absolute value function, $f(x) = |2x - 1|$, is below:

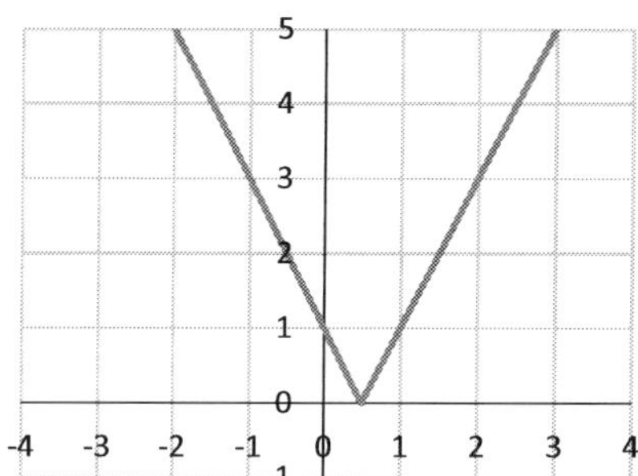

PIECEWISE FUNCTIONS

A **piecewise function** is a function that has different definitions on two or more different intervals. The following, for instance, is one example of a piecewise-defined function:

$$f(x) = \begin{cases} x^2, & x < 0 \\ x, & 0 \leq x \leq 2 \\ (x-2)^2, & x > 2 \end{cases}$$

To graph this function, we'd simply graph each part separately in the appropriate domain. The final graph would look like this:

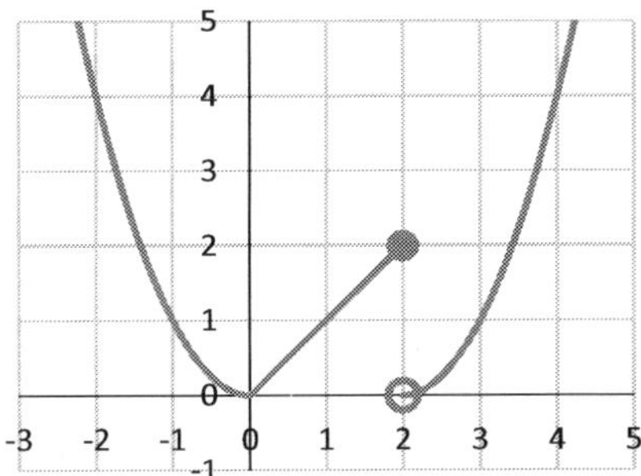

Note the filled and hollow dots at the discontinuity at $x = 2$. This is important to show which side of the graph that point corresponds to. Because $f(x) = x$ on the closed interval $0 \leq x \leq 2$, $f(2) = 2$. The point (2,2) is therefore marked with a filled circle, and the point (2,0), which is the endpoint of the rightmost $(x - 2)^2$ part of the graph but *not actually part of the function*, is marked with a hollow dot to indicate this.

Quadratic Functions

A **quadratic function** is a function in the form $y = ax^2 + bx + c$, where a does not equal 0. While a linear function forms a line, a quadratic function forms a **parabola**, which is a u-shaped figure that either opens upward or downward. A parabola that opens upward is said to be a **positive quadratic function** and a parabola that opens downward is said to be a **negative quadratic function**. The shape of a parabola can differ, depending on the values of a, b, and c. All parabolas contain a **vertex**, which is the highest possible point, the **maximum**, or the lowest possible point, the **minimum**. This is the point where the graph begins moving in the opposite direction. A quadratic function can have zero, one, or two solutions, and therefore, zero, one, or two x-intercepts. Recall that the x-intercepts are referred to as the zeros, or roots, of a function. A quadratic function will have only one y-intercept. Understanding the basic components of a quadratic function can give you an idea of the shape of its graph.

Example graph of a positive quadratic function, $x^2 + 2x - 3$:

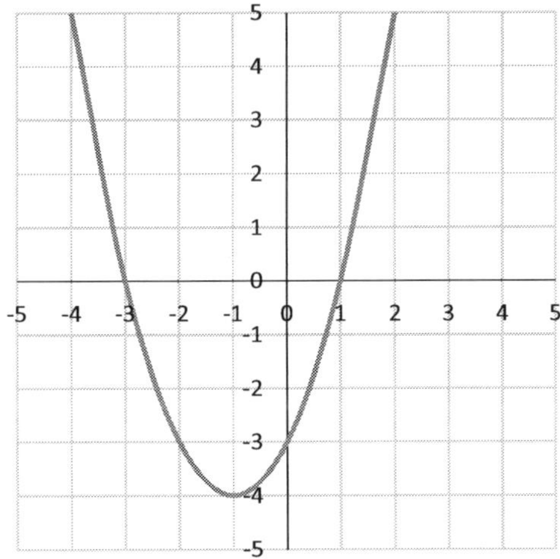

POLYNOMIAL FUNCTIONS

A **polynomial function** is a function with multiple terms and multiple powers of x, such as:

$$f(x) = a_n x^n + a_{n-1}x^{n-1} + a_{n-2}x^{n-2} + \cdots + a_1 x + a_0$$

where n is a non-negative integer that is the highest exponent in the polynomial, and $a_n \neq 0$. The domain of a polynomial function is the set of all real numbers. If the greatest exponent in the polynomial is even, the polynomial is said to be of even degree and the range is the set of real numbers that satisfy the function. If the greatest exponent in the polynomial is odd, the polynomial is said to be odd and the range, like the domain, is the set of all real numbers.

Review Video: Simplifying Rational Polynomial Functions
Visit mometrix.com/academy and enter code: 351038

RATIONAL FUNCTIONS

A **rational function** is a function that can be constructed as a ratio of two polynomial expressions: $f(x) = \frac{p(x)}{q(x)}$, where $p(x)$ and $q(x)$ are both polynomial expressions and $q(x) \neq 0$. The domain is the set of all real numbers, except any values for which $q(x) = 0$. The range is the set of real numbers that satisfies the function when the domain is applied. When you graph a rational function, you will have vertical asymptotes wherever $q(x) = 0$. If the polynomial in the numerator is of lesser degree than the polynomial in the denominator, the x-axis will also be a horizontal asymptote. If the numerator and denominator have equal degrees, there will be a horizontal asymptote not on the x-axis. If the degree of the numerator is exactly one greater than the degree of the denominator, the graph will have an oblique, or diagonal, asymptote. The asymptote will be along the line $y = \frac{p_n}{q_{n-1}}x + \frac{p_{n-1}}{q_{n-1}}$, where p_n and q_{n-1} are the coefficients of the highest degree terms in their respective polynomials.

SQUARE ROOT FUNCTIONS

A **square root function** is a function that contains a radical and is in the format $f(x) = \sqrt{ax + b}$. The domain is the set of all real numbers that yields a positive radicand or a radicand equal to zero. Because square root values are assumed to be positive unless otherwise identified, the range is all real numbers from zero to infinity. To find the zero of a square root function, set the radicand equal to zero and solve for x. The graph of a square root function is always to the right of the zero and always above the x-axis.

Example graph of a square root function, $f(x) = \sqrt{2x + 1}$:

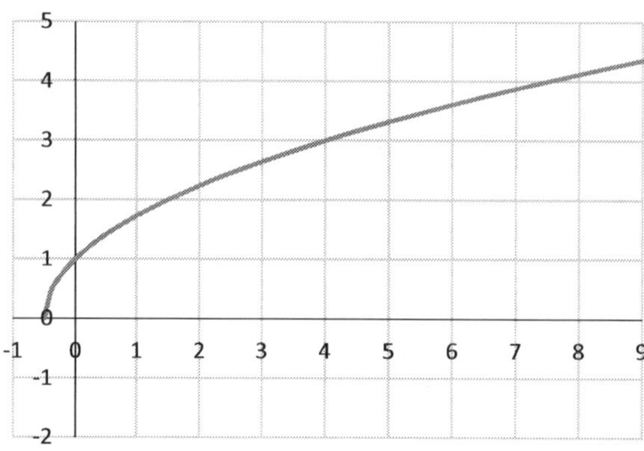

RELATING EQUATIONS TO GRAPHS

You need to be able to match a given graph to the type of equation it represents, whether it be linear, quadratic, or exponential. Questions about bacteria cultures and radioactive isotopes are modeled with exponential equations. Questions about initial fees plus rates associated with a variable are modeled with linear equations. The projectiles of arrows, rocks, balls, missiles or anything that is shot or thrown are modeled with quadratic equations. You should know the general shapes for linear equations (line), quadratic equations (parabola), and exponential equations (steep curve). Also, you should have a firm grasp of the slope-intercept from of a line. When you are working with a linear equation, it is important to avoid making quick, erroneous conclusions about the line. Often, the equation of the line will be written in a form to "hide" the true nature of the line. For example, you may be given an equation like $y - x = k(x + y)$ and asked to determine which is necessarily true of its graph: the graph is a line passing through the origin; the graph is a parabola; the graph is a line with a positive slope; or the graph is a line with a slope of k. At first glance, you might think this is a factored quadratic equation, or you might think it is a linear equation in point-slope form with a slope of k. However, if you rearrange the equation into the slope-intercept form $y = \frac{1+k}{1-k}x$, you can see that the graph of the equation is a line with a y-intercept of zero, which means that the line passes through the origin. Depending on the value of k, the slope of the line can be positive, negative, zero, or undefined.

PRACTICE

P1. Martin needs a 20% medicine solution. The pharmacy has a 5% solution and a 30% solution. He needs 50 mL of the solution. If the pharmacist must mix the two solutions, how many milliliters of 5% solution and 30% solution should be used?

P2. Describe two different strategies for solving the following problem:

Kevin can mow the yard in 4 hours. Mandy can mow the same yard in 5 hours. If they work together, how long will it take them to mow the yard?

P3. A car, traveling at 65 miles per hour, leaves Flagstaff and heads east on I-40. Another car, traveling at 75 miles per hour, leaves Flagstaff 2 hours later, from the same starting point and also heads east on I-40. Determine how many hours it will take the second car to catch the first car by:

(a) Using a table.

(b) Using algebra.

PRACTICE SOLUTIONS

P1. To solve this problem, a table may be created to represent the variables, percentages, and total amount of solution. Such a table is shown below:

	mL solution	**% medicine**	**Total mL medicine**
5% solution	x	0.05	$0.05x$
30% solution	y	0.30	$0.30y$
Mixture	$x + y = 50$	0.20	$(0.20)(50) = 10$

The variable, x, may be rewritten as $50 - y$, so the equation, $0.05(50 - y) + 0.30y = 10$, may be written and solved for y. Doing so gives $y = 30$. So, 30 mL of 30% solution are needed. Evaluating the expression, $50 - y$ for an x-value of 20, shows that 20 mL of 5% solution are needed.

P2. Two possible strategies both involve the use of rational equations to solve. The first strategy involves representing the fractional part of the yard mowed by each person in one hour and setting this sum equal to the ratio of 1 to the total time needed. The appropriate equation is $1/4 + 1/5 = 1/t$, which simplifies as $9/20 = 1/t$, and finally as $t = 20/9$. So, the time it will take them to mow the yard, when working together, is a little more than 2.2 hours.

A second strategy involves representing the time needed for each person as two fractions and setting the sum equal to 1 (representing 1 yard). The appropriate equation is $t/4 + t/5 = 1$, which simplifies as $9t/20 = 1$, and finally as $t = 20/9$. This strategy also shows the total time to be a little more than 2.2 hours.

P3. (a) One strategy might involve creating a table of values for the number of hours and distances for each car. The table may be examined to find the same distance traveled and the corresponding number of hours taken. Such a table is shown below:

Car A		Car B	
x (hours)	*y* (distance)	*x* (hours)	*y* (distance)
0	0	0	
1	65	1	
2	130	2	0
3	195	3	75
4	260	4	150
5	325	5	225
6	390	6	300
7	455	7	375
8	520	8	450
9	585	9	525
10	650	10	600
11	715	11	675
12	780	12	750
13	845	13	825
14	910	14	900
15	975	15	975

The table shows that after 15 hours, the distance traveled is the same. Thus, the second car catches up with the first car after a distance of 975 miles and 15 hours.

(b) A second strategy might involve setting up and solving an algebraic equation. This situation may be modeled as $65x = 75(x - 2)$. This equation sets the distances traveled by each car equal to one another. Solving for x gives $x = 15$. Thus, once again, the second car will catch up with the first car after 15 hours.

Advanced Functions

Step Functions

The double brackets indicate a step function. For a step function, the value inside the double brackets is rounded down to the nearest integer. The graph of the function $f_0(x) = [\![x]\!]$ appears as shown on the left below. In comparison $f(x) = 2\left[\!\left[\frac{1}{3}(x - 1)\right]\!\right]$ is on the right below. The coefficient of 2 shows that it's stretched vertically by a factor of 2 (so there's a vertical distance of 2 units between successive "steps"). The coefficient of $\frac{1}{3}$ in front of the x shows that it's stretched horizontally by a factor of 3 (so each "step" is three units long), and the $x - 1$ shows that it's displaced one unit to the right.

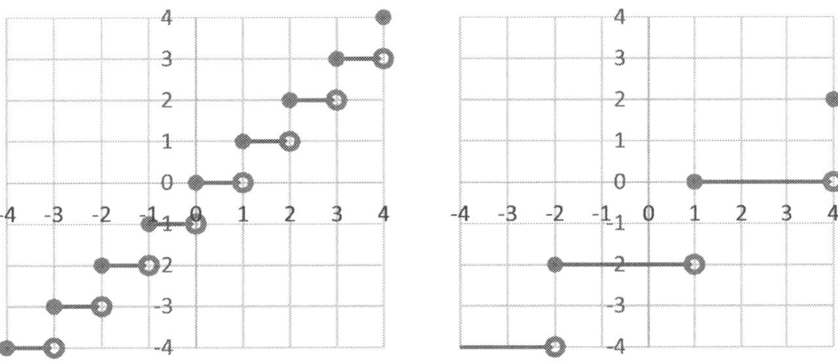

TRANSCENDENTAL FUNCTIONS

Transcendental functions are all functions that are non-algebraic. Any function that includes logarithms, trigonometric functions, variables as exponents, or any combination that includes any of these is not algebraic in nature, even if the function includes polynomials or roots.

EXPONENTIAL FUNCTIONS

Exponential functions are equations that have the format $y = b^x$, where base $b > 0$ and $b \neq 1$. The exponential function can also be written $f(x) = b^x$. Recall the properties of exponents, like the product of terms with the same base is equal to the base raised to the sum of the exponents: $a^x \times a^y = a^{x+y}$ and a term with an exponent that is raised to an exponent is equal to the base of the original term raised to the product of the exponents: $(a^x)^y = a^{xy}$. The graph of an example exponential function, $f(x) = 2^x$, is below:

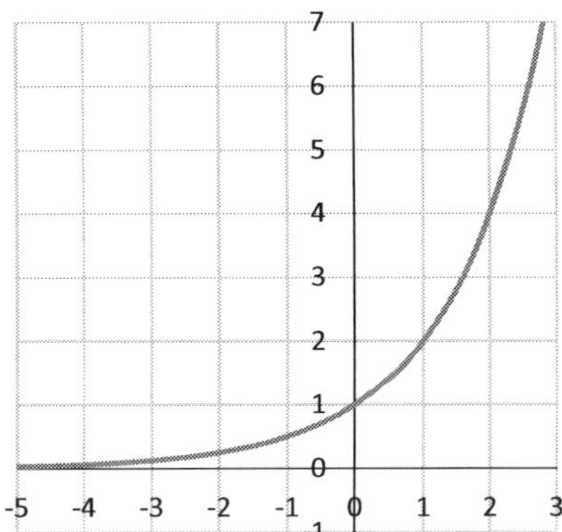

Note in the graph that the y value approaches zero to the left and infinity to the right. One of the key features of an exponential function is that there will be one end that goes off to infinity and another that asymptotically approaches a lower bound. Common forms of exponential functions include:

Geometric sequences: $a_n = a_1 \times r^{n-1}$, where a_n is the value of the nth term, a_1 is the initial value, r is the common ratio, and n is the number of terms. Note that $a_1 \times r^{1-1} = a_1 \times r^0 = a_1 \times 1 = a_1$.

Population growth: $f(t) = ae^{rt}$, where $f(t)$ is the population at time $t \geq 0$, a is the initial population, e is the mathematical constant known as Euler's number, and r is the growth rate.

Compound interest: $f(t) = P\left(1 + \frac{r}{n}\right)^{nt}$, where $f(t)$ is the account value at a certain number of time periods $t \geq 0$, P is the initial principle balance, r is the interest rate, and n is the number of times the interest is applied per time period.

General exponential growth or decay: $f(t) = a(1 + r)^t$, where $f(t)$ is the future count, a is the current or initial count, r is the growth or decay rate, and t is the time.

For example, suppose the initial population of a town was 1,200 people. The population growth is 5%. The current population is 2,400. To find out how much time has passed since the town was founded, we can use the following function:

$$2400 = 1200e^{0.05t}.$$

The general form for population growth may be represented as $f(t) = ae^{rt}$, where $f(t)$ represents the current population, a represents the initial population, r represents the growth rate, and t represents the time. Thus, substituting the initial population, current population, and rate into this form gives the equation above.

The number of years that have passed were found by first dividing both sides of the equation by 1,200. Doing so gives $2 = e^{0.05t}$. Taking the natural logarithm of both sides gives $\ln(2) = ln(e^{0.05t})$. Applying the power property of logarithms, the equation may be rewritten as $\ln(2) = 0.05t \times \ln(e)$, which simplifies as $\ln(2) = 0.05t$. Dividing both sides of this equation by 0.05 gives $t \approx 13.86$. Thus, approximately 13.86 years passed.

Review Video: Biology Application - Exponential Growth Function
Visit mometrix.com/academy and enter code: 336069

Logarithmic Functions

Logarithmic functions are equations that have the format $y = \log_b x$ or $f(x) = \log_b x$. The base b may be any number except one; however, the most common bases for logarithms are base 10 and base e. The log base e is the natural logarithm, or *ln*, expressed by the function $f(x) = \ln x$.

Any logarithm that does not have an assigned value of b is assumed to be base 10: $\log x = \log_{10} x$. Exponential functions and logarithmic functions are related in that one is the inverse of the other. If $f(x) = b^x$, then $f^{-1}(x) = \log_b x$. This can perhaps be expressed more clearly by the two equations: $y = b^x$ and $x = \log_b y$.

The following properties apply to logarithmic expressions:

Property	Description
$\log_b 1 = 0$	The log of 1 is equal to 0 for any base
$\log_b b = 1$	The log of the base is equal to 1
$\log_b b^p = p$	The log of the base raised to a power is equal to that power
$\log_b MN = \log_b M + \log_b N$	The log of a product is the sum of the log of each factor

Property	Description
$\log_b \frac{M}{N} = \log_b M - \log_b N$	The log of a quotient is equal to the log of the dividend minus the log of the divisor
$\log_b M^p = p \log_b M$	The log of a value raised to a power is equal to the power times the log of the value

The graph of an example logarithmic function, $f(x) = \log_2(x+2)$, is below:

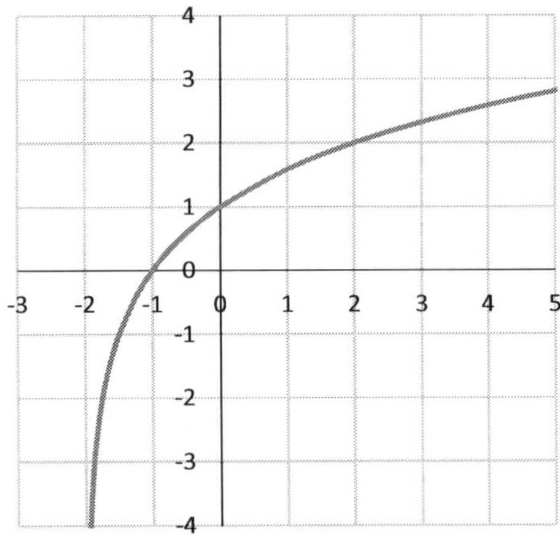

TRIGONOMETRIC FUNCTIONS

Trigonometric functions are periodic, meaning that they repeat the same form over and over. The basic trigonometric functions are sine (abbreviated 'sin'), cosine (abbreviated 'cos'), and tangent (abbreviated 'tan'). The simplest way to think of them is as describing the ratio of the side lengths of a right triangle in relation to the angles of the triangle.

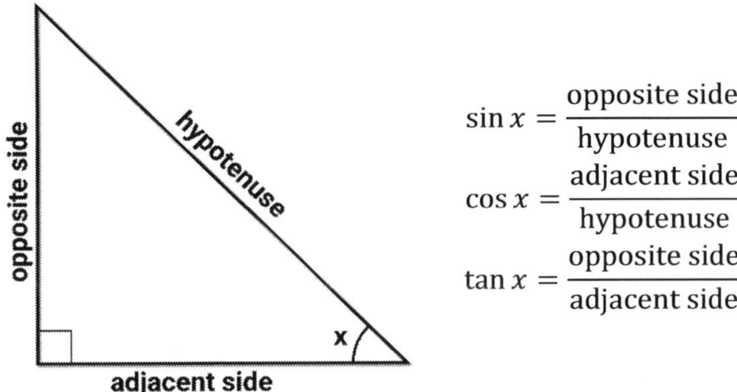

$$\sin x = \frac{\text{opposite side}}{\text{hypotenuse}}$$
$$\cos x = \frac{\text{adjacent side}}{\text{hypotenuse}}$$
$$\tan x = \frac{\text{opposite side}}{\text{adjacent side}}$$

Using sine as an example, trigonometric functions take the form $f(x) = A\sin(Bx + C) + D$, where the **amplitude** is simply equal to A. The **period** is the distance between successive peaks or troughs, essentially the length of the repeated pattern. In this form, the period is equal to ${}^{2\pi}/_{B}$. As for C, this is the **phase shift** or the horizontal shift of the function. The last term, D, is the vertical shift and determines the **midline** as $y = D$.

For instance, consider the function $f(x) = 2 + \frac{3}{2}\sin\left(\pi x + \frac{\pi}{2}\right)$. Here $A = \frac{3}{2}$, $B = \pi$, $C = \frac{\pi}{2}$, and $D = 2$, so the midline is at $y = 2$, the amplitude is $\frac{3}{2}$, and the period is $^{2\pi}/_{\pi} = 2$. To graph this function, we center the sine wave on the midline and extend it to a height above and below the midline equal to the amplitude—so this graph would have a minimum value of $2 - \frac{3}{2} = \frac{1}{2}$ and a maximum of $2 + \frac{3}{2} = \frac{7}{2}$. So, the function would be graphed as follows:

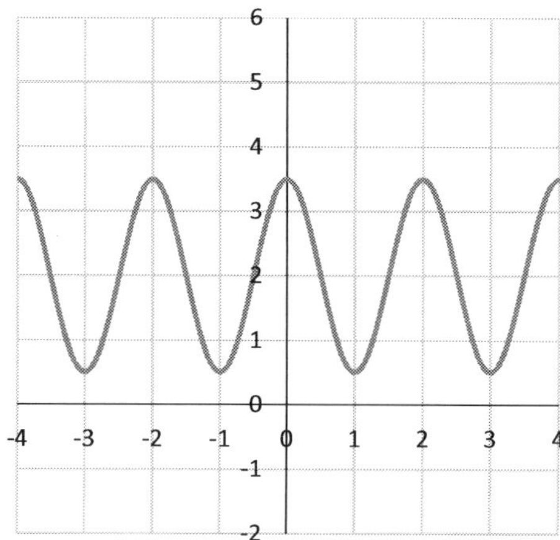

Manipulation of Functions

Translation occurs when values are added to or subtracted from the x or y values. If a constant is added to the y portion of each point, the graph shifts up. If a constant is subtracted from the y portion of each point, the graph shifts down. This is represented by the expression $f(x) \pm k$, where k is a constant. If a constant is added to the x portion of each point, the graph shifts left. If a constant is subtracted from the x portion of each point, the graph shifts right. This is represented by the expression $f(x \pm k)$, where k is a constant.

Stretching, compression, and reflection occur when different parts of a function are multiplied by different groups of constants. If the function as a whole is multiplied by a real number constant greater than 1, $(k \times f(x))$, the graph is stretched vertically. If k in the previous equation is greater than zero but less than 1, the graph is compressed vertically. If k is less than zero, the graph is reflected about the x-axis, in addition to being either stretched or compressed vertically if k is less than or greater than -1, respectively. If instead, just the x-term is multiplied by a constant greater than 1 $(f(k \times x))$, the graph is compressed horizontally. If k in the previous equation is greater than zero but less than 1, the graph is stretched horizontally. If k is less than zero, the graph is reflected about the y-axis, in addition to being either stretched or compressed horizontally if k is greater than or less than -1, respectively.

Algebraic Theorems

According to the **fundamental theorem of algebra**, every non-constant, single variable polynomial has exactly as many roots as the polynomial's highest exponent. For example, if x^4 is the largest exponent of a term, the polynomial will have exactly 4 roots. However, some of these roots may have multiplicity or be non-real numbers. For instance, in the polynomial function $f(x) = x^4 - 4x + 3$, the only real roots are 1 and -1. The root 1 has multiplicity of 2 and there is one non-real root $(-1 - \sqrt{2}i)$.

The **remainder theorem** is useful for determining the remainder when a polynomial is divided by a binomial. The remainder theorem states that if a polynomial function $f(x)$ is divided by a binomial $x - a$, where a is a real number, the remainder of the division will be the value of $f(a)$. If $f(a) = 0$, then a is a root of the polynomial.

The **factor theorem** is related to the remainder theorem and states that if $f(a) = 0$ then $(x - a)$ is a factor of the function.

According to the **rational root theorem,** any rational root of a polynomial function $f(x) = a_n x^n + a_{n-1}x^{n-1} + \cdots + a_1 x + a_0$ with integer coefficients will, when reduced to its lowest terms, be a positive or negative fraction such that the numerator is a factor of a_0 and the denominator is a factor of a_n. For instance, if the polynomial function $f(x) = x^3 + 3x^2 - 4$ has any rational roots, the numerators of those roots can only be factors of 4 (1, 2, 4), and the denominators can only be factors of 1 (1). The function in this example has roots of 1 $\left(\text{or } \frac{1}{1}\right)$ and -2 $\left(\text{or } -\frac{2}{1}\right)$.

Applying the Basic Operations to Functions

For each of the basic operations, we will use these functions as examples: $f(x) = x^2$ and $g(x) = x$.

To find the sum of two functions f and g, assuming the domains are compatible, simply add the two functions together: $(f + g)(x) = f(x) + g(x) = x^2 + x$

To find the difference of two functions f and g, assuming the domains are compatible, simply subtract the second function from the first: $(f - g)(x) = f(x) - g(x) = x^2 - x$.

To find the product of two functions f and g, assuming the domains are compatible, multiply the two functions together: $(f \times g)(x) = f(x) \times g(x) = x^2 \times x = x^3$.

To find the quotient of two functions f and g, assuming the domains are compatible, divide the first function by the second: $\frac{f}{g}(x) = \frac{f(x)}{g(x)} = \frac{x^2}{x} = x\,; x \neq 0$.

The example given in each case is fairly simple, but on a given problem, if you are looking only for the value of the sum, difference, product or quotient of two functions at a particular x-value, it may be simpler to solve the functions individually and then perform the given operation using those values.

The composite of two functions f and g, written as $(f \circ g)(x)$ simply means that the output of the second function is used as the input of the first. This can also be written as $f(g(x))$. In general, this can be solved by substituting $g(x)$ for all instances of x in $f(x)$ and simplifying. Using the example functions $f(x) = x^2 - x + 2$ and $g(x) = x + 1$, we can find that $(f \circ g)(x)$ or $f(g(x))$ is equal to $f(x + 1) = (x + 1)^2 - (x + 1) + 2$, which simplifies to $x^2 + x + 2$.

It is important to note that $(f \circ g)(x)$ is not necessarily the same as $(g \circ f)(x)$. The process is not always commutative like addition or multiplication expressions. It *can* be commutative, but most often this is not the case.

Practice

P1. A professor wishes to invest $20,000 in a CD that compounds annually. The interest rate at his bank is 1.9%. How many years will it take for his account to reach $50,000?

P2. Suppose a new strain of bacteria, after x days, shows a growth rate of 10%. The current count for the new bacteria strain is 100. How many days will pass before the count reaches 1 million bacteria?

P3. Each of the following functions cross the x- and y-axes at the same points. Identify the most likely function type of each graph

(a) 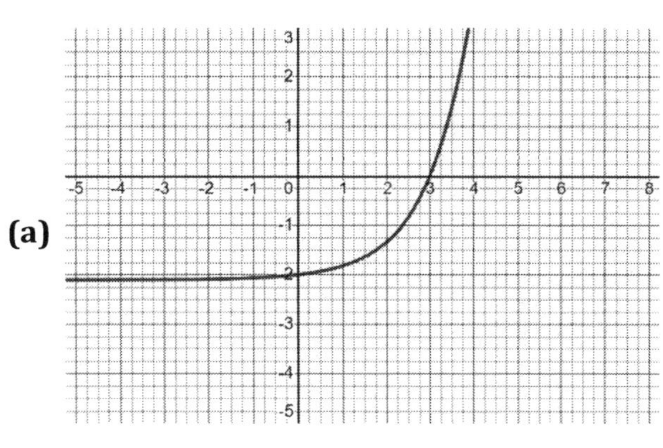

(b) 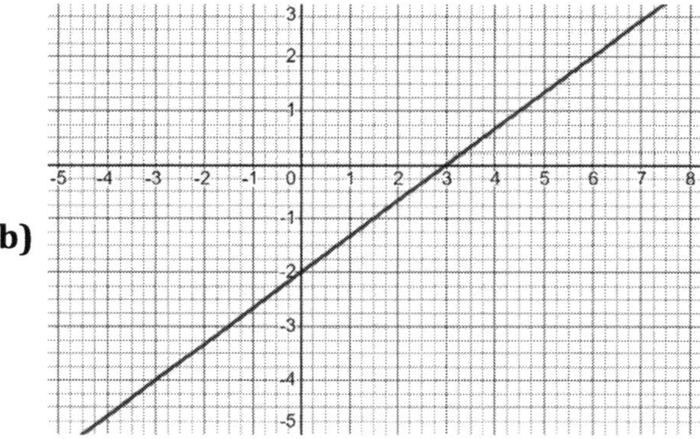

(c) 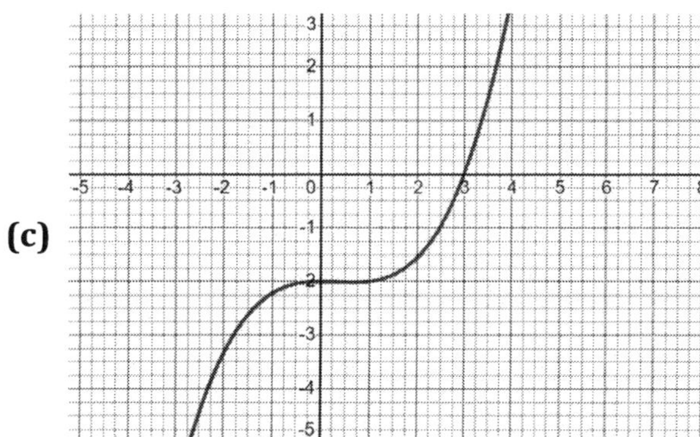

(d) 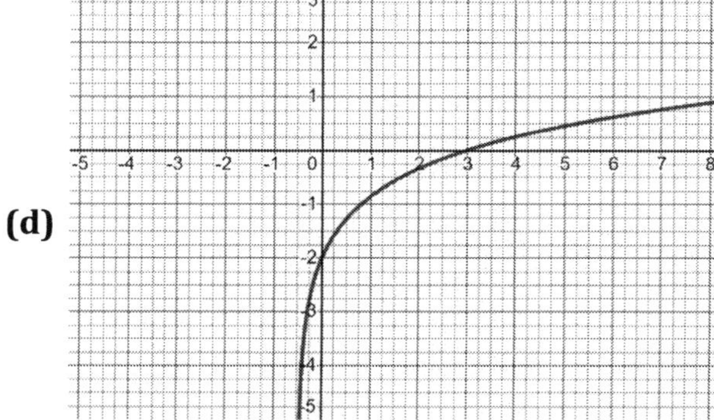

P4. Given the functions $f(x) = -3x + 3$, $g(x) = e^x + 3$, and $h(x) = x^2 - 2x + 1$, perform the following operations and write out the resulting function:

(a) Shift $g(x)$ 4 units to the left and 1 unit up, then compress the new function by a factor of 1/2

(b) $\frac{f(x)}{h(x)}$

(c) $h(g(x))$

(d) $\frac{f(x)+h(x)}{x-1}$

PRACTICE SOLUTIONS

P1. In order to solve this problem, the compound interest formula should be evaluated for a future value of \$50,000, principal of \$20,000, rate of 0.019, and number of years of t. The exponential equation may then be solved by taking the logarithm of both sides. The process is shown below:

$$50{,}000 = 20{,}000\left(1 + \frac{0.019}{1}\right)^t$$

Dividing both sides of the equation by 20,000 gives $2.5 = 1.019^t$. Taking the logarithm of both sides gives $\log(2.5) = t\log(1.019)$. Dividing both sides of this equation by $\log(1.019)$ gives $t \approx 48.68$. Thus, after approximately 49 years, the professor's account will reach \$50,000.

P2. The problem may be solved by writing and solving an exponential growth function, in the form, $f(x) = a(1+r)^x$, where $f(x)$ represents the future count, a represents the current count, r represents the growth rate, and x represents the time. Once the function is evaluated for a future count of 1,000,000, a current count of 100, and a growth rate of 0.10, the exponential equation may be solved by taking the logarithm of both sides.

The problem may be modeled with the equation, $1{,}000{,}000 = 100 \times (1.10)^x$. Dividing both sides of the equation by 100 gives $10{,}000 = 1.10^x$. Taking the logarithm of both sides gives $\log(10{,}000) = x\log(1.10)$. Dividing both sides of this equation by $\log(1.10)$ gives $x \approx 96.6$. Thus, after approximately 97 days, the bacteria count will reach 1 million.

P3. (a) Exponential function – positive, increasing slope

(b) Linear function – positive, continuous slope.

(c) Polynomial function (odd degree) – positive, changing slope. Note that the graph goes off to infinity in opposite quadrants I and III, thus it is an odd degree.

(d) Logarithmic function – positive, decreasing slope

P4. (a) Shifting $g(x)$ to the left 4 units is the same as $g(x+4)$ and shifting the function up one unit is $g(x)+1$. Combining these and multiplying by ½ results in the following:

$$\begin{aligned}\frac{1}{2}(g(x+4)+1) &= \frac{1}{2}\left((e^{x+4}+3)+1\right)\\ &= \frac{e^{x+4}}{2}+2\end{aligned}$$

(b) Factor $h(x)$, noting that it is a perfect square, and be sure to note the constraint on x due to the original denominator of the rational expression:

$$\frac{f(x)}{h(x)} = \frac{-3x+3}{x^2-2x+1} = \frac{-3(x-1)}{(x-1)(x-1)} = \frac{-3}{(x-1)}; x \neq 1$$

(c) Evaluate the composition as follows:

$$\begin{aligned}h\big(g(x)\big) &= (e^x+3)^2 - 2(e^x+3)+1\\ &= (e^x)^2 + 6e^x + 9 - 2e^x - 6 + 1\\ &= e^{2x} + 4e^x + 4\\ &= (e^x+2)^2\end{aligned}$$

(d) Note the constraint on x due to the original denominator of the rational expression:

$$\begin{aligned}\frac{f(x)+h(x)}{x-1} &= \frac{(-3x+3)+(x^2-2x+1)}{x-1}\\ &= \frac{-3(x-1)+(x-1)(x-1)}{x-1}\\ &= -3+(x-1)\\ &= x-4; x \neq 1\end{aligned}$$

Additional Topics in Math

Note: The PSAT has only two questions covering all of the content in this section. Consider focusing on other math topics before spending time on this section.

Questions in this section will test geometric and trigonometric concepts and the Pythagorean Theorem. The student should be familiar with geometric concepts such as volume, radius, diameter, chord length, angle, arc, and sector area. The questions will give certain information about a figure and require the student to solve for some missing information. Any required volume formulas will be provided on the test. The trigonometry questions will require students to use trigonometric ratios and the Pythagorean Theorem to solve problems dealing with right triangles. The student should be able to use these ratios and the Pythagorean Theorem to solve for missing lengths and angle measures in right triangles.

Two-Dimensional Shapes

Triangles

A triangle is a three-sided figure with the sum of its interior angles being 180° The **perimeter of any triangle** is found by summing the three side lengths; $P = a + b + c$. For an equilateral triangle, this is the same as $P = 3a$, where a is any side length, since all three sides are the same length.

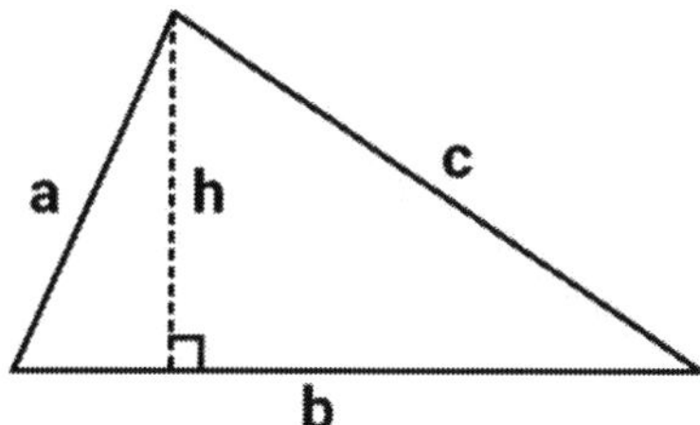

The **area of any triangle** can be found by taking half the product of one side length referred to as the base, often given the variable b and the perpendicular distance from that side to the opposite vertex called the altitude or height and given the variable h. In equation form that is $A = \frac{1}{2}bh$. Another formula that works for any triangle is $A = \sqrt{s(s-a)(s-b)(s-c)}$, where s is the semiperimeter: $\frac{a+b+c}{2}$, and a, b, and c are the lengths of the three sides. Special cases include isosceles triangles: $A = \frac{1}{2}b\sqrt{a^2 - \frac{b^2}{4}}$, where b is the unique side and a is the length of one of the two congruent sides, and equilateral triangles: $A = \frac{\sqrt{3}}{4}a^2$, where a is the length of a side.

Review Video: Area and Perimeter of a Triangle
Visit mometrix.com/academy and enter code: 853779

Parts of a Triangle

An **altitude** of a triangle is a line segment drawn from one vertex perpendicular to the opposite side. In the diagram below, $\overline{BE}$, $\overline{AD}$, and $\overline{CF}$ are altitudes. The length of an altitude is also called the height of the triangle. The three altitudes in a triangle are always concurrent. The point of concurrency of the altitudes of a triangle, O, is called the **orthocenter**. Note that in an obtuse triangle, the orthocenter will be outside the triangle, and in a right triangle, the orthocenter is the vertex of the right angle.

A **median** of a triangle is a line segment drawn from one vertex to the midpoint of the opposite side. In the diagram below, $\overline{BH}$, $\overline{AG}$, and $\overline{CI}$ are medians. This is not the same as the altitude, except the altitude to the base of an isosceles triangle and all three altitudes of an equilateral triangle. The point of concurrency of the medians of a triangle, T, is called the **centroid**. This is the same point as the orthocenter only in an equilateral triangle. Unlike the orthocenter, the centroid is always inside the triangle. The centroid can also be considered the exact center of the triangle. Any shape triangle can be perfectly balanced on a tip placed at the centroid. The centroid is also the point that is two-thirds the distance from the vertex to the opposite side.

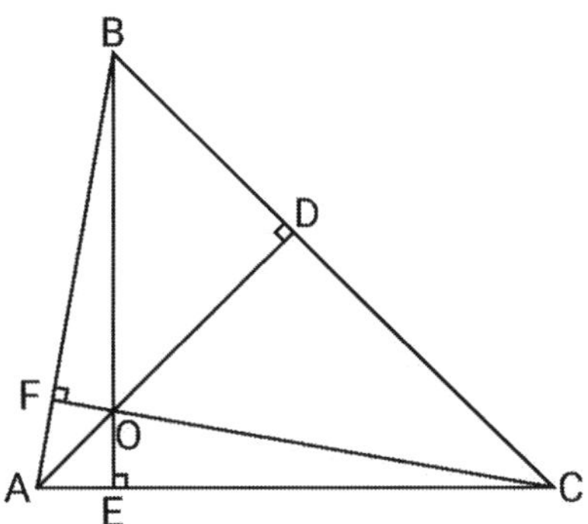

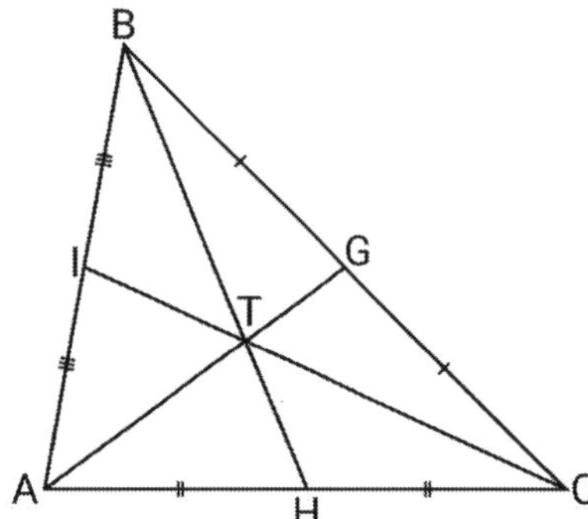

QUADRILATERALS

A **quadrilateral** is a closed two-dimensional geometric figure that has four straight sides. The sum of the interior angles of any quadrilateral is $360°$.

Parallelogram: A quadrilateral that has two pairs of opposite parallel sides. As such it is a special type of trapezoid. The sides that are parallel are also congruent. The opposite interior angles are always congruent, and the consecutive interior angles are supplementary. The diagonals of a parallelogram divide each other. Each diagonal divides the parallelogram into two congruent triangles. A parallelogram has no line of symmetry, but does have 180-degree rotational symmetry about the midpoint.

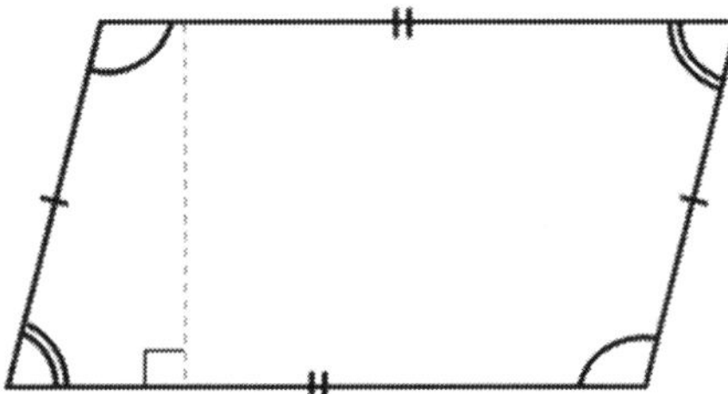

The **area of a parallelogram** is found by the formula $A = bh$, where b is the length of the base, and h is the height. Note that the base and height correspond to the length and width in a rectangle, so this formula would apply to rectangles as well. Do not confuse the height of a parallelogram with the length of the second side. The two are only the same measure in the case of a rectangle.

The **perimeter of a parallelogram** is found by the formula $P = 2a + 2b$ or $P = 2(a + b)$, where a and b are the lengths of the two sides.

Review Video: Parallelogram
Visit mometrix.com/academy and enter code: 129981

Review Video: Area and Perimeter of a Parallelogram
Visit mometrix.com/academy and enter code: 718313

Isosceles trapezoid: A trapezoid with equal base angles. This gives rise to other properties including: the two nonparallel sides have the same length, the two non-base angles are also equal, and there is one line of symmetry through the midpoints of the parallel sides.

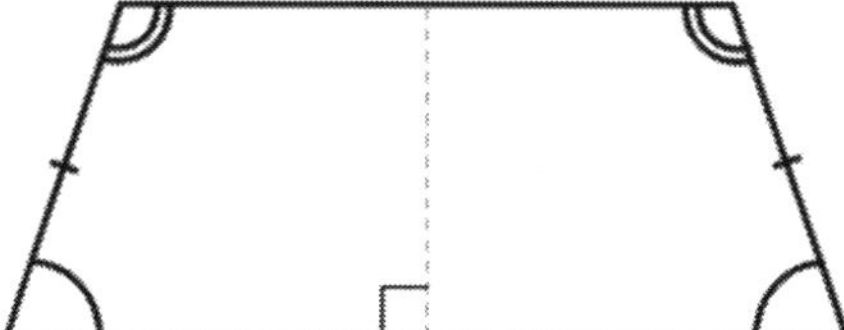

Rectangle: A quadrilateral with four right angles. All rectangles are parallelograms and trapezoids, but not all parallelograms or trapezoids are rectangles. The diagonals of a rectangle are congruent. Rectangles have 2 lines of symmetry (through each pair of opposing midpoints) and 180-degree rotational symmetry about the midpoint.

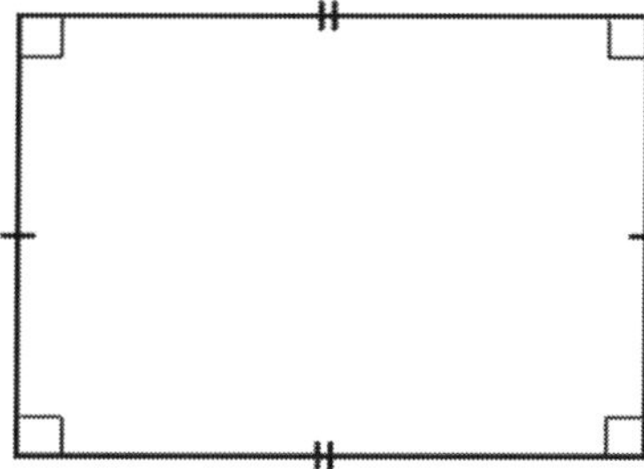

The **area of a rectangle** is found by the formula $A = lw$, where A is the area of the rectangle, l is the length (usually considered to be the longer side) and w is the width (usually considered to be the shorter side). The numbers for l and w are interchangeable.

The **perimeter of a rectangle** is found by the formula $P = 2l + 2w$ or $P = 2(l + w)$, where l is the length, and w is the width. It may be easier to add the length and width first and then double the result, as in the second formula.

Review Video: Area and Perimeter of a Rectangle
Visit mometrix.com/academy and enter code: 933707

Square: A quadrilateral with four right angles and four congruent sides. Squares satisfy the criteria of all other types of quadrilaterals. The diagonals of a square are congruent and perpendicular to each other. Squares have 4 lines of symmetry (through each pair of opposing midpoints and along each of the diagonals) as well as 90-degree rotational symmetry about the midpoint.

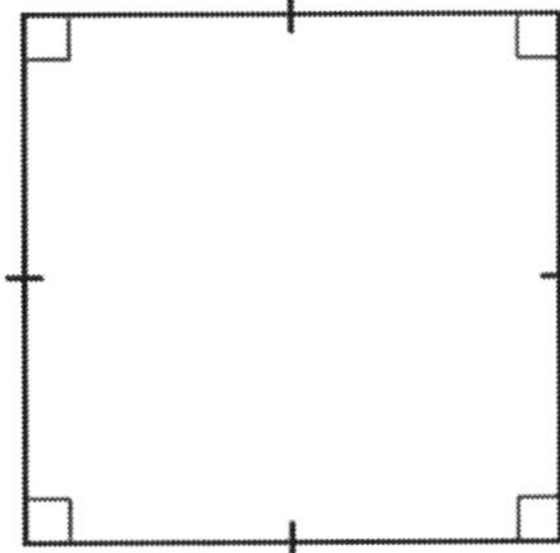

The **area of a square** is found by using the formula $A = s^2$, where s is the length of one side. The **perimeter of a square** is found by using the formula $P = 4s$, where s is the length of one side. Because all four sides are equal in a square, it is faster to multiply the length of one side by 4 than to add the same number four times. You could use the formulas for rectangles and get the same answer.

Review Video: Area and Perimeter of a Square
Visit mometrix.com/academy and enter code: 620902

CIRCLES

The **center** of a circle is the single point from which every point on the circle is **equidistant**. The **radius** is a line segment that joins the center of the circle and any one point on the circle. All radii of a circle are equal. Circles that have the same center, but not the same length of radii are **concentric**. The **diameter** is a line segment that passes through the center of the circle and has both endpoints on the circle. The length of the diameter is exactly twice the length of the radius. Point O in the diagram below is the center of the circle, segments $\overline{OX}$, $\overline{OY}$, and $\overline{OZ}$ are radii, and segment $\overline{XZ}$ is a diameter.

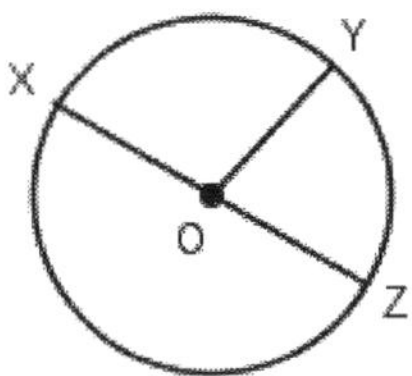

Review Video: Points of a Circle
Visit mometrix.com/academy and enter code: 420746

Review Video: The Diameter, Radius, and Circumference of Circles
Visit mometrix.com/academy and enter code: 448988

The **area of a circle** is found by the formula $A = \pi r^2$, where r is the length of the radius. If the diameter of the circle is given, remember to divide it in half to get the length of the radius before proceeding.

The **circumference** of a circle is found by the formula $C = 2\pi r$, where r is the radius. Again, remember to convert the diameter if you are given that measure rather than the radius.

Review Video: Area and Circumference of a Circle
Visit mometrix.com/academy and enter code: 243015

SOLVING PROBLEMS WITH SIMILARITY AND CONGRUENCE

Congruent figures have the same size and same shape. Similar figures have the same shape but not the same size; their corresponding angles are congruent and their sides are proportional. All circles are similar. All squares are similar; likewise, all regular n-gons are similar to other regular n-gons. These concepts may appear in different types of test questions. For example, if a line is drawn through that triangle such that it is parallel to one side, a triangle similar to the original triangle is formed. The corresponding angles are congruent, and proportional relationships can be used to determine missing side lengths from the given information. Also, if parallel lines are cut by two transversals which intersect between or outside of parallel lines, two similar triangles are formed. If an altitude is drawn from the vertex of an isosceles triangle, two congruent triangles are formed. If an altitude is drawn from the vertex of the right angle to the hypotenuse of a right triangle, the two triangles that are formed are similar to each other and to the original right triangle.

PRACTICE

P1. Find the area and perimeter of the following quadrilaterals:

(a) A square with side length 2.5 cm.

(b) A parallelogram with height 3 m, base 4 m, and other side 6 m.

P2. Calculate the area of a triangle with side lengths of 7 ft, 8 ft, and 9 ft.

PRACTICE SOLUTIONS

P1. (a) $A = s^2 = (2.5 \text{ cm})^2 = 6.25 \text{ cm}^2$; $P = 4s = 4 \times 2.5 \text{ cm} = 10 \text{ cm}$

(b) $A = bh = (3 \text{ m})(4 \text{ m}) = 12 \text{ m}^2$; $P = 2a + 2b = 2 \times 6 \text{ m} + 2 \times 4 \text{ m} = 20 \text{ m}$

P2. Given only side lengths, we can use the semi perimeter to the find the area based on the formula, $A = \sqrt{s(s-a)(s-b)(s-c)}$, where s is the semiperimeter, $\frac{a+b+c}{2} = \frac{7+8+9}{2} = 12$ ft:

$$\begin{aligned} A &= \sqrt{12(12-7)(12-8)(12-9)} \\ &= \sqrt{(12)(5)(4)(3)} \\ &= 12\sqrt{5} \text{ ft}^2 \end{aligned}$$

THREE-DIMENSIONAL SHAPES

You should expect to be asked questions concerning volumes of figures such as rectangular prisms and cylinders. You may be asked to use information such as length of a side, area of a face, or volume of a solid to calculate missing information. Area formulas for circles, rectangles, and triangles and volume formulas for rectangular prisms and cylinders are provided with the test. It is important to understand that the volume calculations may be more complicated than simply applying basic formulas. For example, you may be asked to find the volume of a hexagonal nut and given that the volume of a prism is $V = Bh$, where B is the area of the base and h is the height of the prism. Since you are not given the area formula for a regular hexagon, however, you must find the area by adding the areas of the six equilateral triangles which comprise the hexagon. Once you calculate the area of the base, you can find the volume of a hexagonal prism by multiplying the area of the base and the height; afterward, you must subtract the volume of the cylindrical hole from the volume of the hexagonal prism to find the volume of the hexagonal nut.

SOLIDS

The **surface area of a solid object** is the area of all sides or exterior surfaces. For objects such as prisms and pyramids, a further distinction is made between base surface area (B) and lateral surface area (LA). For a prism, the total surface area (SA) is $SA = LA + 2B$. For a pyramid or cone, the total surface area is $SA = LA + B$.

Review Video: How to Calculate the Volume of 3D Objects
Visit mometrix.com/academy and enter code: 163343

The **surface area of a sphere** can be found by the formula $A = 4\pi r^2$, where r is the radius. The volume is given by the formula $V = \frac{4}{3}\pi r^3$, where r is the radius. Both quantities are generally given in terms of π.

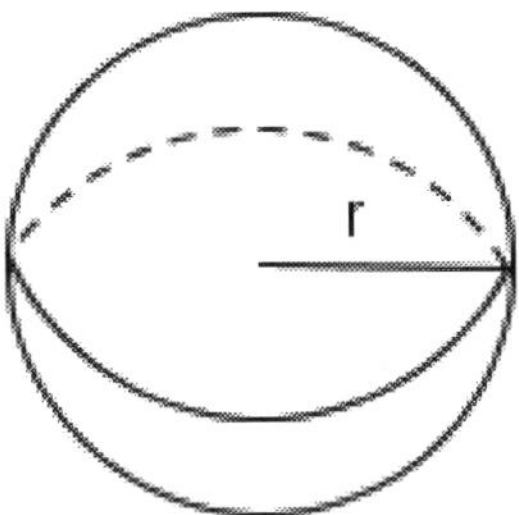

Review Video: Volume and Surface Area of a Sphere
Visit mometrix.com/academy and enter code: 786928

The **volume of any prism** is found by the formula $V = Bh$, where B is the area of the base, and h is the height (perpendicular distance between the bases). The surface area of any prism is the sum of the areas of both bases and all sides. It can be calculated as $SA = 2B + Ph$, where P is the perimeter of the base.

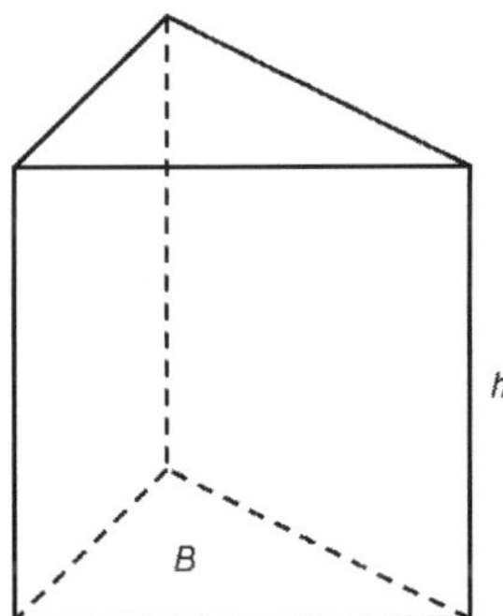

For a **rectangular prism**, the volume can be found by the formula $V = lwh$, where V is the volume, l is the length, w is the width, and h is the height. The surface area can be calculated as $SA = 2lw + 2hl + 2wh$ or $SA = 2(lw + hl + wh)$.

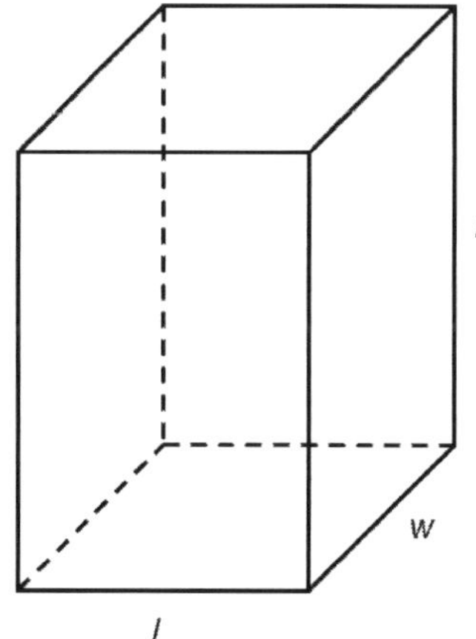

The **volume of a cube** can be found by the formula $V = s^3$, where s is the length of a side. The surface area of a cube is calculated as $SA = 6s^2$, where SA is the total surface area and s is the length of a side. These formulas are the same as the ones used for the volume and surface area of a rectangular prism, but simplified since all three quantities (length, width, and height) are the same.

Review Video: Volume and Surface Area of a Cube
Visit mometrix.com/academy and enter code: 664455

The **volume of a cylinder** can be calculated by the formula $V = \pi r^2 h$, where r is the radius, and h is the height. The surface area of a cylinder can be found by the formula $SA = 2\pi r^2 + 2\pi rh$. The first term is the base area multiplied by two, and the second term is the perimeter of the base multiplied by the height.

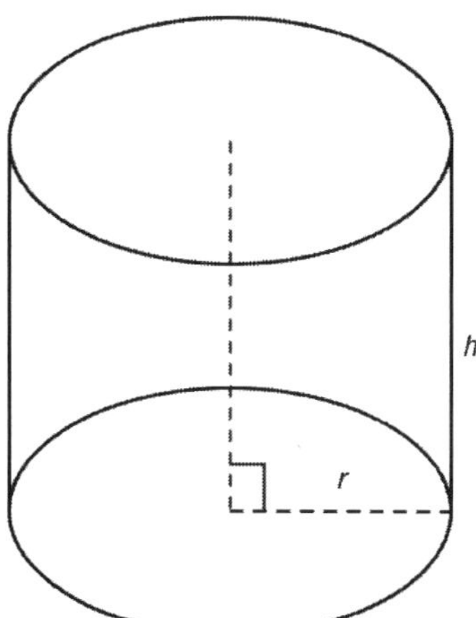

Review Video: Volume and Surface Area of a Right Circular Cylinder
Visit mometrix.com/academy and enter code: 226463

The **volume of a pyramid** is found by the formula $V = \frac{1}{3}Bh$, where B is the area of the base, and h is the height (perpendicular distance from the vertex to the base). Notice this formula is the same as $\frac{1}{3}$ times the volume of a prism. Like a prism, the base of a pyramid can be any shape.

Finding the **surface area of a pyramid** is not as simple as the other shapes we've looked at thus far. If the pyramid is a right pyramid, meaning the base is a regular polygon and the vertex is directly over the center of that polygon, the surface area can be calculated as $SA = B + \frac{1}{2}Ph_s$, where P is the perimeter of the base, and h_s is the slant height (distance from the vertex to the midpoint of one side of the base). If the pyramid is irregular, the area of each triangle side must be calculated individually and then summed, along with the base.

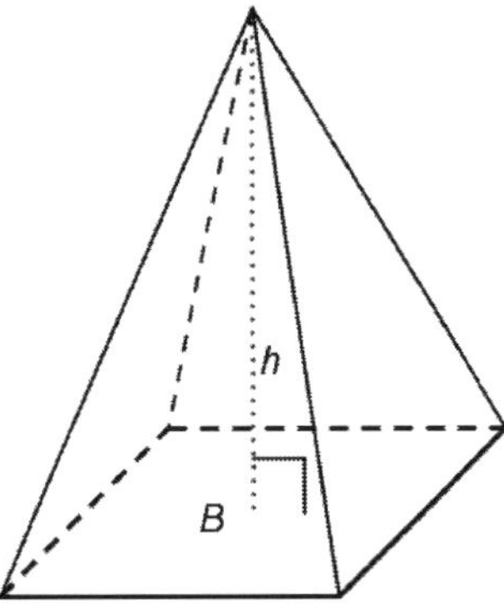

Review Video: Volume and Surface Area of a Pyramid
Visit mometrix.com/academy and enter code: 621932

The **volume of a cone** is found by the formula $V = \frac{1}{3}\pi r^2 h$, where r is the radius, and h is the height. Notice this is the same as $\frac{1}{3}$ times the volume of a cylinder. The surface area can be calculated as $SA = \pi r^2 + \pi rs$, where s is the slant height. The slant height can be calculated using the Pythagorean theorem to be $\sqrt{r^2 + h^2}$, so the surface area formula can also be written as $SA = \pi r^2 + \pi r\sqrt{r^2 + h^2}$.

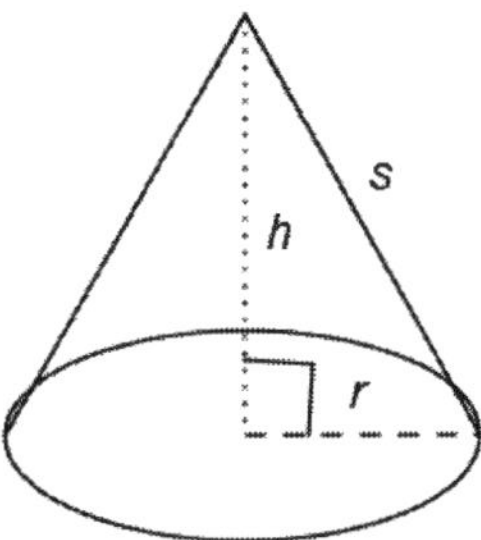

Review Video: Volume and Surface Area of a Right Circular Cone
Visit mometrix.com/academy and enter code: 573574

PRACTICE

P1. Find the surface area and volume of the following solids:

(a) A cylinder with radius 5 m and height 0.5 m.

(b) A trapezoidal prism with base area of 254 mm^2, base perimeter 74 mm, and height 10 mm.

(c) A half sphere (radius 5 yds) on the base of an inverted cone with the same radius and a height of 7 yds.

PRACTICE SOLUTIONS

P1. (a) $SA = 2\pi r^2 + 2\pi rh = 2\pi(5\text{ m})^2 + 2\pi(5\text{ m})(0.5\text{ m}) = 55\pi\text{ m}^2 \cong 172.79\text{ m}^2$;
$V = \pi r^2 h = \pi(5\text{ m})^2(0.5\text{ m}) = 12.5\pi\text{ m}^3 \cong 39.27\text{ m}^3$

(b) $SA = 2B + Ph = 2(254\text{ mm}^2) + (74\text{ mm})(10\text{ mm}) = 1248\text{ mm}^2$;
$V = Bh = (254\text{ mm}^2)(10\text{ mm}) = 2540\text{ mm}^3$

(c) We can find s, the slant height using Pythagoras' theorem, and since this solid is made of parts of simple solids, we can combine the formulas to find surface area and volume:

$$s = \sqrt{r^2 + h^2} = \sqrt{(5\text{ yd})^2 + (7\text{ yd})^2} = \sqrt{74}\text{ yd}$$

$$SA = \frac{4\pi r^2}{2} + \pi rs = \frac{4\pi(5\text{ yd})^2}{2} + \pi(5\text{ yd})(\sqrt{74}\text{ yd}) = (5\pi + 5\pi\sqrt{74})\text{ yd}^2 \cong 150.83\text{ yd}^2$$

$$V = \frac{1}{3}\pi r^2 h = \frac{1}{3}\pi(5\text{ yd})^2(7\text{ yd}) = \frac{35\pi}{3}\text{ yd}^3 \cong 36.65\text{ yd}^3$$

LINES AND PLANES

A **point** is a fixed location in space; has no size or dimensions; commonly represented by a dot. A **line** is a set of points that extends infinitely in two opposite directions. It has length, but no width or depth. A line can be defined by any two distinct points that it contains. A **line segment** is a portion of a line that has definite endpoints. A **ray** is a portion of a line that extends from a single point on that line in one direction along the line. It has a definite beginning, but no ending.

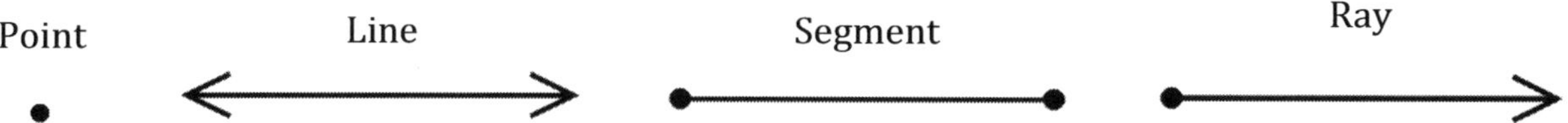

Intersecting lines are lines that have exactly one point in common. **Concurrent lines** are multiple lines that intersect at a single point. **Perpendicular lines** are lines that intersect at right angles. They are represented by the symbol ⊥. The shortest distance from a line to a point not on the line is a perpendicular segment from the point to the line. **Parallel lines** are lines in the same plane that have no points in common and never meet. It is possible for lines to be in different planes, have no points in common, and never meet, but they are not parallel because they are in different planes.

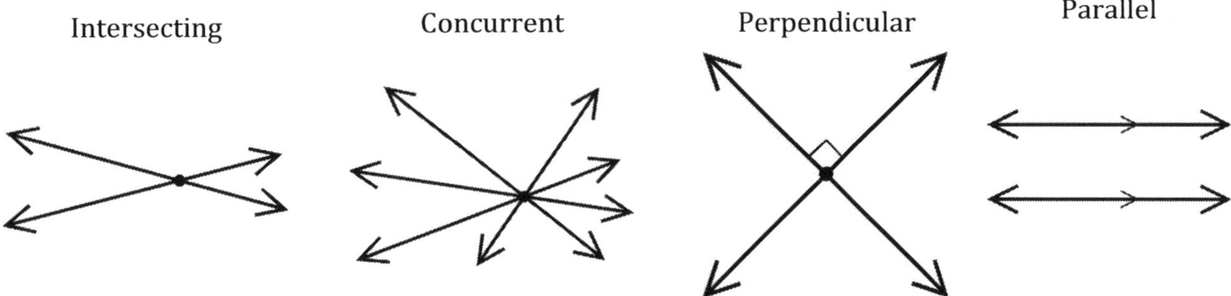

A **transversal** is a line that intersects at least two other lines, which may or may not be parallel to one another. A transversal that intersects parallel lines is a common occurrence in geometry. A **bisector** is a line or line segment that divides another line segment into two equal lengths. A **perpendicular bisector** of a line segment is composed of points that are equidistant from the endpoints of the segment it is dividing.

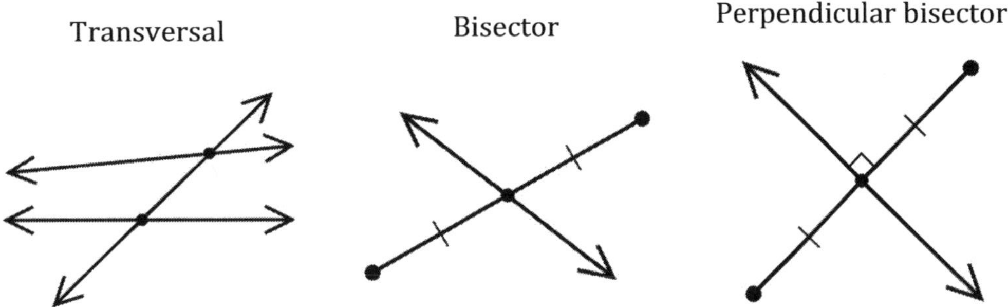

The **projection of a point on a line** is the point at which a perpendicular line drawn from the given point to the given line intersects the line. This is also the shortest distance from the given point to the line. The **projection of a segment on a line** is a segment whose endpoints are the points formed when perpendicular lines are drawn from the endpoints of the given segment to the given line. This is similar to the length a diagonal line appears to be when viewed from above.

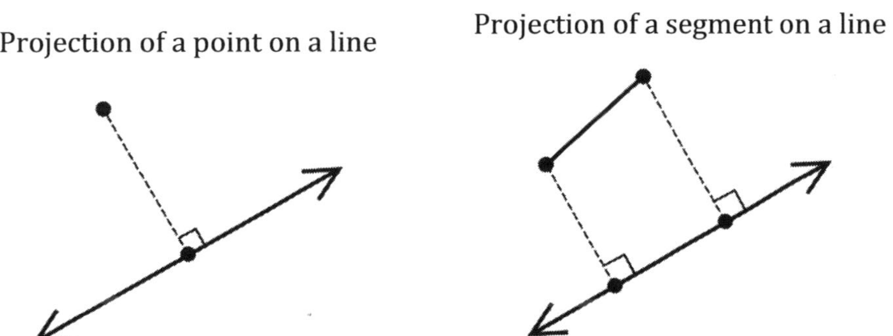

A **plane** is a two-dimensional flat surface defined by three non-collinear points. A plane extends an infinite distance in all directions in those two dimensions. It contains an infinite number of points, parallel lines and segments, intersecting lines and segments, as well as parallel or intersecting rays. A plane will never contain a three-dimensional figure or skew lines, lines that don't intersect and are not parallel. Two given planes are either parallel or they intersect at a line. A plane may intersect a circular conic surface to form **conic sections**, such as a parabola, hyperbola, circle or ellipse.

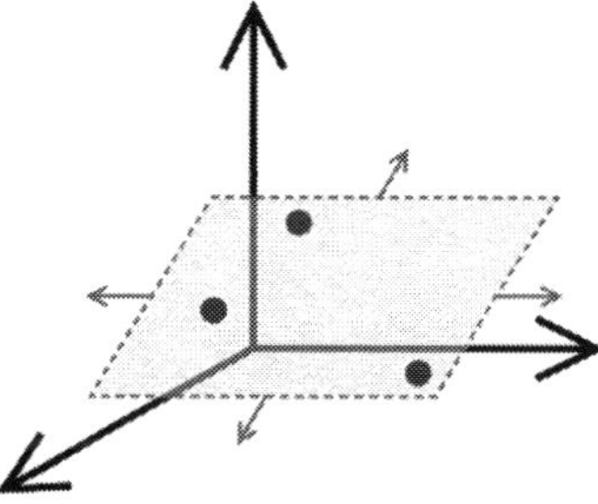

Review Video: Lines and Planes
Visit mometrix.com/academy and enter code: 554267

ANGLES

An **angle** is formed when two lines or line segments meet at a common point. It may be a common starting point for a pair of segments or rays, or it may be the intersection of lines. Angles are represented by the symbol ∠.

The **vertex** is the point at which two segments or rays meet to form an angle. If the angle is formed by intersecting rays, lines, and/or line segments, the vertex is the point at which four angles are formed. The pairs of angles opposite one another are called vertical angles, and their measures are equal.

- An **acute** angle is an angle with a degree measure less than 90°.
- A **right** angle is an angle with a degree measure of exactly 90°.
- An **obtuse** angle is an angle with a degree measure greater than 90° but less than 180°.
- A **straight angle** is an angle with a degree measure of exactly 180°. This is also a semicircle.
- A **reflex angle** is an angle with a degree measure greater than 180° but less than 360°.
- A **full angle** is an angle with a degree measure of exactly 360°.

Two angles whose sum is exactly 90° are said to be **complementary**. The two angles may or may not be adjacent. In a right triangle, the two acute angles are complementary.

Two angles whose sum is exactly 180° are said to be **supplementary**. The two angles may or may not be adjacent. Two intersecting lines always form two pairs of supplementary angles. Adjacent supplementary angles will always form a straight line.

Two angles that have the same vertex and share a side are said to be **adjacent**. Vertical angles are not adjacent because they share a vertex but no common side.

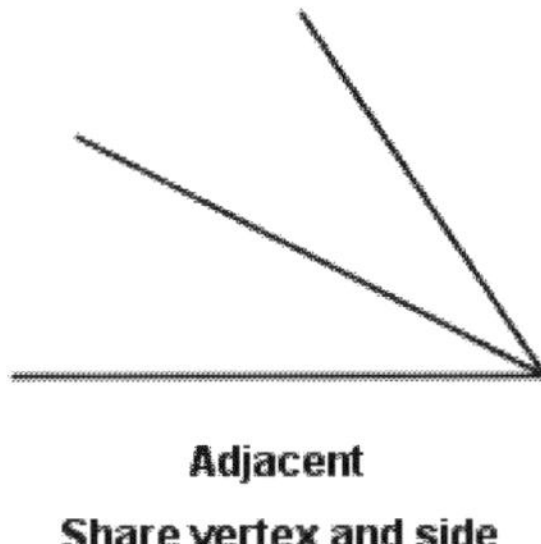

Adjacent
Share vertex and side

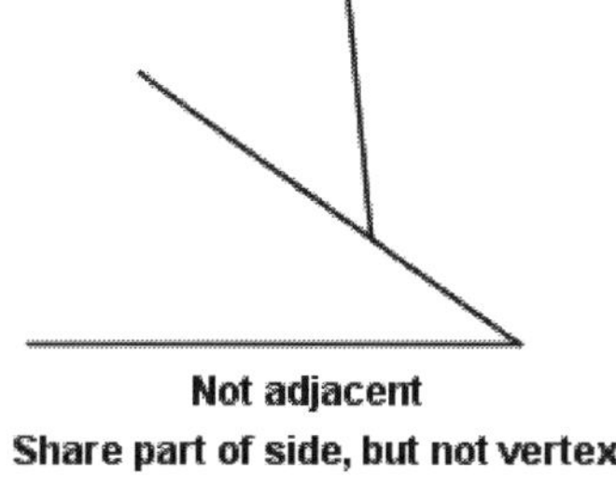

Not adjacent
Share part of side, but not vertex

When two parallel lines are cut by a transversal, the angles that are between the two parallel lines are **interior angles**. In the diagram below, angles 3, 4, 5, and 6 are interior angles.

When two parallel lines are cut by a transversal, the angles that are outside the parallel lines are **exterior angles**. In the diagram below, angles 1, 2, 7, and 8 are exterior angles.

When two parallel lines are cut by a transversal, the angles that are in the same position relative to the transversal and a parallel line are **corresponding angles**. The diagram below has four pairs of corresponding angles: angles 1 and 5; angles 2 and 6; angles 3 and 7; and angles 4 and 8. Corresponding angles formed by parallel lines are congruent.

When two parallel lines are cut by a transversal, the two interior angles that are on opposite sides of the transversal are called **alternate interior angles**. In the diagram below, there are two pairs of alternate interior angles: angles 3 and 6, and angles 4 and 5. Alternate interior angles formed by parallel lines are congruent.

When two parallel lines are cut by a transversal, the two exterior angles that are on opposite sides of the transversal are called **alternate exterior angles**.

Review Video: Angles
Visit mometrix.com/academy and enter code: 264624

In the diagram below, there are two pairs of alternate exterior angles: angles 1 and 8, and angles 2 and 7. Alternate exterior angles formed by parallel lines are congruent.

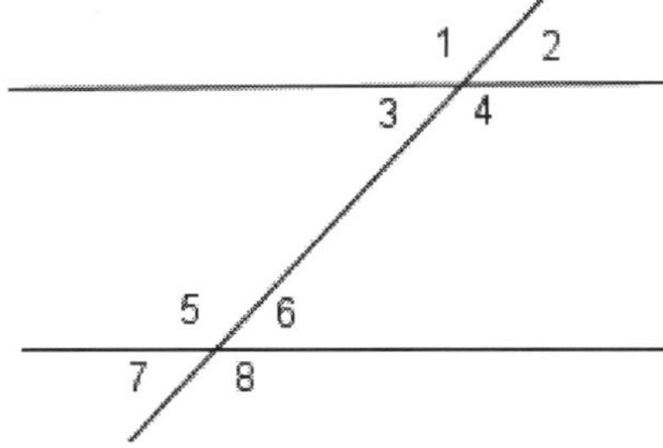

When two lines intersect, four angles are formed. The non-adjacent angles at this vertex are called vertical angles. Vertical angles are congruent. In the diagram, $\angle ABD \cong \angle CBE$ and $\angle ABC \cong \angle DBE$.

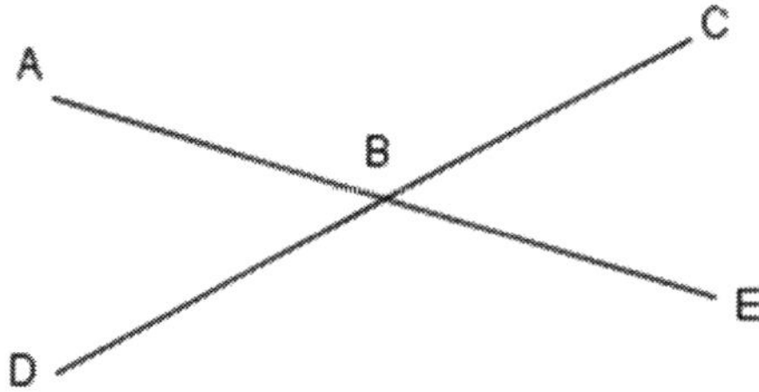

PRACTICE

P1. Find the measure of angles **(a)**, **(b)**, and **(c)** based on the figure with two parallel lines, two perpendicular lines and one transversal:

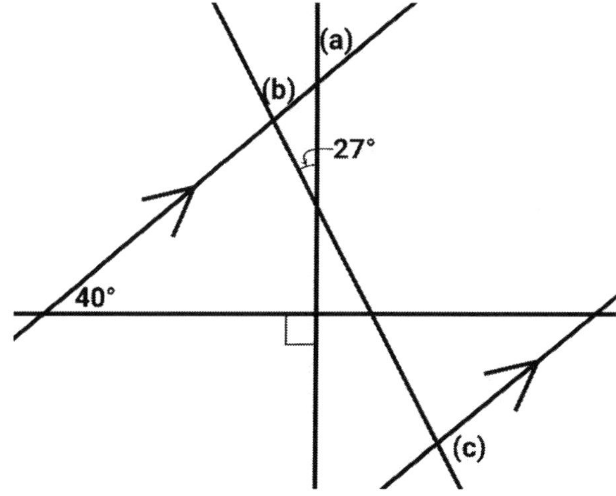

PRACTICE SOLUTIONS

P1. (a) The vertical angle paired with (a) is part of a right triangle with the 40° angle. Thus the measure can be found:

$$90° = 40° + a$$
$$a = 50°$$

(b) The triangle formed by the supplementary angle to (b) is part of a triangle with the vertical angle paired with (a) and the given angle of 27°. Since $a = 50°$:

$$180° = (180° - b) + 50° + 27°$$
$$103° = 180° - b$$
$$-77° = -b$$
$$77° = b$$

(c) As they are part of a transversal crossing parallel lines, angles (b) and (c) are supplementary. Thus $c = 103°$

$$V = \frac{1}{3}\pi r^2 h = \frac{1}{3}\pi (5 \text{ yd})^2 (7 \text{ yd}) = \frac{35\pi}{3} \text{ yd}^3 \cong 36.65 \text{ yd}^3$$

TRIGONOMETRY

PYTHAGOREAN THEOREM

The side of a triangle opposite the right angle is called the **hypotenuse**. The other two sides are called the legs. The Pythagorean theorem states a relationship among the legs and hypotenuse of a right triangle: $a^2 + b^2 = c^2$, where a and b are the lengths of the legs of a right triangle, and c is the length of the hypotenuse. Note that this formula will only work with right triangles.

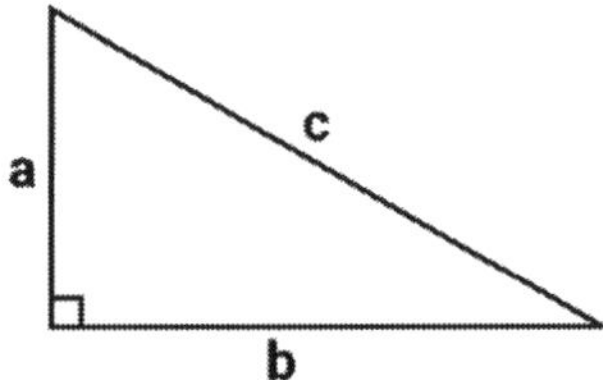

Review Video: Pythagorean Theorem
Visit mometrix.com/academy and enter code: 906576

TRIGONOMETRIC FORMULAS

In the diagram below, angle C is the right angle, and side c is the hypotenuse. Side a is the side opposite to angle A and side b is the side opposite to angle B. Using ratios of side lengths as a means to calculate the sine, cosine, and tangent of an acute angle only works for right triangles.

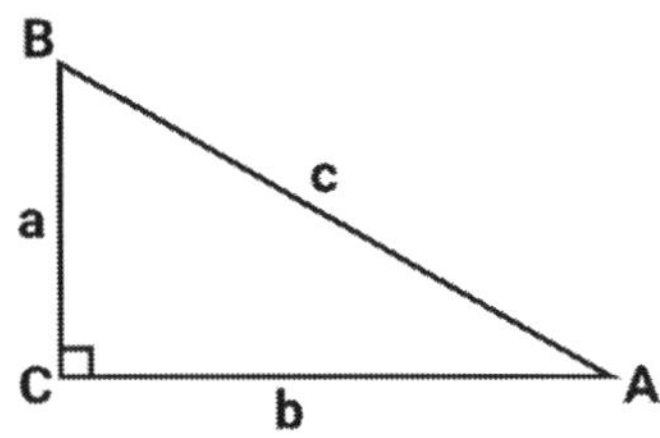

$$\sin A = \frac{\text{opposite side}}{\text{hypotenuse}} = \frac{a}{c} \qquad \csc A = \frac{1}{\sin A} = \frac{\text{hypotenuse}}{\text{opposite side}} = \frac{c}{a}$$

$$\cos A = \frac{\text{adjacent side}}{\text{hypotenuse}} = \frac{b}{c} \qquad \sec A = \frac{1}{\cos A} = \frac{\text{hypotenuse}}{\text{adjacent side}} = \frac{c}{b}$$

$$\tan A = \frac{\text{opposite side}}{\text{adjacent side}} = \frac{a}{b} \qquad \cot A = \frac{1}{\tan A} = \frac{\text{adjacent side}}{\text{opposite side}} = \frac{b}{a}$$

LAWS OF SINES AND COSINES

The **law of sines** states that $\frac{\sin A}{a} = \frac{\sin B}{b} = \frac{\sin C}{c}$, where A, B, and C are the angles of a triangle, and a, b, and c are the sides opposite their respective angles. This formula will work with all triangles, not just right triangles.

The **law of cosines** is given by the formula $c^2 = a^2 + b^2 - 2ab(\cos C)$, where a, b, and c are the sides of a triangle, and C is the angle opposite side c. This is a generalized form of the Pythagorean theorem that can be used on any triangle.

Review Video: Upper Level Trig (Law of Sines)
Visit mometrix.com/academy and enter code: 206844

Review Video: Law of Cosines
Visit mometrix.com/academy and enter code: 158911

PRACTICE

P1. Calculate the following values based on triangle MNO:

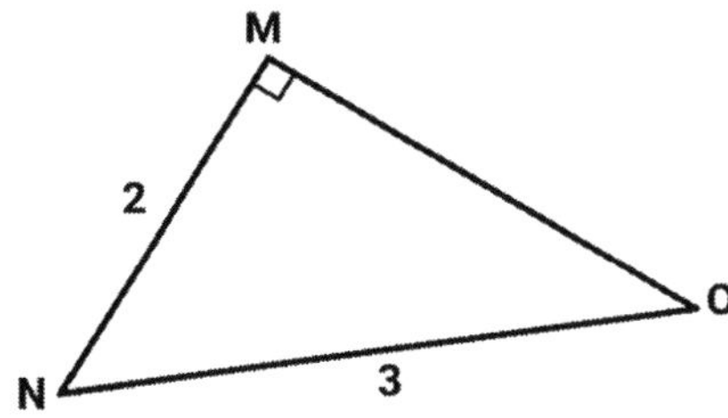

(a) length of $\overline{MO}$

(b) $\sin(\angle NOM)$

(c) area of the triangle, if the units of the measurements are in miles

PRACTICE SOLUTIONS

P1. (a) Since triangle MNO is a right triangle, we can use the simple form of Pythagoras theorem to find the missing side length:

$$\left(\overline{MO}\right)^2 + 2^2 = 3^2$$
$$\left(\overline{MO}\right)^2 = 9 - 4$$
$$\overline{MO} = \sqrt{5}$$

(b) Recall that sine of an angle in a right triangle is the ratio of the opposite side to the hypotenuse. So, $\sin(\angle NOM) = 2/3$

(c) Since triangle MNO is a right triangle, we can use either of the legs as the height and the other as the base in the simple formula for area of a triangle:

$$A = \frac{bh}{2}$$
$$= \frac{(2\text{ mi})(\sqrt{5}\text{ mi})}{2}$$
$$= \sqrt{5}\text{ mi}^2$$

DEGREES, RADIANS, AND THE UNIT CIRCLE

It is important to understand the deep connection between trigonometry and circles. Specifically, the two main units, **degrees** (°) and **radians** (rad), that are used to measure angles are related this way: 360° in one full circle and 2π radians in one full circle: $360° = 2\pi$ rad. The conversion factor relating the two is often stated as $\frac{180°}{\pi}$. For example, to convert $\frac{3\pi}{2}$ radians to degrees, multiply by the conversion factor: $\frac{3\pi}{2} \times \frac{180°}{\pi} = 270°$. As another example, to convert 60° to radians, divide by the conversion factor or multiply by the reciprocal: $60° \times \frac{\pi}{180°} = \frac{\pi}{3}$ radians.

Recall that the standard equation for a circle is $(x-h)^2 + (y-k)^2 = r^2$. A **unit circle** is a circle with a radius of 1 ($r = 1$) that has its center at the origin ($h = 0, k = 0$). Thus, the equation for the unit circle simplifies from the standard equation down to $x^2 + y^2 = 1$.

Standard position is the position of an angle of measure θ whose vertex is at the origin, the initial side crosses the unit circle at the point (1, 0), and the terminal side crosses the unit circle at some other point (a, b). In the standard position, $\sin\theta = b$, $\cos\theta = a$, and $\tan\theta = \frac{b}{a}$.

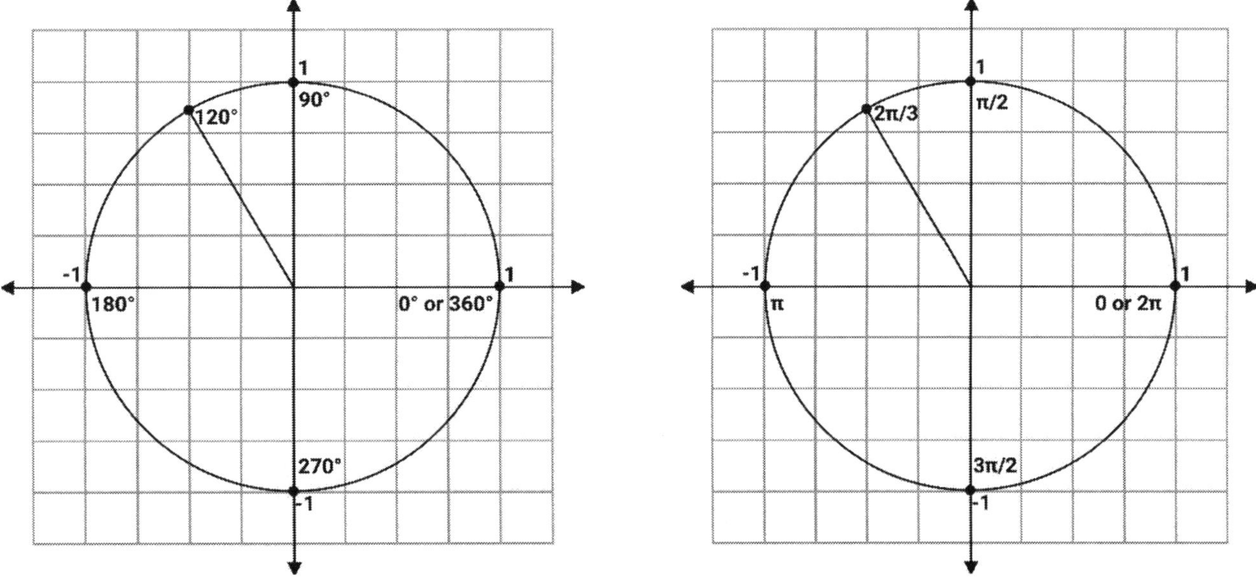

Review Video: Unit Circles and Standard Position
Visit mometrix.com/academy and enter code: 333922

You need to be able to evaluate trigonometric functions of angles in radian measure without your calculator. You may see a question that involves finding $\sin x$ in which $\frac{\pi}{2} < x < \pi$. It is important to be able recognize given intervals which indicate angle-containing quadrants, which are bound by 0, $\frac{\pi}{2}$, π, $\frac{3\pi}{2}$, and 2π.

Basic Trigonometric Functions

Sine

The **sine** (sin) function has a period of 360° or 2π radians. This means that its graph makes one complete cycle every 360° or 2π. Because $\sin 0 = 0$, the graph of $y = \sin x$ begins at the origin, with the x-axis representing the angle measure, and the y-axis representing the sine of the angle. The graph of the sine function is a smooth curve that begins at the origin, peaks at the point $\left(\frac{\pi}{2}, 1\right)$, crosses the x-axis at $(\pi, 0)$, has its lowest point at $\left(\frac{3\pi}{2}, -1\right)$, and returns to the x-axis to complete one cycle at $(2\pi, 0)$.

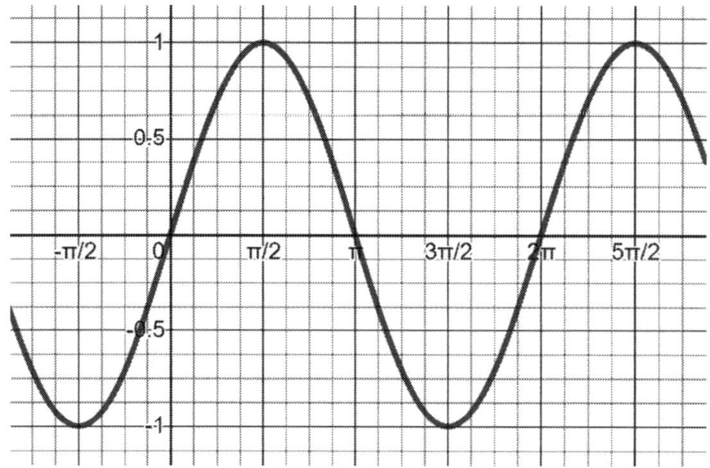

Review Video: Upper Level Trig: Sine
Visit mometrix.com/academy and enter code: 193339

Cosine

The **cosine** (cos) function also has a period of 360° or 2π radians, which means that its graph also makes one complete cycle every 360° or 2π. Because $\cos 0° = 1$, the graph of $y = \cos x$ begins at the point $(0, 1)$, with the x-axis representing the angle measure, and the y-axis representing the cosine of the angle. The graph of the cosine function is a smooth curve that begins at the point $(0, 1)$, crosses the x-axis at the point $\left(\frac{\pi}{2}, 0\right)$, has its lowest point at $(\pi, -1)$, crosses the x-axis again at the point $\left(\frac{3\pi}{2}, 0\right)$, and returns to a peak at the point $(2\pi, 1)$ to complete one cycle.

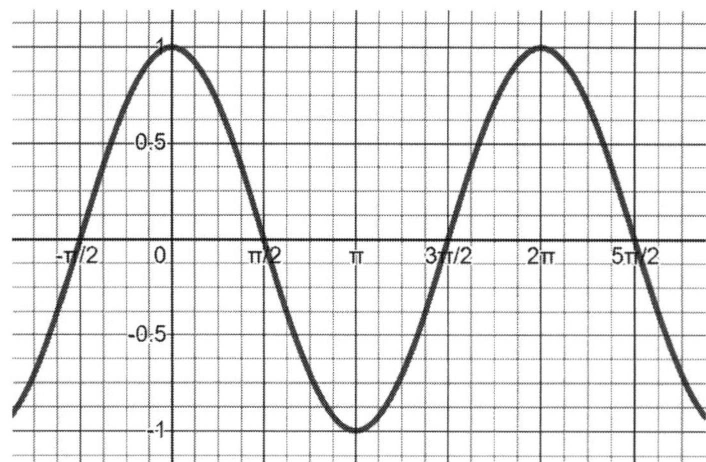

Review Video: Cosine
Visit mometrix.com/academy and enter code: 361120

Tangent

The **tangent** (tan) function has a period of 180° or π radians, which means that its graph makes one complete cycle every 180° or π radians. The x-axis represents the angle measure, and the y-axis represents the tangent of the angle. The graph of the tangent function is a series of smooth curves that cross the x-axis at every 180° or π radians and have an asymptote every $k \times 90°$ or $\frac{k\pi}{2}$ radians, where k is an odd integer. This can be explained by the fact that the tangent is calculated by dividing the sine by the cosine, since the cosine equals zero at those asymptote points.

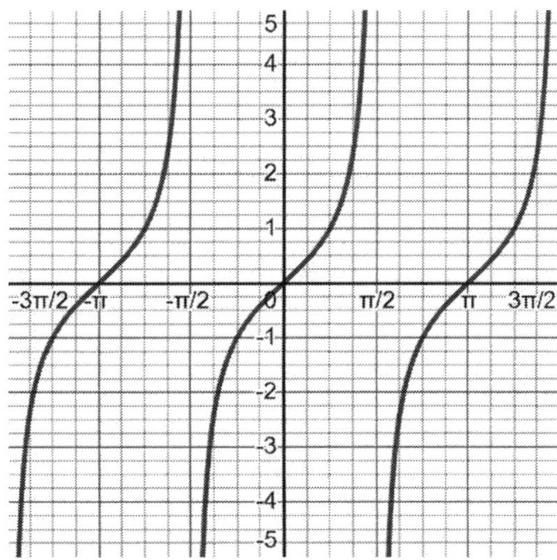

Review Video: Upper Level Trig: Tangent
Visit mometrix.com/academy and enter code: 947639

DEFINED AND RECIPROCAL FUNCTIONS

The tangent function is defined as the ratio of the sine to the cosine: $\tan x = \frac{\sin x}{\cos x}$

To take the reciprocal of a number means to place that number as the denominator of a fraction with a numerator of 1. The reciprocal functions are thus defined quite simply.

Cosecant	$\csc x$	$\frac{1}{\sin x}$
Secant	$\sec x$	$\frac{1}{\cos x}$
Cotangent	$\cot x$	$\frac{1}{\tan x}$

It is important to know these reciprocal functions, but they are not as commonly used as the three basic functions.

Review Video: Defined and Reciprocal Functions
Visit mometrix.com/academy and enter code: 996431

INVERSE FUNCTIONS

Each of the trigonometric functions accepts an angular measure, either degrees or radians, and gives a numerical value as the output. The inverse functions do the opposite; they accept a numerical value and give an angular measure as the output. The inverse of sine, or arcsine, commonly written as either $\sin^{-1} x$ or $\arcsin x$, gives the angle whose sine is x. Similarly:

The inverse of $\cos x$ is written as $\cos^{-1} x$ or $\arccos x$ and means the angle whose cosine is x.
The inverse of $\tan x$ is written as $\tan^{-1} x$ or $\arctan x$ and means the angle whose tangent is x.
The inverse of $\csc x$ is written as $\csc^{-1} x$ or $\text{arccsc}\, x$ and means the angle whose cosecant is x.
The inverse of $\sec x$ is written as $\sec^{-1} x$ or $\text{arcsec}\, x$ and means the angle whose secant is x.
The inverse of $\cot x$ is written as $\cot^{-1} x$ or $\text{arccot}\, x$ and means the angle whose cotangent is x.

Review Video: Inverse of a Cosine
Visit mometrix.com/academy and enter code: 156054

Review Video: Inverse of a Tangent
Visit mometrix.com/academy and enter code: 229055

IMPORTANT NOTE ABOUT SOLVING TRIGONOMETRIC EQUATIONS

Trigonometric and algebraic equations are solved following the same rules, but while algebraic expressions have one unique solution, trigonometric equations could have multiple solutions, and you must find them all. When solving for an angle with a known trigonometric value, you must consider the sign and include all angles with that value. Your calculator will probably only give one value as an answer, typically in the following ranges:

- For $\sin^{-1} x$, $\left[-\frac{\pi}{2}, \frac{\pi}{2}\right]$ or [-90°, 90°]
- For $\cos^{-1} x$, $[0, \pi]$ or [0°, 180°]
- For $\tan^{-1} x$, $\left[-\frac{\pi}{2}, \frac{\pi}{2}\right]$ or [-90°, 90°]

It is important to determine if there is another angle in a different quadrant that also satisfies the problem. To do this, find the other quadrant(s) with the same sign for that trigonometric function and find the angle that has the same reference angle. Then check whether this angle is also a solution.

- In the first quadrant, all six trigonometric functions are positive.
- In the second quadrant, sin and csc are positive.
- In the third quadrant, tan and cot are positive.
- In the fourth quadrant, cos and sec are positive.

If you remember the phrase, "ALL Students Take Classes," you will be able to remember the sign of each trigonometric function in each quadrant. ALL represents all the signs in the first quadrant. The "S" in "Students" represents the sine function and its reciprocal in the second quadrant. The "T" in "Take" represents the tangent function and its reciprocal in the third quadrant. The "C" in "Classes" represents the cosine function and its reciprocal.

DOMAIN, RANGE, AND ASYMPTOTES IN TRIGONOMETRY

The domain is the set of all possible real number values of x on the graph of a trigonometric function. Some graphs will impose limits on the values of x.

The range is the set of all possible real number values of y on the graph of a trigonometric function. Some graphs will impose limits on the values of y.

Asymptotes are lines which the graph of a trigonometric function approaches but never reaches. Asymptotes exist for values of x in the graphs of the tangent, cotangent, secant, and cosecant. The sine and cosine graphs do not have any asymptotes.

DOMAIN, RANGE, AND ASYMPTOTES OF THE SIX TRIGONOMETRIC FUNCTIONS

The domain, range, and asymptotes for each of the trigonometric functions are as follows:

- In the **sine** function, the domain is all real numbers, the range is $-1 \leq y \leq 1$, and there are no asymptotes.
- In the **cosine** function, the domain is all real numbers; the range is $-1 \leq y \leq 1$, and there are no asymptotes.
- In the **tangent** function, the domain is $x \in$ all real numbers; $x \neq \frac{\pi}{2} + k\pi$, the range is all real numbers; and the asymptotes are the lines $x = \frac{\pi}{2} + k\pi$.
- In the **cosecant** function, the domain is $x \in$ all real numbers; $x \neq k\pi$, the range is $(-\infty, -1]$ and $[1, \infty)$, and the asymptotes are the lines $x = k\pi$.
- In the **secant** function, the domain is $x \in$ all real numbers; $x \neq \frac{\pi}{2} + k\pi$, the range is $(-\infty, 1]$ and $[1, \infty)$, and the asymptotes are the lines $x = \frac{\pi}{2} + k\pi$.
- In the **cotangent** function, the domain is $x \in$ all real numbers; $x \neq k\pi$, the range is all real numbers, and the asymptotes are the lines $x = k\pi$.

In each of the above cases, k represents any integer.

TRIGONOMETRIC IDENTITIES

SUM AND DIFFERENCE

To find the sine, cosine, or tangent of the sum or difference of two angles, use one of the following formulas where α and β are two angles with known sine, cosine, or tangent values as needed:

$$\sin(\alpha \pm \beta) = \sin\alpha\cos\beta \pm \cos\alpha\sin\beta$$
$$\cos(\alpha \pm \beta) = \cos\alpha\cos\beta \mp \sin\alpha\sin\beta$$
$$\tan(\alpha \pm \beta) = \frac{\tan\alpha \pm \tan\beta}{1 \mp \tan\alpha\tan\beta}$$

HALF ANGLE

To find the sine or cosine of half of a known angle, use the following formulas where θ is an angle with a known exact cosine value:

$$\sin(\theta/2) = \pm\sqrt{(1 - cos\theta)/2}$$
$$\cos(\theta/2) = \pm\sqrt{(1 + \cos\theta)/2}$$

To determine the sign of the answer, you must recognize which quadrant the given angle is in and apply the correct sign for the trigonometric function you are using. If you need to find an expression for the exact sine or cosine of an angle that you do not know, such as sine 22.5°, you can rewrite the given angle as a half angle, such as $\sin\left(\frac{45°}{2}\right)$, and use the formula above:

$$\sin\left(\frac{45°}{2}\right) = \pm\sqrt{(1-\cos(45°))/2} = \pm\sqrt{\left(1-\frac{\sqrt{2}}{2}\right)/2} = \pm\sqrt{(2-\sqrt{2})/4} = \pm\frac{1}{2}\sqrt{(2-\sqrt{2})}$$

To find the tangent or cotangent of half of a known angle, use the following formulas where θ is an angle with known exact sine and cosine values:

$$\tan\frac{\theta}{2} = \frac{sin\theta}{1+\cos\theta}$$
$$\cot\frac{\theta}{2} = \frac{\sin\theta}{1-\cos\theta}$$

These formulas will work for finding the tangent or cotangent of half of any angle unless the cosine of θ happens to make the denominator of the identity equal to 0.

The Pythagorean theorem states that $a^2 + b^2 = c^2$ for all right triangles. The trigonometric identity that derives from this principle is stated in this way: $\sin^2\theta + \cos^2\theta = 1$

Dividing each term by either $\sin^2\theta$ or $\cos^2\theta$ yields two other identities, respectively:

$$1 + \cot^2\theta = \csc^2\theta$$
$$\tan^2\theta + 1 = \sec^2\theta$$

DOUBLE ANGLES

In each case, use one of the double angle formulas. To find the sine or cosine of twice a known angle, use one of the following formulas:

$$\sin(2\theta) = 2\sin\theta\cos\theta$$

$$\begin{aligned}\cos(2\theta) &= \cos^2\theta - \sin^2\theta \\ &= 2\cos^2\theta - 1 \\ &= 1 - 2\sin^2\theta\end{aligned}$$

To find the tangent or cotangent of twice a known angle, use the formulas where θ is an angle with known exact sine, cosine, tangent, and cotangent values:

$$\tan(2\theta) = \frac{2\tan\theta}{1-\tan^2\theta}$$
$$\cot(2\theta) = \frac{\cot\theta - \tan\theta}{2}$$

Products

To find the product of the sines and cosines of two different angles, use one of the following formulas where α and β are two unique angles:

$$\sin\alpha\sin\beta = \frac{1}{2}[\cos(\alpha-\beta)-\cos(\alpha+\beta)]$$
$$\cos\alpha\cos\beta = \frac{1}{2}[\cos(\alpha+\beta)+\cos(\alpha-\beta)]$$
$$\sin\alpha\cos\beta = \frac{1}{2}[\sin(\alpha+\beta)+\sin(\alpha-\beta)]$$
$$\cos\alpha\sin\beta = \frac{1}{2}[\sin(\alpha+\beta)-\sin(\alpha-\beta)]$$

Complementary

The trigonometric cofunction identities use the trigonometric relationships of complementary angles (angles whose sum is 90°). These are:

$$\cos x = \sin(90° - x)$$
$$\csc x = \sec(90° - x)$$
$$\cot x = \tan(90° - x)$$

Review Video: Complementary Angles
Visit mometrix.com/academy and enter code: 919405

Table of Commonly Encountered Angles

$0° = 0$ radians, $30° = \frac{\pi}{6}$ radians, $45° = \frac{\pi}{4}$ radians, $60° = \frac{\pi}{3}$ radians, and $90° = \frac{\pi}{2}$ radians

$\sin 0° = 0$	$\cos 0° = 1$	$\tan 0° = 0$
$\sin 30° = \frac{1}{2}$	$\cos 30° = \frac{\sqrt{3}}{2}$	$\tan 30° = \frac{\sqrt{3}}{3}$
$\sin 45° = \frac{\sqrt{2}}{2}$	$\cos 45° = \frac{\sqrt{2}}{2}$	$\tan 45° = 1$
$\sin 60° = \frac{\sqrt{3}}{2}$	$\cos 60° = \frac{1}{2}$	$\tan 60° = \sqrt{3}$
$\sin 90° = 1$	$\cos 90° = 0$	$\tan 90° =$ undefined
$\csc 0° =$ undefined	$\sec 0° = 1$	$\cot 0° =$ undefined
$\csc 30° = 2$	$\sec 30° = \frac{2\sqrt{3}}{3}$	$\cot 30° = \sqrt{3}$
$\csc 45° = \sqrt{2}$	$\sec 45° = \sqrt{2}$	$\cot 45° = 1$
$\csc 60° = \frac{2\sqrt{3}}{3}$	$\sec 60° = 2$	$\cot 60° = \frac{\sqrt{3}}{3}$
$\csc 90° = 1$	$\sec 90° =$ undefined	$\cot 90° = 0$

The values in the upper half of this table are values you should have memorized or be able to find quickly and those in the lower half can easily be determined as the reciprocal of the corresponding function.

Review Video: Commonly Encountered Angles
Visit mometrix.com/academy and enter code: 204098

RECTANGULAR AND POLAR COORDINATES

Rectangular coordinates are those that lie on the square grids of the Cartesian plane. They should be quite familiar to you. The polar coordinate system is based on a circular graph, rather than the square grid of the Cartesian system. Points in the polar coordinate system are in the format (r, θ), where r is the distance from the origin (think radius of the circle) and θ is the smallest positive angle (moving counterclockwise around the circle) made with the positive horizontal axis.

To convert a point from rectangular (x, y) format to polar (r, θ) format, use the formula (x, y) to $(r, \theta) \Rightarrow r = \sqrt{x^2 + y^2}; \theta = \arctan\frac{y}{x}$ when $x \neq 0$

Review Video: Rectangular and Polar Coordinate System
Visit mometrix.com/academy and enter code: 694585

Review Video: Converting Between Polar and Rectangular Formats
Visit mometrix.com/academy and enter code: 281325

If x is positive, use the positive square root value for r. If x is negative, use the negative square root value for r. If $x = 0$, use the following rules:

- If $y = 0$, then $\theta = 0$
- If $y > 0$, then $\theta = \frac{\pi}{2}$
- If $y < 0$, then $\theta = \frac{3\pi}{2}$

To convert a point from polar (r, θ) format to rectangular (x, y) format, use the formula (r, θ) to $(x, y) \Rightarrow x = r\cos\theta\,; y = r\sin\theta$

DE MOIVRE'S THEOREM

De Moivre's theorem is used to find the powers of complex numbers (numbers that contain the imaginary number i) written in polar form. Given a trigonometric expression that contains i, such as $z = r\cos x + ir\sin x$, where r is a real number and x is an angle measurement in polar form, use the formula $z^n = r^n(\cos nx + i\sin nx)$, where r and n are real numbers, x is the angle measure in polar form, and i is the imaginary number $i = \sqrt{-1}$. The expression $\cos x + i\sin x$ can be written cis x, making the formula appear in the format $z^n = r^n$ cis nx.

Note that De Moivre's theorem is only for angles in polar form. If you are given an angle in degrees, you must convert to polar form before using the formula.

PRACTICE

P1. Convert the following angles from degrees to radians:

(a) 56°

(b) 12°

(c) 199°

P2. Convert the following angles from radians to degrees:

(a) 3

(b) 3π

(c) 33

P3. Simplify the following trigonometric expressions:

(a) $\frac{\sin x \tan x + \cos x}{\sec x}$

(b) $\frac{4\cos 2x}{\sin^2 2x} + \sec^2 x$

Practice Solutions

P1. Multiply each by the conversion factor $\frac{\pi}{180°}$:

(a) $56° \times \frac{\pi}{180°} \cong 0.977$

(b) $12° \times \frac{\pi}{180°} \cong 0.209$

(c) $199° \times \frac{\pi}{180°} \cong 3.473$

P2. Multiply each by the conversion factor $\frac{180°}{\pi}$:

(a) $3 \times \frac{180°}{\pi} \cong 171.9°$

(b) $3\pi \times \frac{180°}{\pi} = 540° = 180°$

(c) $33 \times \frac{180°}{\pi} \cong 1890.8° \cong 90.8°$

P3. (a) Utilize trigonometric identities and definitions to simplify. Specifically, $\tan x = \frac{\sin x}{\cos x}$, $\sec x = \frac{1}{\cos x}$, and $\sin^2 x + \cos^2 x = 1$:

$$\begin{aligned} \frac{\sin x \tan x + \cos x}{\sec x} &= \left(\sin x \frac{\sin x}{\cos x} + \cos x\right)\cos x \\ &= \frac{\sin^2 x}{\cos x}\cos x + \cos^2 x \\ &= \sin^2 x + \cos^2 x \\ &= 1 \end{aligned}$$

(b) Utilize trigonometric identities and definitions to simplify. Specifically, double angle formulas, $\sin^2 x = (\sin x)^2$, and $\sin^2 x + \cos^2 x = 1$:

$$\begin{aligned}
\frac{4\cos 2x}{\sin^2 2x} + \sec^2 x &= \frac{4(\cos^2 x - \sin^2 x)}{4\sin^2 x \cos^2 x} + \sec^2 x \\
&= \frac{\cos^2 x - \sin^2 x}{\sin^2 x \cos^2 x} + \sec^2 x \\
&= \frac{\cos^2 x}{\sin^2 x \cos^2 x} - \frac{\sin^2 x}{\sin^2 x \cos^2 x} + \sec^2 x \\
&= \frac{1}{\sin^2 x} - \frac{1}{\cos^2 x} + \sec^2 x \\
&= \csc^2 x - \sec^2 x + \sec^2 x \\
&= \csc^2 x
\end{aligned}$$

Circle Properties

Arcs

An **arc** is a portion of a circle. Specifically, an arc is the set of points between and including two points on a circle. An arc does not contain any points inside the circle. When a segment is drawn from the endpoints of an arc to the center of the circle, a sector is formed. A **minor arc** is an arc that has a measure less than 180°. A **major arc** is an arc having a measure of at least 180°. Every minor arc has a corresponding major arc that can be found by subtracting the measure of the minor arc from 360°. A **semicircle** is an arc whose endpoints are the endpoints of the diameter of a circle. A semicircle is exactly half of a circle.

Arc length is the length of that portion of the circumference between two points on the circle. The formula for arc length is $s = \frac{\pi r\theta}{180°}$ where s is the arc length, r is the length of the radius, and θ is the angular measure of the arc in degrees, or $s = r\theta$, where θ is the angular measure of the arc in radians (2π radians $=$ 360 degrees).

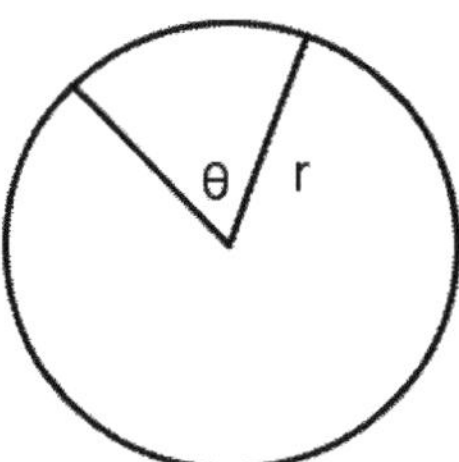

For example, if you are asked to find the length of the arc that subtends a 60° central angle in a circle with a radius of 10 cm, you would solve $s = (10\text{ cm})(60°)\left(\frac{\pi\ rad}{180°}\right)$ to obtain an arc length in centimeters.

Another formula for arc length involving the circumference given by C is $\frac{s}{C} = \frac{\theta}{360°}$ when central angle θ is measured in degrees or $\frac{s}{C} = \frac{\theta}{2\pi}$ when θ is measured in radians. These formulas can be rearranged to solve for s, C, or θ; of course, if you know a circle's circumference, you can also determine its diameter d or radius r using the formula $C = \pi d$ or $C = 2\pi r$.

ANGLES OF CIRCLES

A **central angle** is an angle whose vertex is the center of a circle and whose legs intercept an arc of the circle. The measure of a central angle is equal to the measure of the minor arc it intercepts.

An **inscribed angle** is an angle whose vertex lies on a circle and whose legs contain chords of that circle. The portion of the circle intercepted by the legs of the angle is called the intercepted arc. The measure of the intercepted arc is exactly twice the measure of the inscribed angle. In the following diagram, angle ABC is an inscribed angle. $\widehat{AC} = 2(\text{m}\angle ABC)$

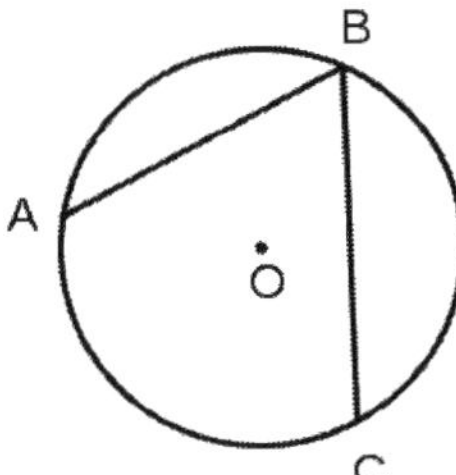

Any angle inscribed in a semicircle is a right angle. The intercepted arc is 180°, making the inscribed angle half that, or 90°. In the diagram below, angle ABC is inscribed in semicircle ABC, making angle ABC equal to 90°.

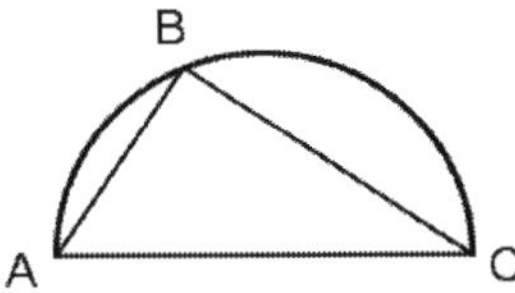

SECANTS, CHORDS, AND TANGENTS

A **secant** is a line that intersects a circle in two points. The segment of a secant line that is contained within the circle is called a **chord**. Two secants may intersect inside the circle, on the circle, or outside the circle. When the two secants intersect on the circle, an inscribed angle is formed.When two secants intersect inside a circle, the measure of each of two vertical angles is equal to half the sum of the two intercepted arcs. Consider the following diagram where $\text{m}\angle AEB = \frac{1}{2}(\widehat{AB} + \widehat{CD})$ and $\text{m}\angle BEC = \frac{1}{2}(\widehat{BC} + \widehat{AD})$.

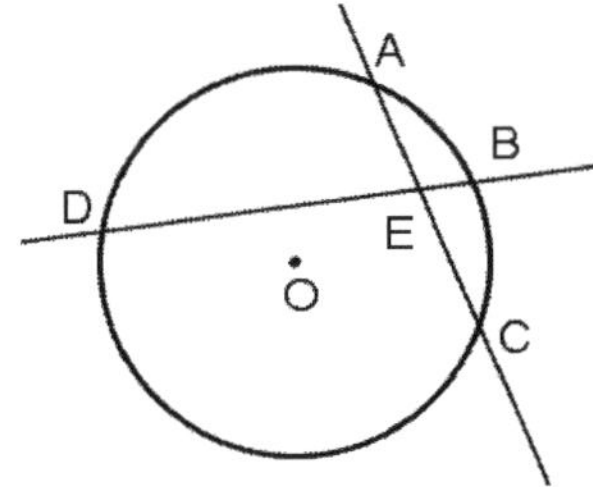

When two secants intersect outside a circle, the measure of the angle formed is equal to half the difference of the two arcs that lie between the two secants. In the diagram below, $m\angle AEB = \frac{1}{2}(\widehat{AB} - \widehat{CD})$.

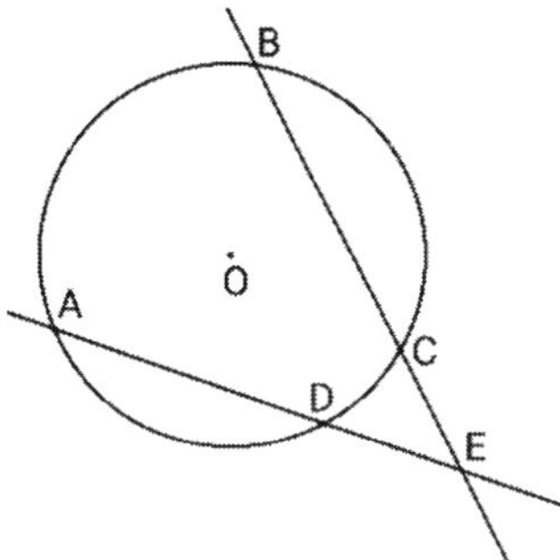

A **tangent** is a line in the same plane as a circle that touches the circle in exactly one point. The point at which a tangent touches a circle is called the **point of tangency**. While a line segment can be tangent to a circle as part of a line that is tangent, it is improper to say a tangent can be simply a line segment that touches the circle in exactly one point.

In the diagram below, $\overleftrightarrow{EB}$ is a secant and contains chord $\overline{EB}$ and $\overleftrightarrow{CD}$ is tangent to circle A. Notice that $\overline{FB}$ is not tangent to the circle. $\overline{FB}$ is a line segment that touches the circle in exactly one point, but if the segment were extended, it would touch the circle in a second point. In the diagram below, point B is the point of tangency.

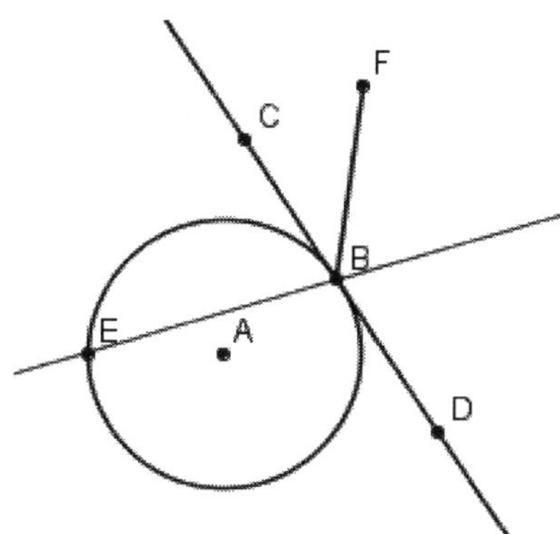

Review Video: Tangent Lines of a Circle
Visit mometrix.com/academy and enter code: 780167

Sectors

A **sector** is the portion of a circle formed by two radii and their intercepted arc. While the arc length is exclusively the points that are also on the circumference of the circle, the sector is the entire area bounded by the arc and the two radii.

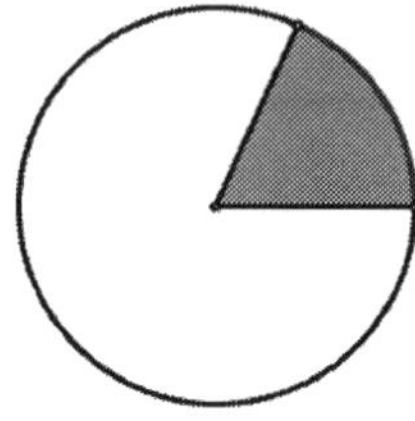

The **area of a sector** of a circle is found by the formula, $A = \frac{\theta r^2}{2}$, where A is the area, θ is the measure of the central angle in radians, and r is the radius. To find the area with the central angle in degrees, use the formula, $A = \frac{\theta \pi r^2}{360}$, where θ is the measure of the central angle and r is the radius.

Review Video: Finding Measurements for Parts of a Circle
Visit mometrix.com/academy and enter code: 417932

On some questions, you may be expected to combine your knowledge of circles with your knowledge of other geometric concepts, such as properties of parallel lines. The formulas for the area and circumference of a circle and the Pythagorean Theorem are provided with the test.

PRACTICE

P1. Given that $\angle DEB = 80°$and $\widehat{BC} = 90°$, determine the following values based on the figure:

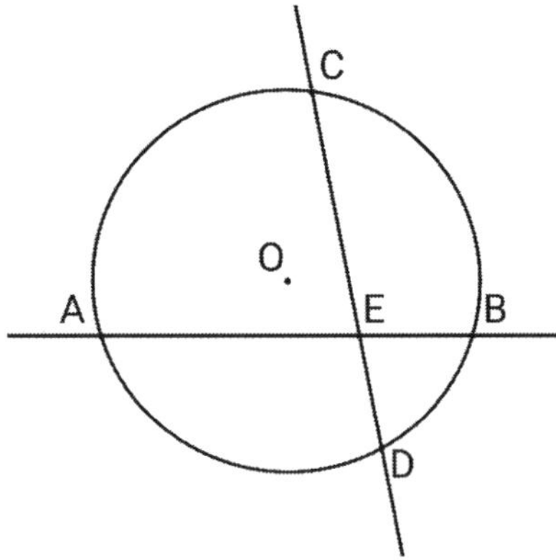

(a) $\widehat{AD}$

(b) $\widehat{DB} + \widehat{CA}$

P2. Given that $\angle OCB = 50°$, $\overleftrightarrow{EF}$ is tangent to the circle at B, and $\overline{CB} = 6$ km, determine the following values abased on the figure:

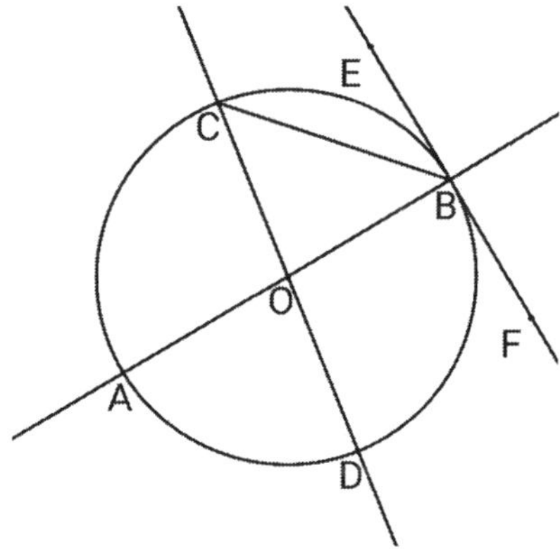

(a) The angle made between $\overleftrightarrow{CD}$ and a line tangent to the circle at A.

(b) The area of the sector of the circle between C and B.

PRACTICE SOLUTIONS

P1. (a). Recall that when two secants intersect inside of a circle, the measure of each of two vertical angles is equal to half the sum of the two intercepted arcs. Also, since $\angle DEB$ and $\angle CEB$are supplementary, the measure of $\angle CEB = 180° - 80° = 100°$ In other words:

$$\begin{aligned}\angle CEB &= \frac{1}{2}(\widehat{BC} + \widehat{AD})\\ 100° &= \frac{1}{2}(90° + \widehat{AD})\\ 200° &= 90° + \widehat{AD}\\ 110° &= \widehat{AD}\end{aligned}$$

(b) Note that the whole circle is divided into four arcs. Thus,

$$\begin{aligned}\widehat{AD} + \widehat{DB} + \widehat{BC} + \widehat{CA} &= 360°\\ 110° + \widehat{DB} + 90° + \widehat{CA} &= 360°\\ \widehat{DB} + \widehat{CA} &= 160°\end{aligned}$$

P2. (a) A line tangent to the circle at A creates a right triangle with one vertex at O, one at A, and the final vertex where $\overleftrightarrow{CD}$ intersects the tangent line, let us call that point G.

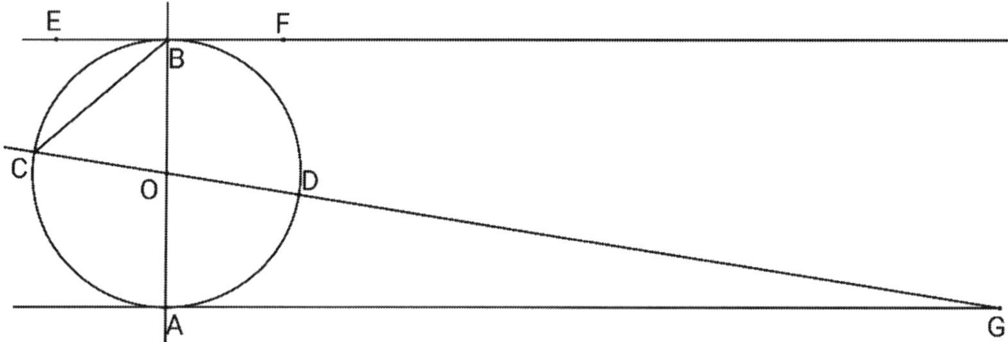

Since AB is a diameter, the line tangent at A is perpendicular to AB, so $\angle OAG = 90°$. The triangle COB has two legs that are the radius of the circle and so must be isosceles. So, $50° \times 2 + \angle COB = 180°$, which means that $\angle COB$ and the vertical angle $\angle GOA$ both equal 80°. Knowing this we can find $\angle AGO$:

$$\begin{aligned}80° + 90° + \angle AGO &= 180°\\ \angle AGO &= 10°\end{aligned}$$

(b) We know $\angle OCB = 50°$ and that triangle COB is isosceles with two legs equal to the radius, so a perpendicular bisector of the triangle as shown will create a right triangle:

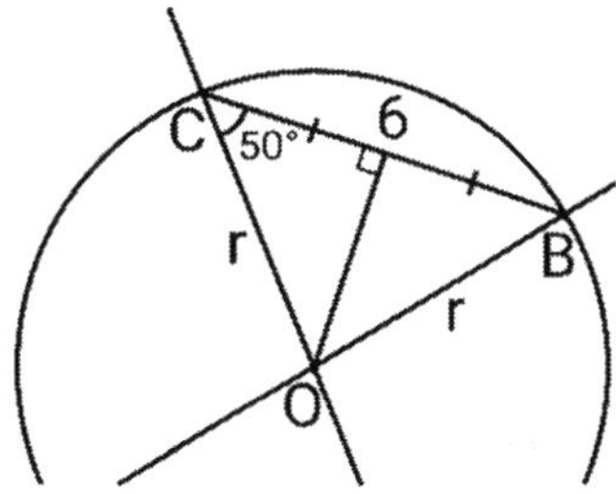

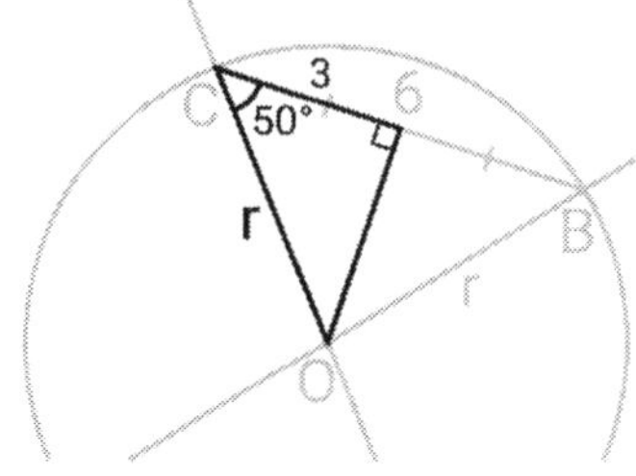

Recall that cosine of an angle in a right triangle is the ratio of the adjacent side to the hypotenuse. Thus, we can find r:

$$\cos 50° = \frac{3}{r}$$
$$r = \frac{3}{\cos 50°}$$

As noted in part (a), $\angle COB = 80°$ so, the area of the sector is:

$$A = \frac{\theta \pi r^2}{360°}$$
$$= \frac{80°\pi\left(\frac{3}{\cos 50°}\right)^2}{360°}$$
$$= \frac{2\pi\left(\frac{9}{\cos^2 50°}\right)}{9}$$
$$= \frac{2\pi}{\cos^2 50°} \cong 15.2 \text{ km}^2$$

TRIANGLE CLASSIFICATION AND PROPERTIES

A **scalene triangle** is a triangle with no congruent sides. A scalene triangle will also have three angles of different measures. The angle with the largest measure is opposite the longest side, and the angle with the smallest measure is opposite the shortest side. An **acute triangle** is a triangle whose three angles are all less than 90°. If two of the angles are equal, the acute triangle is also an **isosceles triangle**. An isosceles triangle will also have two congruent angles opposite the two congruent sides. If the three angles are all equal, the acute triangle is also an **equilateral triangle**. An equilateral triangle will also have three congruent angles, each 60°. All equilateral triangles are also acute triangles. An **obtuse triangle** is a triangle with exactly one angle greater than 90°. The other two angles may or may not be equal. If the two remaining angles are equal, the obtuse triangle is also an isosceles triangle. A **right triangle** is a triangle with exactly one angle equal to 90°. All right triangles follow the Pythagorean theorem. A right triangle can never be acute or obtuse.

The table below illustrates how each descriptor places a different restriction on the triangle:

Angles / **Sides**	**Acute:** All angles < 90°	**Obtuse:** One angle > 90°	**Right:** One angle = 90°
Scalene: No equal side lengths	b, x, z, a, y, c	b, x, z, a, y, c	b, x, z, a, y, c
	$90° > \angle a > \angle b > \angle c$ $x > y > z$	$\angle a > 90° > \angle b > \angle c$ $x > y > z$	$90° = \angle a > \angle b > \angle c$ $x > y > z$

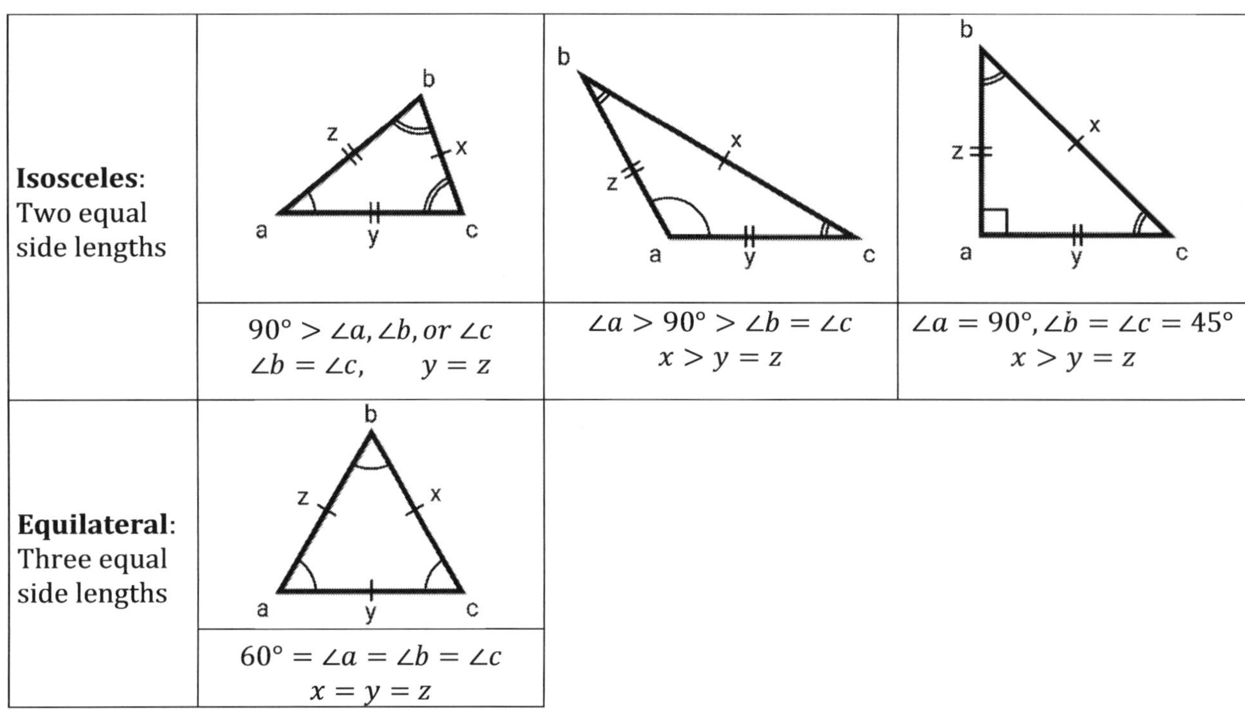

Isosceles: Two equal side lengths	$90° > \angle a, \angle b, or \angle c$ $\angle b = \angle c, \quad y = z$	$\angle a > 90° > \angle b = \angle c$ $x > y = z$	$\angle a = 90°, \angle b = \angle c = 45°$ $x > y = z$
Equilateral: Three equal side lengths	$60° = \angle a = \angle b = \angle c$ $x = y = z$		

Review Video: Introduction to Types of Triangles
Visit mometrix.com/academy and enter code: 511711

SIMILARITY AND CONGRUENCE RULES

Similar triangles are triangles whose corresponding angles are equal and whose corresponding sides are proportional. Represented by AAA. Similar triangles whose corresponding sides are congruent are also congruent triangles.

The triangles can be shown to be **congruent** in 5 ways:

- **SSS**: Three sides of one triangle are congruent to the three corresponding sides of the second triangle.
- **SAS**: Two sides and the included angle (the angle formed by those two sides) of one triangle are congruent to the corresponding two sides and included angle of the second triangle.
- **ASA**: Two angles and the included side (the side that joins the two angles) of one triangle are congruent to the corresponding two angles and included side of the second triangle.
- **AAS**: Two angles and a non-included side of one triangle are congruent to the corresponding two angles and non-included side of the second triangle.
- **HL**: The hypotenuse and leg of one right triangle are congruent to the corresponding hypotenuse and leg of the second right triangle.

Review Video: Similar Triangles
Visit mometrix.com/academy and enter code: 398538

GENERAL RULES FOR TRIANGLES

The **triangle inequality theorem** states that the sum of the measures of any two sides of a triangle is always greater than the measure of the third side. If the sum of the measures of two sides were equal to the third side, a triangle would be impossible because the two sides would lie flat across the third side and there would be no vertex. If the sum of the measures of two of the sides was less than the third side, a closed figure would be impossible because the two shortest sides would never meet. In other words, for a triangle with sides lengths A, B, and C: $A + B > C, B + C > A$, and $A + C > B$

The sum of the measures of the interior angles of a triangle is always 180°. Therefore, a triangle can never have more than one angle greater than or equal to 90°.

In any triangle, the angles opposite congruent sides are congruent, and the sides opposite congruent angles are congruent. The largest angle is always opposite the longest side, and the smallest angle is always opposite the shortest side.

The line segment that joins the midpoints of any two sides of a triangle is always parallel to the third side and exactly half the length of the third side.

Review Video: General Rules (Triangle Inequality Theorem)
Visit mometrix.com/academy and enter code: 166488

You should expect questions requiring you to use the Pythagorean Theorem and trigonometric ratios to find missing side lengths and angles of right triangles. The Pythagorean Theorem as well as the 30°-60°-90° and 45°-45°-90° special right triangles are provided on the test. You should be able to recognize situations in which the Pythagorean Theorem, trigonometry, and special right triangles can be applied. For example, a square can be divided by a diagonal into two 45°-45°-90° triangles. An equilateral triangle can be divided by an altitude into two 30°-60°-90° right triangles. Hexagons can be divided into six equilateral triangles, each of which can be further divided into two 30°-60°-90° triangles. You need to be able to apply the special right triangles to given triangles. For example, if you are given a 45°-45°-90° triangle with a side length of 5 cm, you should be able to determine that the hypotenuse has a length of $5\sqrt{2}$ cm. If you are given a 30°-60°-90° triangle with a short leg of length 3 inches, you should be able to determine that the hypotenuse has a length of 6 inches.

PRACTICE

P1. Given the following pairs of triangles, determine whether they are similar, congruent, or neither (note that the figures are not drawn to scale):

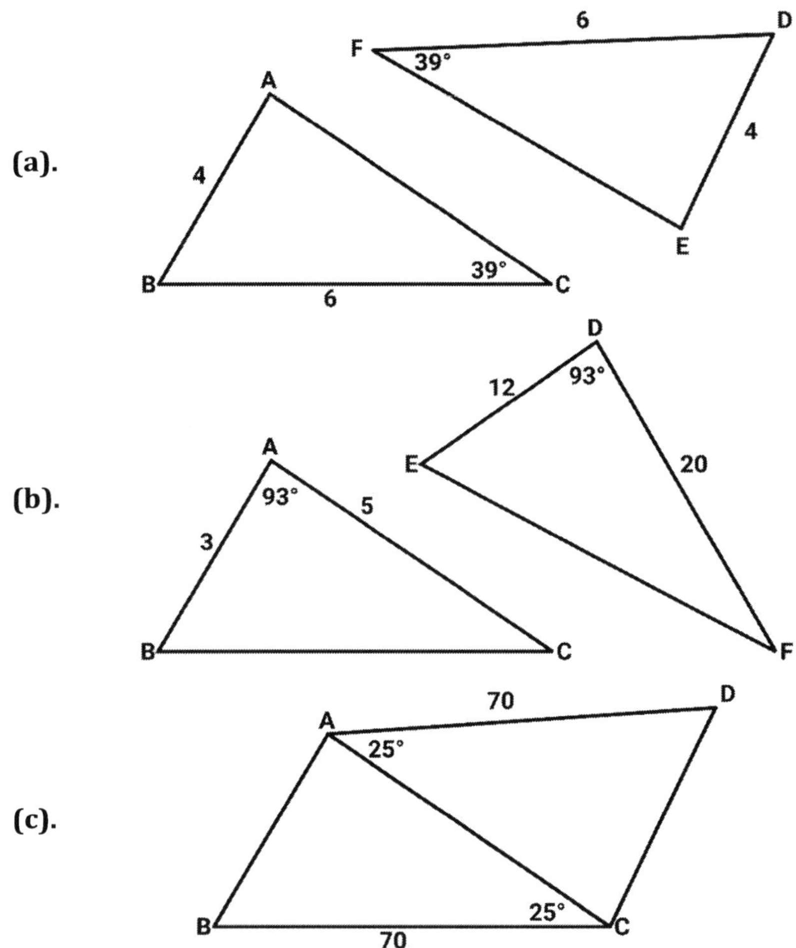

P2. Calculate the following values based on triangle MNO:

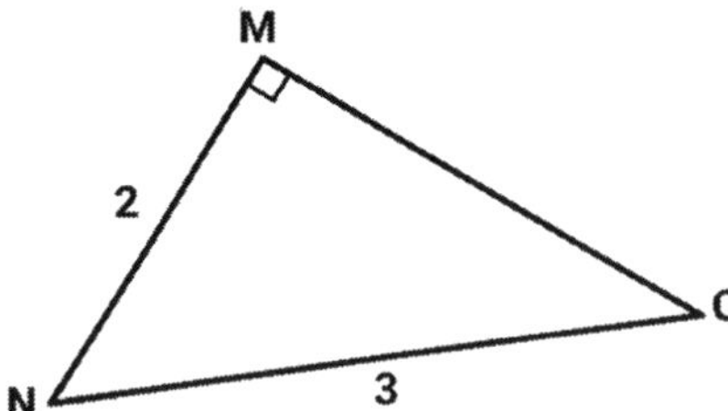

(a) length of $\overline{MO}$

(b) $\sin(\angle NOM)$

(c) area of the triangle, if the units of the measurements are in miles

Practice Solutions

P1. (a). Neither: We are given that two sides lengths and an angle are equal, however, the angle given is not between the given side lengths. That means there are two possible triangles that could satisfy the given measurements. Thus, we cannot be certain of congruence:

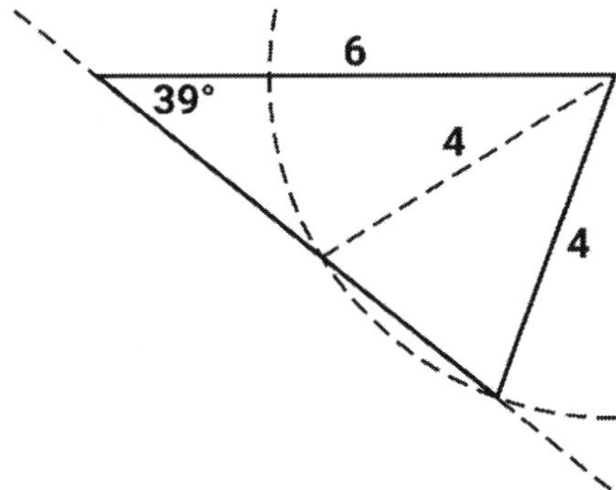

(b) Similar: Since we are given a side-angle-side of each triangle and the side lengths given are scaled evenly $\left(\frac{3}{5} \times \frac{4}{4} = \frac{12}{20}\right)$ and the angles are equal. Thus, $\Delta ABC \sim \Delta DEF$. If the side lengths were equal, then they would be congruent.

(c) Congruent: Even though we aren't given a measurement for the shared side of the figure, since it is shared it is equal. So, this is a case of SAS. Thus, $\Delta ABC \cong \Delta CDA$

P2. (a) Since triangle MNO is a right triangle, we can use the simple form of Pythagoras theorem to find the missing side length:

$$\begin{aligned}\left(\overline{\mathrm{MO}}\right)^2 + 2^2 &= 3^2 \\ \left(\overline{\mathrm{MO}}\right)^2 &= 9 - 4 \\ \overline{\mathrm{MO}} &= \sqrt{5}\end{aligned}$$

(b) Recall that sine of an angle in a right triangle is the ratio of the opposite side to the hypotenuse. So, $\sin(\angle\mathrm{NOM}) = 2/3$

(c) Since triangle MNO is a right triangle, we can use either of the legs as the height and the other as the base in the simple formula for area of a triangle:

$$\begin{aligned}A &= \frac{bh}{2} \\ &= \frac{(2\text{ mi})(\sqrt{5}\text{ mi})}{2} \\ &= \sqrt{5}\text{ mi}^2\end{aligned}$$

Complex Numbers

Complex numbers consist of a real component and an imaginary component. Complex numbers are expressed in the form $a + bi$ with real component a and imaginary component bi. The imaginary unit *i* is equal to $\sqrt{-1}$. That means $i^2 = -1$. The imaginary unit provides a way to find the square root of a negative number. For example, $\sqrt{-25}$ is $5i$. You should expect questions asking you to add, subtract, multiply, divide, and simplify complex numbers. You may see a question that says, "Add $3 + 2i$ and $5- 7i$" or "Subtract $4 + i\sqrt{5}$ from $2 + i\sqrt{5}$." Or you may see a question that says, "Multiply $6 + 2i$ by $8- 4i$" or "Divide $1- 3i$ by $9- 7i$."

Operations on Complex Numbers

Operations with complex numbers resemble operations with variables in algebra. When adding or subtracting complex numbers, you can only combine like terms – real terms with real terms and imaginary terms with imaginary terms. For example, if you are asked to simplify $-2 + 4i- (-3 + 7i)- 5i$, you should first remove the parentheses to yield $-2 + 4i + 3- 7i- 5i$. Combining like terms yields $1- 8i$. One interesting aspect of imaginary number is that if *i* has an exponent greater than 1, it can be simplified. For example, $i^2 = -1$, $i^3 = -i$, and $i^4 = 1$. When multiplying complex numbers, remember to simplify each *i* with an exponent greater than 1. For example, you might see a question that says, "Simplify $(2- i)(3 + 2i)$." You need to distribute and multiply to get $6 + 4i- 3i- 2i^2$. This is further simplified to $6 + i- 2(-1)$, or $8 + i$.

Simplifying Expressions with Complex Denominators

If an expression contains an *i* in the denominator, it must be simplified. Remember, roots cannot be left in the denominator of a fraction. Since *i* is equivalent to $\sqrt{-1}$, *i* cannot be left in the denominator of a fraction. You must rationalize the denominator of a fraction that contains a complex denominator by multiplying the numerator and denominator by the conjugate of the denominator. The conjugate of the complex number $a + bi$ is $a- bi$. You can simplify $\frac{2}{5i}$ by simply multiplying $\frac{2}{5i} \cdot \frac{i}{i}$, which yields $-\frac{2}{5}i$. And you can simplify $\frac{5+3i}{2-4i}$ by multiplying $\frac{5+3i}{2-4i} \cdot \frac{2+4i}{2+4i}$. This yields $\frac{10+20i+6i-12}{4-8i+8i+16}$ which simplifies to $\frac{-2+26i}{20}$ or $\frac{-1+13i}{10}$, which can also be written as $-\frac{1}{10} + \frac{13}{10}i$.

Student-Produced Response

The PSAT test includes some questions that are not multiple choice. Instead, they require you to solve the problem, then fill the exact number into a grid very similar to the one you used to enter your name and address on the form. The grid has a row of four boxes on top, with a column of numbers 0–9, a slash, and a decimal beneath each box.

To fill in the grid, write your answer in the boxes on top, then fill in the corresponding circle underneath. Use the slash to indicate fractions. It's a machine-scored test, so you don't get any credit for the number you write on top — that's strictly to help you fill in the circles correctly. If your answer doesn't fill up all four columns, that's okay. And it doesn't matter whether you left-justify or right-justify your answers. What does matter is that the circles be filled in correctly.

If You Can't Write It Using the Characters Provided, It's Not Right

No student-produced response will be a negative number or a percentage. If you get a negative number, you've made a mistake. Percentages should be expressed as a ratio or decimal; for example, 50% can be written as .50.

Start on the Left

There are a few reasons to start with the first box every time. For one thing, it's faster. It will also help you be as precise as possible. If your answer is <1, though, don't use a leading 0 before the decimal. The PSAT omits the 0 from column one to help you be as precise as possible. For decimals, use as many columns as you can. Don't round or truncate answers. If you calculate an answer to be .125, enter the full number, not .13.

Repeat a Repeating Decimal

Repeating decimals such as .666666 are only counted correct if you fill all the available columns. Either .666 or .667 will get credit. However, .66 will be counted as wrong.

Don't Use Mixed Numbers

If you try to write 2 ½, the computer will think you've written 21/2 and count it wrong. Instead, use the improper fraction form of such numbers; for example, 2 ½ = 5/2.

Use Your Calculator

You brought a calculator; use it. Work the problem twice to make sure you entered all the numbers correctly.

Check Your Work

More than any other questions in the math section, student-produced responses need to be double-checked. Try working the problem backward, plugging answers back into the original equation.

It's Okay to Get Multiple Answers

Some questions may have more than one answer. In that case, any correct answer will do.

In General

Approach the problem systematically. Take time to understand what is being asked for. In many cases, there is a drawing or graph that you can write on. Draw lines, jot notes, do whatever is necessary to create a visual picture and to allow you to understand what is being asked.

PSAT Practice Test

Reading Test

Questions 1-9 are based on the following passage.

This passage is adapted from Louisa May Alcott, Little Women, *originally published in 1868.*

"Christmas won't be Christmas without any presents," grumbled Jo, lying on the rug.

"It's so dreadful to be poor!" sighed Meg, looking down at her old dress.

"I don't think it's fair for some girls to have plenty of pretty things, and other girls nothing at all," added little Amy, with an injured sniff.

"We've got Father and Mother, and each other," said Beth contentedly from her corner.

The four young faces on which the firelight shone brightened at the cheerful words, but darkened again as Jo said sadly, "We haven't got Father, and shall not have him for a long time." She didn't say "perhaps never," but each silently added it, thinking of Father far away, where the fighting was.

Nobody spoke for a minute; then Meg said in an altered tone, "You know the reason Mother proposed not having any presents this Christmas was because it is going to be a hard winter for everyone. She thinks we ought not to spend money for pleasure, when our men in the army are suffering so. We can't do much, but we can make our little sacrifices, and ought to do it gladly. But I am afraid I don't," and Meg shook her head, as she thought regretfully of all the pretty things she wanted.

"But I don't think the little we should spend would do any good. We've each got a dollar, and the army wouldn't be much helped by our giving that. I agree not to expect anything from Mother or you, but I do want to buy Undine and Sintram for myself. I've wanted it so long," said Jo, who was a bookworm.

"I planned to spend mine in new music," said Beth, with a little sigh, which no one heard but the hearth brush and kettle-holder.

"I shall get a nice box of Faber's drawing pencils; I really need them," said Amy decidedly.

"Mother didn't say anything about our money, and she won't wish us to give up everything. Let's each buy what we want, and have a little fun; I'm sure we work hard enough to earn it," cried Jo, examining the heels of her shoes in a gentlemanly manner.

"I know I do—teaching those tiresome children nearly all day, when I'm longing to enjoy myself at home," began Meg, in the complaining tone again.

"You don't have half such a hard time as I do," said Jo. "How would you like to be shut up for hours with a nervous, fussy old lady, who keeps you trotting, is never satisfied, and worries you till you're ready to fly out the window or cry?"

"It's naughty to fret, but I do think washing dishes and keeping things tidy is the worst work in the world. It makes me cross, and my hands get so stiff, I can't practice well at all." And Beth looked at her rough hands with a sigh that anyone could hear that time.

"I don't believe any of you suffer as I do," cried Amy, "for you don't have to go to school with impertinent girls, who plague you if you don't know your lessons, and laugh at your dresses, and label your father if he isn't rich, and insult you when your nose isn't nice."

"If you mean libel, I'd say so, and not talk about labels, as if Papa was a pickle bottle," advised Jo, laughing.

1. Which choice gives the best summary of the problems presented in this passage?

A) The sisters do not have as much money to spend as they would like, and Amy is made fun of at school.
B) Mother forbade any presents this Christmas, and the sisters are unhappy with their responsibilities.
C) Father is away at war, money is scarce, and the sisters are unhappy with their responsibilities.
D) Beth is tired of cleaning and washing dishes, and Father is away at war.

2. Which of the following selections provides the best evidence that this passage takes place during a time of war?

A) Line 1 ("Christmas won't ... any presents")
B) Line 7 ("We haven't ... long time.")
C) Lines 12-13 ("She thinks ... suffering so")
D) Line 16 ("But I ... any good")

3. Based on what is stated in the passage, what do you know to be true about Father?

A) He wants his daughters to spend their money on themselves.
B) He wants his daughters to buy things for each other.
C) He is likely to die in the war.
D) He is not likely to return home in time for Christmas.

4. Which sister does NOT specify what she wants to buy with her money?

A) Amy
B) Beth
C) Jo
D) Meg

5. As used in line 4, the word "injured" most nearly means

A) in pain
B) offended
C) sympathetic
D) sickly

6. Based on the context of the passage, a reader who is unfamiliar with "Undine and Sintram" mentioned in line 18 could conclude it is the name of which of these?

A) A perfume
B) A work of art
C) A work of literature

D) A work of music

7. What do lines 20-21 ("no one ... kettle holder") tell the reader about where Beth is located in the room?

A) She is next to the stove
B) She is next to the window
C) She is next to the kitchen table
D) She is next to the fireplace

8. In line 32, Beth complains of not being able to practice well. To what sort of practicing is Beth referring?

A) Practicing music
B) Practicing drawing
C) Practicing housekeeping
D) Practicing schoolwork

9. Which of the following sentences best describes the theme of this passage?

A) Children should not be required to work outside the home.
B) In time of war, everyone should make sacrifices for the good of the country.
C) Not everyone has the same problems, but everyone has problems.
D) Money should only be spent on oneself, because no one else deserves it.

Questions 10-20 are based on the following two passages.

Both passages are adapted from addresses given by Abraham Lincoln. The first is his Second Inaugural Address *and the second is his* Gettysburg Address.

Passage 1

At this second appearing to take the oath of the Presidential office there is less occasion for an extended address than there was at the first. Then a statement somewhat in detail of a course to be pursued seemed fitting and proper. Now, at the expiration of four years, during which public declarations have been constantly called forth on every point and phase of the great contest which still absorbs the attention and engrosses the energies of the nation, little that is new could be presented. The progress of our arms, upon which all else chiefly depends, is as well known to the public as to myself, and it is, I trust, reasonably satisfactory and encouraging to all. With high hope for the future, no prediction in regard to it is ventured.

On the occasion corresponding to this four years ago all thoughts were anxiously directed to an impending civil war. All dreaded it, all sought to avert it. While the inaugural address was being delivered from this place, devoted altogether to saving the Union without war, insurgent agents were in the city seeking to destroy it without war—seeking to dissolve the Union and divide effects by negotiation. Both parties deprecated war, but one of them would make war rather than let the nation survive, and the other would accept war rather than let it perish, and the war came.

One-eighth of the whole population were colored slaves, not distributed generally over the Union, but localized in the southern part of it. These slaves constituted a peculiar and powerful interest. All knew that this interest was somehow the cause of the war. To strengthen, perpetuate, and extend this interest was the object for which the insurgents would rend the Union even by war, while the Government claimed no right to do more than to restrict the territorial enlargement of it. Neither party expected for the war the magnitude or the duration which it has already attained. Neither anticipated that the cause of the conflict might cease with or even before the conflict itself should cease. Each looked for an easier triumph, and a result less fundamental and astounding. Both read the same Bible and pray to the same God, and each invokes His aid against the other. It may seem strange that any men should dare to ask a just God's assistance in wringing their bread from the sweat of other men's faces, but let us judge not, that we be not judged. The prayers of both could not be answered. That of neither has been answered fully. The Almighty has His own purposes. "Woe unto the world because of offenses; for it must needs be that offenses come, but woe to that man by whom the offense cometh." If we shall suppose that American slavery is one of those offenses which, in the providence of God, must needs come, but which, having continued through His appointed time, He now wills to remove, and that He gives to both North and South this terrible war as the woe due to those by whom the offense came, shall we discern therein any departure from those divine attributes which the believers in a living God always ascribe to Him? Fondly do we hope, fervently do we pray, that this mighty scourge of war may speedily pass away. Yet, if God wills that it continue until all the wealth piled by the bondsman's two hundred and fifty years of unrequited toil shall be sunk, and until every drop of blood drawn with the lash shall be paid by another drawn with the sword, as was said three thousand years ago, so still it must be said "the judgments of the Lord are true and righteous altogether."

With malice toward none, with charity for all, with firmness in the right as God gives us to see the right, let us strive on to finish the work we are in, to bind up the nation's wounds, to care for him who shall have borne the battle and for his widow and his orphan, to do all which may achieve and cherish a just and lasting peace among ourselves and with all nations.

Passage 2

Four score and seven years ago our fathers brought forth on this continent, a new nation, conceived in Liberty, and dedicated to the proposition that all men are created equal.

Now we are engaged in a great civil war, testing whether that nation, or any nation so conceived and so dedicated, can long endure. We are met on a great battle-field of that war. We have come to dedicate a portion of that field, as a final resting place for those who here gave their lives that that nation might live. It is altogether fitting and proper that we should do this.

But, in a larger sense, we cannot dedicate -- we cannot consecrate -- we cannot hallow -- this ground. The brave men, living and dead, who struggled here, have consecrated it, far above our poor power to add or detract. The world will little note, nor long remember what we say here, but it can never forget what they did here. It is for us the living, rather, to be dedicated here to the unfinished work which they who fought here have thus far so nobly advanced. It is rather for us to be here dedicated to the great task remaining before us: that from these honored dead we take increased devotion to that cause for which they gave the last full measure of devotion; that we here highly resolve that these dead shall not have died in vain; that this nation, under God, shall have a new birth of freedom; and that government of the people, by the people, for the people shall not perish from the earth.

10. Why does the author discuss his first inaugural address in Passage 1?

A) To prove that the country could have gone in a different direction.
B) To illustrate how the country had changed since his first inauguration.
C) To show how much he improved the country during his first term.
D) To explain that the country was once a place of peace.

11. In line 16 of Passage 1, the word "peculiar" most nearly means

A) Odd
B) Bizarre
C) Specific
D) Appropriate

12. In lines 28-31 of Passage 1, the author states, "If we shall suppose that... [God] gives to both North and South this terrible war as the woe due to those by whom the offense came..." Which of the following does he provide as evidence of this supposition?

A) Line 20 ("Neither party ... already attained")
B) Line 23 ("Both read ... the other")
C) Lines 27-28 ("Woe unto ... offense cometh")
D) Lines 34-37 ("Yet, if God ... righteous altogether")

13. What is the purpose of the lines 39-42 of Passage 1 ("With malice ... all nations.")?

A) It is a sober remembrance for all who died during the American Civil War.
B) It is a warning that America could face new conflicts with other nations.
C) It is an attempt to forge a new feeling of union and caring between the North and the South.
D) It is a plea to other nations to seek peaceful solutions to conflicts with the United States.

14. Which sentence from Passage 1 supports the idea that the author believed the North and the South did not have equally justifiable reasons for taking part in the war?

A) Lines 13-14 ("Both parties ... war came")

B) Line 17 ("All knew ... the war")
C) Line 21-22 ("Neither anticipated ... should cease")
D) Line 22 ("Each looked ... and astounding")

15. How does the author unite the themes of war and religion in Passage 1?

A) He suggests that the war and its end are parts of God's plan.
B) He says that no man would ask God to help him win a war.
C) He insists that it is God's responsibility, not his own, to resolve the war.
D) He quotes from the Bible liberally to extend an address he knew was too short.

16. In lines 9-10 of Passage 2, the author writes that "the world will little note, nor long remember what we say here, but it can never forget what they did here." Which rhetorical device does the author use?

A) Epiphora
B) Anaphora
C) Repetition
D) Parallelism

17. In line 15 of Passage 2, what is the author most likely emphasizing when he speaks of "freedom"?

A) Freedom from war
B) Freedom for all citizens
C) Freedom to own slaves
D) Freedom to worship God

18. Which of the following comes closest to summarizing the main idea of Passage 2?

A) In dedicating this ground, we must moreover save our democracy so soldiers did not die in vain.
B) In dedicating this ground, we must consecrate and hallow it to honor the soldiers living and dead.
C) In dedicating this ground, we must ensure the world remembers what we said and they did here.
D) In dedicating this ground, we must complete soldiers' unfinished work by declaring a cease-fire.

19. Which idea is overtly included in both passages?

A) Achieving an enduring peace
B) The Civil War being God's will
C) Completing some ongoing tasks
D) Wishing the war would end soon

20. How would the experience of reading Passage 1, a transcript of a speech, most likely differ from seeing and hearing the address delivered in person?

A) The author likely was angry while delivering his address, and this anger is lost in its transcription.
B) The author's original address was much longer than the version that was later transcribed.
C) The author was an impressively tall man and appeared more intimidating when he leaned toward his audience.
D) The author would have been able to use his voice to heighten the emotion in his address.

Questions 21-29 are based on the following passage.

This passage is adapted from Franklin Roosevelt's 1941 State of the Union Address.

Many subjects connected with our social economy call for immediate improvement. We should bring more citizens under the coverage of old-age pensions and unemployment insurance. We should widen the opportunities for adequate medical care. We should plan a better system by which persons deserving or needing gainful employment may obtain it.

I have called for personal sacrifice. And I am assured of the willingness of almost all Americans to respond to that call. A part of the sacrifice means the payment of more money in taxes. In my Budget Message, I will recommend that a greater portion of this great defense program be paid for from taxation than we are paying for today. No person should try, or be allowed, to get rich out of the program; and the principle of tax payments in accordance with ability to pay should be constantly before our eyes to guide our legislation. If the Congress maintains these principles, the voters, putting patriotism ahead of pocketbooks, will give you their applause.

In the future days, which we seek to make secure, we look forward to a world founded upon four essential human freedoms. The first is freedom of speech and expression—everywhere in the world. The second is freedom of every person to worship God in his own way—everywhere in the world. The third is freedom from want—which, translated into world terms, means economic understandings which will secure to every nation a healthy peacetime life for its inhabitants—everywhere in the world. The fourth is freedom from fear—which, translated into world terms, means a world-wide reduction of armaments to such a point and in such a thorough fashion that no nation will be in a position to commit an act of physical aggression against any neighbor—anywhere in the world.

That is no vision of a distant millennium. It is a definite basis for a kind of world attainable in our own time and generation. That kind of world is the very antithesis of the so-called new order of tyranny which the dictators seek to create with the crash of a bomb. To that new order we oppose the greater conception—the moral order. A good society is able to face schemes of world domination and foreign revolutions alike without fear.

Since the beginning of our American history, we have been engaged in change—in a perpetual peaceful revolution—a revolution which goes on steadily, quietly adjusting itself to changing conditions—without the concentration camp or the quick-lime in the ditch. The world order which we seek is the cooperation of free countries, working together in a friendly, civilized society.

This nation has placed its destiny in the hands and heads and hearts of its millions of free men and women; and its faith in freedom under the guidance of God. Freedom means the supremacy of human rights everywhere. Our support goes to those who struggle to gain those rights and keep them. Our strength is our unity of purpose. To that high concept there can be no end save victory.

21. Which of the following does the author give as an example of the "personal sacrifice" mentioned in line 5?

A) Higher taxation
B) Military service
C) Arms reduction
D) Four freedoms

22. Which of the following describes a major theme of the passage?

A) It is important for all people to have access to the benefits of an old-age system that supports citizens when they can no longer work.
B) Patriotic people will feel the need to pay more taxes to the government to obtain certain benefits they would not be able to afford.
C) People who want to work should be able to find work without bias and without undue hardship.
D) There are four basic freedoms that are vital to the health of people: speech, worship, freedom from want, and freedom from fear.

23. The author mentions that several aspects of the social economy need to be improved immediately. Which of the following does he <u>not</u> cite as an example in the passage?

A) Expanding retirement benefits
B) Expanding healthcare benefits
C) Expanding draft by the military
D) Expanding labor opportunities

24. In lines 5-11 ("I have ... their applause."), the author makes the claim that raising taxes is an action that will be enthusiastically supported by a patriotic populace. Which of the following would be an effective counterargument to this claim?

A) Americans are uninterested in pursuing freedom of any kind, and the four freedoms listed here are not considered important.
B) The average citizen already feels overburdened by taxes and feels the money is not being well-spent by the government.
C) Individuals will easily assent to the idea of a greater tax burden since it will naturally lead to a more prosperous state.
D) Patriots of all kinds are part of the natural makeup of America, and some will feel that the support of government is something that should be contemplated and debated.

25. Which of the following most precisely describes what the author means in line 21 when he states, "That is no vision of a distant millennium"?

A) The author believes that these freedoms will no longer be attainable if action is not taken soon.
B) The author believes that, if his policies are enacted, these freedoms will last far into the future.
C) The author believes that these freedoms can only be attained by enacting the policies he has described.
D) The author believes that these freedoms are attainable in the near future.

26. As used in line 22 of the passage, the word "order" most nearly means

A) A command given by a military leader
B) An authoritative decision or direction
C) An arrangement of items in sequence
D) A system of world politics and society

27. As used in line 33 of the passage, the word "end" most nearly means

A) Death
B) Purpose
C) Outcome

D) Conclusion

28. Which selection from the passage best supports the idea that America is constantly evolving toward a better situation?

A) Lines 17-20 ("The fourth ... the world.")
B) Lines 23-25 ("To that new ... without fear.")
C) Lines 26-28 ("Since the beginning ... the ditch.")
D) Lines 30-31 ("This nation ... guidance of God.)

29. Read the following excerpt from an independent commentary on this passage. What idea from the passage is emphasized in this excerpt?

> It highlights the important social issues of the day, the very same issues our nation is struggling with at the moment. What can we do about our elderly? Do class distinctions matter? The fact of the matter is, no one wants to take care of a sickly aging relative, regardless of class. Then again, most of our elderly don't want to live with their offspring, either—rich or poor.

A) the need for a social safety net for the aging populace
B) the need for a lack of social class distinctions
C) the fact that many of the elderly do not want long-term care
D) the idea that people want to live independently

Questions 30-39 are based on the following passage.

The phylum Annelida, named for the Latin word *anellus*, meaning "ring," includes earthworms, leeches, and other similar organisms. In their typical form, these animals exhibit bilateral symmetry, a cylindrical cross section, and an elongate body divided externally into segments (*metameres*) by a series of rings (*annuli*). They are segmented internally as well, with most of the internal organs repeated in series in each segment. This organization is termed *metamerism*. Metameric segmentation is the distinguishing feature of this phylum, and provides it with a degree of evolutionary plasticity in that certain segments can be modified and specialized to perform specific functions. For example, in some species certain of the locomotor *parapodia*, or feet, may be modified for grasping, and some portions of the gut may evolve digestive specializations.

The gut is a straight, muscular tube that functions independently of the muscular activity in the body wall. The Annelida resemble the nematodes, another worm phylum, in possessing a fluid-filled internal cavity separating the gut from the body wall. In both phyla, this cavity is involved in locomotion. However, in the annelids this space is formed at a much later time during the development of the embryo, and presumably evolved much later as well. This fluid-filled internal space is called a true *coelom*.

The annelid excretory and circulatory systems are well developed, and some members of the phylum have evolved respiratory organs. The nervous system offers a particular example of metameric specialization. It is concentrated anteriorly into enlarged cerebral ganglia connected to a ventral nerve cord that extends posteriorly and is organized into repeating segmental ganglia.

This phylum includes members bearing adaptations required for aquatic (marine or freshwater) or terrestrial habitats. They may be free-living entities or exist as parasites. Among the best known are the earthworm *Lumbricus*, the water leech *Hirudo*, and the marine worm *Nereis*.

Graphic 1

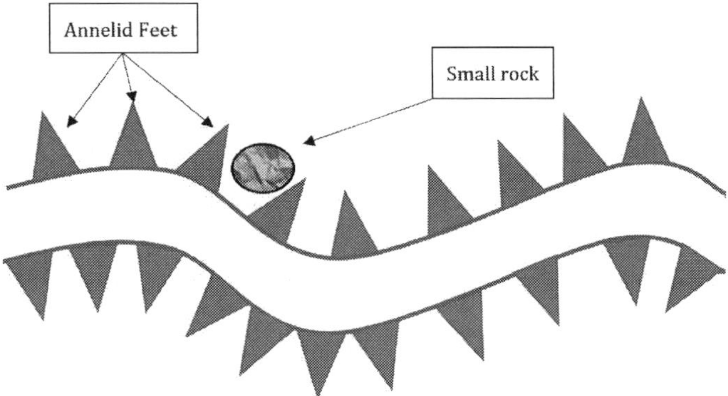

30. What is the purpose of this passage?

A) To describe the annelid nervous system.
B) To describe the annelid digestive system.
C) To introduce distinctive features of annelid anatomy.
D) To define metamerism.

31. The main difference between the Annelida and all other animal phyla is that

A) the Annelida are worms.
B) the Annelida include the leeches.

C) the Annelida are metameric.
D) the Annelida are aquatic.

32. One evolutionary advantage of segmentation is that

A) Segmented animals have many feet.
B) Segmented animals have a fluid-filled coelom.
C) Segments can specialize to perform certain functions.
D) Segments can evolve into more advanced forms of life.

33. What is meant by the term *metamerism* used in line 5?

A) Segmentation of the anatomy
B) A series of rings
C) Bilateral symmetry
D) Evolutionary plasticity

34. What is meant by the term *parapodia* used in line 8?

A) Specialization
B) Grasping appendages
C) Locomotion
D) Feet

35. Lines 10-15 discuss annelids and nematodes. Which of the following best describes how the author relates the characteristics of these two phyla?

A) Compare and contrast
B) Parts and whole
C) Cause and effect
D) Relative importance

36. The purpose of the paragraph in lines 20-22 in the passage is to

A) give familiar examples of members of the annelid phylum.
B) show that annelids may be parasites.
C) tell the reader that annelids may be adapted to aquatic environments.
D) show that there are many annelids in nature and that they are adapted to a wide variety of habitats.

37. Which of the following selections provides evidence to support the statement that metamerism confers some evolutionary flexibility?

A) Line 6 ("Metameric segmentation ... this phylum")
B) Lines 8-9 ("in some species ... digestive specializations")
C) Lines 10-11 ("The gut ... body wall")
D) Lines 11-13 ("The Annelida ... in locomotion")

38. Some annelids form features to perform certain functions. Which function does Graphic 1 seem to be illustrating?

A) Annelid feet may be used for locomotion or movement.
B) Annelid feet may be used for climbing.
C) Annelid feet may be able to produce secretions.
D) Annelid feet may be used to grasp things.

39. After the first sentence, which of the following describes the structure of this passage relative to the paragraph content sequence?

A) Body parts; body systems; types, habitats, names; distinctive feature
B) Distinctive feature; body parts; body systems; types, habitats, names
C) Body systems; distinctive feature; types, habitats, names; body parts
D) Types, habitats, names; distinctive feature; body parts; body systems

Questions 40-49 are based on the following passage.

The planet Pluto was discovered in 1930 by an American astronomer named Clyde Tombaugh and was quickly added to our list of planets. Pluto keeps an elliptical orbit with a period of about 248 years where it occasionally crosses the orbit of Neptune. Pluto is even known to have several moons! Since 1978, five moons have been confirmed! Despite all of this, Pluto's status as a planet has been challenged recently, demoting it to a dwarf planet.

In 2006, the International Astronomical Union (IAU) met to establish a definition for planets. Until this meeting, there was surprisingly no formalized definition for a planet, all the while, more and more celestial bodies have been discovered all throughout our solar system. If strict rules weren't applied, any number of would-be planets could be added to our taxonomy.

The IAU created a checklist of needs to qualify an object as a planet. First, the object must have an orbit around the Sun. Many objects get caught in the gravity of the Sun, but very few actually enter a regular orbit.

Second, a planet must have enough mass to assume what is called hydrostatic equilibrium. This simply means that the gravity of the planet is strong enough to form a nearly spherical shape. Lucky for Pluto, it meets the first two conditions!

The third condition is where Pluto falls short: a planet must have "cleared the neighborhood" of its own orbit. The planet's gravity, which is a result of its mass, must be strong enough that it either absorbs other objects that cross its path or will fling them out of the way. Pluto is simply not massive enough to protect itself from the interference of other planets and objects that come into contact with it. The dwarf planet's orbital path also is more irregular than that of other planets, likely because of the gravitational interference of other objects. All eight of the other planets in our solar system seem mostly unaffected by objects and have a very stable orbit. As a result, Pluto has been reclassified as a dwarf planet for the time being.

Even with clear reasoning, there is a huge pushback regarding Pluto's status as a dwarf planet. Many scientists point out that asteroids remain near Earth and Jupiter, indicating that even our own planet has not cleared its neighborhood of other bodies. Just a century ago, the existence of Pluto was not yet confirmed. Now the tug of war between science and sentimentality holds Pluto's fate. Perhaps the advancement of technology will further expand our knowledge of these mid-sized celestial bodies and help us understand this cherished pseudo-planet.

Pluto's Estimated Mass (1931-2006)	
Year	Mass (as a multiple of Earth's mass)
1931	1
1948	0.1 or 1/10
1976	0.01 or 1/100
1978	0.0015 or 1/650
2006	0.00218 or 1/459

40. Which of the following best states the purpose of the passage?

A) To entertain the reader with the differences between dwarf-planets and planets, using Pluto as an example.
B) To describe the differences between planets and dwarf-planets and produce excitement for future research.
C) To persuade the reader that Pluto's reclassification to a dwarf-planet is a good thing and has valid reasoning.
D) To inform the reader of Pluto's reclassification to a dwarf-planet and the reasoning behind the decision.

41. Which of the following does the passage list as a scientific reason in favor of Pluto being considered a planet?

A) Pluto has cleared its neighborhood.
B) Pluto has a regular orbit around the sun.
C) Pluto has a moon.
D) Pluto has always been a planet.

42. What is a probable definition for "celestial bodies" as found in line 8 of the passage?

A) Large objects in space
B) Meteors and meteorites
C) Unconfirmed planets
D) Dwarf planets with moons

43. What does it mean for an object to have hydrostatic equilibrium as found in line 13?

A) It has equal parts water and air.
B) Its mass in water helps it form into a spherical shape.
C) Its gravity is strong enough to hold a spherical shape.
D) The mass of the planet holds it in a steady shape without changing.

44. As used in line 19, the word "massive" most nearly means

A) taking up space
B) having mass
C) moving quickly
D) rotating consistently

45. Which of the following is the best stand-in for the word "sentimentality" as used in line 27?

A) rationalism
B) empiricism
C) ethics
D) nostalgia

46. What stance does the author hold regarding the status of Pluto as a dwarf planet.

A) He disagrees with the status and wants Pluto to be reinstated as a planet because the definition of a planet is inconsistent.
B) He agrees with the status because it is consistent with the IAU's guidelines.
C) He gives neither opinion but desires more information to make a clear determination.
D) He disagrees because Pluto has always been called a planet and should not be changed.

47. Review the chart entitled "Pluto's Estimated Mass from 1915 to 2006." What is the general trend over time regarding the estimation of Pluto's mass?

A) Pluto's estimated mass largely remained the same
B) Pluto's estimated mass increased over time.
C) Pluto's estimated mass had no real trend over time.
D) Pluto's estimated mass decreased over time.

48. Does the chart support Pluto's reclassification from planet to dwarf planet as its estimated mass has changed?

A) Yes, because a planet must have a large enough mass to clear its neighborhood, and Pluto's mass is estimated much lower than before.
B) Yes, because Pluto has retained a spherical shape, even though the estimated mass has changed.
C) No, because there is not enough information to support Pluto's reclassification.
D) No, because Pluto's estimated mass has increased over time, but it continues to have an unstable orbit.

49. Of the following, which would be the most suitable title for this passage?

A) Distinguishing Planets from Moons
B) The IAU's Taxonomy of Celestial Bodies
C) Pluto: Science vs. Sentiment
D) A Planet Once Again

Writing and Language Test

Questions 1–11 are based on the following passage.

A symbol of industry and perseverance, beavers have figured in literature, cartoons, and art for centuries. They have been valued in past centuries by the wealthy, who prized their fur for hats and coats, and they have been despised by farmers for the destruction of trees and stopping up of waterways. But while beavers are familiar figures, many of their contributions [1] were not as widely known. Their diligent building habits accomplish more than simply piling up sticks and creating ponds. Their dams serve not only as a barricade for the [2] beaver's benefit, but they also filter sediment and pollutants such as nitrogen and phosphorus from the water. Additionally, the dams aid the environment by trapping soil that is eroding from the land [3] upstream; slowing the loss and aiding the growth of crops on these lands.

1.

A) NO CHANGE
B) is
C) are
D) was

2.

A) NO CHANGE
B) beavers'
C) land's
D) their

3.

A) NO CHANGE
B) upstream, which is slowing
C) upstream; which slows
D) upstream, slowing

At one time the beaver population in North America numbered in the [4] ten's or possibly even hundred's of millions, but in the 17th century their numbers were decimated due to the demand for fur. In fact, the fur trade led to a conflict called the Beaver Wars (also known as the French and Iroquois Wars) between 1629 and 1701. Due to the extensive trapping for fur and the more recent use of their glands for perfume and medicine, the US beaver population has [5] declined sharply in the past few centuries.

4.

A) NO CHANGE
B) ten's, or possibly even hundred's
C) tens—or possibly even hundreds
D) tens or possibly even hundreds

5.

A) NO CHANGE
B) declines sharply
C) sharp declined
D) declined in a sharp way

With protective measures in place, beavers are now beginning to make a comeback in the US, but a new population brings its own problems. For example, the building of their dams [6] destroy trees and can hinder use of the water, so there is a question of how to encourage beavers while protecting natural resources and private property. Property owners can use several methods to discourage [7] beavers, wrapping tree trunks in metal mesh, spraying repellant on trees and bushes along the water, and setting traps. The wire mesh prevents the beavers from chewing the bark and thereby killing the trees. The repellant discourages beavers from eating the sprayed foliage because of [8] it's unpleasant taste. Finally, beavers can be trapped and relocated, [9] which encouraging them to settle in a new place.

Despite the aggressive fur trapping and the fact that many view these rodents as pests, beavers have shown resilience by continuing to thrive and adapt as necessary. Their colonies can be found throughout most of North America, as well as areas of South America, Asia, and Europe. [10] However, beavers are still in danger of extinction and need special protection.

[11]

6.

A) NO CHANGE
B) destroys
C) are destroying
D) destroyed

7.

A) NO CHANGE
B) beavers;
C) beavers:
D) beavers

8.

A) NO CHANGE
B) its
C) their
D) theirs

9.

A) NO CHANGE
B) that is encouraging
C) encouraging
D) encourage

10. How should the author modify the closing statement to best summarize the selection?

A) NO CHANGE
B) Sometimes they need to be settled in a new place, but this gives beavers a chance to thrive while keeping property undamaged.
C) All that beavers really want is to live in peace, building their dams.
D) Although beavers may bring challenges, their contributions make them an invaluable environmental asset.

11. The author is considering adding an anecdote about beavers devastating the crop on a small farm. To which paragraph should this be added?

A) the 1st paragraph
B) the 2nd paragraph
C) the 3rd paragraph
D) it should not be added

Questions 12–22 are based on the following passage.

What do wedding invitations, ancient Eastern pottery, and medieval books have in common? Each is likely to contain examples of calligraphy, a style of writing that has been used for [12] millennium in cultures around the world. Calligraphy, literally meaning "beautiful writing," has been used as an expression of history, belief, and beauty for people groups from a variety of religions, values, and socioeconomic levels. Some cultures view it as an artistic form of writing, while others consider it pure art. While these cultures represent a diverse tradition, calligraphy is generally divided into two [13] categories: Eastern and Western.

12.

A) NO CHANGE
B) a millennia
C) millennia
D) more than a millennia

13.

A) NO CHANGE
B) categories.
C) categories;
D) categories-

Eastern calligraphy, in particular, is not merely a writing style but a respected art form—superior to painting—that can be seen in manuscripts, vases, and even decoration on weapons. [14] The roots, in China, of calligraphy can be traced back more than 2,000 years. An elite Chinese education, as far back as the Han dynasty, included training in calligraphy. Several distinct styles developed, as each ancient kingdom had a unique set of characters. However, each style had careful [15] guidelines, such as the order of the brushstrokes when creating each character.

Calligraphy has also played a significant role in the Arab world. Heavily employed in a religious setting, [16] copying manuscripts or creating Islamic art were common uses of calligraphy. Beginning in the late 1900s, [17] calligraphy was used in the Hurufiyya movement to create modern art while seeking to preserve its distinctly Arabic influence.

14.

A) NO CHANGE
B) In China, the roots of calligraphy
C) The roots of calligraphy, in China
D) The roots of, in China, calligraphy

15.

A) NO CHANGE
B) tools
C) history
D) meaning

16.

A) NO CHANGE
B) calligraphy was commonly used in copying manuscripts or creating Islamic art
C) common uses of calligraphy included copying manuscripts or creating Islamic art
D) frequently calligraphy was used to copy manuscripts or create Islamic art

17.

A) NO CHANGE
B) calligraphy was employed in the Hurufiyya movement
C) the Hurufiyya movement invented calligraphy
D) the Hurufiyya movement used calligraphy

Like Islamic calligraphy, Western calligraphy was most commonly used for copying religious manuscripts before the invention of the printing press. [18] In large part this was due to the fact that very few outside of the monasteries were literate. This began to change when Charlemagne rose to power in the late eighth century. He made a great effort to promote scholarship and the literary arts, including contributions to book-copying centers. [19] Charlemagne was never able to learn to write himself.

After the printing press came into use, the creation of hand-copied books naturally declined, [20] so calligraphy remained in practice and continues to this day. In fact, a modern calligraphy movement began in the late [21] 1800s and is still flourishing more than a century later. Some calligraphers continue to use tools very similar to the ones employed centuries ago, while others use technology to create their designs. [22] Although not everyone uses this technology, it proves that calligraphy has moved into the modern world.

18.

A) NO CHANGE
B) Altogether
C) Completely
D) Somewhat

19. Where is the best place for this sentence?

A) NO CHANGE
B) At the beginning of this paragraph, because it gives background for why Charlemagne advocated for writing.
C) In the previous paragraph, as a transition to this one.
D) It should be removed from the selection because the information is not relevant.

20.

A) NO CHANGE
B) however
C) yet
D) because

21.

A) NO CHANGE
B) 1800's
C) 18th century
D) eighteenth century

22. Which of the following sentences would make a good conclusion to the selection?

A) NO CHANGE
B) Calligraphy has lasted for thousands of years in China, truly standing the test of time.
C) Bridging the gap between the written word and art, and between diverse cultures, calligraphy is an enduring tradition.
D) Thanks to the various world religions, the ancient art of calligraphy has been preserved for today's audience.

Questions 23–33 are based on the following passage and supplementary material.

The familiar notes of Joplin's [23] "The Entertainer," for many, bring back memories of chasing the local ice cream truck, wrinkled dollar bills in hand. Choosing from a brightly colored menu and slowly eating drippy ice cream bars was a quintessential part of childhood summers for many. Today these trucks are [24] lesser common than a couple of decades ago, leading some to wonder why ice cream is no longer as popular. However, despite the vanishing ice cream trucks, the consumption of frozen treats remains a [25] depleting business. As society has changed, the method of attracting customers has also adapted.

23.

A) NO CHANGE
B) The Entertainer,
C) The Entertainer,
D) the entertainer

24.

A) NO CHANGE
B) less common
C) less uncommon
D) not as uncommon

25.

A) NO CHANGE
B) shaky
C) volatile
D) booming

1.[26] Increasing, health is a concern for Americans, and ice cream consumption has steadily decreased since the turn of the century. *2.* Concerns over fat and sugar content have caused many to blacklist the treat in favor of healthier options. *3.* [27] Whether yogurt is a healthy alternative to ice cream is debatable, particularly as servings can be larger and toppings can add hundreds of sugar-dense calories. *4.* One of these options is frozen yogurt, which has grown into a thriving business in recent decades. *5.* The trucks that cruised neighborhoods at one time [28] are replaced with thousands of tiny shops offering self-serve yogurt and toppings. *6.* Even so, frozen yogurt is providing significant competition to the ice cream industry as consumers eagerly respond to the lower-calorie offering.

26.

A) NO CHANGE
B) Greater
C) Greatly
D) Increasingly

27. Where is the best place for this sentence?

A) NO CHANGE
B) After sentence 4
C) After sentence 5
D) After sentence 6

28.

A) NO CHANGE
B) were
C) have been
D) is

[29] Ice cream remains an overwhelmingly popular treat, both in the US and around the globe. [30] Although ice cream and frozen yogurt sales have stagnated in the US, worldwide consumption of ice cream is on the rise. To meet the demand at home and abroad, the US produces large amounts of ice cream, close to a billion gallons per year. Much of this goes to neighboring nations: the US exports 60,000 metric tons just to Canada, Mexico, and the Caribbean. Since the origin of ice cream can be traced all the way back to 200 B.C. in China, and since China is the most populous nation in the world, it is not surprising that it is also the world's greatest consumer of ice cream, though several nations, including New Zealand, the US, and Australia, consume more per person. [31]

Gallons of Frozen Dessert Sold Annually in the US

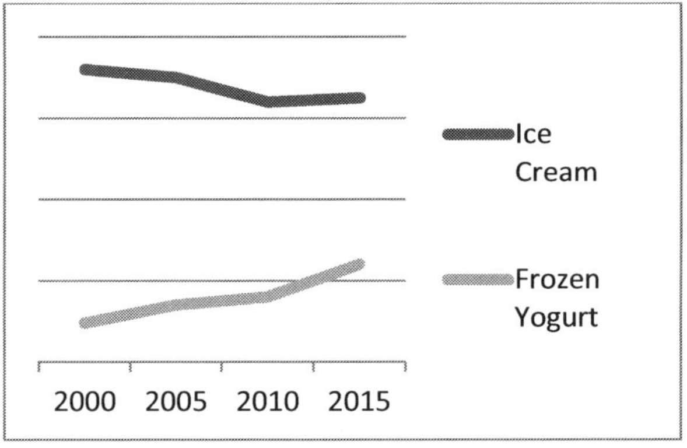

29. How can the author best transition from the previous paragraph?

A) NO CHANGE
B) Because of the popularity of frozen yogurt, ice cream remains
C) Due to this competition, ice cream is no longer
D) Despite the competition, ice cream remains

30. Which of the following statements best uses the information given in the graph?

A) NO CHANGE
B) Even though ice cream sales have dropped slightly in the US since 2000, as frozen yogurt sales climb
C) While frozen yogurt sales have boomed in the last decade
D) Despite declining interest in ice cream over the past several years

31. Which of the following facts would be useful to add to this paragraph?

A) NO CHANGE
B) The amount of ice cream produced per year by Blue Bell
C) The amount of ice cream consumed per year in China
D) The most popular flavor of frozen yogurt

It seems [32] unusual that while frozen yogurt may be the new trend, ice cream is still a beloved American—and global—dessert. And as healthier options continue to arise, the market is projected to keep increasing. So [33] while you may not hear the tinny notes of an ice cream truck in your neighborhood this summer, your options for a cold, sweet treat are only increasing. [33]

32.

A) NO CHANGE
B) unexpected
C) apparent
D) unlikely

33.

A) NO CHANGE
B) whether
C) however
D) unfortunately

Questions 34–44 are based on the following passage.

A young 13th-century mathematician named Leonardo of Pisa is [34] guilty of introducing the Hindu-Arabic numeral system (0, 1, 2 ...) to the Western world. Though he received little recognition in his day, his work had a lasting impact on modern society, permanently changing the way mathematics was [35] viewed, and calculations were performed. Although Leonardo (sometimes known as Leonardo Bonacci or Leonardo Fibonacci) [36] was young, he was very knowledgeable, today he is virtually unknown except for one famous contribution: the Fibonacci sequence. [37] Sadly, the sequence wasn't even his own discovery, as it had been well known for centuries prior to appearing in his book *Liber Abaci* (or *Book of Calculation*).

34.

A) NO CHANGE
B) responsible for
C) the one who was
D) in charge of

35.

A) NO CHANGE
B) viewed;
C) viewed:
D) viewed

36. Which of the following is the best introduction for this sentence?

A) NO CHANGE
B) lived centuries ago, his work endures
C) is famous for many things
D) made numerous other contributions to mathematics

37.

A) NO CHANGE
B) Ironically
C) Disappointingly
D) Tragically

1. The Fibonacci sequence, sometimes called "nature's secret code," is an infinite pattern. *2.* Rather than a simple, linear sequence such as 1, 3, 5, 7..., this sequence is more complex. *3.* Each term is achieved by adding the two previous terms: 1, 1, 2, 3, 5.... *4.* Graphing the numbers creates a steep curve. *5.* [38] This curve is represented in various ways in nature. *6.* It can be seen in the growth pattern of many sunflower seeds, the curve of a shell, and even the whorl of a galaxy. *7.* [39] The Fibonacci sequence is closely related to the Golden Ratio, which also appears in various objects, as well as manmade structures. *8.* [40] Although this sequence only appears in select aspects of nature, it illustrates how nature always follows a pattern.

38. What is the best way to combine the underlined portion?

A) NO CHANGE
B) This curve shows up in almost every part of nature, such as the
C) This curve is represented in a variety of natural forms, including the
D) Fibonacci can be seen in numerous ways in nature, such as the

39. Which sentence best supports the main idea of the paragraph?

A) NO CHANGE
B) Not all sunflowers follow this design; approximately 20% have a different but equally intricate pattern.
C) Although Fibonacci never knew the extent of his discovery, he revolutionized mathematics.
D) Following this design allows plants to optimize their efficiency, fitting the maximum number of seeds into a given space.

40. What is the best location for this sentence?

A) NO CHANGE
B) after sentence 4
C) after sentence 6
D) DELETE, because this sentence does not fit in this paragraph

Although the number sequence has been studied and used in a variety of [41] ways, Fibonacci's introduction of the numeral system is arguably a much greater contribution. Originally this system was developed in India well over 1,000 years ago, and it offers a mathematical system much more [42] challenging to advanced mathematics, such as the algebra that is now the bane of many students. Prior to the Hindu-Arabic system, the Western world relied on Roman numerals and instruments such as the abacus. These are more complicated for calculations, and Roman numerals are also more challenging when writing out long numbers. Fibonacci included decimal places along with the ten digits of the Arabic system. While numbers are written differently in different parts of the world, the general system is accepted worldwide.

When Fibonacci introduced the *modus Indorum* ("method of the Indians," as he called the Hindu-Arabic system), he could not have [43] prophesied that his work would spread around the world. [44] Yet every time you glance at a clock, make a purchase, or count the number of donuts in the box, you should thank Fibonacci for his system. The modern world relies on the contribution of this young, little-known Italian mathematician.

41.

A) NO CHANGE
B) ways:
C) ways;
D) ways

42.

A) NO CHANGE
B) difficult
C) conducive
D) agreeable

43.

A) NO CHANGE
B) understood
C) known
D) foretold

44. Does this sentence fit in the selection?

A) Yes, because the supporting examples are relevant
B) Yes, because it sums up the main idea of the selection
C) No, because the examples are not relevant
D) No, because the tone does not fit with the rest of the selection

Math – No Calculator

Questions 1–13 are multiple choice. Questions 14–17 are grid-in.

1. A taxi ride costs $4.25 for the first mile and $0.70 for each mile after the first. Which of the following functions $c(d)$ gives the total cost (in dollars) of traveling d miles ($d \geq 1$)?

A) $c(d) = 3.55 + 0.70(d + 1)$
B) $c(d) = 3.55 + 0.70(d - 1)$
C) $c(d) = 4.25 + 0.70d$
D) $c(d) = 4.25 + 0.70(d - 1)$

2. Which of these expresses the equation $y = 4x - 2$ as x in terms of y?

A) $x = 4y - 2$

B) $x = -4y + 2$

C) $x = \frac{1}{4}y + 2$

D) $x = \frac{1}{4}y + \frac{1}{2}$

3. Which of the following is equivalent to the inequality $2|x + 3| - 9 \geq -1$.

A) $-1 \leq x \leq 7$
B) $-7 \leq x \leq 1$
C) $x \leq -1$ and $x \geq 7$
D) $x \leq -7$ and $x \geq 1$

4. The solution to which of the following systems of inequalities is graphed below?

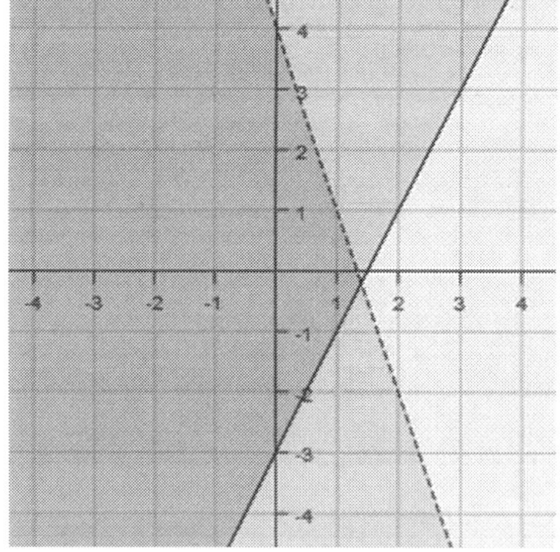

A) $y < -3x + 4$
$4x - 2y \leq 6$
B) $y \geq 2x - 3$
$y < 3x + 4$
C) $x < -3y + 4$
$y + 3 \leq 2x$
D) $y > 4 - 3x$
$y \leq 2x - 3$

5. Which of the following is the correct graph of the system of inequalities below?

$$x - y > 1$$
$$2x + y > 2$$

a. 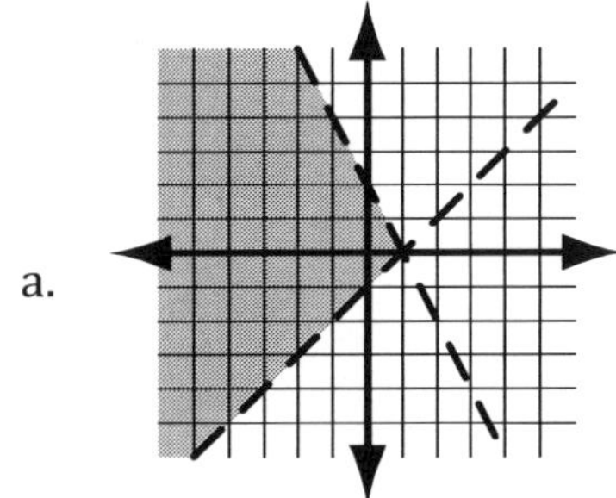

c. 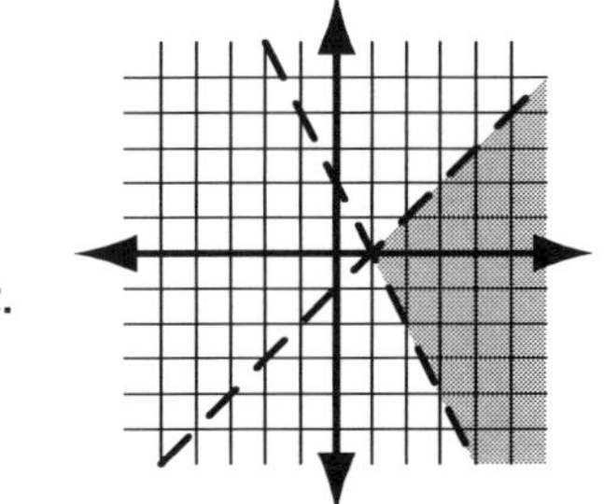

b. 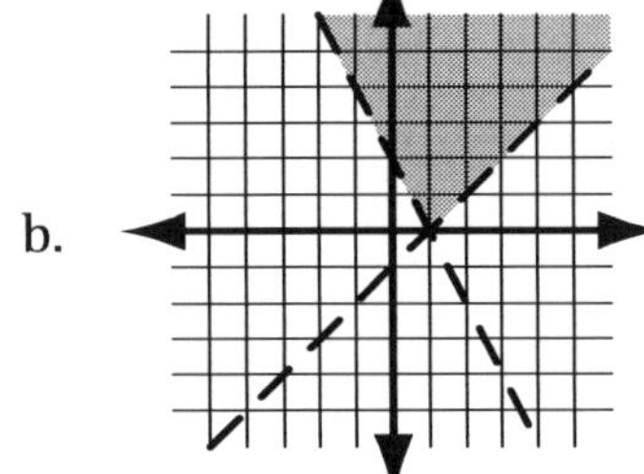

d. 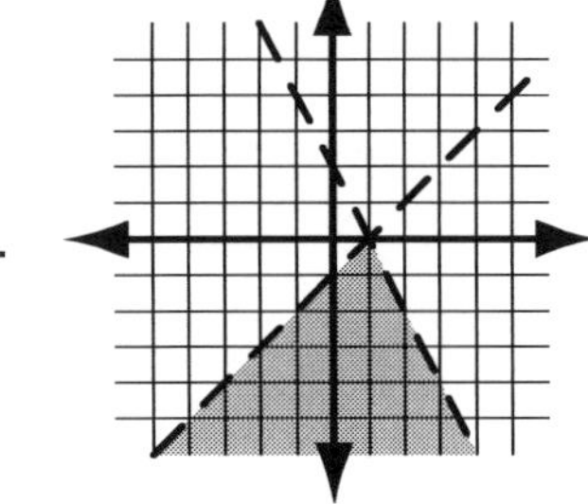

6. Which of the following is equivalent to $3 - 2x < 5$?

A) $x < 1$
B) $x > 1$
C) $x < -1$
D) $x > -1$

7. A certain exam has 30 questions. A student gets 1 point for each question he gets right and loses half a point for a question he answers incorrectly; he neither gains nor loses any points for a question left blank. If *C* is the number of questions a student gets right and *B* is the number of questions he leaves blank, which of the following represents his score on the exam?

A) $C - \frac{1}{2}B$
B) $C - \frac{1}{2}(30 - B)$
C) $C - \frac{1}{2}(30 - B - C)$
D) $(30 - C) - \frac{1}{2}(30 - B)$

8. A building has a number of floors of equal height, as well as a thirty-foot spire above them all. If the height of each floor in feet is *h*, and there are *n* floors in the building, which of the following represents the building's total height in feet?

A) $n + h + 30$
B) $nh + 30$
C) $30n + h$
D) $30h + n$

9. If $x + y > 0$ when $x > y$, which of the following cannot be true?

A) $x = 6$ and $y = -1$
B) $x = -3$ and $y = 0$
C) $x = -4$ and $y = -3$
D) $x = 3$ and $y = -3$

10. Simplify the expression $\frac{x^2+2x-24}{5x-20}$.

A) $\frac{x-4}{5}$

B) $\frac{x+6}{5}$

C) $\frac{(x-4)(x+6)}{5(x-4)}$

D) $\frac{(x+4)(x+6)}{5(x-4)}$

11. Simplify the expression $x^6 \times (3x)^2$.

A) $3x^8$
B) $3x^{12}$
C) $9x^8$
D) $9x^{12}$

12. A theater manager estimates that he will sell 600 tickets to a play if he prices tickets at \$10 each. He also estimates that he will sell fifty fewer tickets for every dollar the price is raised or fifty more tickets for every dollar the price is lowered. Write a function $r(x)$ for the estimated revenue if the theater raises the price by x dollars.

A) $r(x) = -50x^2 - 100x + 6000$
B) $r(x) = -50x^2 + 100x + 6000$
C) $r(x) = 50x^2 - 1100x - 6000$
D) $r(x) = 50x^2 + 1100x + 6000$

13. Compare the graphs of $f(x) = 3^x$ and $g(x) = 3^{x+1}$.

A) The graph of g is the graph of f shifted one unit down.
B) The graph of g is the graph of f shifted one unit up.
C) The graph of g is the graph of f shifted one unit to the left.
D) The graph of g is the graph of f shifted one unit to the right.

14. Exponential functions grow by equal factors over equal intervals. By what factor does the exponential function $f(x) = 3 \times 2^x$ grow over every interval whose length is 3?

Grid your answer.

15. A librarian makes 50% more per hour for each hour that he works in excess of 40 hours each week. The linear function $s(h) = 27h + 720$ represents his weekly salary (in dollars) if he works h hours more than 40 hours that week. For example, his weekly salary is $s(10) = 990$ dollars if he works 50 hours in one week (because $10 + 40 = 50$). What is his hourly wage (in dollars) after he has already worked the initial 40 hours in one week?

Grid your answer.

16. Calculate the sixth term $f(6)$ of the sequence defined as:

$$f(n) = \begin{cases} 1 & n = 1, 2 \\ f(n-1) + 2f(n-2) & n > 2 \end{cases}$$

Grid your answer.

17. Consider the function $f(x) = (x-3)(x^2 - x - 2)$. What is the sum of all values of x for which the graph of the function intersects the x-axis?

Grid your answer.

Math – Calculator

Questions 1–27 are multiple choice. Questions 28–31 are gridded.

1. Solve the following system of equations.

$$y = 3x + 2$$
$$2x + y = 7$$

A) $x = -1, y = 5$
B) $x = -1, y = 9$
C) $x = 1, y = 5$
D) $x = 1, y = 9$

2. The table below lists values for x and $f(x)$.

x	$f(x)$
1	2
2	5
3	10
4	17
5	26

Which of the following equations describes the relationship between x and $f(x)$?

A) $f(x) = x + 1$
B) $f(x) = x^2$
C) $f(x) = (-x)^2$
D) $f(x) = x^2 + 1$

3. Which of the following equations represents the relationship between x and y, shown in the table below?

x	y
−3	−21
−1	−3
0	6
2	24
5	51

A) $y = 9x + 6$
B) $y = 7x$
C) $y = 3x + 18$
D) $y = 12x + 6$

4. The mean test grade on Ms. Juarez's biology final was 86, while the median test grade was 82.5. What could explain the difference between these two values?

A) Most students scored less than 80.
B) Most students scored between 82.5 and 86.
C) Several students had low, outlying scores, pulling the median down.
D) Several students had high, outlying scores, pulling the mean up.

5. If the two lines $2x + y = 0$ and $y = 3$ are plotted on a typical xy coordinate grid, at which point will they intersect?

A) (-1.5, 3)
B) (1.5, 3)
C) (-1.5, 0)
D) (4, 1)

6. What is the value of $\frac{x^3+2x}{x+3}$ when $x = -1$?

A) $-\frac{3}{2}$

B) $-\frac{2}{3}$

C) $\frac{1}{2}$

D) $\frac{3}{4}$

7. What is the value of $\frac{2x-2}{x-3}$ when $x = -1$?

A) 0
B) 1
C) 2
D) -2

8. Simplify: $4(-3 + 5i) + 6(1 - 3i)$.

A) $18 + 38i$
B) $13 + 18i$
C) $-6 + 2i$
D) $-6 - 2i$

9. An MP3 player is set to play songs at random from the fifteen songs it contains in its memory. Any song can be played at any time, even if it is repeated. There are 5 songs by Band A, 3 songs by Band B, 2 by Band C, and 5 by Band D. If the player has just played two songs in a row by Band D, what is the probability that the next song will also be by Band D?

A) 1 in 5
B) 1 in 3
C) 1 in 9
D) 1 in 27

10. 9.5% of the people in a town voted for a certain proposition in a municipal election. If the town's population is 51,623, about how many people in the town voted for the proposition?

A) 3,000
B) 5,000
C) 7,000
D) 10,000

11. A reporter for a school newspaper surveys the students at the school to ask if they prefer chocolate, vanilla, or strawberry ice cream. Of the students who answer her question, 35% prefer vanilla, and 40% prefer chocolate. What percent of the students she surveyed prefer strawberry?

A) 15%
B) 25%
C) 45%
D) There is not enough information to say.

12. Liz runs a woodworking stand at a community market. She purchases a friend's handmade pens for $15 each to sell along with her own goods. To make a profit, she marks the pens up by 30%. On the last day of the market, she marks down everything by 20%. How much are the pens now?

A) $15.60
B) $15.90
C) $16.64
D) $17.90

13. Mrs. Patterson's classroom has sixteen empty chairs. All the chairs are occupied when every student is present. If 2/5 of the students are absent, how many students make up her entire class?

A) 16 students
B) 32 students
C) 24 students
D) 40 students

14. The probability that Alisha chooses a philosophy class is 0.30. The probability that she chooses a qualitative methods class, given that she chooses a philosophy class, is 0.40. Finally, the probability she chooses a philosophy class or a qualitative methods class is 0.62. What is the probability she chooses a qualitative methods class?

A) 0.32
B) 0.38
C) 0.44
D) 0.52

Question 15 is based on the following figure (not drawn to scale):

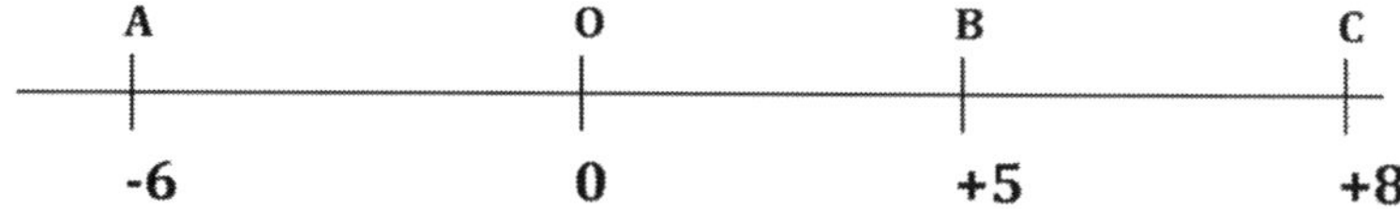

15. In the figure, A, B, and C are points on the number line, where O is the origin. What is the ratio of the distance $\overline{BC}$ to distance $\overline{AB}$?

A) 3:5
B) 8:5
C) 8:11
D) 3:11

16. The numbers of volunteers in different states are shown in the table below. Which of the following statements is true?

Texas	8	17	18	19	20	21	21	21	22	28	29	31	41	45	48
New Mexico	7	11	15	29	30	30	31	33	34	36	37	42	44	44	45

A) The numbers of volunteers in Texas have a greater median and mean.
B) The numbers of volunteers in Texas have a greater median and a smaller mean.
C) The numbers of volunteers in Texas have a smaller median and mean.
D) The numbers of volunteers in Texas have a smaller median and a greater mean.

17. Marcus is purchasing hamburger patties and hot dogs for a community barbecue. He needs a total of 500, and plans to buy at least twice as many hot dogs as hamburgers. Which of the following systems of equations/inequalities represents his purchase, if *x* represents hamburgers and y represents hot dogs?

A) $x \geq y$
$2x + y = 500$

B) $x \geq 2y$
$x + y = 500$

C) $x \leq 2y$
$2x + 3y = 500$

D) $2x \leq y$
$x + y = 500$

18. Given the table shown below, what is the probability that a student is a Democrat or prefers math?

	History	**Science**	**Math**	**Total**
Democrat	13	30	37	80
Republican	20	38	12	70
Total	33	68	49	150

A) $\frac{129}{150}$

B) $\frac{46}{75}$

C) $\frac{37}{150}$

D) $\frac{37}{80}$

Questions 19 and 20 are based on the following table:

Kyle bats third in the batting order for the Badgers baseball team. The table below shows the number of hits that Kyle had in each of 7 consecutive games played during one week in July.

Day of Week	Number of Hits
Monday	1
Tuesday	2
Wednesday	3
Thursday	1
Friday	1
Saturday	4

19. What is the mode of the numbers in the distribution shown in the table?

A) 1
B) 2
C) 3
D) 4

20. What is the mean of the numbers in the distribution shown in the table?

A) 1
B) 2
C) 3
D) 4

Questions 21 and 22 refer to the following information.

The table below records the amount of sleep that a group of students had the night before a test, the number of students in each group, and the test scores of each group.

	Group 1	Group 2	Group 3
Amount of Sleep	<6.5 hrs	6.5–7.5 hrs	>7.5 hrs
Number of Students	6	4	2
Test Scores	83, 77, 89, 68, 91, 72	82, 88, 77, 90	86, 93

21. What is the probability that a randomly chosen student slept less than 6.5 hours and scored in the 80s?

A) $\frac{1}{4}$

B) $\frac{1}{6}$

C) $\frac{2}{9}$

D) $\frac{5}{12}$

22. Which group has the lowest mean score?

A) Group 1
B) Group 2
C) Group 3
D) multiple groups share the lowest mean

23. Solve the equation $\sqrt{4x-3}+2=x$ for x.

A) $x = 1$
B) $x = 7$
C) $x = -1$ and $x = 7$
D) $x = 1$ and $x = 7$

24. If $f(x)$ is a quadratic function with roots at $x = -4$ and $x = 6$, what is $f(x)$?

A) $f(x) = x^2 - 24$
B) $f(x) = x^2 - 10x + 24$
C) $f(x) = x^2 - 2x - 24$
D) $f(x) = x^2 + 2x - 24$

25. Which of the following represents the sum of $\frac{3}{x+2} + \frac{x}{x^2+10x+16}$?

A) $\frac{3}{x+2}$
B) $\frac{x+6}{x+8}$
C) $\frac{2(x+6)}{(x+2)(x+8)}$
D) $\frac{4(x+6)}{(x+8)(x+2)}$

26. Which of the following represents the product of $(4x^3 - 2x + 4)(x - 8)$?

A) $4x^4 - 32x^3 + 18x - 32$
B) $4x^4 - 32x^3 - 18x^2 - 2x - 12$
C) $4x^4 - 32x^3 - 2x^2 + 20x - 32$
D) $4x^4 - 28x^3 - 2x^2 + 16x - 4$

27. In the figure, *ABCD* is a parallelogram. The angles are m∠$B = (3x)°$ and m∠$C = (4x + 5)°$. Find m∠A.

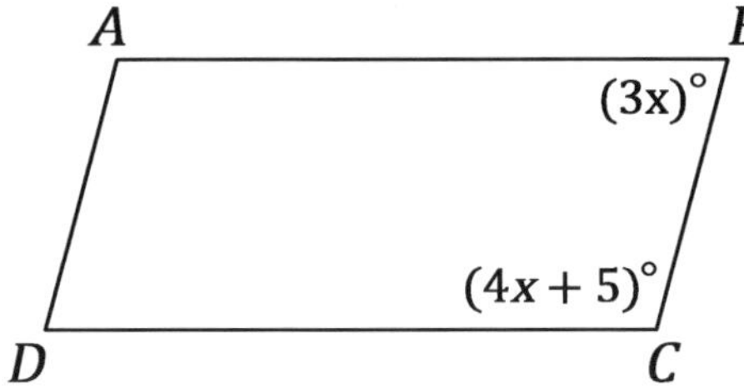

A) m∠$A = 95°$
B) m∠$A = 100°$
C) m∠$A = 105°$
D) m∠$A = 110°$

28. In the figure, the radius of circle *C* is 8. What is the area of the shaded sector, rounded to the nearest tenth?

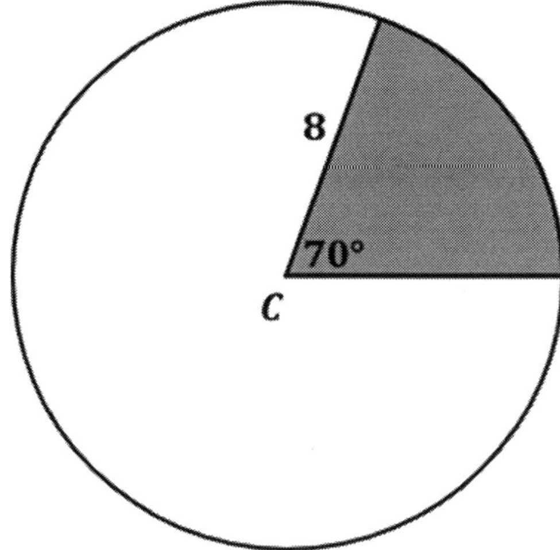

Grid your answer.

29. The figure shows the shape of a large swimming pool in a Las Vegas resort. The pool is a rectangle with semicircles on either end. If the pool is 8 ft deep throughout, what is the volume of the pool in cubic feet, rounded to the nearest whole number?

Grid your answer.

30. In the figure, ΔABC is an equilateral triangle with sides of length 10 in. Circle O is inscribed in this triangle, so that it is tangent to ΔABC at three points, the midpoint of each side. What is the radius of circle O rounded to the nearest tenth?

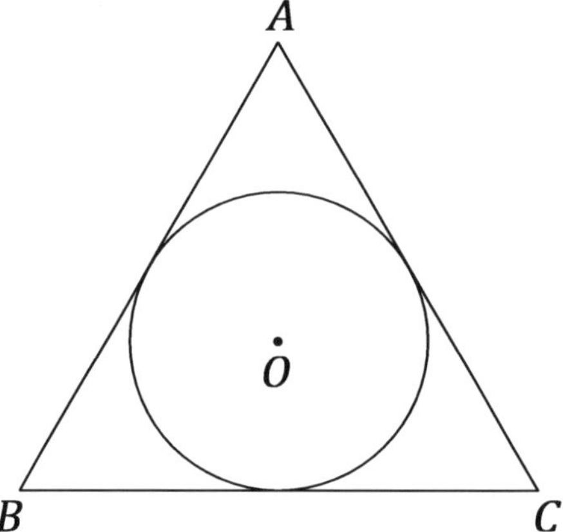

Grid your answer.

31. A seller purchases wholesale merchandise and makes a profit by selling it for more than she paid for it. When she purchases an item, she adds 25% to the price she paid for it, and lists it for sale at that price. If an item does not sell within 6 months, she places it on clearance, and reduces the price by 10%. What is her percentage profit on clearance items, rounded to the nearest tenth of a percent?

Grid your answer.

Answer Key and Explanations

Reading Test

1. Choice A is the best answer. Choice B is incorrect because Mother did not forbid any presents. Choices C and D give some of the problems presented in the selection, but do not offer a complete summary. Lines 2-4 ("It's so dreadful ... injured sniff") indicate that the girls are poor and hint at being unable to purchase even nice clothes. In line 34-35 ("I don't believe ... nose isn't nice."), Amy describes suffering at the hands of "impertinent girls," implying that she is made fun of by other girls, likely at school.

2. Choice C is the best answer. Of the options listed, Choice C is the only one that refers to men suffering in the army. Choice A references a lack of Christmas presents but does not mention the reason for this. Choice B talks about the girls not having their father with them for some indefinite period of time, but that does not by itself imply that there is a war going on. Choice D discusses the limited usefulness of their theoretical monetary contributions.

3. Choice D is the best answer. We know from the very first line in the passage that Christmas is approaching and Jo's comment in line 7 ("We haven't ... long time") indicates that their father is not expected to return home anytime soon. Thus, the most reasonable inference is that he is not likely to return home in time for Christmas. Although the sisters are all concerned about their father's wellbeing, there is nothing to indicate that he is likely to die, as in Choice C. Similarly, we have no indication about his preference for what his daughters do with their money as in Choices A and B.

4. Choice D is the best answer. The other sisters all specify what they want to buy: Amy in line 22 ("I shall ... drawing pencils"), Beth in line 20 ("I planned ... new music"), and Jo in line 18 ("I do ... for myself"). We are given no indication as to what Meg wants.

5. Choice B is the best answer. In the context of the sentence, Amy's sniff indicates that her sense of fairness, vanity, and pride has been offended. While Amy is indeed sympathetic to the sentiments expressed by her sisters as in Choice C, injured would not be a word used to express that. There is nothing in this passage indicating Amy has been physically harmed as in Choice A, or is ill as in Choice D.

6. Choice C is the best answer. *Undine and Sintram* (de la Motte Fouqué, 1855) is a novella based on a fairy tale. The reader who is unfamiliar with this title can deduce it from the context of lines 18 and 19: after saying "I do want to buy Undine and Sintram for myself," the following sentence reads, "'I've wanted it so long,' said Jo, who was a bookworm." The author would not mention that Jo was a bookworm in this sentence unless the item named were a book.

7. Choice D is the best answer. The presence of a hearth brush and kettle-holder indicate a fireplace. The fact that the fireplace "hears" Beth's sigh when no one else does means that Beth is close to it.

8. Choice A is the best answer. Previously, Beth has said that she plans to spend her dollar on new music (Line 20), so the inference that can be made here is that Beth would like to be practicing music. Drawing (Choice B) is what Amy does. She says she will buy Faber's drawing pencils with her dollar. Housework (Choice C) is what Beth complains makes it difficult for her to practice. Schoolwork (Choice D) is what Amy complains about after Beth's complaint.

9. Choice C is the best answer. As the sisters discuss their situation, it is clear that each one of them faces a particular set of challenges. They all desire things that they do not have, and they are all required to do things they would prefer not to. The passage also indicates that their father is away fighting in a war. Although one of the sisters mentions that there are other girls who have plenty of pretty things, the overarching sense of the passage is that everyone has their own troubles.

10. Choice B is the best answer. In lines1-2 of passage 1 ("At this second...at the first."), his second inaugural address, Lincoln discusses his first address, describing how the first actions in the coming Civil War were just beginning to take place. The country had suffered much since then as the war got underway and continued throughout his first term as president. This change in the nation inspired the plea for an end to the hostilities that dominates his second inaugural address.

11. Choice C is the best answer. "Peculiar" can mean odd (Choice A) or bizarre (Choice B), but these make no sense in this context. "Peculiar" can also mean specific (Choice C), unique, particular, distinctive, or characteristic, which is the meaning in this case, because in lines 16-17, Lincoln was referring to the specific and unique situation that, "One-eighth of the whole population were colored slaves, not distributed generally over the Union, but localized in the southern part of it," and the specific interest these slaves constituted. Appropriate (Choice D) is another synonym offered by a thesaurus for the second (correct) meaning, but its denotation of suitable or fitting does not make sense in this context as specific, unique, particular, distinctive, etc. does.

12. Choice C is the best answer. Lincoln's Biblical quotation established the subsequent supposition that the war is an example of the woe for causing offenses described in the quotation (just as previously in the same sentence he supposed American slavery was one of the offenses that must needs come). Choice A does not support the supposition that God gave the war as woe; if anything, it supports his contention that despite their basic differences regarding slavery. In line 14, it is said that "both parties deprecated war." Choice B reinforces the parallelism and comparison/contrast established in lines 12-15 ("saving the Union without war/destroy it without war"; "make war rather than let the nation survive/accept war rather than let it perish") and continued in lines 21-23 ("Neither...expected....Neither anticipated....Each looked for....") rather than supporting that war was God's giving both sides woe for offenses. Choice D supports that even though everyone wanted the war to end soon ("Fondly...away", penultimate sentence), if it lasted longer it would be God's will.

13. Choice C is the best answer. Lincoln's final paragraph, lines 39-42 of passage 1 ("With malice toward...with all nations."), issues a plea for "malice toward none, with charity for all." This statement represents an attempt to heal the pain that existed between the North and South during the Civil War. Lincoln wants the United States to reunite and move on from the war as a solid, individual, caring nation.

14. Choice A is the best answer. Lincoln believed that the South was wrong for making war by trying to secede from the union, and the North was right for trying to maintain the union by refusing to accept the hostile action. The quote in lines 14-15 ("Both parties ... war came.") shows he believed the actions of the North were more justifiable than those of the South.

15. Choice A is the best answer. In lines 35-38 of passage 1, Lincoln states that "if God wills that it [the war] continue ... until every drop of blood drawn with the lash shall be paid by another drawn with the sword, as was said three thousand years ago, so still it must be said 'the judgments of the Lord are true and righteous altogether.'" This statement indicates Lincoln's believe that the war was a product of God's will.

16. Choice D is the best answer. By using the same syntactic structure in "what we say here" and "what they did here", Lincoln employed parallel structure to reinforce his message contrasting words vs. deeds. Epiphora (Choice A), epistrophe, is repeating the same words/phrases at the *ends* of sentences/clauses. An example in Lincoln's Gettysburg Address is: "that government of the people, by the people, for the people..." in its final sentence. Choice B, Anaphora, is repeating the same words/phrases at the *beginnings* of clauses/sentences, as Dickens did in the opening of *A Tale of Two Cities*: "It was the best of times, it was the worst of times, it was the age of wisdom, it was the age of foolishness..." etc. (he used "it was" 10 times in one sentence). Repetition (Choice C) involves simply repeating the same word/phrase/clause multiple times. Parallelism/parallel structure does not require exact word repetition, but symmetrical sentence/clause structure arranging the same parts of speech in the same word order.

17. Choice B is the best answer. The closest meaning is freedom for all citizens, which would include slaves. Lincoln issued the Emancipation Proclamation over nine months before the Gettysburg Address, but the Civil War was still being fought over the issue of slavery. In line 10-16 ("It is for us...from the earth."), he called for "us the living" to finish the "unfinished work" of the soldier and "highly resolve that these dead shall not have died in vain" by giving the nation a "new birth of freedom". Without reaffirming the nation's bases of freedom and equality, the nation would "perish from the earth" and the soldiers would have died in vain. The entire paragraph, lines 7-16 ("But, in a larger sense... perish from the earth."), leads up to this meaning. Choice A is wrong because this does not indicate freedom from war: the speech does not say ending the war would bring freedom; but by restoring the nation's original foundations of freedom and equality for which soldiers fought, the dead would not die in vain—not that soldiers should be freed from fighting the war as in Choice C. Slavery violated the foundations of US democracy; hence Choice D makes no sense in this context.

18. Choice A is the best answer. Lincoln was reminding his audience that the nation was formed with the ideas of liberty and equality as foundations—seen symmetrically in the opening and closing sentences—and reasoning that upholding those ideals was the best way to honor the soldiers who fought for that nation. Choice B is not the main idea as he explicitly stated in the third lines 7-8 ("we cannot consecrate – we cannot hallow – this ground") because the soldiers had done so "far beyond our poor power to add or detract." He continues to say their deeds will never be forgotten even though his and others' words would—making Choice C incorrect. Completing soldiers' unfinished work refers not to declaring a cease-fire (Choice D) in particular, but to ensuring the nation's democratic government and its founding principles would not "perish from the earth."

19. Choice C is the best answer. In the Second Inaugural Address, Lincoln said in line 40 of passage 1, "...let us strive on to finish the work we are in..." and in the Gettysburg Address, lines 10-11 of passage 2, "...to be dedicated here to the unfinished work which they who fought here have thus far so nobly advanced." He spoke of Choices A, B, and D in the former speech, but not overtly in the latter.

20. Choice D is the best answer. Lincoln delivered his Second Inaugural Address after a time of great hardship for the United States. His plea for the country's resolution of its severe problems must have been an emotional experience for the president, and his voice must have conveyed this emotionality as he read the speech. As a result, reading the transcript could not have quite the same emotional impact as hearing it in person. The tone of the address is not anger (Choice A), but rather the desire for reconciliation and peace. For the same reason, Choice C is also not the best choice since the speaker is not seeking to intimidate those listening. Choice B is not relevant to the different experiences of reading and hearing.

21. Choice A is the best answer. Following the phrase, "I have called for personal sacrifice" in line 5, the author states, "A part of the sacrifice means the payment of more money in taxes" for "a greater portion of this great defense program" in lines 6-8. While he called for taxpayers to support the military, in this passage he did not equate personal sacrifice with serving in the military (Choice B). While he described worldwide arms reduction (Choice C), he did not equate this with personal sacrifice, but with the fourth freedom: freedom from fear. The four freedoms (Choice D) he identified were "essential human freedoms", i.e., things all human beings had rights to, not examples of personal sacrifice.

22. Choice D is the best answer. There are four basic freedoms that are vital to the health of people: speech, worship, freedom from want, and freedom from fear. This speech is typically referred to as the "Four Freedoms" speech. In it, the author articulates the basic freedoms he believes in. These freedoms are the central focus of the speech, since it supports the other ideas that he is focusing on (i.e., social issues). Choice A is a single detail in the speech, Choice B is not articulated, and Choice C is not in the speech.

23. Choice C is the best answer. In this passage, there is no mention of expanding the draft of citizens into military service. As examples of aspects of the social economy needing "immediate improvement," the author cited, "We should bring more citizens under the coverage of old-age pensions...."; "We should widen the opportunities for adequate medical care"; and "We should plan a better system by which persons deserving or needing gainful employment may obtain it."

24. Choice B is the best answer. The argument that needs to be evaluated is that people will be happy to give more money in taxes to the government. It would be safe to raise the counterargument that the general population may already believe they are paying enough in taxes and don't think the government is spending that money wisely. Not everyone will be happy to give more to the government to spend. Choices A and D do not address the question. Choice C agrees with the author's premise.

25. Choice D is the best answer. In stating, "That is no vision of a distant millennium," the author is saying that we do not have to wait hundreds or thousands of years to see the freedoms that he has described become reality. While the author would likely agree with some or all of the statements listed in the other answer choices, none of them reflects the meaning of the statement in question.

26. Choice D is the best answer. After describing the four freedoms he identified, the author states that the vision of a world founded on those freedoms was "attainable in our own time and generation" and that it would be "the very antithesis of the so-called new order of tyranny," referring to the "order" that dictators wanted to impose. He further described the "cooperation of free countries, working together in a friendly, civilized society" as "the world order which we seek." This context establishes that "order" most nearly means a system of world politics and society rather than a military leader's command (Choice A), an authoritative decision or direction (Choice B), or an arrangement in sequence (Choice C).

27. Choice C is the best answer. FDR spoke of freedom, defining it in line 31 as "the supremacy of human rights everywhere." This is the "high concept" he refers to in the following line 33. In this context, the "end" of victory does not mean death, as in Choice A. It does not precisely mean purpose (Choice B), as in the common phrase "a means to an end" (a way of achieving a purpose): he was not saying victory was the only purpose of the concept, but rather that this concept could have no other outcome (Choice C) or result than victory. "End" can also mean conclusion (Choice D), i.e., the termination or finishing of something, which does not fit the meaning in this context quite as precisely as in Choice C because it does not imply cause and effect as "outcome" does.

28. Choice C is the best answer. The sentence found in lines 26-28, "Since the beginning of our American history, we have been engaged in change—in a perpetual peaceful revolution—a revolution which goes on steadily, quietly adjusting itself to changing conditions—without the concentration camp or the quick-lime in the ditch" is the only statement listed here that directly supports the idea that FDR thought that America is constantly moving toward a better way of life.

29. Choice A is the best answer. It emphasizes the need for a social safety net for the aging populace. While the other ideas in Choices B and C are clearly mentioned in the blog, they are not derived from the speech. Choice A is the only one that discusses an idea that shows up in the speech.

30. Choice C is the best answer. The passage describes several distinctive features of annelid anatomy and tells how some of them differ from other worms. Descriptions of the annelid anatomy can be found throughout the passage, whereas the other answer choices are too specific, though they are mentioned.

31. Choice C is the best answer. The text defines metameres as segments, and discusses segmentation as the distinguishing feature of the phylum.

32. Choice C is the best answer. In lines 6-8 ("Metameric segmentation...specific functions."), the text gives the example of feet specializing into grasping organs to illustrate this evolutionary advantage of segmental plasticity. It gives specific examples, but describes the helpfulness of segmentation for performing specialized functions.

33. Choice A is the best answer. The term "metamerism" is defined in lines 4-5 ("They are...termed metamerism.") of the selection as an organization of the anatomy into segments.

34. Choice D is the best answer. The term parapodia is defined in lines 8-9 ("For example...digestive specializations.").

35. Choice A is the best answer. The author compares annelids and nematodes when he describes both as having a fluid-filled internal *coelum* or cavity separating the body wall and gut, and both having this cavity involved in their locomotion. The author also contrasts the two phyla in that annelids develop this cavity much later during both embryonic growth (and presumably evolutionary progress). None of the other answer choices accurately reflect the structure of this paragraph.

36. Choice D is the best answer. In lines 20-21 ("This phylum...terrestrial habitats."), tell us that annelids can live in salt or fresh water and on land, and then gives examples of each in the following sentences. This helps demonstrate that there are many types of annelids and that they live in a variety of habitats. Choices A, B, and C are wrong because they do not represent all of the information presented in these lines. Choice D is the most comprehensive choice.

37. Choice B is the best answer. The author mentions the adaptability of metameres in line 7, noting that "certain segments can be modified and specialized." The author then gives examples of how this is seen in lines 8-9: "certain of the locomotor *parapodia*, or feet, may be modified for grasping, and some portions of the gut may evolve digestive specializations."

38. Choice D is the best answer. The text gives the example of parapodia modified for grasping. The graphic shows a set of Annelid legs that seem to be grabbing a small rock.

39. Choice B is the best answer. After the initial topic sentence, lines 1-9 ("The phylum...digestive specializations.") discuss metameric segmentation as a distinctive feature of annelids. The, lines 10-15 ("The gut...true coelom") discuss annelid body parts, i.e., the gut, body wall, and *coelum*, including their functions, development, and differences and similarities of the latter between annelids and nematodes. Lines 16-19 ("The annelid...segmental ganglia.") then discuss annelid body systems, including excretory, circulatory, respiratory, and nervous. Finally, lines 20-22 ("This phylum...worm Nereis.") include annelid habitat adaptations and names three well-known types.

40. Choice D is the best answer. The passage puts Pluto forth as the main topic, but goes into depth about the reclassification and the reasoning behind Pluto's reclassification, primarily in lines 16-20 ("The third...with itself."). Choice A is wrong because the passage was not primarily for entertainment and the focus was on Pluto, not primarily distinguishing planets and dwarf-planets. Choice B is wrong because the purpose was not to excite people about future research as much as it was to discuss past research. Choice C is wrong because the passage was not persuasive in tone. The author held a primarily informative stance throughout the passage and did not seem to take a side on the matter.

41. Choice B is the best answer. Lines 10-18 ("The IAU...own orbit") provide the three requirements for an object to be a planet. Choice B does refer to a required quality of a planet, that it has a regular orbit. Pluto does, in fact, have a regular orbit around the sun, though it is not as regular as the 8 true planets. Pluto has not cleared its neighborhood, making Choice A wrong. Pluto has a moon, but this is not considered a requirement for a planet, making Choice C wrong. Finally, some may argue that because Pluto was a planet, it should remain a planet, but this is not a scientific basis of reasoning.

42. Choice A is the best answer. The passage does not give any clarification on what a celestial body is. The passage implies that there are many celestial bodies in our solar system, and that some could have been confirmed as planets. This indicates that some are unconfirmed planets, but also implies that some would not be considered planets or dwarf planets. Meteors and meteorites are not discussed and are too specific of a definition for celestial body. The only definition that fits in the context is Choice A, any object in space.

43. Choice C is the best answer. As described in lines 13-14 ("Second, a planet...spherical shape."), a planet is said to be in hydrostatic equilibrium when its gravity is enough to cause it to form into a nearly spherical shape. Despite the prefix '-hydro', This principal does not refer to water in any way.

44. Choice B is the best answer. In line 17, the author explains that a planet must have sufficient gravity to clear its neighborhood, further elaborating that this gravity is a result of the planet's mass. Thus, when the author says that Pluto is not massive enough, he is referring specifically to the planet's mass. A planet's size is often related to its mass, but it is the mass and not the size of the planet that provides the gravitational attraction.

45. Choice D is the best answer. Nostalgia is the best stand-in for sentimentality, as sentimentality and nostalgia both refer to an emotional attachment. Choice B, Empiricism, and Choice A, rationalism, are both more related to science than to sentiment and emotions. Choice C, Ethics, does not fit, as there is no moral dilemma about Pluto's status as a planet.

46. Choice C is the best answer. He gives neither opinion. The author is mainly neutral to this change and only points out what historically has taken place. In lines 28-29 ("Perhaps the...pseudo-planet."), the author does advocate for advancement of technology to help understand these matters further.

47. Choice D is the best answer. Pluto's estimated mass decreased over time, indicating that scientists had likely been largely overestimating Pluto's mass and are getting more precise with time. The estimate for 2006 breaks the trend by increasing the estimated mass, but the chart still shows a recognizable downward trend as a whole.

48. Choice A is the best answer. The passage states in lines 17-18 ("The planet's...of the way.") that a planet's gravity, as a result of its mass, is how it clears its neighborhood. The chart shows a decline in Pluto's estimated mass over time, showing less confidence in Pluto's ability to clear its neighborhood.

49. Choice C is the best answer. Choice A is not correct because the passage does not discuss moons specifically, though it does hint at a major theme of the passage, in that it describes distinguishing planets from other large celestial bodies. Choice B is a good second choice because the majority of the passage includes a description of qualifications of a planet, however, a taxonomy implies discussing many types of bodies. Choice B also does not include Pluto in the topic, which is the primary focus of the passage. Choice D is wrong because Pluto has not been made a planet once again, therefore contradicting the passage. Choice C is correct because the passage as a whole is describing Pluto, giving scientific reasoning for it being changed in status to a dwarf planet. The sentiment aspect comes into play primarily in the final paragraph, lines 24-29 ("Even with clear...pseudo-planet"), as it discusses the major pushback against Pluto's reclassification. That pushback is largely founded in emotion, rather than rationality.

Writing and Language

1. Choice C is the best answer. The sentence is in present tense and the subject (contributions) is plural, so "are" is correct. Answer choice B would be used with a singular subject. Answer choices A and D would be used in a past tense sentence.

2. Choice B is the best answer. The correct answer is beavers', because it refers to multiple animals, not just one (A). The sentence is referring to the benefit of the beavers, not the land (C). Using "their" (D) could refer to the beavers but would not flow grammatically: "the their benefit."

3. Choice D is the best answer. The correct answer is "upstream, slowing." Using a semicolon (A or C) is not correct because the clause after the semicolon is not an independent clause (a portion that could be a stand-alone sentence). Using "upstream, which is slowing" (B) adds unnecessary verbiage and confuses the subject.

4. Choice D is the best answer. "Tens" and "hundreds" are plural, not possessive, so A and B are incorrect. The clause "or possibly even hundreds" could be set off with commas or dashes, but would need punctuation on both ends, so C is incorrect (and B is also incorrect for this reason). Answer choice D uses the correct plural forms and omits all punctuation for "or possibly even hundreds," which is grammatically correct.

5. Choice A is the best answer. The sentence is grammatically correct as it is written. Answer choice B is incorrect because it uses present tense, rather than referring to an event that began in the past and is ongoing. Answer choice C is incorrect because the verb (declined) needs an adverb (sharply) rather than an adjective (sharp). Answer choice D adds unnecessary verbiage, which can confuse the meaning.

6. Choice B is the best answer. The correct answer is "destroys" because the subject (building) is singular, not plural (A), and the sentence is in present tense. Do not be confused by the direct object "dams," which is plural. Answer choice C is incorrect because the subject is singular. Answer choice D is incorrect because the sentence is in present tense, not past.

7. Choice C is the best answer. A colon is correct here because it can be used to introduce a list. Lists should not be introduced with commas (A) or semicolons (B), nor should punctuation between the clause and the list be absent (D).

8. Choice B is the best answer. The correct answer is "its," which is the possessive form of "it." In contrast, "it's" (A) is incorrect because it refers to the contraction of the words "it is." Using "their" or "theirs" (C and D) is incorrect because the subject (foliage) is singular.

9. Choice C is the best answer. The correct answer is "encouraging," which is a present participle modifying the verbs "trapped" and "relocated." It would be correct to write, "which encourages," but not "which encouraging" (A) or "that is encouraging" (B). Finally, "encourage" (D) is an incorrect form of verb for a participle phrase.

10. Choice D is the best answer. The main point of the selection, as can be seen in the opening paragraph, is that beavers make important contributions to the environment. Choices A and B may be true, but are not the main point and therefore poor choices for summarizing. Answer choice C is a subjective opinion.

11. Choice C is the best answer. The third paragraph mentions the destruction beavers can cause, so it would be the best place for this anecdote.

12. Choice C is the best answer. The word "millennia" is plural, while "millennium" is singular. Thus "a millennia" (B and D) are grammatically incorrect, as is using "millennium" (A) without an article.

13. Choice A is the best answer. A colon is used to define or introduce something, such as a new term or a list. Here the sentence is defining or explaining the two categories, so a colon is correct. A period (B) is incorrect because the part of the sentence after the punctuation ("Eastern and Western") is not a complete sentence. A semicolon (C) cannot be used because it is used to separate two independent clauses, and "Eastern and Western" is not a stand-alone sentence. While a dash could potentially be used here, a hyphen (D) is incorrect because it is only used for joining words (such as "well-being"), rather than joining clauses.

14. Choice B is the best answer. Answer choice B is best because it is the most readable. Answer choices A and D divide the phrase "the roots of calligraphy," which makes comprehension more difficult. Answer choice C is an awkward way of sharing the location.

15. Choice A is the best answer. The sentence is referring to a set of rules or guidelines that govern each style of calligraphy.

16. Choice B is the best answer. As it is written, this sentence has a dangling modifier. The subject of the sentence should be "calligraphy," but answer choices A, C, and D place other words directly after the comma, which makes these words appear to be the subject and leads to confusion.

17. Choice D is the best answer. It is better to begin the clause with "the Hurufiyya movement" to stay in active voice rather than passive voice (so A and B are incorrect). Calligraphy was invented long before the Hurufiyya movement, so answer choice C is incorrect.

18. Choice A is the best answer. The sentence is saying that the main reason calligraphy was mostly used for religious methods is that most of those who could write were in the monasteries, where religious works were copied. So it might not be the only reason (as answer choices B and C state) but it is the main reason (so answer choice D is incorrect).

19. Choice D is the best answer. The detail about Charlemagne is interesting and explains why he may have encouraged scholarship, but is not a helpful supporting detail for this paragraph on Western calligraphy, or for the selection as a whole.

20. Choice C is the best answer. The clause beginning with the underlined word is in contrast to the previous clause, so answer choices A and D are incorrect because they imply agreement. Answer choice B is incorrect because the word "however" needs different punctuation: it would need to be preceded by a semicolon and followed by a comma.

21. Choice A is the best answer. An apostrophe (B) is incorrect because the date is plural, not a contraction or possessive. The eighteenth century refers to the 1700s, more than two centuries ago, so answer choices C and D are incorrect.

22. Choice C is the best answer. Answer choice A is incorrect because it only addresses the idea of modern calligraphy that was introduced in this paragraph, rather than summarizing the whole selection. Answer choice B is incorrect because it focuses on China rather than both Eastern and Western cultures that the selection included. Answer choice D is incorrect because religion is not the only reason calligraphy survived. Answer choice C sums the ideas explored in the selection.

23. Choice A is the best answer. Titles of musical works are enclosed in quotation marks, not italics like a book title (B).

24. Choice B is the best answer. The correct phrase is "less common." The term "lesser" (A) is typically used when comparing two items in quantity or quality. Saying that something is less, or not as, uncommon (C and D) means that it is more common, which does not fit the meaning of the text.

25. Choice D is the best answer. The sentence sets up a contrast in the first half of the sentence, stating that trucks are less common now than in the past. The use of the word "while" alerts us to the contrast, so we can expect that the following information is something that does not fit with declining ice cream trucks. The word that best contrasts with this decline is "booming." Both "depleting" (A) and "shaky" (B) are in line with a declining business and do not fit with "while." The word "volatile" (C) implies both upswings and downswings in business, which does not smoothly contrast with the decline in trucks.

26. Choice D is the best answer. The adverb "increasingly" is the correct opening for this sentence. "Increasing" (A) is an adjective and is not appropriate to open a sentence without the noun it is modifying (although it would be acceptable to write, "Health is an **increasing** concern for Americans"). "Greater" (B) is also an adjective, and "greatly" (C) does not convey the idea that the concern is growing.

27. Choice D is the best answer. The concerns about frozen yogurt's nutrition should be brought up after the subject of frozen yogurt has been introduced, which happens in sentences 4–5. Sentence 6 then answers the nutrition concerns by stating that "even so," frozen yogurt remains popular, so it is a good sentence to follow the underlined statement.

28. Choice C is the best answer. The sentence is written in present tense, so "were" (B) is incorrect. However, it is referring to an action that has already occurred, so "are" (A) and "is" (D) are incorrect. Using the present perfect "have been" is correct.

29. Choice D is the best answer. The previous paragraph closes by stating that frozen yogurt is providing competition to the ice cream industry. Answer choice A does not address this competition. Answer choice B is illogical, stating that ice cream sales are high because of the competition. Answer choice C gives wrong information by stating that ice cream is no longer popular. Only answer choice D provides the correct contrast: that ice cream is still popular even though frozen yogurt is providing competition.

30. Choice B is the best answer. The graph shows that ice cream sales declined slightly in the US between 2000 and 2015, while frozen yogurt sales rose. Answer choice B reflects this. Answer choice A incorrectly states that sales of both ice cream and frozen yogurt have stagnated, implying lack of growth or some decline. Answer choice C leaves out the information on ice cream and fails to mention that the sales are in the US (which is significant since the second part of the sentence refers to worldwide consumption). Answer choice D also fails to mention that the declining sales are in the US, which makes the sentence confusing.

31. Choice C is the best answer. It would be useful to add some extra data to support the points of the selection, so answer choice A is incorrect. The amount of ice cream produced by a single company (B) is not necessarily helpful since no mention is made of specific companies or how many are producing ice cream. Since the paragraph mentions that China consumes the most ice cream in the world, it would be useful to add the amount, so answer choice C is correct. Flavors of frozen yogurt (D) are not relevant to the point of the selection, which focuses on amounts eaten and the competition between frozen yogurt and ice cream.

32. Choice C is the best answer. The sentence draws a conclusion that should be obvious from the previous paragraphs: that ice cream is still popular in the US. This conclusion is not unusual (A), unexpected (B), or unlikely (D). Rather it is very apparent (C).

33. Choice A is the best answer. The role of the underlined word is to set up a contrast, stating that even though ice cream trucks are no longer common, there are many frozen dessert options. The word "while" (A) best fits this. "Whether" (B) implies uncertainty, and "however" (C) and "unfortunately" (D) do not fit grammatically in this sentence.

34. Choice B is the best answer. The point of the sentence is that Leonardo introduced a numeral system to the Western world. It would be confusing to say he was "guilty of" introducing it (A) because it is a positive accomplishment rather than a crime. Answer choice C is incorrect because it uses awkward and weak wording. Answer choice D is incorrect because it was not something he was tasked with. The correct wording is that Leonardo was responsible for introducing the numeral system. This does not mean that he was given the responsibility to do so, but simply that he is known for being the person to do so.

35. Choice D is the best answer. No punctuation is necessary before the conjunction since there are only two items in this list.

36. Choice D is the best answer. The idea of the sentence is that this mathematician is only known for one thing today. Answer choice A makes a point that is likely true, that Leonardo was young but knowledgeable, but this information is not relevant to the main point, nor is it grammatically correct because of the comma splice (the comma after "knowledgeable" joins two independent clauses, which can only be done by a semicolon or period). Answer choice B states that "his work endures," which contradicts the rest of the sentence that states only one thing endures. This choice also has a comma splice issue. Answer choice C also contradicts by stating that Leonardo is famous for many things. Answer choice D correctly points out that although Leonardo made many mathematical contributions, he is known for only one of these today.

37. Choice B is the best answer. It is ironic that the one thing Fibonacci is known for was actually discovered by someone else. Even though he was a brilliant mathematician, very little of his own work is known. While some may consider the news sad, disappointing, or tragic, the tone of the sentence indicates that this is an interesting, almost amusing fact.

38. Choice C is the best answer. As the selection is written (A), it is choppy, as one short sentence follows a previous short sentence. Answer choice B incorrectly states that the sequence appears in almost every part of nature. With only three examples, we cannot assume the series is pervasive. Answer choice D says that Fibonacci, rather than his sequence, can be seen in nature. Only answer choice C smoothly connects the two sentences without changing or adding information.

39. Choice D is the best answer. The main idea of the paragraph can be gathered from the previous sentences: the Fibonacci sequence is a pattern often seen in nature. Answer choice A is incorrect because it introduces a new topic. Answer choice B is incorrect because it adds a contradictory detail with no information to reconcile it to the main point. Answer choice C is incorrect because it makes unfounded assumptions and claims (that Fibonacci didn't know the extent of his discovery and that he revolutionized mathematics, neither of which can be proven). Further, these statements have nothing to do with the main point of this paragraph. Answer choice D is correct because it gives a supporting detail about the topic of the Fibonacci sequence in nature.

40. Choice D is the best answer. The information in the underlined portion is unsupported (the selection offers no evidence that nature always follows a pattern) and is not relevant. Even if nature did always follow a pattern, this information does not support the points about the Fibonacci sequence.

41. Choice A is the best answer. The sentence is introduced with an adverb clause so should be followed by a comma. A colon (B) is incorrect because the following portion of the sentence is not a definition or list. A semicolon (C) is incorrect because the introductory clause is not an independent clause (so it cannot be a stand-alone sentence). Leaving out punctuation entirely (D) would make the sentence confusing, with no discernible pauses.

42. Choice C is the best answer. The idea of the sentence is that the Arabic system makes mathematical calculations more possible. Thus "challenging" (A) or "difficult" (B) would not fit. "Agreeable" (D) is a positive term but not the correct connotation.

43. Choice C is the best answer. Fibonacci could not have known future events. While prophecy (A) and foretelling (D) are associated with predicting future events, the passage is not suggesting anything related to this kind of prediction (typically associated with religious or mythological prediction). We have no way of knowing whether Fibonacci could have understood the magnitude of the system spreading through the world (B).

44. Choice D is the best answer. The examples are potentially useful, but the sentence is written in a much more casual tone than the rest of the selection. It uses second person ("you"), which does not appear anywhere else, and then directly addresses the reader, urging him or her, illogically (since Fibonacci is not alive), to thank the mathematician.

Math – No Calculator

1. Choice D is correct. The function for the cost of a taxi ride is a combination of a constant function for the first mile and a linear function for the rest of the ride. The constant function is $c_1(d) = 4.25$ since the cost of the first mile is \$4.25. For the linear part, subtract 1 from d to exclude the first mile, and then multiply the result by 0.70 since it costs \$0.70 per mile. The result is $c_2(d) = 0.70(d - 1)$. Finally, write the function for the total cost of the taxi ride by adding the two functions.

$$\begin{aligned} c(d) &= c_1(d) + c_2(d) \\ &= 4.25 + 0.70(d - 1) \end{aligned}$$

Although not necessary for answering the question, note that this function can also be simplified:

$$\begin{aligned} c(d) &= 4.25 + 0.70d - 0.70 \\ &= 3.55 + 0.70d \end{aligned}$$

2. Choice D is correct.

$$\begin{aligned} y &= 4x - 2 \\ y + 2 &= 4x \\ \frac{y+2}{4} &= x \\ \frac{y}{4} + \frac{2}{4} &= x \\ \frac{1}{4}y + \frac{1}{2} &= x \\ x &= \frac{1}{4}y + \frac{1}{2} \end{aligned}$$

3. Choice D is correct. Solve the inequality:

$$\begin{aligned} 2|x + 3| - 9 &\geq -1 \\ 2|x + 3| &\geq 8 \\ |x + 3| &\geq 4 \end{aligned}$$

$$\begin{array}{ll} x + 3 \geq 4 & -(x + 3) \geq 4 \\ x \geq 1 & x + 3 \leq -4 \\ & x \leq -7 \end{array}$$

4. Choice A is correct. The positively sloped line has a slope of 2 and a y-intercept of -3; the line is solid, and the region above the line is shaded. Therefore, the graph illustrates the solution to the inequality $y \geq 2x - 3$.

The negatively sloped line has a slope of -3 and a y-intercept of 4; the line is dashed, and the region below the line is shaded. Therefore, the graph illustrates the solution to the inequality $y < -3x + 4$.

In choice A, the second inequality when solved for y is equivalent to $y \geq 2x - 3$.

$$\begin{aligned} 4x - 2y &\leq 6 \\ -2y &\leq -4x + 6 \\ y &\geq 2x - 3 \end{aligned}$$

(The direction of the inequality sign changes when multiplying or diving by a negative number.) The solution of the system of inequalities is shown by the region where the two sets of shading overlap.

5. Choice C is correct. The four choices all have the two lines that mark the boundaries of the inequalities plotted identically; the only difference is which sides are shaded. It's therefore not necessary to check that the lines are correct; simply determine which of the areas bounded by the lines pertain to the system of inequalities. One way to do that is to pick a point in each region and check whether it satisfies the inequalities. For instance, in the region on the left, we can pick the origin, $(0,0)$. Since $0 - 0 \ngtr 1$ and $2(0) + 0 \ngtr 2$, this does not satisfy either inequality. From the top region we can choose, for example, the point $(0,3)$. $0 - 3 \ngtr 1$, so this fails to satisfy the first inequality. From the bottom region we can choose, for instance, $(0,-2)$. $0 - (-2) > 1$, so the first inequality is satisfied, but $2(0) + (-2) \ngtr 2$, so the second is not. Finally, from the rightmost region we can choose, for example, the point $(2,0)$. $2 - 0 > 1$ and $2(2) + 0 > 2$, so both inequalities are satisfied; this is the only region that should be shaded in.

6. Choice D is correct. To simplify the inequality $3 - 2x < 5$, we can first subtract 3 from both sides:

$$3 - 2x - 3 < 5 - 3 \Rightarrow -2x < 2$$

Now, we can divide both sides of the inequality by -2. When an inequality is multiplied or divided by a negative number, its direction changes ($<$ becomes $>$, $\leq$ becomes $\geq$, and vice versa). So $-2x < 2$ becomes $\frac{-2x}{-2} > \frac{2}{-2}$, or $x > -1$.

7. Choice C is correct. If the exam has 30 questions, and the student answered C questions correctly and left B questions blank, then the number of questions the student answered incorrectly must be $30 - B - C$. He gets one point for each correct question, or $1 \times C = C$ points, and loses $\frac{1}{2}$ point for each incorrect question, or $\frac{1}{2}(30 - B - C)$ points. Therefore, one way to express his total score is $C - \frac{1}{2}(30 - B - C)$.

8. Choice B is correct. If there are n floors, and each floor has a height of h feet, then to find the total height of the floors, we just multiply the number of floors by the height of each floor: nh. To find the total height of the building, we must also add the height of the spire, 30 feet. So, the building's total height in feet is $nh + 30$.

9. Choice D is correct. First, test each expression to see which satisfies the condition $x > y$. This condition is only met for answer choices A and D, so only these need to be considered further. Test those choices to see which satisfy the inequality $x + y > 0$. It can be seen that this inequality holds for choice A, but not for choice D, since $x + y = 3 + (-3) = 3 - 3 = 0$. In this case $x + y$ is not greater than 0.

10. Choice B is correct. To simplify the expression, first factor the numerator and the denominator. To factor the numerator, use trial-and-error to find two numbers whose sum is 2 and whose product is -24, and then put those numbers into the form $(x + \_)(x + \_)$. For the denominator, factor out the common factor, which is 5.

$$\frac{x^2 + 2x - 24}{5x - 20} = \frac{(x+6)(x-4)}{5(x-4)}$$

Now there is a common factor, $(x-4)$, in both the numerator and the denominator. Therefore, you can further simplify the expression by cancelling it out.

$$\frac{(x+6)(x-4)}{5(x-4)} = \frac{x+6}{5}$$

11. Choice C is correct. To simplify the expression, first simplify the expression with parentheses. To raise $3x$ to the third power, raise both 3 and x to the third power separately.

$$\begin{aligned} x^6 \times (3x)^2 &= x^6 \times 3^2 \times x^2 \\ &= x^6 \times 9x^2 \end{aligned}$$

Next, multiply the two terms. Since they have the same base and are being multiplied together, add the exponents of the like base, x.

$$\begin{aligned} x^6 \times 9x^2 &= 9x^{6+2} \\ &= 9x^8 \end{aligned}$$

12. Choice B is correct. Revenue is the total amount of money the theater makes from ticket sales. In this case, the revenue is the price of each ticket multiplied by the total number of tickets sold. So, to find the estimated revenue, find the price and the number of tickets sold after the price is raised by x dollars. Then multiply the two quantities together. If the price of a ticket starts at $10, then the price after it is raised by x dollars will be $10+x$ dollars. In addition, we are told that the theater sells 50 fewer tickets for every dollar the price is raised. Therefore, the total number of tickets that are sold will be $600-50x$. Calculate the revenue function $r(x)$ by multiplying the expressions and simplify the result.

$$\begin{aligned} r(x) &= (10+x)(600-50x) \\ &= -50x^2 + 100x + 6000 \end{aligned}$$

13. Choice C is correct. To transform $f(x)$ into $g(x)$, you have to replace x with $x+1$. This transformation results in a translation, or shift, of the graph. Specifically, for a particular x, $g(x)$ returns the value of the function $f(x)$ one unit further along the x-axis (to the right). This results in shifting the graph one unit to the left.

14. The correct answer is 8. The length of an interval is the difference between its endpoints. For example, the length of the interval [2, 4] is 2. To determine how the given function grows over an interval of length 3, determine the value of f at each endpoint of that interval. Since exponential functions grow by equal factors over equal intervals, you can use any interval of length 3, and your answer will apply to all such intervals. For example, you can use the interval [0,3]:

$$\begin{aligned} f(0) &= 3 \cdot 2^0 \\ &= 3 \cdot 1 \\ &= 3 \end{aligned}$$

$$\begin{aligned} f(3) &= 3 \cdot 2^3 \\ &= 3 \cdot 8 \\ &= 24 \end{aligned}$$

Since $f(0)=3$ and $f(3)=24$, the function grows by a factor of $\frac{24}{3}=8$ over this interval.

15. The correct answer is 27. The linear function $s(h) = 27h + 720$ starts at 720 when $h = 0$ and increases by 27 every time h increases by 1. Therefore, for every hour after 40, the librarian earns \$27.

16. The correct answer is 21. Since the function is defined recursively, you need to calculate all of the first six terms. The first and second terms are already given in the problem as $f(1) = 1$ and $f(2) = 1$. To calculate the third term, $f(3)$, take the previous term and add two times the term that is two back:

$$f(3) = f(2) + 2f(1) = 1 + 2 = 3$$

The fourth term is similarly calculated:

$$f(4) = f(3) + 2f(2) = 3 + 2 = 5$$

Continuing in this way, you will find that the first six terms of the sequence are 1, 1, 3, 5, 11, 21. Therefore, the sixth term of the sequence is 21.

17. The correct answer is 4: $f(x) = (x - 3)(x^2 - x - 2)$ is a cubic equation written as a product of a linear factor and a quadratic factor, $x - 3$ and $x^2 - x - 2$, respectively. The quadratic expression $x^2 - x - 2$ can be further factored to $(x - 2)(x + 1)$, so $f(x) = (x - 3)(x^2 - x - 2) = (x - 3)(x - 2)(x + 1)$. The graph of the function crosses the x axis at any point at which the value of $f(x) = 0$. To find the x-intercepts, solve $f(x) = 0 = (x - 3)(x - 2)(x + 1)$ using the zero-product property.

$$x - 3 = 0 \qquad x - 2 = 0 \qquad x + 1 = 0$$
$$x = 3 \qquad x = 2 \qquad x = -1$$

Then the sum is $3 + 2 + (-1) = 4$

Math – Calculator

1. Choice B is correct. Notice that the given system has two equations, and each equation has two variables, x and y. Therefore, the solution of the system of equations must have values for each of the two variables. To find the solution, you can use algebraic methods, graphs, tables, or matrices. For the purposes of this explanation, we will use an algebraic method called substitution.

To begin, notice that the first equation already has y isolated on the left side. Therefore, substitute the left side, $3x + 2$, for y into the second equation, and then solve for x.

$$\begin{aligned} 2x + y &= 7 \\ 2x + (3x + 2) &= 7 \\ 5x &= 5 \\ x &= 1 \end{aligned}$$

To find the value of y, substitute 1 for x in the first equation.

$$\begin{aligned} y &= 3(1) + 2 \\ &= 3 + 2 \\ &= 5 \end{aligned}$$

Therefore, the solution of the given system of equations is $x = 1, y = 5$. Check this solution on your own by substituting the values into the second equations to make sure that you get a true equality.

2. Choice D is correct. For each value of x, $f(x) = x^2 + 1$,

$$\begin{aligned} f(1) &= (1)^2 + 1 = (1)(1) + 1 = 1 + 1 = 2 \\ f(2) &= (2)^2 + 1 = (2)(2) + 1 = 4 + 1 = 5 \\ f(3) &= (3)^2 + 1 = (3)(3) + 1 = 9 + 1 = 10 \\ f(4) &= (4)^2 + 1 = (4)(4) + 1 = 16 + 1 = 17 \\ f(5) &= (5)^2 + 1 = (5)(5) + 1 = 25 + 1 = 26 \end{aligned}$$

3. Choice A is correct. The slope (or ratio of the change in y-values per change in corresponding x-values) may first be calculated. Using the points, (−3, −21) and (−1, −3), the slope can be written as $\frac{-3-(-21)}{-1-(-3)}$ or 9. The slope can be substituted into the slope-intercept form of an equation, or $y = mx + b$, to find the y-intercept. Doing so gives $y = 9x + b$. Substituting the x- and y-values of any ordered pair will reveal the y-intercept. The following may be written: $-21 = 9(-3) + b$; solving for b gives $b = 6$. Thus, the equation that represents the relationship between x and y is $y = 9x + 6$.

4. Choice D is correct. The median is the score in the middle: half of the students scored higher than 82.5 and half scored lower. The mean is the average, which is calculated by adding all the scores together and dividing by the number of students. Since the mean is higher than the median, this means that some of the students scored high, well above the median, which pulls the mean up above the median grade.

5. Choice A is correct. Since the second line, $y = 3$, is horizontal, the intersection must occur at a point where $y = 3$. If $x = -1.5$, the equation describing the line is satisfied: $2 \times (-1.5) + 3 = 0$.

6. Choice A is correct. To evaluate $\frac{x^3+2x}{x+3}$ at $x = -1$, substitute in -1 for x in the expression:

$$\frac{(-1)^3 + 2(-1)}{(-1) + 3} = \frac{(-1) + (-2)}{2} = \frac{-3}{2} = -\frac{3}{2}$$

7. Choice B is correct. To solve this problem, all we need to do is substitute -1 for every x in the expression and then simplify:

$$\frac{2(-1) - 2}{(-1) - 3} = \frac{-2 - 2}{-4} = \frac{-4}{-4} = 1$$

8. Choice C is correct. Start by distributing each coefficient across the parentheses. Next add the complex binomials. Complex numbers have a real part, a, and an imaginary part, b, and are usually written as $a + bi$. When adding imaginary numbers, add the real parts and the imaginary parts separately:

$$4(-3 + 5i) + 6(1 - 3i) = -12 + 20i + 6 - 18i = (-12 + 6) + (20i - 18i) = -6 + 2i$$

9. Choice B is correct. The probability of playing a song by any band is proportional to the number of songs by that band, divided by the total number of songs, or $\frac{5}{15} = \frac{1}{3}$ for Band D. The probability of playing any particular song is not affected by what has been played previously, since the choice is random.

10. Choice B is correct. The number of people who voted for the proposition is 9.5% of 51,623. If we only require an approximation, we can round 9.5% to 10%, and 51,623 to 50,000. Then 9.5% of 51,623 is about 10% of 50,000, or $(0.1)(50{,}000) = 5{,}000$.

11. Choice B is correct. Since all students who answered her survey said they prefer one of the three flavors; the percentages must add up to 100%. Therefore, the percentage of students who prefer strawberry is:

$$100\% - (35\% + 40\%) = 100\% - 75\% = 25\%$$

12. Choice A is correct. Liz ordinarily sells each pen for 30% more than (or 130% of) her cost:

$$\$15.00 \times 1.3 = \$19.50$$

For the last day of market, she takes 20% off (or sells it for 80% of) the ordinary sale price:

$$\$19.50 \times 0.8 = \$15.60$$

The marked down price is $15.60.

13. Choice D is correct. Since 16 chairs are empty, and this represents 2/5 of the total enrollment, then the full class must consist of $\frac{5}{2}(16) = 40$ students.

14. Choice C is correct. The problem may be solved by writing $P(p \text{ or } q) = P(p) + P(q) - P(p \text{ and } q)$. The probability for philosophy or qualitative and the probability for philosophy may be substituted giving $0.62 = 0.30 + P(q) - P(p \text{ and } q)$. Next find the probability that she chooses both philosophy and qualitative by using the formula, $P(p \text{ and } q) = P(p) \times P(q|p)$. Substituting the probabilities of 0.30 and 0.40 gives $P(p \text{ and } q) = 0.30 \times 0.40$, or 0.12. Now, the probability of 0.12

may be substituted into the original equation, giving $0.62 = 0.30 + P(q) - 0.12$. Solving for $P(q)$ gives a probability of 0.44. Thus, there is a 0.44 probability that Alisha chooses a qualitative methods class.

15. Choice D is correct. Since the figure represents the number line, the distance from point A to point B will be the difference, B-A, which is $5 - (-6) = 11$. The distance from point B to point C will be the difference, C-B, which is $8 - 5 = 3$. So, the ratio $\overline{BC} : \overline{AB}$ will be 3:11.

16. Choice C is correct. The median number of volunteers in Texas is 21, with a mean of approximately 25.9. The median number of volunteers in New Mexico is 33, with a mean of approximately 31.2. Thus, the median and mean numbers of volunteers in Texas are smaller.

17. Choice D is correct. If there are at least twice as many hot dogs (y) as hamburgers (x), then necessarily $y \geq 2x$, or $2x \leq y$. And since hot dogs and hamburgers must add up to 500, then $x + y = 500$.

18. Choice B is correct. The probability may be written as $P(A \text{ or } B) = P(A) + P(B) - P(A \text{ and } B) = \frac{80}{150} + \frac{49}{150} - \frac{37}{150}$, which simplifies to $P(A \text{ or } B) = \frac{46}{75}$.

19. Choice A is correct. The mode is the number that appears most often in a set of data. If no item appears most often, then the data set has no mode. In this case, Kyle achieved one hit a total of three times, two hits twice, three hits once, and four hits once. One hit occurred the most times, and therefore the mode of the data set is 1.

20. Choice B is correct. The mean, or average, is the sum of the numbers in a data set, divided by the total number of items. This data set contains seven items, one for each day of the week. The total number of hits that Kyle had during the week is the sum of the numbers in the right-hand column, or 14. This gives Mean $= \frac{14}{7} = 2$.

21. Choice B is correct. There are two students who slept less than 6.5 hours and scored in the 80s. We can add the number of students in each group to find the total number who took the test: $6 + 4 + 2 = 12$. So, the probability is 2 out of 12, or $\frac{1}{6}$.

22. Choice A is correct. We calculate the mean of each group by adding the scores and dividing by the number in each group. The mean of the first group is: $\frac{83+77+89+68+91+72}{6} = 80$

The mean of the second group is: $\frac{82+88+77+90}{4} = 84.25$

The mean of the third group is: $\frac{86+93}{2} = 89.5$

23. Choice B is correct. You can solve the equation using graphs, tables, or algebraic methods. For this explanation, we will approach the problem algebraically. To begin, isolate the square-root sign on the left side by subtracting 2 from both sides.

$$\sqrt{4x - 3} + 2 = x$$
$$\sqrt{4x - 3} = x - 2$$

Then square both sides of the equation and simplify the result.

$$\left(\sqrt{4x-3}\right)^2 = (x-2)^2$$
$$4x - 3 = x^2 - 4x + 4$$

Now solve the resulting equation by moving everything to one side and factoring the resulting quadratic equation.

$$x^2 - 8x + 7 = 0$$
$$(x-7)(x-1) = 0$$

$$x = 7 \text{ and } x = 1$$

Therefore, the possible solutions are $x = 1$ and $x = 7$. Unfortunately, whenever you must square both sides of an equation to solve it, you run the risk of finding an incorrect solution. Consequently, we cannot automatically say that the solutions are $x = 1$ and $x = 7$. We need to check these solutions in the original equation. To do this, substitute them into the given equations and make sure that the result is a true statement.

$x = 1$
$\sqrt{4 \times 1 - 3} + 2 = 1$
$\sqrt{1} + 2 = 1$
$1 + 2 = 1$
$false$

$x = 7$
$\sqrt{4 \times 7 - 3} + 2 = 7$
$\sqrt{25} + 2 = 7$
$5 + 2 = 7$
$true$

Since only $x = 7$ leads to a true statement, the solution is $x = 7$.

24. Choice C is correct. The roots of a quadratic function $f(x)$ are the values of x for which $f(x) = 0$. Quadratic functions may have two real roots, two imaginary roots, or one real double root. A quadratic function written in the form $f(x) = (x-a)(x-b)$ has roots at $x = a$ and $x = b$. Therefore, to find $f(x)$, substitute the given roots for a and b into $f(x) = (x-a)(x-b)$ and simplify.

$$\begin{aligned} f(x) &= (x-a)(x-b) \\ &= \big(x-(-4)\big)(x-6) \\ &= (x+4)(x-6) \\ &= x^2 - 2x - 24 \end{aligned}$$

25. Choice D is correct. The denominator of the second rational expression may be factored as $(x+8)(x+2)$. Thus, the least common denominator of the two rational expressions is $(x+8)(x+2)$. Multiplying the top and bottom of the first fraction by $(x+8)$, we see that $\frac{3}{x+2} = \frac{3\,(x+8)}{(x+2)(x+8)}$. The sum may be written as $\frac{3(x+8)+x}{(x+8)(x+2)}$, which simplifies to $\frac{4x+24}{(x+8)(x+2)}$. Factoring out a 4 in the numerator gives: $\frac{4(x+6)}{(x+8)(x+2)}$.

26. Choice C is correct. Distributing each term in the expression, $x - 8$, across each term in the trinomial, gives:

$$4x^4 - 2x^2 + 4x - 32x^3 + 16x - 32$$

Writing the expression in standard form gives:

$$4x^4 - 32x^3 - 2x^2 + 20x - 32$$

27. Choice C is correct. In a parallelogram, consecutive angles are supplementary; that is, the sum of their measures is 180°. Use this to write an equation and then solve for x.

$$\begin{aligned} m\angle B + m\angle C &= 180° \\ (4x + 5) + (3x) &= 180 \\ 7x + 5 &= 180 \\ 7x &= 175 \\ x &= 25 \end{aligned}$$

Now use this value to find $m\angle B$ and $m\angle C$.

$$\begin{aligned} m\angle B &= 3x \\ &= 3(25) \\ &= 75° \end{aligned} \qquad \begin{aligned} m\angle C &= 4x + 5 \\ &= 4(25) + 5 \\ &= 105° \end{aligned}$$

In a parallelogram, opposite sides are congruent. Thus, $m\angle A = m\angle C = 105°$.

28. The correct answer is 39.1. The area of a circle is given by the formula $A = \pi r^2$, where r is the length of the radius. A sector is a slice of a circle bounded by two radii. Its area is proportional to the angle between the two radii bounding the sector. Thus, the area of a sector with angle θ (in degrees) is given by the formula

$$A = \pi r^2 \times \frac{\theta}{360}$$

Substitute the value of the radius and angle into this formula and simplify. Round the result to the nearest tenth.

$$\begin{aligned} A &= \pi(8)^2 \times \frac{70}{360} \\ &= 64\pi \times \frac{70}{360} \\ &\approx 39.1 \end{aligned}$$

29. The correct answer is 2825. The pool is a prism, so its volume is calculated by using the formula $V = Bh$, where B is the area of the base (i.e. the area of the given shape) and h is the height (i.e. the depth) of the swimming pool. First calculate B by adding the areas of the rectangle and two semicircles.

The area of the rectangle is given by the formula $A = lw$. Thus,

$$\begin{aligned} A_{\text{rectangle}} &= lw \\ &= 20 \text{ ft} \times 12 \text{ ft} \\ &= 240 \text{ ft}^2 \end{aligned}$$

Now notice that the diameter of each semicircle is 12 ft, so their radius is $r = 12 \div 2 = 6$ ft. Put together, the two semicircles form a complete circle, whose area is given by the formula $A = \pi r^2$. Thus, the total area of the semicircles is

$$\begin{aligned} A_{\text{semicircles}} &= \pi r^2 \\ &= \pi \times (6\text{ ft})^2 \\ &= 36\pi\text{ ft}^2 \\ &\approx 113.10\text{ ft}^2 \end{aligned}$$

Then add the two areas to find the total area of the swimming pool.

$$\begin{aligned} B &= A_{\text{rectangle}} + A_{\text{semicircles}} \\ &\approx 240\text{ ft}^2 + 113.10\text{ ft}^2 \\ &= 353.10\text{ ft}^2 \end{aligned}$$

Finally, use this value to find the volume of the pool. Recall that its depth is given as 8 ft in the problem.

$$\begin{aligned} V &= Bh \\ &\approx 353.10\text{ ft}^2 \times 8\text{ ft} \\ &\approx 2825\text{ ft}^3 \end{aligned}$$

30. The correct answer is 2.9. The first step is to draw into the diagram what we are told or can deduce. The circle intercepts the triangle at the midpoints of its sides, so draw a radius that meets the midpoint of AB (marked D below). Next, draw a line from A to the center, noting that this line bisects $\angle BAC$; thus, $m\angle DAO = \frac{1}{2} \times 60° = 30°$. Since D is the midpoint of AB, we know that $AD = \frac{1}{2}(AB) = 5$.

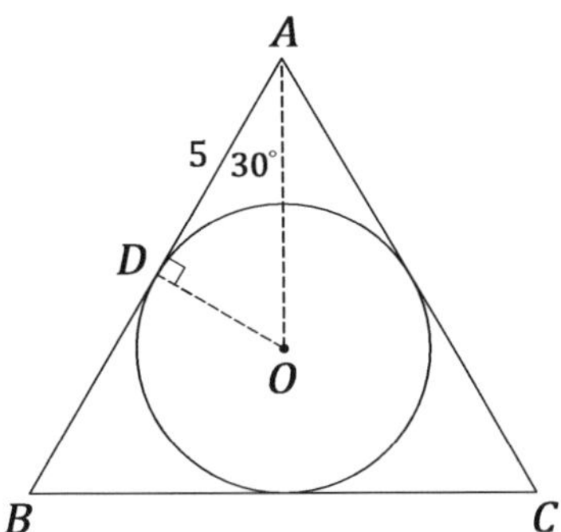

Now we can see that ΔADO is a 30-60-90 triangle. In a 30-60-90 triangle, the ratio of the lengths of the sides is $1{:}\sqrt{3}{:}\,2$. In this triangle, 5 corresponds to $\sqrt{3}$ and the radius r corresponds to 1. Use a proportion to calculate r:

$$\begin{aligned} \frac{1}{\sqrt{3}} &= \frac{r}{5} \\ r\sqrt{3} &= 5 \\ r &= \frac{5}{\sqrt{3}} \approx 2.9 \end{aligned}$$

31. The correct answer is 12.5. Suppose the seller purchases an item for \$100. She then adds 25% to the price she paid for it and lists it for sale at regular price:

$$\text{Regular} = \$100 + 25\% \times \$100 = \$100 + \$25 = \$125$$

If that \$125 item does not sell in 6 months, it is placed on clearance and marked down by 10%:

$$\text{Clearance} = \$125 - 10\% \times \$125 = \$125 - \$12.50 = \$112.50$$

Calculate her profit on the clearance as a percentage of what she paid for it:

$$\text{Profit} = \frac{\text{price sold for} - \text{price paid for}}{\text{price paid for}}$$

$$\text{Profit} = \frac{112.5-100}{100} = \frac{12.5}{100} = 12.5\%.$$

How to Overcome Test Anxiety

Just the thought of taking a test is enough to make most people a little nervous. A test is an important event that can have a long-term impact on your future, so it's important to take it seriously and it's natural to feel anxious about performing well. But just because anxiety is normal, that doesn't mean that it's helpful in test taking, or that you should simply accept it as part of your life. Anxiety can have a variety of effects. These effects can be mild, like making you feel slightly nervous, or severe, like blocking your ability to focus or remember even a simple detail.

If you experience test anxiety—whether severe or mild—it's important to know how to beat it. To discover this, first you need to understand what causes test anxiety.

Causes of Test Anxiety

While we often think of anxiety as an uncontrollable emotional state, it can actually be caused by simple, practical things. One of the most common causes of test anxiety is that a person does not feel adequately prepared for their test. This feeling can be the result of many different issues such as poor study habits or lack of organization, but the most common culprit is time management. Starting to study too late, failing to organize your study time to cover all of the material, or being distracted while you study will mean that you're not well prepared for the test. This may lead to cramming the night before, which will cause you to be physically and mentally exhausted for the test. Poor time management also contributes to feelings of stress, fear, and hopelessness as you realize you are not well prepared but don't know what to do about it.

Other times, test anxiety is not related to your preparation for the test but comes from unresolved fear. This may be a past failure on a test, or poor performance on tests in general. It may come from comparing yourself to others who seem to be performing better or from the stress of living up to expectations. Anxiety may be driven by fears of the future—how failure on this test would affect your educational and career goals. These fears are often completely irrational, but they can still negatively impact your test performance.

Review Video: 3 Reasons You Have Test Anxiety
Visit mometrix.com/academy and enter code: 428468

Elements of Test Anxiety

As mentioned earlier, test anxiety is considered to be an emotional state, but it has physical and mental components as well. Sometimes you may not even realize that you are suffering from test anxiety until you notice the physical symptoms. These can include trembling hands, rapid heartbeat, sweating, nausea, and tense muscles. Extreme anxiety may lead to fainting or vomiting. Obviously, any of these symptoms can have a negative impact on testing. It is important to recognize them as soon as they begin to occur so that you can address the problem before it damages your performance.

Review Video: 3 Ways to Tell You Have Test Anxiety
Visit mometrix.com/academy and enter code: 927847

The mental components of test anxiety include trouble focusing and inability to remember learned information. During a test, your mind is on high alert, which can help you recall information and stay focused for an extended period of time. However, anxiety interferes with your mind's natural processes, causing you to blank out, even on the questions you know well. The strain of testing during anxiety makes it difficult to stay focused, especially on a test that may take several hours. Extreme anxiety can take a huge mental toll, making it difficult not only to recall test information but even to understand the test questions or pull your thoughts together.

Review Video: How Test Anxiety Affects Memory
Visit mometrix.com/academy and enter code: 609003

Effects of Test Anxiety

Test anxiety is like a disease—if left untreated, it will get progressively worse. Anxiety leads to poor performance, and this reinforces the feelings of fear and failure, which in turn lead to poor performances on subsequent tests. It can grow from a mild nervousness to a crippling condition. If allowed to progress, test anxiety can have a big impact on your schooling, and consequently on your future.

Test anxiety can spread to other parts of your life. Anxiety on tests can become anxiety in any stressful situation, and blanking on a test can turn into panicking in a job situation. But fortunately, you don't have to let anxiety rule your testing and determine your grades. There are a number of relatively simple steps you can take to move past anxiety and function normally on a test and in the rest of life.

Review Video: How Test Anxiety Impacts Your Grades
Visit mometrix.com/academy and enter code: 939819

Physical Steps for Beating Test Anxiety

While test anxiety is a serious problem, the good news is that it can be overcome. It doesn't have to control your ability to think and remember information. While it may take time, you can begin taking steps today to beat anxiety.

Just as your first hint that you may be struggling with anxiety comes from the physical symptoms, the first step to treating it is also physical. Rest is crucial for having a clear, strong mind. If you are tired, it is much easier to give in to anxiety. But if you establish good sleep habits, your body and mind will be ready to perform optimally, without the strain of exhaustion. Additionally, sleeping well helps you to retain information better, so you're more likely to recall the answers when you see the test questions.

Getting good sleep means more than going to bed on time. It's important to allow your brain time to relax. Take study breaks from time to time so it doesn't get overworked, and don't study right before bed. Take time to rest your mind before trying to rest your body, or you may find it difficult to fall asleep.

Review Video: The Importance of Sleep for Your Brain
Visit mometrix.com/academy and enter code: 319338

Along with sleep, other aspects of physical health are important in preparing for a test. Good nutrition is vital for good brain function. Sugary foods and drinks may give a burst of energy but this burst is followed by a crash, both physically and emotionally. Instead, fuel your body with protein and vitamin-rich foods.

Also, drink plenty of water. Dehydration can lead to headaches and exhaustion, especially if your brain is already under stress from the rigors of the test. Particularly if your test is a long one, drink water during the breaks. And if possible, take an energy-boosting snack to eat between sections.

Review Video: How Diet Can Affect your Mood
Visit mometrix.com/academy and enter code: 624317

Along with sleep and diet, a third important part of physical health is exercise. Maintaining a steady workout schedule is helpful, but even taking 5-minute study breaks to walk can help get your blood pumping faster and clear your head. Exercise also releases endorphins, which contribute to a positive feeling and can help combat test anxiety.

When you nurture your physical health, you are also contributing to your mental health. If your body is healthy, your mind is much more likely to be healthy as well. So take time to rest, nourish your body with healthy food and water, and get moving as much as possible. Taking these physical steps will make you stronger and more able to take the mental steps necessary to overcome test anxiety.

Review Video: How to Stay Healthy and Prevent Test Anxiety
Visit mometrix.com/academy and enter code: 877894

Mental Steps for Beating Test Anxiety

Working on the mental side of test anxiety can be more challenging, but as with the physical side, there are clear steps you can take to overcome it. As mentioned earlier, test anxiety often stems from lack of preparation, so the obvious solution is to prepare for the test. Effective studying may be the most important weapon you have for beating test anxiety, but you can and should employ several other mental tools to combat fear.

First, boost your confidence by reminding yourself of past success—tests or projects that you aced. If you're putting as much effort into preparing for this test as you did for those, there's no reason you should expect to fail here. Work hard to prepare; then trust your preparation.

Second, surround yourself with encouraging people. It can be helpful to find a study group, but be sure that the people you're around will encourage a positive attitude. If you spend time with others who are anxious or cynical, this will only contribute to your own anxiety. Look for others who are motivated to study hard from a desire to succeed, not from a fear of failure.

Third, reward yourself. A test is physically and mentally tiring, even without anxiety, and it can be helpful to have something to look forward to. Plan an activity following the test, regardless of the outcome, such as going to a movie or getting ice cream.

When you are taking the test, if you find yourself beginning to feel anxious, remind yourself that you know the material. Visualize successfully completing the test. Then take a few deep, relaxing breaths and return to it. Work through the questions carefully but with confidence, knowing that you are capable of succeeding.

Developing a healthy mental approach to test taking will also aid in other areas of life. Test anxiety affects more than just the actual test—it can be damaging to your mental health and even contribute to depression. It's important to beat test anxiety before it becomes a problem for more than testing.

Review Video: Test Anxiety and Depression
Visit mometrix.com/academy and enter code: 904704

Study Strategy

Being prepared for the test is necessary to combat anxiety, but what does being prepared look like? You may study for hours on end and still not feel prepared. What you need is a strategy for test prep. The next few pages outline our recommended steps to help you plan out and conquer the challenge of preparation.

Step 1: Scope Out the Test

Learn everything you can about the format (multiple choice, essay, etc.) and what will be on the test. Gather any study materials, course outlines, or sample exams that may be available. Not only will this help you to prepare, but knowing what to expect can help to alleviate test anxiety.

Step 2: Map Out the Material

Look through the textbook or study guide and make note of how many chapters or sections it has. Then divide these over the time you have. For example, if a book has 15 chapters and you have five days to study, you need to cover three chapters each day. Even better, if you have the time, leave an extra day at the end for overall review after you have gone through the material in depth.

If time is limited, you may need to prioritize the material. Look through it and make note of which sections you think you already have a good grasp on, and which need review. While you are studying, skim quickly through the familiar sections and take more time on the challenging parts. Write out your plan so you don't get lost as you go. Having a written plan also helps you feel more in control of the study, so anxiety is less likely to arise from feeling overwhelmed at the amount to cover.

Step 3: Gather Your Tools

Decide what study method works best for you. Do you prefer to highlight in the book as you study and then go back over the highlighted portions? Or do you type out notes of the important information? Or is it helpful to make flashcards that you can carry with you? Assemble the pens, index cards, highlighters, post-it notes, and any other materials you may need so you won't be distracted by getting up to find things while you study.

If you're having a hard time retaining the information or organizing your notes, experiment with different methods. For example, try color-coding by subject with colored pens, highlighters, or post-it notes. If you learn better by hearing, try recording yourself reading your notes so you can listen while in the car, working out, or simply sitting at your desk. Ask a friend to quiz you from your flashcards, or try teaching someone the material to solidify it in your mind.

Step 4: Create Your Environment

It's important to avoid distractions while you study. This includes both the obvious distractions like visitors and the subtle distractions like an uncomfortable chair (or a too-comfortable couch that makes you want to fall asleep). Set up the best study environment possible: good lighting and a comfortable work area. If background music helps you focus, you may want to turn it on, but otherwise keep the room quiet. If you are using a computer to take notes, be sure you don't have any other windows open, especially applications like social media, games, or anything else that could distract you. Silence your phone and turn off notifications. Be sure to keep water close by so you stay hydrated while you study (but avoid unhealthy drinks and snacks).

Also, take into account the best time of day to study. Are you freshest first thing in the morning? Try to set aside some time then to work through the material. Is your mind clearer in the afternoon or evening? Schedule your study session then. Another method is to study at the same time of day that you will take the test, so that your brain gets used to working on the material at that time and will be ready to focus at test time.

Step 5: Study!

Once you have done all the study preparation, it's time to settle into the actual studying. Sit down, take a few moments to settle your mind so you can focus, and begin to follow your study plan. Don't give in to distractions or let yourself procrastinate. This is your time to prepare so you'll be ready to fearlessly approach the test. Make the most of the time and stay focused.

Of course, you don't want to burn out. If you study too long you may find that you're not retaining the information very well. Take regular study breaks. For example, taking five minutes out of every hour to walk briskly, breathing deeply and swinging your arms, can help your mind stay fresh.

As you get to the end of each chapter or section, it's a good idea to do a quick review. Remind yourself of what you learned and work on any difficult parts. When you feel that you've mastered the material, move on to the next part. At the end of your study session, briefly skim through your notes again.

But while review is helpful, cramming last minute is NOT. If at all possible, work ahead so that you won't need to fit all your study into the last day. Cramming overloads your brain with more information than it can process and retain, and your tired mind may struggle to recall even previously learned information when it is overwhelmed with last-minute study. Also, the urgent nature of cramming and the stress placed on your brain contribute to anxiety. You'll be more likely to go to the test feeling unprepared and having trouble thinking clearly.

So don't cram, and don't stay up late before the test, even just to review your notes at a leisurely pace. Your brain needs rest more than it needs to go over the information again. In fact, plan to finish your studies by noon or early afternoon the day before the test. Give your brain the rest of the day to relax or focus on other things, and get a good night's sleep. Then you will be fresh for the test and better able to recall what you've studied.

Step 6: Take a practice test

Many courses offer sample tests, either online or in the study materials. This is an excellent resource to check whether you have mastered the material, as well as to prepare for the test format and environment.

Check the test format ahead of time: the number of questions, the type (multiple choice, free response, etc.), and the time limit. Then create a plan for working through them. For example, if you have 30 minutes to take a 60-question test, your limit is 30 seconds per question. Spend less time on the questions you know well so that you can take more time on the difficult ones.

If you have time to take several practice tests, take the first one open book, with no time limit. Work through the questions at your own pace and make sure you fully understand them. Gradually work up to taking a test under test conditions: sit at a desk with all study materials put away and set a timer. Pace yourself to make sure you finish the test with time to spare and go back to check your answers if you have time.

After each test, check your answers. On the questions you missed, be sure you understand why you missed them. Did you misread the question (tests can use tricky wording)? Did you forget the information? Or was it something you hadn't learned? Go back and study any shaky areas that the practice tests reveal.

Taking these tests not only helps with your grade, but also aids in combating test anxiety. If you're already used to the test conditions, you're less likely to worry about it, and working through tests until you're scoring well gives you a confidence boost. Go through the practice tests until you feel comfortable, and then you can go into the test knowing that you're ready for it.

Test Tips

On test day, you should be confident, knowing that you've prepared well and are ready to answer the questions. But aside from preparation, there are several test day strategies you can employ to maximize your performance.

First, as stated before, get a good night's sleep the night before the test (and for several nights before that, if possible). Go into the test with a fresh, alert mind rather than staying up late to study.

Try not to change too much about your normal routine on the day of the test. It's important to eat a nutritious breakfast, but if you normally don't eat breakfast at all, consider eating just a protein bar. If you're a coffee drinker, go ahead and have your normal coffee. Just make sure you time it so that the caffeine doesn't wear off right in the middle of your test. Avoid sugary beverages, and drink enough water to stay hydrated but not so much that you need a restroom break 10 minutes into the test. If your test isn't first thing in the morning, consider going for a walk or doing a light workout before the test to get your blood flowing.

Allow yourself enough time to get ready, and leave for the test with plenty of time to spare so you won't have the anxiety of scrambling to arrive in time. Another reason to be early is to select a good seat. It's helpful to sit away from doors and windows, which can be distracting. Find a good seat, get out your supplies, and settle your mind before the test begins.

When the test begins, start by going over the instructions carefully, even if you already know what to expect. Make sure you avoid any careless mistakes by following the directions.

Then begin working through the questions, pacing yourself as you've practiced. If you're not sure on an answer, don't spend too much time on it, and don't let it shake your confidence. Either skip it and come back later, or eliminate as many wrong answers as possible and guess among the remaining ones. Don't dwell on these questions as you continue—put them out of your mind and focus on what lies ahead.

Be sure to read all of the answer choices, even if you're sure the first one is the right answer. Sometimes you'll find a better one if you keep reading. But don't second-guess yourself if you do immediately know the answer. Your gut instinct is usually right. Don't let test anxiety rob you of the information you know.

If you have time at the end of the test (and if the test format allows), go back and review your answers. Be cautious about changing any, since your first instinct tends to be correct, but make sure you didn't misread any of the questions or accidentally mark the wrong answer choice. Look over any you skipped and make an educated guess.

At the end, leave the test feeling confident. You've done your best, so don't waste time worrying about your performance or wishing you could change anything. Instead, celebrate the successful completion of this test. And finally, use this test to learn how to deal with anxiety even better next time.

Review Video: 5 Tips to Beat Test Anxiety
Visit mometrix.com/academy and enter code: 570656

Important Qualification

Not all anxiety is created equal. If your test anxiety is causing major issues in your life beyond the classroom or testing center, or if you are experiencing troubling physical symptoms related to your anxiety, it may be a sign of a serious physiological or psychological condition. If this sounds like your situation, we strongly encourage you to seek professional help.

How to Overcome Your Fear of Math

The word *math* is enough to strike fear into most hearts. How many of us have memories of sitting through confusing lectures, wrestling over mind-numbing homework, or taking tests that still seem incomprehensible even after hours of study? Years after graduation, many still shudder at these memories.

The fact is, math is not just a classroom subject. It has real-world implications that you face every day, whether you realize it or not. This may be balancing your monthly budget, deciding how many supplies to buy for a project, or simply splitting a meal check with friends. The idea of daily confrontations with math can be so paralyzing that some develop a condition known as *math anxiety*.

But you do NOT need to be paralyzed by this anxiety! In fact, while you may have thought all your life that you're not good at math, or that your brain isn't wired to understand it, the truth is that you may have been conditioned to think this way. From your earliest school days, the way you were taught affected the way you viewed different subjects. And the way math has been taught has changed.

Several decades ago, there was a shift in American math classrooms. The focus changed from traditional problem-solving to a conceptual view of topics, de-emphasizing the importance of learning the basics and building on them. The solid foundation necessary for math progression and confidence was undermined. Math became more of a vague concept than a concrete idea. Today, it is common to think of math, not as a straightforward system, but as a mysterious, complicated method that can't be fully understood unless you're a genius.

This is why you may still have nightmares about being called on to answer a difficult problem in front of the class. Math anxiety is a very real, though unnecessary, fear.

Math anxiety may begin with a single class period. Let's say you missed a day in 6th grade math and never quite understood the concept that was taught while you were gone. Since math is cumulative, with each new concept building on past ones, this could very well affect the rest of your math career. Without that one day's knowledge, it will be difficult to understand any other concepts that link to it. Rather than realizing that you're just missing one key piece, you may begin to believe that you're simply not capable of understanding math.

This belief can change the way you approach other classes, career options, and everyday life experiences, if you become anxious at the thought that math might be required. A student who loves science may choose a different path of study upon realizing that multiple math classes will be required for a degree. An aspiring medical student may hesitate at the thought of going through the necessary math classes. For some this anxiety escalates into a more extreme state known as *math phobia*.

Math anxiety is challenging to address because it is rooted deeply and may come from a variety of causes: an embarrassing moment in class, a teacher who did not explain concepts well and contributed to a shaky foundation, or a failed test that contributed to the belief of math failure.

These causes add up over time, encouraged by society's popular view that math is hard and unpleasant. Eventually a person comes to firmly believe that he or she is simply bad at math. This belief makes it difficult to grasp new concepts or even remember old ones. Homework and test grades begin to slip, which only confirms the belief. The poor performance is not due to lack of ability but is caused by math anxiety.

Math anxiety is an emotional issue, not a lack of intelligence. But when it becomes deeply rooted, it can become more than just an emotional problem. Physical symptoms appear. Blood pressure may rise and heartbeat may quicken at the sight of a math problem – or even the thought of math! This fear leads to a mental block. When someone with math anxiety is asked to perform a calculation, even a basic problem can seem overwhelming and impossible. The emotional and physical response to the thought of math prevents the brain from working through it logically.

The more this happens, the more a person's confidence drops, and the more math anxiety is generated. This vicious cycle must be broken!

The first step in breaking the cycle is to go back to very beginning and make sure you really understand the basics of how math works and why it works. It is not enough to memorize rules for multiplication and division. If you don't know WHY these rules work, your foundation will be shaky and you will be at risk of developing a phobia. Understanding mathematical concepts not only promotes confidence and security, but allows you to build on this understanding for new concepts. Additionally, you can solve unfamiliar problems using familiar concepts and processes.

Why is it that students in other countries regularly outperform American students in math? The answer likely boils down to a couple of things: the foundation of mathematical conceptual understanding and societal perception. While students in the US are not expected to *like* or *get* math, in many other nations, students are expected not only to understand math but also to excel at it.

Changing the American view of math that leads to math anxiety is a monumental task. It requires changing the training of teachers nationwide, from kindergarten through high school, so that they learn to teach the *why* behind math and to combat the wrong math views that students may develop. It also involves changing the stigma associated with math, so that it is no longer viewed as unpleasant and incomprehensible. While these are necessary changes, they are challenging and will take time. But in the meantime, math anxiety is not irreversible—it can be faced and defeated, one person at a time.

False Beliefs

One reason math anxiety has taken such hold is that several false beliefs have been created and shared until they became widely accepted. Some of these unhelpful beliefs include the following:

There is only one way to solve a math problem. In the same way that you can choose from different driving routes and still arrive at the same house, you can solve a math problem using different methods and still find the correct answer. A person who understands the reasoning behind math calculations may be able to look at an unfamiliar concept and find the right answer, just by applying logic to the knowledge they already have. This approach may be different than what is taught in the classroom, but it is still valid. Unfortunately, even many teachers view math as a subject where the best course of action is to memorize the rule or process for each problem rather than as a place for students to exercise logic and creativity in finding a solution.

Many people don't have a mind for math. A person who has struggled due to poor teaching or math anxiety may falsely believe that he or she doesn't have the mental capacity to grasp mathematical concepts. Most of the time, this is false. Many people find that when they are relieved of their math anxiety, they have more than enough brainpower to understand math.

Men are naturally better at math than women. Even though research has shown this to be false, many young women still avoid math careers and classes because of their belief that their math abilities are inferior. Many girls have come to believe that math is a male skill and have given up trying to understand or enjoy it.

Counting aids are bad. Something like counting on your fingers or drawing out a problem to visualize it may be frowned on as childish or a crutch, but these devices can help you get a tangible understanding of a problem or a concept.

Sadly, many students buy into these ideologies at an early age. A young girl who enjoys math class may be conditioned to think that she doesn't actually have the brain for it because math is for boys, and may turn her energies to other pursuits, permanently closing the door on a wide range of opportunities. A child who finds the right answer but doesn't follow the teacher's method may believe that he is doing it wrong and isn't good at math. A student who never had a problem with math before may have a poor teacher and become confused, yet believe that the problem is because she doesn't have a mathematical mind.

Students who have bought into these erroneous beliefs quickly begin to add their own anxieties, adapting them to their own personal situations:

I'll never use this in real life. A huge number of people wrongly believe that math is irrelevant outside the classroom. By adopting this mindset, they are handicapping themselves for a life in a mathematical world, as well as limiting their career choices. When they are inevitably faced with real-world math, they are conditioning themselves to respond with anxiety.

I'm not quick enough. While timed tests and quizzes, or even simply comparing yourself with other students in the class, can lead to this belief, speed is not an indicator of skill level. A person can work very slowly yet understand at a deep level.

If I can understand it, it's too easy. People with a low view of their own abilities tend to think that if they are able to grasp a concept, it must be simple. They cannot accept the idea that they are capable of understanding math. This belief will make it harder to learn, no matter how intelligent they are.

I just can't learn this. An overwhelming number of people think this, from young children to adults, and much of the time it is simply not true. But this mindset can turn into a self-fulfilling prophecy that keeps you from exercising and growing your math ability.

The good news is, each of these myths can be debunked. For most people, they are based on emotion and psychology, NOT on actual ability! It will take time, effort, and the desire to change, but change is possible. Even if you have spent years thinking that you don't have the capability to understand math, it is not too late to uncover your true ability and find relief from the anxiety that surrounds math.

Math Strategies

It is important to have a plan of attack to combat math anxiety. There are many useful strategies for pinpointing the fears or myths and eradicating them:

Go back to the basics. For most people, math anxiety stems from a poor foundation. You may think that you have a complete understanding of addition and subtraction, or even decimals and percentages, but make absolutely sure. Learning math is different from learning other subjects. For example, when you learn history, you study various time periods and places and events. It may be important to memorize dates or find out about the lives of famous people. When you move from US history to world history, there will be some overlap, but a large amount of the information will be new. Mathematical concepts, on the other hand, are very closely linked and highly dependent on each other. It's like climbing a ladder – if a rung is missing from your understanding, it may be difficult or impossible for you to climb any higher, no matter how hard you try. So go back and make sure your math foundation is strong. This may mean taking a remedial math course, going to a tutor to work through the shaky concepts, or just going through your old homework to make sure you really understand it.

Speak the language. Math has a large vocabulary of terms and phrases unique to working problems. Sometimes these are completely new terms, and sometimes they are common words, but are used differently in a math setting. If you can't speak the language, it will be very difficult to get a thorough understanding of the concepts. It's common for students to think that they don't understand math when they simply don't understand the vocabulary. The good news is that this is fairly easy to fix. Brushing up on any terms you aren't quite sure of can help bring the rest of the concepts into focus.

Check your anxiety level. When you think about math, do you feel nervous or uncomfortable? Do you struggle with feelings of inadequacy, even on concepts that you know you've already learned? It's important to understand your specific math anxieties, and what triggers them. When you catch yourself falling back on a false belief, mentally replace it with the truth. Don't let yourself believe that you can't learn, or that struggling with a concept means you'll never understand it. Instead, remind yourself of how much you've already learned and dwell on that past success. Visualize grasping the new concept, linking it to your old knowledge, and moving on to the next challenge. Also, learn how to manage anxiety when it arises. There are many techniques for coping with the irrational fears that rise to the surface when you enter the math classroom. This may include controlled breathing, replacing negative thoughts with positive ones, or visualizing success. Anxiety interferes with your ability to concentrate and absorb information, which in turn contributes to greater anxiety. If you can learn how to regain control of your thinking, you will be better able to pay attention, make progress, and succeed!

Don't go it alone. Like any deeply ingrained belief, math anxiety is not easy to eradicate. And there is no need for you to wrestle through it on your own. It will take time, and many people find that speaking with a counselor or psychiatrist helps. They can help you develop strategies for responding to anxiety and overcoming old ideas. Additionally, it can be very helpful to take a short course or seek out a math tutor to help you find and fix the missing rungs on your ladder and make sure that you're ready to progress to the next level. You can also find a number of math aids online: courses that will teach you mental devices for figuring out problems, how to get the most out of your math classes, etc.

Check your math attitude. No matter how much you want to learn and overcome your anxiety, you'll have trouble if you still have a negative attitude toward math. If you think it's too hard, or just have general feelings of dread about math, it will be hard to learn and to break through the anxiety. Work on cultivating a positive math attitude. Remind yourself that math is not just a hurdle to be cleared, but a valuable asset. When you view math with a positive attitude, you'll be much more likely to understand and even enjoy it. This is something you must do for yourself. You may find it helpful to visit with a counselor. Your tutor, friends, and family may cheer you on in your endeavors. But your greatest asset is yourself. You are inside your own mind – tell yourself what you need to hear. Relive past victories. Remind yourself that you are capable of understanding math. Root out any false beliefs that linger and replace them with positive truths. Even if it doesn't feel true at first, it will begin to affect your thinking and pave the way for a positive, anxiety-free mindset.

Aside from these general strategies, there are a number of specific practical things you can do to begin your journey toward overcoming math anxiety. Something as simple as learning a new note-taking strategy can change the way you approach math and give you more confidence and understanding. New study techniques can also make a huge difference.

Math anxiety leads to bad habits. If it causes you to be afraid of answering a question in class, you may gravitate toward the back row. You may be embarrassed to ask for help. And you may procrastinate on assignments, which leads to rushing through them at the last moment when it's too late to get a better understanding. It's important to identify your negative behaviors and replace them with positive ones:

Prepare ahead of time. Read the lesson before you go to class. Being exposed to the topics that will be covered in class ahead of time, even if you don't understand them perfectly, is extremely helpful in increasing what you retain from the lecture. Do your homework and, if you're still shaky, go over some extra problems. The key to a solid understanding of math is practice.

Sit front and center. When you can easily see and hear, you'll understand more, and you'll avoid the distractions of other students if no one is in front of you. Plus, you're more likely to be sitting with students who are positive and engaged, rather than others with math anxiety. Let their positive math attitude rub off on you.

Ask questions in class and out. If you don't understand something, just ask. If you need a more in-depth explanation, the teacher may need to work with you outside of class, but often it's a simple concept you don't quite understand, and a single question may clear it up. If you wait, you may not be able to follow the rest of the day's lesson. For extra help, most professors have office hours outside of class when you can go over concepts one-on-one to clear up any uncertainties. Additionally, there may be a *math lab* or study session you can attend for homework help. Take advantage of this.

Review. Even if you feel that you've fully mastered a concept, review it periodically to reinforce it. Going over an old lesson has several benefits: solidifying your understanding, giving you a confidence boost, and even giving some new insights into material that you're currently learning! Don't let yourself get rusty. That can lead to problems with learning later concepts.

Teaching Tips

While the math student's mindset is the most crucial to overcoming math anxiety, it is also important for others to adjust their math attitudes. Teachers and parents have an enormous influence on how students relate to math. They can either contribute to math confidence or math anxiety.

As a parent or teacher, it is very important to convey a positive math attitude. Retelling horror stories of your own bad experience with math will contribute to a new generation of math anxiety. Even if you don't share your experiences, others will be able to sense your fears and may begin to believe them.

Even a careless comment can have a big impact, so watch for phrases like *He's not good at math* or *I never liked math*. You are a crucial role model, and your children or students will unconsciously adopt your mindset. Give them a positive example to follow. Rather than teaching them to fear the math world before they even know it, teach them about all its potential and excitement.

Work to present math as an integral, beautiful, and understandable part of life. Encourage creativity in solving problems. Watch for false beliefs and dispel them. Cross the lines between subjects: integrate history, English, and music with math. Show students how math is used every day, and how the entire world is based on mathematical principles, from the pull of gravity to the shape of seashells. Instead of letting students see math as a necessary evil, direct them to view it as an imaginative, beautiful art form – an art form that they are capable of mastering and using.

Don't give too narrow a view of math. It is more than just numbers. Yes, working problems and learning formulas is a large part of classroom math. But don't let the teaching stop there. Teach students about the everyday implications of math. Show them how nature works according to the laws of mathematics, and take them outside to make discoveries of their own. Expose them to math-related careers by inviting visiting speakers, asking students to do research and presentations, and learning students' interests and aptitudes on a personal level.

Demonstrate the importance of math. Many people see math as nothing more than a required stepping stone to their degree, a nuisance with no real usefulness. Teach students that algebra is used every day in managing their bank accounts, in following recipes, and in scheduling the day's events. Show them how learning to do geometric proofs helps them to develop logical thinking, an invaluable life skill. Let them see that math surrounds them and is integrally linked to their daily lives: that weather predictions are based on math, that math was used to design cars and other machines, etc. Most of all, give them the tools to use math to enrich their lives.

Make math as tangible as possible. Use visual aids and objects that can be touched. It is much easier to grasp a concept when you can hold it in your hands and manipulate it, rather than just listening to the lecture. Encourage math outside of the classroom. The real world is full of measuring, counting, and calculating, so let students participate in this. Keep your eyes open for numbers and patterns to discuss. Talk about how scores are calculated in sports games and how far apart plants are placed in a garden row for maximum growth. Build the mindset that math is a normal and interesting part of daily life.

Finally, find math resources that help to build a positive math attitude. There are a number of books that show math as fascinating and exciting while teaching important concepts, for example: *The Math Curse; A Wrinkle in Time; The Phantom Tollbooth;* and *Fractals, Googols and Other Mathematical Tales*. You can also find a number of online resources: math puzzles and games, videos that show math in nature, and communities of math enthusiasts. On a local level, students can compete in a variety of math competitions with other schools or join a math club.

The student who experiences math as exciting and interesting is unlikely to suffer from math anxiety. Going through life without this handicap is an immense advantage and opens many doors that others have closed through their fear.

Self-Check

Whether you suffer from math anxiety or not, chances are that you have been exposed to some of the false beliefs mentioned above. Now is the time to check yourself for any errors you may have accepted. Do you think you're not wired for math? Or that you don't need to understand it since you're not planning on a math career? Do you think math is just too difficult for the average person?

Find the errors you've taken to heart and replace them with positive thinking. Are you capable of learning math? Yes! Can you control your anxiety? Yes! These errors will resurface from time to time, so be watchful. Don't let others with math anxiety influence you or sway your confidence. If you're having trouble with a concept, find help. Don't let it discourage you!

Create a plan of attack for defeating math anxiety and sharpening your skills. Do some research and decide if it would help you to take a class, get a tutor, or find some online resources to fine-tune your knowledge. Make the effort to get good nutrition, hydration, and sleep so that you are operating at full capacity. Remind yourself daily that you are skilled and that anxiety does not control you. Your mind is capable of so much more than you know. Give it the tools it needs to grow and thrive.

Thank You

We at Mometrix would like to extend our heartfelt thanks to you, our friend and patron, for allowing us to play a part in your journey. It is a privilege to serve people from all walks of life who are unified in their commitment to building the best future they can for themselves.

The preparation you devote to these important testing milestones may be the most valuable educational opportunity you have for making a real difference in your life. We encourage you to put your heart into it—that feeling of succeeding, overcoming, and yes, conquering will be well worth the hours you've invested.

We want to hear your story, your struggles and your successes, and if you see any opportunities for us to improve our materials so we can help others even more effectively in the future, please share that with us as well. **The team at Mometrix would be absolutely thrilled to hear from you!** So please, send us an email (support@mometrix.com) and let's stay in touch.

If you'd like some additional help, check out these other resources we offer for your exam:
http://MometrixFlashcards.com/PSAT

Additional Bonus Material

Due to our efforts to try to keep this book to a manageable length, we've created a link that will give you access to all of your additional bonus material.

Please visit http://www.mometrix.com/bonus948/psat to access the information.

Made in the USA
Las Vegas, NV
03 October 2021

31651515R00168